Side effects of the modernisation of EU competition law

Modernisation of EU competition law as a challenge to the enforcement system of EU competition law and EU law in general

Side effects of the modernisation of EU competition law

Modernisation of EU competition law as a challenge to the enforcement system of EU competition law and EU law in general

Proefschrift

ter verkrijging van de graad van doctor aan de Universiteit van Tilburg, op gezag van de rector magnificus, prof. dr. Ph. Eijlander, in het openbaar te verdedigen ten overstaan van een door het college voor promoties aangewezen commissie in de aula van de universiteit om op vrijdag 15 oktober 2010 om 10.15 uur

door

Laura Yvonne Marie-Louise Parret,
geboren op 2 april 1969 te Leuven.

Promotores:

Prof. dr. P. Larouche
Prof. dr. L.A.J. Senden

Promotiecommissie:

Prof. dr. A. Prechal
Prof. dr. T. Tridimas
Prof. dr. W. Wils
Prof. dr. J. Boone

Cover image
Charlie Chaplin in Modern Times (1936), screenshot

Production Wolf Legal Publishers
P.O. Box 31051, 6503 CB Nijmegen, The Netherlands

A commercial edition of this book will be published by Wolf Legal Publishers.

Table of contents

Preface

As shown on the cover, Charlie Chaplin is stuck in the machinery of modernisation. Modern Times are fascinating but complicated. They present a challenge.

Finalising this book has certainly also been a challenge, in more ways than I would have imagined. I have come a long way from the days I did not know why I went to study law. It is still somewhat of a mystery to me, but at some point, I developed a real passion for it, especially for the law as a system, as a phenomenon, as a dynamic machinery in which I myself, and most people I know, work.

The academic exercise I undertook in the previous months, was like nothing I have ever done before. It was not only finishing the last article but mostly the task of bringing the different articles together. I wanted to model them into one story. Many of my ideas about how competition law evolved these last fifteen years, are contained in this book. In that respect it is like closing a chapter. If this book is now finished, it also means I have proven to myself that I am ready to do real academic work. The subjects that I want to explore further in the near future are already there in the making. And in that respect it is more of a beginning than an end.

I wish to thank Prof. Pierre Larouche and Prof. Linda Senden for their invaluable support and help. It is thanks to Pierre that this book finally materialised. His idea to make a thesis in the form of a collection of articles (still very much a novelty in law) and his discrete encouragement at the right moment and the right time, were really crucial. Linda's support and input was also decisive. Her professionalism and her broader perspective in EU law, as well as her patience and thorough reading of the last pieces, helped me enormously.

I thank the other members of the commission for their contribution and stimulating input: Prof. Takis Tridimas, Prof. Sacha Prechal, Prof. Jan Boone, Prof. Wouter Wils. I admire the work of every one of you, since long before this thesis, and I appreciate your support.

The department of European and International Public Law has become a big family since I started there. It is an inspiring and stimulating environment to work in. Linda Senden and I go back a long way as colleagues and friends. A particular word of thanks for Willem van Genugten, whom I consider to be my mentor in many ways. Thanks to Leigh Hancher, Conny Rijken and all the other colleagues, and especially to Helen Staples, who gracefully accepted the task of correcting my English in the conclusions but who did more than just that. I am grateful to Femke Bijleveld, Sietske Trommelen, Eefje de Volder and Eva Bezem who each did their share of practical and editing work.

If I stayed on in Tilburg around 2007 when my professional career in practice took another turn, it was thanks to the challenging and interesting colleagues and activities of the Tilburg Law and Economics Center. TILEC is a real success story and I hope to be able to follow its further development.

There are three persons I wish to thank in particular and who have been important in my career so far. Gerard van der Wal, Sacha Prechal and Stefaan Raes have more in common than they probably realize. Each in their own discipline (advocate, academic, judge and in combinations) they have shown me the way in terms of necessary skills and high standards of quality and professional integrity. I have the greatest respect and sympathy for each of them.

I pay tribute to Koen Lenaerts whose enthusiasm in teaching European law twenty years ago was so contagious. At the Brussels bar, in the various lawyers associations in which I was active, in the Dutch and Belgian world of European law and competition law and at university, so many people inspired me. I dare not make a list, out of fear of forgetting some.

I have chosen another route to get to this academic title than the other members of my family, but without them, it would not have happened. Have I proven that law is science? Probably not. But does it really matter? I thank my parents for teaching me curiosity, openness of mind and the value of eternal doubt. I thank my sister for showing the way and for simply making me feel that she was always close to me even though we are seperated by distance.

I thank Steven van Steenkiste, my very dear friend, for accepting to be part of this important moment with me. Equally I greet Elisabetta Manunza, who is a real soulmate, who not only stands by my side for the defense but also gave valuable advice in the last phase.

And finally, Dominique, who found the right argument to convince me to bring this project to an end. He knows only too well that my choice to combine teaching, writing and practising the law is, at times, a truly exhausting exercise. He is the toughest of all to please, that is why his input is so valuable.

My dearest daughter Anna. She is already a master in logic and reasoning and she has bargained for so many things that I must do for her once this project is finished, that there are busy times ahead. She is my eternal sunshine.

Laura Parret
1 September 2010

Chapter 1

Introduction

This thesis brings five articles together written between 2005 and 2010, more or less one written every year. The title "Side effects of modernisation - Modernisation as a challenge to the enforcement system of EU competition law and EU law in general" formulates the subject of all the different articles.

The term modernisation is well known and often used in competition circles. However, it is used to identify a variety of different trends. It is also, being a neutral and general term, not at all self-evident outside of competition law what it actually means. Therefore, at the outset, a short explanation of the concepts of modernisation and side effects in the title seems helpful. This introduction also describes the personal motivation, the sources of inspiration and the background of this book well as the methodological approach that is closely related thereto.

The term modernisation is meant to cover a complex of different developments that took place in EU competition law over the last years. Modernisation has a substantive component and a more procedural and institutional component. Both are addressed in this book, in particular from the perspective of the enforcement of the law.[1] In the end, one of the result of bringing these articles together has been that together they clearly show how both aspects of modernisation are related. This shall be highlighted in the conclusions and final remarks in chapter 7.

Substantive modernisation is a process that started somewhere at the end of the '90's and, in short, the term is used to refer to the introduction of a more economic approach in competition law, more in particular the cartel prohibition of Article 101 TFEU and, to a lesser extent, Article 102 TFEU. In one area after the other, substantive EU rules were reformed, going from the rules on vertical agreements to the rules on horizontal agreements and followed, much later, by the announcement of new policy orientations for abuse of dominance. More attention for economic analysis and the market circumstances in a case, implying more cooperation between lawyers and economists, was the subject at at the heart of these reforms. The other side

---

1 This means that when it comes to the substantive component of modernisation, the analysis does not concern the reforms from a substantive perspective (for example new provisions of the law, new policy for certain agreements, new concepts in the legal assessment of behaviour) but shall deal in various ways with the impact that these reforms have had on the legal system as a whole and on the enforcement system in particular. Enforcement is defined as the application of the law in individual cases in a particular procedural and institutional framework, in such as a way that rights can be invoked and are guaranteed, and that duties and obligations are fulfilled.

of the story was having less hard rules and per se prohibitions and more self-assessment by companies.[2]

The other development that is covered by the term modernisation is the process of decentralisation, which was mainly initiated by Regulation 1/2003 of 16 December 2002 of the Council (joined as appendice). This aspect of modernisation, namely the decentralisation in EU competition law refers, in particular, to the increased involvement of national judges and national competition authorities in the enforcement of EU competition law (and not only possibly their own national law). Where the judges are concerned, the great novelty was the introduction of the legal exception of Article 101 (3) TFEU and the abolishment of the notification system at the Commission. Where the competition authorities are concerned, they were given a clear role to play as the enforcers of EU law in their own national jurisdictions.[3]

Very early on when the project for this book surfaced, the term "side effects" came to mind. It aims at developments that are not the core content, nor the purpose as such of modernisation as defined above, but that appeared as ancillary or side effects. To explain why the term side effects seemed to fit with all the different contributions and the collection thereof, reference is made to certain elements in the medical definition of the term. Side effects of a medical treatment are mostly unintended, sometimes perceived in a negative way, and they are usually difficult to predict and to treat. They are also very individually determined. If not treated adequately, they can become worse than the disease that the main treatment had set out to cure. Side effects are effects on other aspects of health than the one that is targeted with the treatment. To measure whether or not it is worthwhile to endure side effects, and to explain where they come from, it is necessary to take a more global perspective (the general health and living conditions of a person) as opposed to looking only at the specific problem the cure wants to treat. All these elements seemed to fit well to the subject and approach in this collection of articles.

Certain side effects on the system of enforcement of EU competition law are provoked by, or closely related to important recent substantive and procedural developments in competition law. Some of these side effects are singled out in these articles because, from an individual perspective, they seemed particularly interesting and sometimes worrying or problematic.[4]

---

[2] References to specific reforms can be found throughout the different chapters.

[3] Again, throughout the different chapters, more detailed references can be found to the new provisions and the rights and duties of judges and authorities in this new modernised context.

[4] Chapter 3 on interstate trade is somewhat of an exception to the extent that I was asked for a contribution to a book with a predetermined subject whereas all the other articles where the result of a particular personal interest. However, chapter 3 does seem to be in coherence with the others when it comes to the approach and the common themes that shall be discussed further in chapter 7. The most

These last remarks on the choice of the term "side effects" might also explain why the different pieces do not contain much detailed and technical examination of particular aspects of modernisation. This thesis is motivated by the willingness to explore more theoretical ways to observe and study competition law, drawing on the interest and experience as a more all round EU lawyer, and combined with a great interest in procedure and due process in general.[5]

The tile also presents modernisation as a challenge, both to the enforcement system of EU competition law as well as to the enforcement of EU law more in general. The term challenge is meant in a positive way: the side effects of modernisation that are identified should make us reflect thoroughly on an number of aspects of the enforcement system, allowing us to improve it as we go along. The reference to EU law in general is inspired by the fact that many issues described in the articles can be useful to study for lawyers not active in competition law and certain developments might also have repercussions well beyond competition law.

Translated in terms of approach and methodology, all articles attempt to take a broader perspective: competition law is part of the legal system of the European Union, Union law, and the law of Member States. Competition law should and cannot be isolated from developments elsewhere in the law. Also, both in practice and in academic reflections the underlying question is often: Is, and if so why, should competition law be different than any other area of law? And also, do inherent characteristics of competition law justify differences when it comes to the enforcement of the law?[6] This critical, almost sceptical, attitude towards the "world of competition law" is certainly a factor of influence. Perhaps taking more of a panoramic view on competition law can also contribute to its development, rather than always concentrating on the latest technical development. Also, modernised competition law does not only require lawyers to be open to what economics have to offer. Especially when it comes to enforcing the law and the many open legal questions that currently exist in that respect, profound knowledge and reflection from a broader legal perspective can also be useful:

---

important reason is that the research question underlying the article, is inspired by the general methodological approach to look at competition law in a broader EU law context. The study of the interstate clause is especially interesting in that respect because it is a concept present in all areas of internal market law.

5 The opportunity for detailed examination of the law in all its ins and outs exists on a daily basis in the practice of the law and in other writings. Although competition law was part of daily work since the beginning in 1993, in practice, at least until 2007, I have always had the benefit of dealing with other areas of EU law. Since 2007 the focus of work and interest is very much on procedure in a broad sense.

6 These questions are mentioned here because they explain the personal motivation, the way the law is practiced and studied, the choice of subjects and the common approach. They are not to be seen as a central research question for which this thesis formulates an answer. The particularity of this thesis being a collection of articles which were not all written with a pre-existing intention to bundle them, makes it difficult to formulate a single research question retroactively.

competition law is a fairly young discipline and its procedural framework is under construction.[7] The question if and how competition law is similar or different than other areas of the law also helps to keep an open mind and to avoid overspecialization and tunnel vision.

The research is certainly influenced as well by increasing cooperation with non-lawyers and a more multidisciplinary context, both in practice as well as in the academic setting. A "law and economics" context can have a variety of beneficial effects, many of which have been extensively described and studied over the last years. A perhaps less obvious effect of the confrontation of law and economics in practice and academic work, is the doubt about the role and significance of the law as a whole and the self-evidence of legal concepts and principles that we use so easily on a daily basis (see below: proof, effectiveness). In my case, the confrontation of law and economics contributed to a growing interest, not primarily for doing multidisciplinary work myself but, on the contrary, for research touching on the basics of our legal systems (see below: objectives of a legal system, judicial protection). In other words, for typically legal issues. In that respect this thesis is also forward-looking: it can hopefully serve as a basis for exploring some intriguing, more theoretical, issues further in the near future: the role of procedure, the relationship between substantive law and procedural law, the way the legal system adapts itself to non-legal considerations, lawmaking as opposed to policy in the European Union.

Every one of the articles is reproduced in this thesis in the form in which it was published.[8] Chapter 6 is an exception because it has not yet been published at the time this manuscript was completed.

---

7 One obvious example is given here from experience: most competition lawyers have some familiarity with human rights, at least are aware of the right to a fair trial and the rights of defense. However, the straightforward application of human rights case-law depends on the pre-existing question whether human rights protection can indeed be invoked in the area of competition law and how. The procedural framework is in fact a mixture of e.g. human rights, principles of good administration, general principles of law common to most member states, certain quasi-criminal features, and typically EU institutional and substantive elements. When difficulties arise in the enforcement of the law in a case this often implies, in my personal view, the question as to which are the right sources of law to draw inspiration from. Equally in academic reflection, and when constructing further the enforcement system, it seems valid to sometimes take a panoramic approach on competition law and its enforcement before focusing again on a specific legal issue.

8 This implies for example that the numbering of the treaties is not adapted to the Lisbon Treaty in chapters 2 until 5. A table of equivalence is added in appendice at the end of this book. Given the fact that each article was a stand-alone project, it also means that in the introductory part of each one of them, the same elements are often described as the relevant context and there might be some repetition involved. However, the choice was made to simply reproduce the articles as they were written because it seems the best way to show the evolution over time. Also, it is important to note that the idea to bring a number of articles together in a thesis, did not yet exist when the first one (chapter 2) was written. The idea appeared

The first article (written and published in 2005) concerns judicial protection and modernisation of competition law and combines my interest for the subject of judicial protection and in particular, access to court for individuals, with the area I worked in most in practice, competition law. This article entitled "*Judicial protection after Modernisation of Competition law*" is chapter 2. The research question at the basis of this article was whether the system put into place by Regulation 1/2003 could result in an increase in the lack of judicial protection for individuals as a side effect of the modernisation and decentralisation it wished to achieve.

The second article (written and published in 2006) was originally published in Dutch in a book on the changing role of the interstate trade concept. My article entitled "*Intrastate equals interstate*" (translation) covers the perspective of competition law and aims to examine if and how the concept of interstate trade plays a role in this area of Union law. It therefore also touches on the relationship between competition law and European Union law in general, in particular here the law of the internal market. This article is chapter 3 below. It addresses a specific legal requirement in the application of competition law and also questions how this will be affected by modernisation.

The third article (written and presented as a paper in 2007, published in 2008) deals with proof, a subject of growing importance in competition law. The approach was one inspired by the interaction with economists, both in practice as well as in the Tilburg Law and Economics Center. This article proposes a pragmatic view on issues of proof and is entitled "*Sense and nonsense of rules on proof in cartel cases: How to reconcile a more economics based approach to competition law with more attention for rules on proof*"; it forms Chapter 4. Growing interest for a typically legal issue such as proof, is considered a side effect of modernisation.

The next article is a project which took the longest to develop, although the first drafts date back to 2005-2006. The first version was finished end of 2008 and published in April 2009 as a TILEC discussion paper. It was also presented in a substantially revised version as a paper at a conference in Bonn in May 2010 and it was published as an article in August 2010. It builds on the changes that competition law has undergone through the modernisation process and the uncertainty this has caused about the objectives that EU competition law and policy wishes to protect. The article "*Should we know what we are protecting? Yes we should!*" is chapter 5. The subtitle is *A plea for a solid and comprehensive debate about the objectives of EU competition law and policy.* It expresses a feeling of confusion at the

---

around the time the third article (chapter 4 on proof) was being written and the fourth one (chapter 5 on objectives) was already underway. Therefore there was no a priori choice of a general theme to be expressed in different articles. The coherence and the common ideas are to a large extent a spontaneous process. Chapter 7 expresses and structures these common ideas.

normative foundations of modernised competition law and policy. This confusion is also qualified as a side effect of modernisation.

Chapter 6 contains the last article (written mostly in 2009, to be submitted for publication in 2010) which again combines the research interests of judicial protection, procedural law and competition enforcement. It is entitled "*Decentralisation of competition law: sacrificing procedural autonomy?*" The subtitle is *Autonomy versus effectiveness: a well known conflict in EU law revisited and its impact on the question of future harmonisation in the area of enforcement of competition law.* The article was finalized in March 2010. It pinpoints the trend towards increasing convergence of national procedural law and wonders what place there still is for the EU law concepts of effectiveness and procedural autonomy in that respect.

In Chapter 7, the conclusions of each article are recalled and summarized and, where appropriate, certain aspects are briefly updated. The purpose is not to provide for a full fletched update of the (older) articles but to show more clearly the continuity between the different pieces and to highlight some common themes by way of conclusion.

Although self-standing articles, there are a number of recurring common themes that appear throughout them. Four of these themes shall be discussed further by way of conclusions in chapter 7, they are:

(1) The relationship between competition law and the internal market
(2) Substantive modernisation as a challenge to the enforcement system
(3) Modernisation from an organizational perspective: the complicated relationship between decentralisation, convergence and consistency
(4) Modernisation as a challenge to the system of judicial protection.

Chapter 2

Judicial protection after modernisation of competition law*

The entry into force of Regulation 1/2003 has far-reaching implications for the enforcement of the EC competition rules. However, it does not deal with access to justice or the judicial protection of companies involved in competition cases. This article argues that the current legal framework in EC competition law lacks attention for some important issues of judicial protection. Certain characteristics of the modernised and decentralised system of competition law enforcement in the post 1 May 2004 era, add to pre-existing problems in that respect. Generally speaking the lack of judicial protection under the pre-modernisation system was mainly a result of the strict rules on the admissibility of direct actions under Article 230 EC Treaty, which left some decisions or acts of the Commission outside the scope of judicial review. In that respect, the most important reasons for concern in the new system are the number of (formal) individual decisions taken by the Commission, the further increase of soft law instruments and the creation of a number of new types of decisions by the Commission and within the network of competition authorities. This article focuses particularly on access to courts as one of the most fundamental elements of the right to effective judicial protection. The subject seems all the more relevant in light of recent developments in other areas of Community law highlighting the growing importance of the principle of adequate judicial protection in the Community legal order. The author calls upon the Community courts to continue to play an important role in the new modernised system of EC competition law.

1. The legal framework: developments in the area of judicial protection

1.1 Definition

When reference is made here to *legal protection* or *judicial protection* this shall mean the possibility for private parties to challenge a decision of the Commission, which concerns them, in a court of law. This shall be any decision which involves the application of the competition rules laid down in the EC Treaty.[10] The right to effective legal protection is part of the Community legal order. Access to a court is the most important component

---

* This article was published in *Legal Issues of Economic Integration*, 2005, 32 (4), p. 339-368. It was finalized on 1 July 2005.

[10] Individuals should be able to enforce all rights they derive directly from Community law: ECJ Case 222/84, *Johnston* [1986] ECR 1651 [18]. Merger control decisions are not the focus of attention here even though the case-law in this area shall be referred to where it is considered relevant.

of this general principle. Every individual who considers himself wronged by a measure which deprives him of a right or an advantage under Community law must have access to a remedy against that measure and be able to obtain complete judicial protection.[11]

The requirement of judicial protection is part of the rights protected under Article 6 and 13 of the European Convention on Human Rights.[12] Article 47 of the Charter of Fundamental Rights of the European Union also expresses the right to an effective remedy and to a fair trial. [13] The Court has referred to the fact that the principle is common to the constitutional traditions of the Member States.

According to many authors, there is a (special) need for full jurisdiction in competition cases because the Community acts (Commission decisions) can result in the imposition of considerable fines thus qualifying as "decisions" within the meaning of Article 6 ECHR.[14] Such full jurisdictional control means review not only of the possible sanction that was imposed but also of all the facts and of their legal assessment.

Access to a judge therefore on the centralised Community level means access to the Community Courts. In order to compare the levels of judicial protection before and after the entry into force of Regulation 1/2003, the following questions shall be addressed: do parties have a right to a (motivated) decision and is the decision open to appeal in front of a court? If access to a court can be established, the standard of review adopted by the

---

[11] See Opinion of Advocate General Darmon, Case C-97/91, *Borelli* [1992] ECR I-6313, par. 31. See H. Schermers and D. Waelbroeck, *Judicial protection in the European Union* (The Hague: Kluwer Law International, 2001) 46 and following. This has been emphasized at numerous occasions in relation to the national courts' duties under Article 10 EC; see also M. Brealey and M. Hoskins, *Remedies in EC law* (London: Sweet & Maxwell, 1998) 99-107.

[12] One of the standard cases of the Court for Human Rights in Strasbourg is *Golder v United Kingdom* (Appl no 4451/70) (1975) Series A no 18: the Court held that the detailed fair trial guarantees under Article 6 would be useless if it were impossible to start court proceedings in the first place; see also J. Jacobs and R. White, *European Convention on Human Rights* (Oxford: OUP, 2002)151-155.

[13] Charter of Fundamental rights of the European Union [2000] OJ C 364/1; the Charter has now been integrated into the Treaty establishing a Constitution for Europe (Constitutional Treaty) [2004] OJ C 310.

[14] D. Waelbroeck and D. Fosselard, 'Should the Decision Making Power in EC Antitrust Procedures be left to an Independent Judge? The impact of the European Convention of Human Rights on EC Antitrust Procedures' (1994) 14 *Yearbook of European Law* 111 and following; Schermers and Waelbroeck, *Judicial Protection in the EU* (above n 2) 48-49; K. Lenaerts and J. Vanhamme, 'Procedural rights of private parties in the Community administrative process' (1997) 34 *Common Market Law Review* 531, 555.

courts and the scope of the appeal are also relevant to determine the level of judicial protection, which is why this issue is also briefly addressed.[15]

1.2 The increasing importance of the right to effective judicial protection

Before examining the level of judicial protection in the light of recent changes in competition law, some developments in case-law and legislation outside the field of competition law shall first be very briefly described so far as they relate to effective judicial protection.

1.2.1 Case law on Article 230 EC Treaty

Recent case-law in Luxembourg has again drawn attention to the much discussed admissibility criteria of Article 230 EC Treaty. The fourth paragraph of Article 230 EC Treaty confers the right on individuals to lodge a direct appeal against acts of Community institutions provided certain admissibility criteria are met. Such a direct appeal is possible against acts addressed to a particular individual or against acts which, although in the form of a regulation or addressed to another person, in fact directly and individually concern him. One of the most controversial subjects in the past (outside of competition law) was the strict test applied for the interpretation of 'individual concern' in relation to acts of a general nature.[16]

In its judgement in the *Jégo-Quéré* case of 3 May 2002, the Court of First Instance stated that it was time to review existing case-law on the possibility of private parties attacking Community measures of a general nature.[17] The Court of First Instance proposed a new criterion for analysing 'individual concern'. The reasoning of the CFI was largely based on the principle of effective judicial review based on the European Convention on Human Rights. The Court referred to the Opinion of the Advocate General in *UPA* who also called for a reform of the case-law in this area.[18] The judgement in Jégo-Quéré appeared to offer new opportunities to potential applicants, but the sense of victory did not last long.[19] In its judgement of 25 July 2002,

---

15 See J. Jans, R. de Lange, S. Prechal and R. Widdershoven, *Inleiding tot het Europees bestuursrecht*, 2nd edition (Nijmegen: Ars Aequi, 2002) 81 for additional elements.

16 See: A. Arnull, 'Private applicants and the action for annulment since Codorniu' (2001) 38 *Common Market Law Review* 7 and the overview in the Opinion of Advocate General Jacobs in Case C-50/00P, *UPA* [2002] ECR I-6677. Jacobs refers to what was identified as a serious gap in the system of judicial remedies of Community law.

17 CFI Case T-177/01, *Jégo-Quéré et Cie SA/Commission* [2002] ECR II-2365.

18 Opinion of Advocate General Jacobs (above n 16); the new criterion Jacobs proposed for "individual concern" was different: see par. 60 of the Opinion.

19 Paragraph 51 of the judgement. the CFI stated that an individual should be considered as "*individually concerned by a Community measure of general application that concerns him directly if the measure in question affects his legal*

Union de Pequenos Agricultores, the Court of Justice refused to depart from the settled case-law to allow more actions by private parties to be brought under Article 230 EC.[20] More specifically, the Court seemed to indicate that a more flexible interpretation of "individual concern", in cases where there is no effective judicial review for parties, goes further than the text of the EC Treaty allows.[21] The judgement contains a striking paragraph concluding that it is not unlikely that a reform of the existing system of remedies is necessary, but it is up to the Member States to take the initiative in that respect.[22]

Commentary on this small revolution initiated by the CFI and promptly questioned by the ECJ, has been varied: some regretted that the ECJ did not take the opportunity to open up locus standi for individuals[23] and others argued that there is no gap in judicial protection under Community law and no need to lament the rejection of a re-interpretation of Article 230. This last line of the argument places great emphasis on the important duties the national judges have to ensure judicial protection.[24]

These developments show that this general principle has become such an important part of the Community legal order that even the Court (carefully) questioned the instruments that the Treaties currently offer individuals for challenging acts of the institutions.[25] The thorough analysis made by

---

position, in a manner which is both definite and immediate, by restricting his rights or by imposing obligations on him".

20 ECJ Case C-50/00P, *Union de Pequenos Agricultores* [2002] ECR I-6677.

21 See for first comments on the judgement: S. Prechal and L. Parret, 'Zaak C-50/00 P, Unión de Pequeños Agricultores t. Raad van de Europese Unie' (2003) 1 *Sociaal-Economische Wetgeving* 35.

22 Par. 45. The judgement was confirmed in the judgement of 1 April 2004 in the appeal against the CFI's judgement in ECJ Case C-263/02 P *Jégo-Quéré* [2004] ECR I-03425. The differences of opinion expressed by the Community judges came to the attention of the Convention working on a Constitution for the European Union. On this aspect of "Constitutional dialogue": D. Hanf, 'Talking with "the pouvoir constituant" in times of constitutional reform: The European Court of Justice on Private Applicants' Access to Justice' (2003) 10 *Maastricht Journal of European & Comparative Law* 265.

23 Amongst the most disappointed: F. Ragolle, 'Access to justice for private applicants in the Community legal order: recent Revolutions' (2003) 28 *European Law Review* 90; A. Arnull, 'April shower for Jégo-Quéré' (2004) 29 *European Law Review* (2004) 287.

24 See J. Temple Lang, 'Actions for Declarations that Community Regulations are invalid: the duties of National Courts under Article 10 EC' (2003) 28 *European Law Review* 102 and X. Groussot, 'The EC System of Legal Remedies and Effective Judicial Protection: does the system really need reform?' (2003) 30 *Legal Issues of Economic Integration* 221; P. Nihoul, 'Le recours des particuliers contre les actes Communautaires de portée générale' (2002) 96 *J.T. Droit Européen* 38.

25 It should be said that the Court had already raised the issue in 1995 in a paper for the IGC before the Treaty of Amsterdam. For remarkable comments on this subject from the President of the CFI, see B. Vesterdorf, 'The Community Court system ten

Advocate General Jacobs in *UPA* and the many comments in literature questioning whether the Community judicial system is in line with the right to effective judicial protection, also provide a basis for the analysis made in this article.

1.2.2 Other developments

The growing importance of the principle of judicial protection in the Community legal order is demonstrated also by a number of other developments over the last years. Reference is made first to direct and indirect harmonisation of national procedural law to ensure effective enforcement of rights derived from Community law. [26,27] As a result, the principle of procedural autonomy of Member States is slowly eroding. This follows not only from new legislation but also from the case law. Judges should set aside domestic legislation, administrative practice or the established case-law of the national jurisdictions, if this is necessary to ensure that the rights that private parties derive from Community law can be enforced.[28] The right to effective judicial protection for individuals has been at the heart of the reasoning of the ECJ in these cases.[29] The same standards do not seem to apply however to remedies in a national context on the one hand and remedies before the Community Courts on the other.[30]

---

years from now and beyond: challenges and possibilities' (2003) 28 *European Law Review* 303.

26 Council Directive 89/665/EEC of 21 December 1989 on the coordination of the laws, regulations and administrative provisions relating to the application of review procedures to the award of public supply and public works contracts [1989] OJ L 395/33.
E-commerce Directive: Directive 2000/31/EC of the European Parliament and of the Council of 8 June 2000 on certain legal aspects of information society services, in particular electronic commerce, in the Internal Market ('Directive on electronic commerce') [2000] OJ L 178/1.
Consumer guarantees Directive: Directive 1999/44/EC of the European Parliament and of the Council of 25 May 1999 on certain aspects of the sale of consumer goods and associated guarantees [1999] OJ L 171/12 and Directive 98/27/EC of the European Parliament and of the Council of 19 May 1998 on injunctions for the protection of consumers interests [1998] OJ L 166/ 51.

27 There is also growing direct harmonisation by way of regulations which is more well-known: one of the most important recent examples being Council Regulation (EC) 1206/2001 of 28 May 2001 on cooperation between courts of the Member States in taking evidence in civil and commercial matters [2001] OJ L 174/1.

28 ECJ Case C-129/00, *Commission/Italy* [2003] ECR I-14637; See J. McKendrick, 'Modifying Procedural Autonomy: Better Protection for Community Rights' (2000) 8 *European Review of Private Law* (2000) 565.

29 See for example ECJ *Commission/Italy* (above n 28); ECJ case C-453/00, *Kühne & Heinz*, [2004] ECR I-00837.

30 Reference is made to the reluctance of the ECJ to open up Article 230 EC described above. In general on remedies at a national level see: J. Lonbay and A Biondi (ed.) *Remedies for Breach of EC Law*, (Chichester, Wiley, 1997); W. Van Gerven, 'Of rights, remedies and procedures' 37 *Common Market Law Review* (2000), 501; T. Eilmansberger 'The relationship between rights and remedies in EC law": in search of the missing link' (2004) 41 *Common Market Law Review* 1199.

The incorporation of fundamental human rights into the Community legal order has been another important factor in the development of the right to effective judicial protection. The Treaty on the European Union and now the Constitutional Treaty contain references to the European Convention on Human Rights. [31] The rights laid down in the convention are recognised as general principles of law that are part of the Community legal system.[32] The case-law of the European Court for Human Rights, which has fleshed out the right to an effective remedy, also forms part of the Community legal order.[33] In the meantime this case-law is also evolving. An interesting example is the judgement in the Posti case where the analysis of the ECHR demonstrates that Article 6(1) requires not just the availability of a judicial remedy but also requires that in practice the remedies can be considered adequate.[34]

There are also some new provisions relating to the judicial system in the Constitutional Treaty.[35] In the provisions dealing with the Court of Justice, the Constitutional Treaty now consolidates the principle that Member States must provide remedies sufficient to ensure effective legal protection in the areas covered by Union law.[36] The necessary legal instruments must exist for effective enforcement. This obligation therefore now has an explicit constitutional status.

Finally, the Constitutional Treaty contains a modified article on the admissibility of direct actions by individuals against Community acts.[37] The text of the new provision is as follows:

> *'Any natural or legal person may, ..., institute proceedings against an act addressed to that person or which is of direct and individual concern to him or her, and against a regulatory act which is of direct concern to him or her and does not entail implementing measures.'*

The current text of the fourth paragraph of Article 230 EC Treaty can be recalled:

> *'Any natural or legal person may...institute proceedings against a decision addressed to that person or against a decision, although in the form of a*

---

31 Articles II-107, II-111 and 112 of the Constitutional Treaty (above n 13).

32 Articles I-7 and II-47 of the Constitutional Treaty (above n 13).

33 See ECJ Case C-94/00, *Roquette Frères* [2002] ECR 9011.

34 *Posti and Rahko v Finland* (Appl no 27824/95) ECHR Reports 2002 VI.

35 Constitutional Treaty (above n 13).

36 Article I-29.

37 Article III-365 of the Constitution. See Groussot (above n 24). Apparently, one of the proposals discussed in the working groups was an explicit reference to Article 230(4) in Article 47 of the Charter which states the right to effective judicial protection. See also Memorandum by Prof. T. Tridimas on these discussions and his proposal for improving access to court, www.publications.parliament.uk/pa/ld200304/lolselect/ldeucom/47/47we20.htm.

regulation or a decision addressed to another person, is of direct and individual concern to the former.´ [38]

Notwithstanding the questions of interpretation that can be expected with regards to this new provision (if of course it ever enters into force), the amendment of the provision providing a legal basis for direct appeals by individuals also demonstrates the growing importance of the individual's right to judicial review. The creation of a possible appeal of individuals against an act of a general nature can be seen as quite an important step considering the legal systems in the Member States.

2. Modernisation of competition law

Modernisation, brought about by Regulation 1/2003, has been the subject of numerous comments in legal literature. Particular reference is made here also to one of the previous editions of Legal Issues, which contains several outstanding contributions about this subject.

In many, if not most cases, market related issues are now at the heart of the decision of a competition authority applying Articles 81 and 82 and the merger rules.[39] This means that, to a large extent, market analysis determines the outcome of a case. Market analysis does not merely involve establishing facts but applying a number of legal concepts such as the relevant market, an appreciable restriction of competition and market power. Therefore, if parties wish to obtain annulment of a decision, they should be able to obtain full review by a court of the market analysis contained in the contested decision.

In this article Regulation 1/2003 is viewed from a specific angle, namely the impact it will have on the existing level of judicial protection for individual companies at the EC level. The Regulation and its accompanying Notices raise a number of issues from the point of view of judicial protection.

2.1 Commission (individual) decisions

Now that national authorities and judges can give full application to Article 81 EC, the Commission has declared that it wants to focus on the major pan-European cases, hardcore cartels and/or those cases that are suitable for setting an example on grounds of policy.[40][41], There will no longer be any

---

38 The phrase "and against a regulatory act which is of direct concern to him or her and does not entail implementing measures" clearly refers to regulations such as those referred to in the Jégo-Quéré and UPA cases.

39 Meaning qualifying facts as being compatible or not with the rules.

40 See also Commission Policy Document on proactive competition policy: Commission (EC) 'A Proactive Competition Policy for a Competitive Europe' (Communication) COM (2004) 293 final, 20 april 2004: available at http://europa.eu.int/comm/competition/publications/proactive/en.pdf.

exemption decisions but there are various types of decisions the Commission can of course still take in individual cases.[42]

Within this category, there are formal decisions based directly on Regulation 1/2003 and other decisions. Article 7 Regulation 1/2003 provides that the Commission may require that undertakings end an infringement of Article 81 or 82. This is of course not new. However, it continues by stating that the Commission may impose on undertakings behavioural or structural remedies, which are proportionate to the infringement and necessary to bring the infringement to an end. Article 9 also gives a new competence to the Commission: if commitments are offered by parties to meet concerns raised by the Commission during the procedure, the Commission may by decision make those binding on the undertakings. Such a decision shall then conclude that there are no longer legal grounds for action by the Commission.[43]

The Commission can also adopt a "finding of inapplicability" if required by the Community public interest.[44] The main purpose of this provision appears to have been to limit the concerns of legal security that were often expressed with regard to the abolition of the notification system. It is said that undertakings will not have a right to such a decision but the Commission might decide to adopt one where it would clarify the law and ensure its consistent application throughout the Community.[45]

The list of possible Commission decisions addressed to individuals should also include the so-called guidance letters.[46] Guidance letters are not regulated in Regulation 1/2003 itself but by a separate notice.[47] Parties can address a memorandum to the Commission setting out why they require guidance and why their case raises a novel point of law. The conditions set

---

41 I. Atanasiu and C. Ehlermann, 'The modernisation of EC antitrust law: consequences for the future role and function of the EC Courts' (2002) 23 *European Competition Law Review* 72. For more general comments and a critical assessment of modernisation see A. Riley, 'EC Antitrust Modernisation: the Commission does very nicely, thank you', in two parts, (2003) 24 *European Competition Law Review* 604 and 657.

42 Will there be more or less individual Commission decisions under the new system? Opinions on this issue are not unequivocal in literature: see Ehlermann and Atanasiu (above n 41), they assume that there will be more decisions.

43 See comments: R. Whish, *Competition Law,* 5th edn (London: Lexis Nexis UK, 2003) 257.

44 Article 10 of Council Regulation (EC) No 1/2003/EC on the implementation of the rules on competition laid down in Articles 81 and 82 of the Treaty [2003] OJ L1/1.

45 Recital 14.

46 Recital 38 of Regulation 1/2003. From the beginning of the modernisation plans the Commission had promised that undertakings would still have a limited possibility to get informal guidance.
Have these guidance letters now replaced entirely the system of comfort letters?

47 Commission Notice on informal guidance relating to novel questions concerning Articles 81 and 82 of the EC Treaty that arise in individual cases (guidance letters) [2004] OJ C101/78.

out in the Notice relate to the importance of the case (in terms of financial interests of the parties) and the absence of pending court procedures on the same issues.

Presumably, these guidance letters will now replace the practice of comfort letters previously used by the Commission to informally end cases and let its views be known. The conditions for guidance letters are strict, however; the question is whether at some point new informal versions of the above-mentioned individual decisions shall turn up again. Comfort letters were a source of criticism, because of their unsatisfactory legal status so there will be some reticence. This issue has not been debated much either in the Commission documents prior to Regulation 1/2003 or in literature.

2.2 Use of soft law

Regulation 1/2003 is accompanied by six notices that are essential to the new modernised system.[48] These notices clearly contain much more than a simple consolidation of existing practice and case-law. In some areas, they introduce new concepts and new conditions for the application of Article 81 EC.[49] In other instances, they introduce new rules of a more procedural nature.[50] Soft law is adopted unilaterally by the Commission and, although on the basis of (older) established case law, it is not (formally) binding upon courts, it is of major importance in individual cases notwithstanding the lack of appeal.[51] The soft law created by the Commission in this area also has a harmonising effect because its rules frequently serve as a source of inspiration for the application of national competition law. This increases its

---

48 Commission Notice on cooperation within the Network of Competition Authorities [2004] OJ C101/43; Commission Notice on the co-operation between the Commission and the courts of the EU Member States in the application of Articles 81 and 82 EC [2004] OJ C 101/54; Commission Notice on the handling of complaints by the Commission under Articles 81 and 82 of the EC Treaty [2004] OJ C 101/65; Commission Notice on informal guidance (above n 47); Commission Notice - Guidelines on the effect on trade concept contained in Articles 81 and 82 of the Treaty [2004] OJ C 101/81; Commission Notice - Guidelines on the application of Article 81(3) of the Treaty [2004] OJ C 101/97.

49 This is the case for the Notice on Article 81 (3) EC which in fact not only gives new elements for the application of the conditions in Article 81 (3) but also contains a very important part on Article 81 (1) and the way it should be applied, which is more than a mere consolidation of current practice and case-law; for comments see L. Hancher and P. Lugard, ' Honey, I Shrunk the Article! A critical assessment of the Commission's Notice on Article 81(3) of the EC Treaty' (2004) 25 *European Competition Law Review* 410.

50 Co-operation in the network, with national judges; the possibility for individuals to obtain so-called guidance letters; see for a thorough study and criticism on the increased use of soft law: L. Senden, *Soft Law in European Community Law, its relationship to Legislation* (Oxford: Hart Publishing, 2005).

51 A judge could indirectly challenge the validity of soft law through a preliminary question and a party to national proceedings should be able to invoke the exception of illegality against soft law instruments. For an example of an exception of illegality (Article 241), see CFI Case T-23/99 *LRAF* [2002] ECR II-1705.

importance for daily competition practice even more. The term "soft law" indeed applies to the type of act but not to its contents.

2.3 Inter-network decisions[52]

There are a number of "inter-network" decisions that the Commission can take on the basis of Regulation 1/2003: the decision to transmit documents (Article 11.2), the decision to request a NCA to transmit documents relating to pending case (Article 11.4), the decision to take over a case previously dealt with by a NCA (Article 11.6), the decision to exchange information (Article 12), the decision to suspend a case being dealt with at another level, and the decision to reject a complaint on the ground that a NCA is already dealing with the case or has dealt with it (Article 13). The possibilities for parties to challenge these decisions shall be discussed below.

2.4. Amicus curiae system

Then there is finally the special category of "amicus curiae" cases. Article 15 of Regulation 1/2003 provides for a novel route of intervention by the Commission in cases pending before the national courts. Different scenarios are possible: the Commission can be asked by the court to provide information via a position or opinion on questions concerning the application of the competition rules; the Commission, acting on its own initiative, may submit written observations to the courts of the Member States and if permitted by the court, oral observations are also possible.[53]

3. Right to a decision before and after[54]

The question of whether a party has a right to obtain a decision on behalf of the Commission is obviously an essential prerequisite to the possibility to exercise one's right of judicial review.

3.1 Applicants

It is difficult to determine whether an applicant had a right to a decision after having notified an agreement for exemption or negative clearance under

---

52 Needless to say the term "decision" is used here in the widest possible sense, not referring to a decision as defined in the Treaty. Only new decisions are dealt with here: the existing infringement decision and the rejection of a complaint are not mentioned in this part.

53 The last paragraph of Article 15 provides that the NCA or Commission may request the relevant court of the Member States to transmit or insure the transmission to them of any documents necessary for the assessment of the case in preparation of the observations mentioned. See also the Notice on co-operation with national courts (above n 48).

54 The term "decision" used here refers to an act closing an investigation by the Commission, which can be the subject of an appeal in a court of law, in other words a "decision" within the meaning of Article 230 EC.

the "old" system. Article 4 of Regulation 17 did not contain an obligation for the Commission to take a decision, only an obligation for parties to notify in order to obtain an exemption.[55] Some have argued that such a right must exist because notifications of new agreements do not benefit from provisional validity, and it would be contrary to the principle of legal certainty if parties could be held to wait indefinitely for a Commission decision.[56] The case-law has confirmed on numerous occasions that the Commission has certain discretionary powers. However, the case-law usually cited in support of this margin of discretion relates to complaint cases and thus might not be conclusive.[57] The Court of Justice had ruled that the rejection of a request for an exemption must be adequately motivated[58] but there is no clear-cut case to say that applicants had a right to a decision when they applied for an exemption or a negative clearance.

In a system where there are no longer any formal notifications, the question of the right to a decision now only concerns companies requesting the Commission to look at their case in the absence of a formal request. This might be to obtain a decision on the non-applicability of the provisions laid down in Articles 81 and 82.[59]However, it appears from the above that there was no clearly defined right to a decision under the "old system" when a notification was made. It seems very unlikely therefore that a right to obtain a negative clearance of declaration of non-application will exist under Regulation 1/2003.

The question of a right to a decision might also occur in case informal guidance is requested. The Notice on guidance letters contains an implicit statement by the Commission that parties shall have no right for the Commission to act upon a request for such a letter.[60] It goes without saying that such a statement is not binding and could be overruled by the Community Courts. However, it does not seem likely that the courts would rule in favour of a right to guidance because this might lead to, in effect, reinstating a notification procedure.[61]

---

55 Commission Notice on cooperation between national courts and the Commission in applying Articles 85 and 86 of the EEC Treaty [1993] OJ C 39/6.

56 Commentaire Mégret, *Le droit de la CEE, Tome 4 Concurrence.* 2nd edn (Bruxelles: Editions de l'Université de Bruxelles, 1997) 448 and J. Temple Lang, 'Community Antitrust law - Compliance and enforcement' (1981) *Common Market Law Review* 335.

57 For example CFI Case T-24/90, *Automec v Commission* [1992] ECR II-2223.

58 For example ECJ Case 19 and 20/74, *Kali & Salz* [1975] ECR 499.

59 This is the new possibility in Article 10. There is no longer a form required for this: it is not set up as a procedure initiated by a notification but rather as a possibility the Commission has to look at an individual case that is important for policy reasons. Nevertheless there is little reason to see why this might not happen after a request from a company.

60 Commission Notice on informal guidance (above n 47). Paragraph 17 states that the Commission shall inform parties if a guidance letter is not issued.

61 A remaining issue here is whether the practice of comfort letters shall be completely replaced by these guidance letters or not.

It is argued here that the Commission should be obliged to motivate the rejection of such a request in a similar way as the Courts have required for the rejection of complainant in the past (see below). There is no other forum to challenge the Commission's refusal than before the Community courts and the existence of a decision is a prerequisite for an appeal. A parallel approach to the case-law described giving complainants a right to a motivated rejection seems entirely justifiable.[62]

All in all, there are fewer cases in which the Commission can be asked to take an individual decision now. Perhaps the lack of a right to a decision at the Community level will also be compensated by the possibilities of ensuring judicial protection at the national level. Nevertheless, the only instrument that exists for the moment to obtain legal security in complicated cases is the procedure for guidance letters. It certainly cannot be taken for granted that legal certainty can be obtained at a national level.[63]

3.2 Complainants

In relation to complaints, the Courts have frequently stated that the Commission can set priorities with a view to the Community interest. It can consider the importance of the infringement to the common market and the likelihood of establishing the infringement but the Commission may also take account of other factors, such as the economical significance of the case.[64] Complainants only have a right to a motivated rejection of their complaint: the Commission is required to substantiate its arguments why the complaint is rejected because there is no Community interest.[65] There is therefore no right for complainants to a formal infringement decision although the Courts are willing to carry out extensive judicial review to examine whether a rejection is adequately motivated.[66]

---

62 One could imagine that in the context of national litigation parties are required to demonstrate that they did everything in their means to assess their complex agreements: would they then have to refer to the fact that they tried to obtain a guidance letter from the Commission? The refusal of that guidance shall have an impact on that litigation and the wording shall be decisive. If the national judge is in doubt about the wording of the letter, would preliminary questions be possible? The judge could suspend proceedings in a similar way as described in the Notice on co-operation with national judges.

63 Many competition authorities have an enforcement system very similar to the new Regulation 1/2003 system and have decided to also abolish exemptions. The possibility to obtain informal guidance shall differ from Member State to Member State. Furthermore, important as the role of national courts may be for private enforcement, parties seeking legal certainty shall not have often (if ever) access to "preventive" judicial review. There are also still many obstacles to private enforcement: see Riley (above n 41).

64 C. Kerse and N. Khan, *EC Antitrust procedure* (London: Sweet & Maxwell, 1998) 90 and following.

65 CFI Case T-37/92, *BEUC/Commission* [1994] ECR II-285, ECJ Case C-119/97 P, *UFEX* [1999] ECR I-1341.

66 Kerse and Khan (above n 64) and C. Kerse, 'The complaint in Competition Cases: a Progress Report' (1997) 34 *Common Market Law Review* 213 and following.

The possibility for complainants to take their case to a national court justifies in part the discretionary powers granted to the Commission.[67] In its efforts to decentralise the application of competition rules, the Commission has strongly encouraged bringing cases at a national level.[68] It has taken quite a clear view in this: *"there is not normally a sufficient Community interest in examining a case where the plaintiff is able to secure adequate protection of his rights before the national courts. In these circumstances the complaint will normally be filed."* The CFI has taken a less radical view. If a case involving the complainant is pending before a national court, this is a factor that the Commission can take into account. However, the fact that a case could be brought before a national court is not reason alone to reject a complaint.[69] Given the further decentralisation that took place recently this is interesting case-law to bear in mind. A form has now been drafted for complaints and the Commission has published a Notice, which aims to promote complaints.[70] The Notice repeats the established principle that complainants have no right to a decision.[71]

3.3 Right to a decision after modernisation?

The existence of private enforcement at a national level does not justify the lack of a right to a decision for applicants. This is especially true for the decisions which the Commission can take on the basis of Regulation 1/2003 and which cannot be replaced by a national judgement or decision. Applicants of formal or informal decisions should have a right to a decision. An indirect argument can be found in par. 75 of the CFI judgement in Automec II. The Court first reiterates that complainants have no right to obtain a decision regarding the existence or otherwise of the infringement. It then continues: "It follows that the Commission cannot be required to give a decision in that connection unless the subject-matter of the complaint falls within its exclusive purview, as in the case of the withdrawal of an exemption granted under Article 85 (3) of the Treaty." Does the Court mean that there is a right to a decision when a case falls within the scope of the exclusive competence of the Commission?[72]Such an interpretation, which seems desirable, would impose a right to a decision in various situations under the new system.

---

67 See also par. 17 of the new Commission Notice on handling complaints (above n 48).

68 See both 1993 Commission Notice on co-operation with national courts (above n 55) as well as 1997 Commission Notice on co-operation with national competition authorities [1997] OJ C 313/3.

69 CFI, *Automec v Commission* (above n 57).

70 See above n 48.

71 Par.27-28, 4-45. It is noted that the Notice seems to indicate that the requirement of a legitimate interest shall be increasingly important and might therefore constitute an additional obstacle, par. 33-40.

72 See above n 69.

Parallel to the case-law on complaints, applicants should have at least a right that the Commission "defines its position" which is not the same as a formal decision). There is currently no legal basis for that right, nor is there clear jurisprudence in that respect. However, if such a right does not exist, the complainants are in a better position than the companies concerned (applicants) since they have been given the right, by legislation and by the Courts, to a motivated rejection of their complaint.[73]

Finally, a separate question might also be whether companies that are subject of an investigation based on a compliant should have a right to the rejection of such a complaint by the Commission. According to the case-law mentioned above, the answer seems also to be negative even though in practice a complaint can cause great economic and reputational damage. In (national) damage proceedings the absence of a clear decision confirming there has or has not been an infringement can be an obstacle.

4. Admissibility under Article 230 EC: appeal possible before and after?[74]

In terms of judicial protection, the condition that an act must be challengeable to be open to review under Article 230 EC Treaty and, in some cases, the requirement that parties have a real interest to bring a case were the most debated issues.[75]

The Courts have always taken a non-formalistic approach. To be challengeable, an act must be of a binding character, it must produce legal effects and be definitive.[76] The contents of the act shall be examined.[77] An illustrative example of this approach is a case where an oral statement was considered appealable by the CFI.[78] Regardless of this seemingly liberal approach by the Courts, several types of decisions of the Commission in competition cases have nevertheless been considered non-appealable in the past.

---

73 CFI Case T-28/90, *Asia Motor France* [1992] ECR II-2285.

74 Article 232 is not addressed here.

75 T. Hartley, *The foundations of European Community Law* (Oxford: OUP, 2003) 356 and following; and P. Craig and G. De Burca, *EU law, Text, Cases and Materials.* 3th edn (Oxford: OUP, 2003) 333-337 on the standard of protection of fundamental rights in Competition proceedings and on review of legality, 506-507.

76 See ECJ in PVC cases correcting the CFI on this point: ECJ Case C-137/92 P, *PVC* [1994] ECR I- 2555 [47-52] and also CFI Case T- 70 and 71/92, *Florimex* [1997] ECR II-693.

77 This approach is not specific to competition cases but common to all cases on the admissibilty of individual appeals, see Schermers and Waelbroeck (above n 11) 317. On "legal effects": 336 and following.

78 CFI Case T-3/93, *Air France* [1994] ECR II-121.

4.1 Addressees

As far as the addressees of a formal Commission decision are concerned, the following types of decisions occurred under Regulation 17: an infringement decision on the basis of Article 81 and 82 EC Treaty[79], a negative clearance on the same basis[80], a decision granting an exemption from Article 81 (1)[81] a decision to revoke the benefit of an exemption[82] or an interim order.[83] In the case of addressees, problems of admissibility of an action before the CFI could arise in the case of an appeal against a negative clearance or an exemption or in case they wish to attack a particular part of the infringement decision and not only the operative part. Do parties have sufficient interest in bringing such a case?

The admissibility of an application against a negative clearance could be a problem: the CFI has considered such an act unchallengeable because it gives satisfaction to the companies concerned. The Court found that by its nature, a negative clearance is not capable of altering the legal position of parties.[84] Therefore an appeal against the reasoning of such a clearance might not be admissible.

An exemption decision by definition implied that the prohibition of Article 81 (1) EC applies; a party might have an interest in contesting that there is an appreciable restriction of competition or in contesting the market definition that is the basis for the Commission's finding that it has a dominant position within the meaning of Article 82 EC. In principle, it is possible to bring an action against a part of an act without bringing the other parts in dispute.[85] An unfavourable provision in the operative part of the decision can be annulled.[86] Grounds of a decision can be annulled if they are a necessary support for the operative part of the decision. However, the requirement of

---

79 Article 3 Regulation 17.

80 Article 2 Regulation 17.

81 Article 81 (3) and Article 4 Regulation 17. An appeal can lead to annulment of the entire exemption; see CFI Case T-374/94, *European Night Services* [1998] ECR II-3141.

82 Article 8 Regulation 17: the regulation only mentioned revocation of an individual exemption; however the benefit of a block exemption was revoked in some cases, see ECJ Case C-279/98 P, *Langnese* [1998] ECR I-5609. Some of the block exemption regulations grant this possibility to the Commission, see for vertical agreements, Article 6 of Commission Regulation (EC) No 2790/1999 of 22 December 1999 on the application of Article 81(3) of the Treaty to categories of vertical agreements and concerted practices [1999] OJ L 336/21.

83 See also L. Ritter, W. Braun and F. Rawlinson, *European Competition Law: a practitioners guide.* 2nd edn (The Hague: Kluwer Law International, 2000) 910-911.

84 CFI Case T-138/89, *Nederlandse bankiersvereniging and Nederlandse Vereniging van Banken v. Commission of the European Communities (Dutch Banks)* [1992] ECR II-2181.

85 Schermers and Waelbroeck (above n 11) 346.

86 ECJ Case 17/74, *Transmarine Ocean Paint* [1974] ECR 1063.

"sufficient interest" makes the case-law in this area somewhat unpredictable.

There seems little doubt that formal decisions based on Regulation 1/2003 shall be appealable acts by companies to whom they are addressed under Article 230 EC in the same way as before under Regulation 17. Article III-365 of the Constitution constitutes a status quo for applicants.

An interesting question is whether there might be an admissibility issue if an addressee challenges only the remedies imposed on it or the wording of the commitments that the Commission makes binding in its decision. These are new questions to the extent that neither remedies nor commitments were dealt with formally under Regulation 17, the predecessor of Regulation 1/2003, although clearly the practice existed.[87] The courts also have experience with remedies in the area of merger control.[88]

4.2 Third parties

First, the right to appeal by third parties against decisions addressed to another company or association for violation of EC competition law: according to the case law, the effects of an exemption decision are similar to a rejection of a complaint for the complainant and a direct appeal against such a decision must fulfil the conditions of Article 230 EC.[89] If there was a legitimate interest in filing a complaint but this was not actually done, the admissibility of an action proves more problematic.[90] Finally, a negative clearance decision might be detrimental to the rights of third parties but it is not always obvious that locus standi exists because the Courts require a sufficient legitimate interest.[91]

The case of a rejection of a complaint is clearer. It is established case-law that a final rejection of a complaint can be challenged before the CFI by a complainant. However, the judicial review is limited to the question whether the Commission adequately stated its reasons for not pursuing the case. The distinction with the right to an actual infringement decision remains;[92] the requirements for a rejection of a complaint cannot be the same as those for a

---

87 See Woodpulp case: ECJ Case C-89/85, *Woodpulp* [1993] ECR I-1307: the commitments are a corollary of an act of the Commission against which an action should be possible.

88 See case-law discussed below (Coca Cola and Lagardère).

89 CFI Case T-17/93 *Matra Hachette* [1994] ECR II-595.

90 CFI Case T-114/92 *Bureau Européen des Médias de l'Industrie Musicale (BEMIM) v. Commission of the European Communities* [1995] ECR II-00147.

91 CFI *Dutch Banks* (above n 75), in that case however the applicants' interest was seen to be uncertain. If the applicant did not actively participate in the proceedings but can demonstrated that he was not aware thereof or badly informed, the appeal might be admissible: the CFI decided this in a merger case, CFI Cases T-96/92 and T-12/93, *Comité Central d'Entreprise de la Société Générale des Grandes Sources and others v Commission of the European Communities* [1995] ECR II-2479.

92 CFI Case T-87/92, *Kruidvat* [1996] ECR II-1931.

formal decision; even though in some cases the scrutiny by the Court (also of the market analysis) is quite detailed.[93]

A decisive element in the case-law allowing complainants locus standi against individual decisions (not addressed to them) in competition cases was the fact that they were often involved in the procedure before the Commission.[94]The question is then whether the abolition of the notification procedure shall have any impact on their position. If they introduce a complaint on the basis of Article 7, 2nd paragraph of Regulation 1/2003 and the relevant Notice, they can claim to have a procedural position. If the Commission would have merely heard them as an interested party in an informal way, it shall be less obvious because, in the absence of a (formal) complaint or an investigation ex officio, the Commission shall not be under an obligation to hear interested parties. Again here the new provision in the Constitution does not seem to alter the position of complainants in the future.[95] It seems advisable that interested parties make sure they have clearly manifested themselves in an early stage of a Commission investigation to have a stronger case at the Courts in terms of admissibility.

4.3 Informal individual decisions[96]

Now we turn again to the informal decisions that have always been part of the practice of the Commission and that shall continue to exist, be it in some new shapes and sizes.

Competition cases were often closed with different types of informal decisions: negative clearance comfort letter, the statement that the agreement is covered by a block exemption or Notice, the agreement is contrary to 81 (1) EC but seems eligible for an exemption 81 (3) EC, discomfort letter: no decision intended but likely infringement (usually reference to national competition law).[97]

The two last types mentioned, could be highly unsatisfactory for parties. Even though it is established case-law that the letters are not binding as

93 For example CFI Case T-65/96, *Kisk Glass & Co. Ltd v Commission of the European Communities* [2000] ECR II-1885; CFI case T- 197/97 and 198/97, *Weyl Beef Products BV, Exportslachterij Chris Hogeslag BV and Groninger Vleeshandel BV v Commission of the European Communities* [2001] ECR II-303.

94 These cases were also referred to as quasi-judicial determination cases where the ECJ was more willing to accept standing under Article 230 (4) EC.

95 The requirements of "direct and individual concern" still exists, unless we would consider that a Commission decision on the basis of Articles 7 or 10 of Regulation 1/2003 would constitute a "regulatory act" (new category of standing, see above under 37) in which case only direct concern needs to be demonstrated.

96 I concentrate here on decisions that contain a substantive decision and less on decisions of a more procedural nature such as for example the refusal to grant access to file.

97 Kerse, *EC Antitrust procedure* (above n 64) 238 and following.

decisions on the courts[98], they can serve as bad precedents in private litigation. Moreover, the Commission can change its mind afterwards.[99] The Courts seemed to (implicitly) suggest some kind of higher value when the Commission published its intentions in the OJ but it is not clear whether it would help parties much in arguing locus standi.[100]

To be challengeable, an act must be of a binding character, it must produce legal effects and be definitive. In IBM it was formulated as follows: *"any measure the legal effects of which are binding on, and capable of affecting the interests of the applicant by bringing about a distinct change in his legal position is an act or decision which may be the object of an action under Article 230"*.[101] On this basis an appeal against an Article 19(3) Notice has been rejected by the CFI.[102]

There do not seem to be many precedents of direct appeals against comfort letters by addressees. A major obstacle is the fact that comfort letters could be qualified as a "provisional" position taken by the Commission at a given moment in time. Acts of the Commission that are of a mere procedural, provisional or preliminary nature, are not considered appealable.[103] It can be expected that this reasoning is (shall be) again the argument to refuse access to courts with regards to several types of (new) informal decisions after modernisation.

Yet the "provisional" character of comfort letters was clearly different from the category of preparatory acts such as a statement of objections, against which the Courts have also refused locus standi.[104] In the case of a

---

98 D. Stevens, 'The "Comfort letter": Old Problems, New Developments' (1994)15 *European Competition Law Review* 81.

99 Some comfort letters were preceded by an Article 19 (3) publication; the Commission announced this as an effort to increase their legal value; Comp. Rep. 1991. This was done mainly after the criticism following the judgements in the Perfume cases, see Kerse (above n 64).

100 ECJ Case 253/78 and I-3/79, *Guerlain* [1980] ECR 2327 and CFI *Langnese* (above n 78).

101 ECJ Case 60/81, *IBM* [1981] ECR 2639; also Automec I: CFI Case T- 64/89, *Automec* [1990] ECR II-367.

102 CFI Case T-74/92, *Ladbroke* [1995] ECR II-115.

103 Lenaerts and Arts mention the following as being relevant factors to determine whether an appeal against "procedural" decisions should be possible: is it a "decision which is independent of the final decision" and would "an appeal against the final decision award adequate protection". Likewise, a decision not to treat certain documents as confidential is appealable but a decision refusing to comply with a request for disclosure of a document from a file, is not. In the last case the possible unlawfulness of the decision can be attacked in an application against the final decision, see K. Lenaerts and D. Arts, *Procedural Law of the European Union* (London: Sweet & Maxwell, 1999) 148.

104 A statement of objections is not appealable; the same attitude was taken with regards the opening of an investigation, minutes made during an inspection, refusal to grant access to the file, the announcement of the reopening of a competition procedure, see for others Schermers and Waelbroeck (above n 2) 353.

statement of objections a definitive decision will still follow and that decision shall be a possible subject of appeal; in the case of comfort letters and other informal (final) decisions, the whole purpose is to avoid a formal decision.[105] Secondly, in practice, they have the same effects as the closing of a case, which casts doubts on their provisional nature.[106] Finally, they are provisional because the Commission might reach a different conclusion at a later stage or on the basis of new facts. However, that particular argument does not seem valid either because the same is true for the application of a block exemption or the benefit of an individual decision, which can be withdrawn.

An important case that takes a more liberal approach, is the Stork case.[107] The Court found it important that in cases of decisions drawn up in a procedure involving several stages, measures which definitively determine a position of the institution upon the conclusion of that procedure, should be open to challenge. Interesting here was the fact that the letters mentioned that the case could be reopened if new points or facts of law would appear, but this was not considered convincing enough by the Court to refuse admissibility.[108]

Informal decisions of the Commission should be open to appeal if they contain an assessment of the factual and legal position of a party in such a way that this has consequences not only for the parties but possibly for third parties' rights. The starting point is the IBM criterion mentioned above. The more modern case-law which skips the requirement "challengeable act" under 230 (4) and goes straight to "direct and individual concern" can just as well be used. It would be consistent with the general trend in the case-law on Article 230 EC that no longer considers the type of act important to determine the admissibility of the appeal.

Unfortunately many valuable arguments have also been rejected in this respect by the Courts. In the *Coca Cola judgement* of 22 March 2000, the applicant sought annulment of a merger decision of the Commission in

---

105 There are some indications that an appeal might be possible if a comfort letter is reasoned in the same way as a decision: Commission (EC) 25th report on competition policy COM (1996) 126 final, reference to ATR/Alenia/Aerospace,128.

106 If the effects are similar to an exemption because the letter explains that the conditions of Article 81 (3) EC are fulfilled, the CFI has accepted the case in Koelman: CFI Case T-575/93, *Koelman* [1996] ECR II-1.

107 CFI Case T-241/97, *Stork Amsterdam bv/Commission* [2000] ECR II-309. The CFI ruled that a comfort letter definitively rejecting a complaint and closing the file may be a subject of an action, since it has the content and the effect of a decision, in as such as it closes the investigation, contains an assessment of the agreements in question and prevents the applicants from requiring the reopening of the investigation unless they put forward new evidence.

108 The Commission Notice on informal guidance (above n 47) gives the Commission the right to change its views, par. 24 but as in Stork, this should not be an obstacle.

which a notified operation was approved.[109] Many arguments were brought forward to show that the decision has important and lasting consequences for the company involved, but the CFI rejected them all. It is difficult to reconcile the approach in that case with the judgement in *Lagardère Canal+* in which the CFI demonstrated greater willingness to review the Commission's position.[110] In both cases, many arguments were put forward on the basis of the parties' right to effective judicial review. These cases demonstrate that the case-law on the admissibility of direct appeals against decisions of the Commission is not always coherent.

4.4 The right to appeal new informal individual decisions

The Notice on informal guidance implies that guidance letters shall not be decisions of the Commission within the meaning of the present Article 249 EC.[111] That statement is obviously not enough to "protect" these letters from review by the Court of First Instance. A priori there is no reason for these informal decisions, or any new types that might be taken, to be treated differently than other existing types of decisions such as comfort letters in the pre-modernisation days.

The main issue is arguing the effects on the economical and legal position of parties.[112] These effects shall clearly often exist. If a comfort letter (before) or a guidance letter (after) has similar effects as a decision, it should be a possible subject of appeal under 230 (4) EC. A clear indication could be when a letter is reasoned in a similar way as a decision. Furthermore, the CFI has accepted a public statement (letters) by the Commission on a merger as a decision.[113] An important consideration of the Court was that the Commission has apparently taken and announced a decision on the application of the EC rules on merger control, after having analysed its competence with regards to the operation.[114]

If access to the Community courts is not granted, no other access to a judge will exist for parties to challenge the findings of the Commission.[115] There is a striking difference in this respect between the current text of Article 230 EC on the one hand and Article III-365 of the Constitutional on the other

---

[109] CFI Case T-125/97 and 127/97, *Coca Cola* [2000] ECR II-1733.

[110] CFI Case T-251/00, *Lagardère Canal+* [2002] ECR I-4825.

[111] Par. 25.

[112] See the formula that the CFI had proposed in the Jégo Quéré case (cited above in note 17) for appeals against acts of a general nature: a party shall be individually concerned if the measure affects his legal position, in a manner that is both definite and immediate, by restricting his rights of by imposing obligations on him (par. 51).

[113] CFI, *Air France* (above n 78).

[114] The consequence being that the authorities of the Member States are competent and can apply their own laws. For the parties concerned the announcement implies they did not have to notify the Commission. Competitors might see an immediate change in their marker position.

[115] The latter within the meaning of Article 6 ECHR.

hand. The reference to decisions has disappeared: an appeal is possible against acts addressed to a person or acts that are of direct or individual concern to him. From the perspective of the right to effective judicial review, it would therefore not be appropriate to limit this to the acts enumerated in Article I-33 of the Constitution. The intention of the legislator was to consolidate the existing case-law whereby the effects on the legal position of parties is what constitutes the nature of the act.

4.5 Inter-Network decisions

A recent article examined the new EU network of competition authorities in the light of the European Convention on Human Rights and the Charter of Fundamental rights of the EU. The issue of access to court was not discussed, but surprisingly the focus was only on a right to a fair hearing and other guarantees protecting defendants in criminal proceedings.[116]

The network of competition authorities is meant to provide a flexible and efficient way for the allocation of cases at the correct level. The introduction of formal procedures and obstacles could possibly make the system less efficient. However these worthy objectives do not justify a lack of involvement of the judiciary in the functioning of the network. The growing importance of the right to effective judicial protection should have an impact on the network, at least as far as the Commission's decisions are concerned. When the Commission operates within the network, it does so in the legal framework of Community law (the EC Treaty, Regulation 1/2003 and procedural regulations such as 773/2004), and as a Community institution it is only subject to judicial control by the Court of First Instance and the Court of Justice.

The Commission as well as national competition authorities have made several statements that inter-network decisions are merely of a procedural nature.[117] However, even on the basis of existing case law, the possibility of access to courts cannot be disregarded that easily. It is not impossible for example to demonstrate that a decision of the Commission to refer a case to a national competition authority is liable to affect the rights of parties. An important precedent for this can be found in the Philips case.

In this 2003 judgement, the Court of First Instance accepted the admissibility of an appeal against the decision of the Commission to refer a

[116] The general conclusion in the article that the structure and the functioning of the EU network of competition authorities does not appear to be incompatible with the requirements of the European Convention on human rights and of the Charter of fundamental rights of the EU, seems to be drawn too readily; W. Wils, *The EU Network of Competition Authorities, the European Convention on Human Rights and the Charter of Fundamental Rights of the EU,* paper presented at the EUI in 2002: http://www.iue.it/RSCAS/Research/Competition/2002.shtml (papers).

[117] See for example par. 31 of the Notice on cooperation: decisions of allocation are a mere division of labour.

merger to a national competition authority. The reasoning of the Court of First Instance is interesting and relevant for this subject. The CFI first examines the existence of direct effect and formulates the following criterion: *"it must be examined whether the referral decision is capable of directly and automatically affecting the applicant's legal position or whether these effects will arise from the decision adopted by the national competition authorities."*[118] The Court states that the direct effect must be examined in the light of the purpose of the measure. The purpose of referral under the merger regulation rules is to transfer responsibility. The lack of actual effect on the competitive position of parties on the relevant market does not exclude direct effect. The effect of the referral is to exclude the application of the EC merger rules (both lawfulness and procedural rights) and to subject the concentration to exclusive review by national competition authorities ruling under their national law. This last element may lead some to reject this judgement because under Regulation 1/2003 a competition authority or court can (and sometimes must) judge a case on the basis of the EC provisions and not (only) national law. However, there are a number of reasons why it is believed this judgement is nevertheless a valuable precedent.

First of all, national competition law is not necessarily similar to EC law from a procedural point of view; therefore the review cannot entirely be "considered comparable as regards its scope and effects."[119] More importantly two arguments of the CFI apply entirely to the situation within the network: by terminating the procedure under Regulation 1/2003, a referral deprives parties of the procedural rights they have at a Community level[120] and the referral precludes parties from relying on the judicial protection which they enjoy under the Treaty, more specifically the opportunity to bring a subsequent action before the CFI under Article 230 EC.[121] The CFI does not mention the judgements in Jégo or UPA discussed above, presumably because they were about the condition "individual concern" whereas the arguments in Philips relate to "direct concern". Nevertheless it must be said there is some tension between the cases mentioned.[122]

There seems to be an additional argument for the admissibility of appeals against referral decisions on the basis of Article 11 of Regulation 1/2003. The Notice on co-operation describes the *rules of allocation* of cases within the network. It appears from these rules that authorities, including the Commission, have to establish, e.g. a material link between the possible

---

118 CFI Case T-119/02, *Philips* [2003] ECR 1433.

119 Par. 283.

120 Regulation 1/2003 (above n 44) and Commission Regulation (EC) No 773/2004 of 7 April 2004 relating to the conduct of proceedings by the Commission pursuant to Articles 81 and 82 of the EC Treaty [2004] OJ L 123/18.

121 Par. 285.

122 See especially par. 290 and 297 of Philips where the link with the availability of national remedies is made; in UPA the Court said that this should not be a factor of importance when evaluating individual concern.

infringements on the one hand and the territory on the other hand. This involves an evaluation of the effect on trade between Member States, an assessment of the activities of parties, the definition of the relevant market, the value and the location of evidence etc. It must be clear that, at least potentially, a referral decision shall contain or be based on a position on these issues that can have legal effects for the parties concerned.[123]

Other types of inter-network decisions that can be taken by the Commission in the network were identified above: should they be treated differently in the light of effective judicial review? First of all, there is the issue of exchange of information: reference is made both to the transmission of documents under Article 11 as well as the exchange of information under Article 12 Regulation 1/2003. Admittedly, such decisions by the Commission might be considered even more as referrals, as merely of a procedural nature. However, if the exchange of information leads to a transfer of responsibility and an investigation opened by the Commission is subsequently closed at the Community level, the reasoning from the Philips judgement described above, might apply. The same can be said about the decisions on the basis of Article 13 of Regulation 1/2003 where the Commission can close a case because a national competition authority is already dealing with it. Another situation that should justify judicial review to guarantee the protection of parties would be a dispute about the confidential nature of information.[124]

4.6 Amicus curiae interventions

Before the national judge a debate can take place about the content of the Commission's written submissions in the framework of the new amicus curiae system based on Article 15 of Regulation 1/2003. The Commission seems to assume that these submissions shall be merely factual elements that the national courts can take into account, like the opinions that were already granted under the old Notice on co-operation between the Commission and the courts. In fact, the problems from a point of view of judicial protection are very similar here as those arising from the use of soft law (see below). It does not seem acceptable that these submissions would be immune from any form of judicial review, especially if they play a decisive role in the resolution of the dispute.

4.7 Soft law?

Will the increased use of soft law have an impact on procedural rights of parties? The increase of soft law can raise questions mainly at a national level: these policy documents often containing new rules and concepts are

---

[123] This "test" is in line with the approach taken by Advocate General Jacobs in ECJ *UPA* (above n 16).

[124] The Notice on co-operation in the network recalls that the terms professional secrecy and confidentiality are Community law concepts (above n 39), at par. 28.

formally not binding but of great importance in national litigation.[125] At a centralised level, it seemed very unlikely that an individual direct appeal against an instrument of soft law was possible under the (old) text of Article 230 EC Treaty.[126] It remains to be seen how the new text of the Constitution shall be interpreted in the future because it contains an interesting new possibility to act against regulatory acts. It shall perhaps be difficult for parties to argue that they have an interest in obtaining standing to challenge notices, guidelines and similar documents.[127] There is however an issue of judicial protection here because these instruments of soft law often contain very detailed rules that, even though theoretically only being "an interpretation" by the Commission, cannot be actually called into question in a national context.[128] The only possibility to challenge these instruments of soft law would be an exception of illegality on the basis of Article 241 EC or the possibility of preliminary questions by the national court: this requires the pre-existence of a dispute in court.[129]

5. The Courts approach to judicial review

5.1 Standard of review

Assuming an applicant has locus standi, the level of judicial protection is also determined by the standard of review adopted by the judiciary. Much depends on the level of self-restraint adopted by the courts.[130]

It is relevant to make a distinction between decisions involving sanctions and other decisions. Where sanctions are involved, Article 229 EC Treaty provides for full review by the courts. Article 31 of Regulation 1/2003 sets out the principle of unlimited jurisdiction to review decisions where the Commission has fixed a fine or periodic penalty payment. The Court of Justice may cancel, reduce or increase the fine or penalty payment imposed.

---

[125] In practice national judges are reluctant to set aside soft law instruments but the case-law of the Court of Justice is nevertheless very clear.

[126] I exclude individual "soft law" like comfort letters and refer only to notices and guidelines of a more general nature.

[127] Parties must prove a vested and continued interest in the annulment of the contested measure see CFI *Kruidvat* (above n 92) and CFI *Dutch Banks* (above n 84).

[128] The new provision in Article II-365 might inspire some however to argue that these acts of the Commission are "regulatory acts". This would then mean only direct concern has to be demonstrated.

[129] In this respect the ECJ's recent judgement in the PVC case is of great interest, (above n 76): It seems to acknowledge the possibility of an exception of illegality and it is also very clear on the obligation for the Commission to respect its own Notices.

[130] M. Siragusa, "Judicial review of competition decisions under EC law" – a lecture by Mario Siragusa of Cleary, Gottlieb, Steen & Hamilton given at the Competition Commission on 21 September 2004; Lenaerts and Vanhamme, *Procedural rights of private parties* (above n 14) 559.

In other cases, Article 230 EC implies that review is limited to the legality of the decisions. There is no clear definition in EC law of the standard of review to be adopted by the Community Courts in general; neither is there a definition specific to competition law. The same can be said for the other key concepts of burden and the standard of proof for the Commission or the complainant. The Courts have developed their own case-law which, in the area of competition, shows slightly different approaches towards the scope of judicial review according to the subject matter of the appeal.

There is a tendency for the Courts to leave discretion to the Commission when evaluating facts and economical considerations.[131] In many judgements the Courts has considered that where there is a complex economic situation, Community institutions have a *margin of appreciation* or *power of appraisal*, not only as to measures to be taken but also to the assessment of the facts.[132] In competition cases the Court seemed willing to leave fairly wide (discretionary?) powers to the Commission, particularly where exemptions on the basis of Article 81 (3) EC are concerned and in the review of the legality of Commission decisions rejecting complaints for alleged breaches of competition rules. Very often in these last situations the Courts limited themselves to examining whether the decision is based on a materially incorrect appreciation of the facts or contains a manifest error of assessment.[133] The Court of First Instance, mostly supported by the Court, seems more willing to review in depth the assessment of facts under Article 81 (1) EC in direct appeals against Commission decisions.

There seems to be noticeable distinction therefore between, on the one hand, the comprehensive judicial review the Courts have often carried out under Article 81(1) EC Treaty[134] and the more limited judicial review that can be found in other cases mainly applications of Article 81 (3).[135] One of the

---

[131] Article 33 of the ECSC Treaty might have been a source of inspiration: in addition to similar conditions as in Article 173 EEC, the article stated *"the Court may not, however, examine the evaluation of a situation, resulting from economic facts or circumstances..., save where the Commission is alleged to have misused its powers or to have manifestly failed to observe the provisions of the Treaty..."* Ehlermann denies the existence of such self-restraint, 'Community Competition Procedures' in: Lord Slyn of Hadley and S Pappas (eds), *Procedural Aspects of EC Competition Law* (Maastricht: European Institute of Public Administration, 1995) 9, but explicitly refers to it in Ehlermann and Atanasiu (above n 41). Similarly K. Lenaerts and D. Gerard also argue that there is no longer a "self-imposed limited control", 'Decentralisation of EC Competition Law Enforcement: Judges in the Frontline' (2004) 27 *World Competition: law and economics review* 313 [340].

[132] Schermers & Waelbroeck, on the difference between "margin of appreciation" and "discretionary powers", see D. Bailey, 'Scope of Judicial review under Article 81' (2004) 41 *Common Market Law Review* 1327; also Jacobs, F, *Court of Justice Review in Competition cases*, (New York, Fordham University, 1987) 541.

[133] Ehlermann and Atanasiu (above n 41).

[134] Meaning they will review a decision to the maximum extent possible under Article 230 and in case of fines, under Article 229, see Bailey (above n 125) 1333.

[135] Limited judicial review meaning the CFI will confine its review to whether the lawfulness of the decision is vitiated by error of law or fact, procedural impropriety,

reasons that had been identified by the Courts for limiting the scope of judicial review important in this context relates to the *complex economic analysis* inherent to many competition cases. Other reasons worthwhile mentioning are the procedural rules before the Community courts and the institutional balance. Many Commission decisions determine the law and set standards that are really policy decisions. The Courts will be reluctant to replace the Commission's view on such issues with their own. The jurisprudence on non-compete obligations is a good example.[136]

It must be said that even in judgements that might qualify as *comprehensive* judicial review, the Courts will generally not actually assess the facts again nor evaluate the actual value of the evidence brought by parties. Therefore judicial review in some competition cases, even by the CFI, can most likely not be considered as full and unlimited judicial review within the meaning of the ECHR.[137]

Recent case-law has shown again that the CFI is willing to review in great detail the assessment of the Commission whether or not a concentration is compatible with the common market.[138] The Court of Justice has endorsed this approach in the recent judgements upon appeal.[139] Finally there is a slow and gradual trend towards less deference towards economic appraisal through an appraisal of the Commission's (adequate) statement of reasons.[140] The recent case-law of the Community courts indicates that the Commission will have to investigate the facts of every case very thoroughly and must attain a sufficient standard of proof. This is also why some have predicted an increase in workload for the Community courts: more cases will be brought and the depth of analysis by the Courts shall increase.[141]

---

defective reasoning or a manifest error of assessment, see Bailey (above n 132) 1333.

136 See ECJ Case 42/84, *Remia* [1985] ECR 2545; why four years and not three; why for that matter *de minimis* at 5% and not 8%? These are the type of policy choices by the Commission that the Courts shall not interfere with; the same can be said most likely for all the thresholds that modernised competition law contains. See also Jacobs (above n 132) 572.

137 Schermers and Waelbroeck (above n 2) 48; Waelbroeck and Fosselard (above n 14).

138 CFI Case T-5/02 *Tetra Laval* [2002] ECR II-4381; CFI Case T-342/99 *Airtours* [2002] ECR II-2585; CFI Case T-310/01 *Schneider* [2002] ECR II-4071. For comments on the standard of proof, see D. Bailey, 'Standard of Proof in EC Merger proceedings: a common law perspective' (2003) 40 *Common Market Law Review* 845.

139 ECJ Cases C-12/03 & C-13/03, *Commission of the European Communities v Tetra Laval BV* [2005] ECR 987, 1113.

140 For example: CFI Cases T-374, 375, 384 and 388/94, *European Night Services* [1998] ECR II-3141.

141 Ehlermann and Atanasiu (above n 14).

5.2 The impact of modernisation?

The self-restraint operated by the Community courts with regard to Commission decisions was often present in appeals against exemption decisions. This category of appeals is now part of history. In which cases shall the CFI still play a role, and how should the Courts define their role after modernisation?

The rights of complainants seem not to have changed. The CFI shall still be able to examine the rejection of complaints by the Commission. It would not be a good idea for the Community courts to render the admissibility or the review of such cases more difficult in the post- modernisation area. The existence of the national alternatives should not lead to any restrictions at a Community level. A recent study carried out for the Commission has shown that there are astonishingly little cases before the national courts. Reference is also made to the Air France judgement where the CFI stated that the possible existence of remedies before the national courts cannot preclude the possibility of contesting the legality of a decision adopted by a Community institution directly before the Community judicature under Article 230 EC.[142]

The self-imposed restraint of the Courts in the presence of complex economic considerations is no longer, if ever it was, appropriate, and it does injustice to the great competence developed by the CFI in competition cases. Where Article 81(3) is concerned, national judges are now required to apply the conditions for an exception, and the Commission's Notice describes the conditions to be applied in such a way that the exercise seems void of policy considerations. There is no reason why the Community courts should not be able to deal with economic considerations just as the national judges do.

Secondly, as argued on a number of occasions above, the only way individuals can currently obtain review of Commissions decisions is by the Community courts. Effective judicial protection would be denied if factual and economical considerations cannot be subject of the review.[143]

Further, the fact that the Commission has a power of appraisal and has the institutional task of designing the Community's competition policy does not automatically imply that judicial review should not be comprehensive. In cases where policy considerations obviously play a role there might be some argument to defend a more marginal approach. However, this is not the case for the majority of appeals. Going back to appeals against the rejection of a complaint, review by the Courts should verify whether the Commission has

---

142 CFI Case Air France (above n 78). In a way the ECJ said the same in UPA and Jégo by denying that the alternative remedies at a national level should be relevant in a given case to determine whether the direct appeal is admissible.

143 As defended by Tiili and Vanhamme this is best done through comprehensive review instead of the alternative route of the adequate statement of reasoning which leads to a less satisfactory result for applicants.

carefully examined the complaint and taken into account all facts and economic considerations notwithstanding the principle that the complainant does not have a right to an infringement decision which, as defended above, seems justified by the existence of the national route for complainants.[144]

For complainants, enforcement is possible on both the national level and Community level; this is much less the case for parties to an agreement. In their case, lack of a right to a decision and subsequently locus standi is more problematic from the viewpoint of the right to effective judicial review and the related principle of legal certainty. It is submitted that both the principle of effective judicial protection now generally recognised as a key element of the Community legal order, as well as the modernisation of competition law, justify that comprehensive judicial review becomes the rule against individual decisions taken in the framework of Regulation 1/2003 and limited or marginal review the exception.[145]
Finally, there is another specific characteristic of the centralised enforcement system that supports the argument that comprehensive judicial review should be the rule. It relates to the fact that the Commission has both the investigative as well as the decision making powers.[146] This reinforces the need for full review by a court of law after the decision has been taken.

5.3 The Role of the Community Courts after Modernisation: Concluding Remarks

It is likely that the Courts shall in any case play an important role through the preliminary rulings procedure: national courts can refer any question dealing with the interpretation of competition rules [147] and the validity of

---

[144] However, this alternative is far from very much promoted a guarantee that adequate judicial protection shall be obtained; see Riley (above n 41) for a very pessimistic view, p. 607 and following.

[145] The same thesis is defended, be it on some other grounds, in the excellent paper by V.Tiili and J. Vanhamme, 'The power of appraisal of the Commission vis à vis the powers of judicial review of the Communities Court of First Instance and Court of Justice' *22 Fordham International Law Journal* (1999) 885. Ehlermann and Atanasiu also call for a "normal standard of review" (above n 41).

[146] It has been raised that this is a separate problem with regards to the ECHR; see D. Waelbroeck and D. Fosselard (above n 14). Interestingly enough in another article 'The combination of the investigative and prosecutorial function and the adjudicative function in EC Antitrust Enforcement: a legal and economic analysis' (2004) 27 *World Competition: Law and Economics Review* 201, W. Wils argues that possible problems arising from the Commissions double function under the European Convention are reduced because of the existence in the EC system of judicial review by the Community Courts. The point that is made here is precisely that in many cases such review does not exist because of the lack of a right to a decision and the admissibility criteria under Article 230 EC.

[147] This includes both interpretation of concepts of EC competition law as well as (by renvoi) questions of national competition law based there on, see ECJ Case C-7/97, *Oscar Bronner* [1998] ECR I-7791. B. Vesterdorf expects preliminary references to increase due to Regulation 1/2003 and enlargement (above n 16) 317. K. Lenaerts and D. Gerard, 'Decentralisation of EC Competition Law

Community measures. It has been defended above that national judges should not hesitate to challenge the validity of, e.g. soft law or amicus curiae intervention and, if necessary, put questions to the ECJ.

In general, however, the modernised system seems to give a less prominent role to the Community courts in terms of judicial review because more cases are expected to take place at a national level. The individual's right to an effective remedy on the basis of Community law, is assumedly fulfilled independently of the level at which he can obtain judicial relief. For those individuals for whom alternative judicial review on a national level is really possible, there does not seem to be a problem.[148] However, judicial review of Commission decisions is never possible at a national level.

The discussion recalls the debate that took place following Advocate General Jacobs Opinion in *UPA* and the CFI's judgement in *Jégo* that followed, briefly described above. The question both the Advocate General and the CFI struggled with was whether the existence of indirect means to challenge acts of the Community by way of preliminary questions (Article 234 EC), an exception of illegality (Article 241 EC) or an action for damages (Article 235 and 288), was enough to ensure effective judicial remedies for individuals. If national procedures involving an indirect challenge of a decision of the Commission are effective, then one might accept the Community courts to step back. For individual decisions and inter-network decisions, such indirect challenges are not sufficient.

It was defended above that locus standi should exist for direct appeals against a number of existing decisions where it is presently still difficult to bring an appeal and secondly locus standi should exist for a number of new decisions under Regulation 1/2003. A "test" for admissibility was proposed. Moreover, a case was made for systematic comprehensive review by the CFI.

A possible criticism might be that this will increase the workload of the Courts and that the existing procedural framework has not been suitably adapted. Although this might be a valid argument, there are three reasons why it should not be decisive. Firstly, every individual has the right to effective judicial protection. The natural consequence of the importance of this principle elsewhere in Community law should lead to respect being accorded to it also in the area of competition law. The Courts should be encouraged to apply the same standards to themselves as those they apply to the national judge when he is responsible for providing for remedies for

---

Enforcement' (above n 122), on Community courts at p. 338. Because of enlargement and decentralisation more referrals can be expected. See on competence of NCA's: ECJ Case C-53/03, *Syfait e.a* [2005] ECJ I-04609.

148 In UPA the ECJ rejected the relevance of the existence of national remedies because this would imply an examination of the system of a given Member State in each case. This is a plausible argument. However here we refer to the possibility of national review in terms of the competence of national judges as opposed to Community Courts, leaving aside the actual chances of obtaining relief.

breach of EC law at the national level. Secondly, there is room for creativity in the procedural framework in which the Courts now operate.[149] Reference is made to the changes already made by the Treaty of Nice and to the future Constitutional Treaty. Use might be made of the specialised tribunals; an adapted fast track procedure seems appropriate for appeals against decisions within the network and in the amicus curiae system. Use of witnesses and experts might be increased. Thirdly, a thorough review of the enforcement system at a Commission level might be considered because of the growing criticism that the Commission both investigates and sanctions. Such a reform would compensate to a certain extent the current limited role that the Community judges play.

In the absence of legislative initiatives, we might expect answers from the Courts to these new questions in the near future, particularly in relation to issues of admissibility of direct appeals. There is a basis in the existing case-law to allow for more of a role for the Courts than the Commission so far leads us to believe in its Notices and public statements. Whilst competition law was undergoing modernisation in recent years, there have been several developments outside this area that reinforce the importance of every individual's right to an adequate level of judicial protection. case-law in the competition law area has always been somewhat more lenient towards locus standi than in other areas of Community law because of the seriousness of the sanctions involved and it should continue to do so.

It would be an exaggeration to state that the level of judicial protection for individuals at the centralised level of enforcement has dramatically decreased. A fair assessment is that some existing problems have not been solved, and some new questions have been raised. It will be up to the Community courts again to attempt to find some answers.

---

[149] Original ideas expressed by D. Goyder, *EC Competition Law* (Oxford: OUP, 2003) 561.

Chapter 3

Intrastate equals interstate*

The particularities of the role of the interstate requirement in competition law

Both Articles 81 and 82 EC Treaty require practices to affect trade between Member States to fall within the scope of the prohibitions that they contain. In other areas of EC law, such as for example free movement of goods or services, the Treaty also only applies is there is "interstate effect". The purpose of this article is to highlight the particularities of the interstate requirement in competition law and to reflect on its further evolution taking into account the modernisation package of 2004 which included Commission guidelines on the effect on trade between Member States.

First, the concept is defined by reference to the case-law. Then the interpretation of the interstate clause as a condition for the application of the competition rules is discussed. Reference is made to the link with free movement, the extensive interpretation of the concept and some specific developments in the case-law. The role of the requirement is then briefly addressed. In a second part of the article, Reg. 1/2003 and modernisation (decentralisation) are brought into the picture and the Commissions guidelines are described in some more detail. By way of conclusion, attention is drawn to the fact that the requirement of interstate effect has never stopped competition law to apply to, what in other areas of EC law would be called, internal situations.

1. Introduction[150]

The purpose of this article is to highlight the particularities of the interstate criterion in the specific area of competition law and to reflect on its further development.

It is often said elsewhere in Community law that the requirement of interstate trade is fading or becoming less important.[151] By this it is usually meant that the Community judges have gradually expanded the application of Community law to internal situations. As a consequence, more national

* This article is the translation of a chapter entitled 'Europees mededingingsrecht: intrastaat is gelijk aan interstaat', in: E. Manunza and L. Senden (eds.), *De EU: de interstatelijkheid voorbij?* (Nijmegen: Wolf Publishers, 2006). The article was closed on 1 March 2006.

150 This article is a translation from Dutch.

151 The changing role of the interstate clause in other areas of Community law was the subject of other chapters in the book in which this contribution was published. It is relevant to keep in mind what the general theme of the book was, when reading this particular chapter.

rules are being screened for their compatibility with Community law, even if this is not strictly necessary for the accomplishment of the internal market. This widens the impact of Community law. In turn, the consequence might be loss of autonomy for Member States, both where substantial law is concerned as well as in the area of procedures (procedural autonomy).

It can surely be said also in competition law that the impact of Community law has increased significantly. However, the situation is not quite the same. Is the interstate trade clause still relevant? The answer is probably affirmative, mostly due to developments that are specific to competition law. However, the role of the interstate criterion is different.

Competition law does not deal with state regulation but with prohibitions that are directly applicable to companies. We are not in a situation where a citizen or a company is in conflict with its own or another Member State. Concept such as U-turn or reversed discrimination, are not relevant here. The scenarios are very different. This can be illustrated by a hypothetical example.

A company A from the United States might find itself before a judge in Italy in a conflict concerning the validity of a non-compete clause in an agreement concluded with the Greek company C. The contract might concern the sale of pharmaceuticals on the Italian and Greek market. If the judge considers that clause to be restrictive of competition, the clause might be null and void on the basis of the cartel prohibition laid down in Article 81 of the EC Treaty. The fact that two parties are involved that are not resident in Italy, is totally irrelevant. In this particular dispute two companies are involved in commercial litigation. The judge will have to establish whether the contract has effects on competition within the common market and whether the trade between Member States is affected. However international this dispute may seem, it is possible that Community law does not apply. On the contrary, it is also possible that such a clause in a contract between for example two Dutch companies, falls within the scope of application of Article 81 EC Treaty.

The condition "may affect trade between Member States" is mentioned both in the cartel prohibition of Article 81 of the EC Treaty as well as the prohibition of abuse of a dominant position in Article 82 EC Treaty. The purpose here is not to provide an overview of the different types of agreements and behaviour in relation to the condition of interstate trade. Rather, the purpose is to examine how the concept has developed and which has been the impact of the entering into force of Regulation 1/2003 of 16 December 2002. This contribution therefore does not include an exhaustive discussion of the concept of interstate trade but rather aims to provide some thoughts and comments in the light of recent developments.

First, the condition of interstate trade shall briefly be defined and described on the basis of practice of the European Commission and the jurisprudence of the Court of First instance and the Court of Justice of the European Communities. This shall include the practice with regards to agreements and behaviour limited to a Member State. The entry into force of Regulation 1/2003 shall then be examined from the perspective of interstate effect. This will obviously also include a description of the Notice of the Commission in which the concept has been explained. Finally, a related concept (the Community interest) is introduced and some conclusive remarks shall be made.

2. General context

2.1 Definition of interstate trade

Article 81 (agreements) en 82 (abuse) EC Treaty both contain the condition that the behaviour of companies has to "affect trade between Member States". It is a condition for the application of both prohibitions but it is also a criterion to determine competences.

In the absence of real "travaux prèparatoires", it is assumed that the condition was included to leave sufficient margin for Member States to regulate the economy within their Member State in an independent way. However, it shall appear hereinafter that the Court of Justice has not let itself be restricted by that to enlarge the scope of application of both prohibitions. Since the very beginning, the link was made to the common market. It is interesting for example to refer to the Explanatory Memorandum of the Dutch law approving the EEC Treaty:

> *"With these words the Treaty has aimed to draw a line between cartels and dominant positions which affect the functioning of a common market, and those which only have a local significance and are therefore uninteresting from a Community point of view".*[152]

There are also a number of linguistic peculiarities to be mentioned. First of all, the term "affect trade between Member States".

The different linguistic versions of the Treaty have slightly different wording. In some languages (such as in Dutch) a negative word is added (ongunstig) giving rise to questions in the case law. Is every affectation on trade between Member States sufficient or does it have to be a negative one? The Court of Justice ended this debate quite soon by referring to the objectives of the provisions. According to the Court the essence is whether:

> *"The concept of "agreements...which may affect trade between member states" is intended to define, in the law governing cartels, the boundary*

---

[152] Cited in Mulder & Mok, *Kartelrecht* (Deventer: Kluwer, 1962) 215. It is also explained there that the origin of the condition of effect on interstate trade can be found in U.S. antitrust law.

between the areas respectively governed by Community law and national law. In this connexion what is particularly important is whether the agreement is capable of constituting a threat, either direct or indirect, actual or potential, to freedom of trade between Member States in a manner which may harm the attainment of the objectives of a single market between state".[153]

In another famous case, also still cited as a standard in this area, it is formulated as follows:

"It must be possible to foresee with a sufficient degree of probability on the basis of a set of objective factors of law or of fact that the agreement in question may have an influence, direct or indirect, actual or potential, on the pattern of trade between member states. The influence thus foreseeable must give rise to a fear that the realization of a single market between Member States might be impeded. In this respect, it is necessary to consider in particular whether the agreement is capable of bringing about a partitioning of the market in certain products between member states.".[154]

This means that in principle, an increase in interstate trade can also be taken into account, not only a negative impact.

Furthermore, the wording of Articles 81 and 82 EC also mentions "*may* affect". This means that in competition law it has been clear from the start that potential affectation was also envisaged. It has also become apparent from the standard phrases cited above, that the Court has used an interpretation very similar to the formula used in free movement: any direct or indirect, actual or potential obstacle to trade, can be taken into account.

In these general remarks about the definition of interstate trade, it is appropriate to say something also about the term "trade".

In the context of Community law it is not surprising that it is an autonomous concept and, according to the Court, a very broad one. Trade does not only cover goods but also services and loss of profits to another Member State.[155] The concept basically covers any cross-border economic activity. "Between Member States" implies that there must be an impact on cross-border economic activities between at least two Member States: this

---

153 ECJ Cases 54/64 & 58/64, *Consten and Grundig* [1966] ECR (1966) 571.

154 ECJ Case 56/65, *Société Technique Minière (L.T.M.) v Maschinenbau Ulm GmbH (M.B.U.)* [1966] 416. See also W van Gerven, *Kartelrecht: Europese Gemeenschap* (Deventer: Tjeenk Willink, 1997) 86.

155 ECJ Case 172/80, *Gerhard Züchner v Bayerische Vereinsbank AG* [1981] ECR 2021. Other examples: R. Burnley, 'Interstate revisited: the jurisdictional criterion for articles 81 and 82', (2002) 23 *European Competition Law Review* 217.

can be part of one Member State and not necessarily the whole territory.[156] Finally, the question of interstate trade is clearly a different from the one concerning the definition of the relevant market. Even if the relevant market is national or even regional, there can be an effect on trade between Member States.[157]

2.2 Appreciability

The extensive interpretation of the condition of interstate trade since the beginning of European competition law, allowed the Commission to bring nearly all agreements under Article 81 EC Treaty. A possible correction came in the judgement Völk/Vervaecke in which the Court determined that agreements can escape the application of Article 81 EC Treaty if they have only an insignificant influence on interstate trade.[158] Since then it is acknowledged that Article 81 EC Treaty contains a condition of appreciability.

In the meanwhile, the Commission was overcome by notifications of agreements under the regime of Regulation 17 and welcomed the Courts judgement. The Commission based its *de minimis* policy on this judgement.[159] It has to be said in the following notices and case-law that there has always been a certain confusion surrounding appreciability: does it apply to the restriction of competition itself or to the trade between Member States? In the *de minimis N*otice of 2001, the Commission implicitly recognizes that there has been some unclarity surrounding this concept and makes the distinction more clear.[160] This is now confirmed in the Notice on interstate trade of 2004 which shall be discussed under 3.3.[161] It is now generally recognised that the condition of appreciability applies both to the restriction of competition as well as to the trade between Member States.

156 CFI Case T-213/95, *Stichting Certificatie Kraanverhuurbedrijf (SCK) and Federatie van Nederlandse Kraanbedrijven (FNK) v Commission of the European Communities* [1997] ECR II-1739.

157 Commission Notice laying down guidelines on the effect on trade concept contained in Articles 81 and 82 of the Treaty [2004] OJ C 101/7, point 22 and chapter 3.2.

158 ECJ Case 5/69 *Franz Völk v S.P.R.L. Ets J. Vervaecke* [1969] ECR 295.

159 The first Notice dates back to 1970 : Commission Notice of 2 June 1970 [1970] OJ/1; the current Notice is Commission Notice on agreements of minor importance which do not appreciably restrict competition under Article 81 (1) of the Treaty (de minimis) [2001] OJ C 368/7.

160 Ibid.

161 Commission Notice laying down guidelines on the effect on trade (above n 157).

3. Further interpretation of the interstate condition in practice and jurisprudence

3.1 Relation with free movement

Since the Consten & Grundig judgement of the Court, in each case the overall legal and factual elements of the case have to be taken into account to determine whether an agreement or behaviour can directly or indirectly, effectively or potentially, have an influence on the trade between Member States.

It is good to note that this definition was laid down by the Court even before the famous similar ruling in Dassonville with regards to the free movement of goods.[162]

Did the Court find the inspiration in Consten & Grundig when clarifying this concept of "measures of having equivalent effect"? In any case, this shows how Community competition rules as well as the rules on free movement of goods are fundamentally instrumental to the same higher goal which is the common market.[163]

In the meantime, the focus in competition law has been more fighting restrictions of competition as such, rather than accomplishing the common market. This is perhaps a difference with the jurisprudence and the area of free movement where the Court seems to have particular attention for those areas where the Community legislator as well as the Member States failed to eliminate obstacles to free movement.[164]

3.2 Extensive interpretation

It appears from the short description above that the condition of interstate trade was never a major obstacle for the application of Articles 81 and 82 of

---

162 ECJ Case 8/74, *Dassonville* [1974] ECR 837: "all trading rules enacted by Member States which are capable of hindering, directly or indirectly, actually or potentially, intra-community trade are to be considered as measures having an effect equivalent to effective restrictions" (rec. 5).

163 On the convergence between rules on free movement and rules on competition, K. Mortelmans, 'Towards convergence in the application of the rules on free movement and on competition' (2001) 38 Common Market Law Review 613. Also J. Faull, 'Effect on trade between Member States and Community: Member State jurisdiction' (Fordham Corporate Law Institute) New York [1990] 485. The internal markt has not lost its significance as an important principle of interpretation, see Opinion of Advocate General Poiares Maduro, case 205/03 P, 10 November 2005, rec. 51.

164 See recent articles by R. Wezenbeek, 'Consumer and competition policy: the Commission's perspective and the example of transport' (2006) 17 *European Business Law Review* 73; H. Vedder, 'Competition law and consumer protection: how Competition can be used to Protect Consumers Even better – or Not' (2006) 17 *European Business Law Review* 83.

the EC Treaty in specific cases. It has to be said that the Commission did not particularly give much attention to this condition when dealing with individual cases.[165]

The Court of Justice had also stated that the effect on trade between Member States is usually the consequence of several factors which might not each individually be decisive.[166] With regards to interstate trade the burden of proof was not important: proof had to be delivered that agreements as a whole, could possibly appreciably influence the trade between Member States.[167]

The extensive interpretation of this condition was sometimes criticised, even by implying that the Commission as well as the Court of Justice exceeded their competences. However, all in all there was little opposition to the flexible attitude of the Commission, supported therein by the Courts.[168]

It is not required either that every single part of an agreement, including every single restriction of competition, affects commerce. If the agreement as a whole has an interstate effect, Community law shall apply to the whole agreement, including those elements of the agreement which do not as such affect trade between Member States.[169]

The wide interpretation which is applied, makes it easy to apply the cartel prohibition just as well as the prohibition on abuse of a dominant position to cases where interstate effect is not so obvious. Agreements between an undertaking from a Member State and an undertaking from a third country can for instance have as a result that the trade between Member States is affected.[170] In the case of vertical agreements, the theory of cumulative effect was developed. In some cases, on the basis of that theory, an agreement shall have to be looked at in the context of a network of similar agreements of which it is a part. It is only when looking at the network of similar

---

165 For comments see R. Burnley, (above n 155); W. van Gerven, (above n 154); J Faull (above n 163). In this lastly mentioned article the author states: "Many commentators conclude that it is hard to find something which may not affect trade between Member States".

166 ECJ case C-250/92, *Gottrup-Klim* [1994] ECR I-5641; also ECJ Joined Cases C-215/96 & C-216/96, *Bagnasco* [1999] ECR I-135, rec. 47.

167 Court of Justice 21 January 1999, Bagnasco, cited in previous note. According to Faull: "The reasonably foreseeable effect on the reasonably foreseeable development of trade", (above n 163).

168 Criticism increased also after the entry into force of the Treaty of Maastricht and the introduction of the principle of subsidiarity, see in this perspective P. Bos, 'Towards a Clear Distribution of Competence between EC and National Competition Authorities' (1995) 16 *European Competition Law Review* 410.

169 ECJ Case 193/83, *Windsurfing* [1986] ECR I-611; ECJ case C-266/97 P *Vereniging van Groothandelaren in Bloemkwekerijen* [2000] ECR I-2135.

170 ECJ Case 51/75, *EMI/CBS* [1976] ECR I-811; J. Faull and A. Nikpay, *The EC law of Competition* (Oxford: Oxford University Press, 1999) 100.

agreements that the effect on interstate trade shall be evaluated. Brewery contracts are classical examples in this respect.[171]

3.3 Two approaches

A distinction is often made between two approaches that can be found in the case-law concerning the condition of interstate trade. Both eventually find their justification in the accomplishment of the internal market.[172]

The first method to establish whether the condition is met, is based on effective or potential changing streams of trade. This approach is usually taken and follows from the standard case-law of the Court described above.

A second way to look at interstate trade has less to do with the impact on the trade within the common market but more with the effects on the structure of competition on the market. Most examples of this approach are to be found in applications of Article 82 EC Treaty. In the case United Brands, the Court said the following:

> *"...it is immaterial whether this behaviour relates to trade between Member States once it has been shown that such elimination will have repercussions on the patterns of competition in the common market "*.[173]

The so-called structural criterion was also applied by the Commission in some cartel cases.[174] This structural approach was partly the basis for the readiness of the application of 81 and 82 EC to internal or national situations.[175] This is addressed in the following section.

3.4 Internal situation?

In this context it is necessary to examine those cases where only one Member State seems to be involved, at least at first sight. We could refer to these cases as so-called internal situations. Where competition law is concerned, it is necessary to specify that it is not the place of establishment of companies that is relevant but the internal situation refers to a case where the effects of possible infringing behaviour are only felt in one particular Member State.

---

[171] ECJ Case 23/67, *Brasserie de Haecht* [1976] ECR 512; ECJ Case C-234/89, *Stergios Delimitis v Henninger Bräu AG* [1991] ECR I-935.

[172] R Wesseling, 'Subsidiarity in Community Antitrust law: setting the right agenda' (1997) 22 *European Law Review* 35; also J. Faull (above n 163).

[173] ECJ case 27/76, *United Brands* [1978] ECR 207.

[174] For example Commission Decision 91/299/EEC of 19 December 1990 relating to a proceeding under Article 86 of the EEC Treaty [1991] OJ L 152/21.

[175] Not always without criticism, see Opinion of Advocate General Mischo case 246/86 *SC Belasco* [1989] ECR I-2117.

On the condition of "effect on trade between Member States", Verloren van Themaat wrote already in the early days of competition law: *"It is clear that many cartels will fall under this prohibition whilst having only participating companies from one Member State. It is crystal clear that this will be the case for import and export cartels. Undoubtfully cartel agreements taking place in economic sectors where export is a substantial part of business, will almost always fulfill this condition"* (own translation).[176]

According to established case-law, agreements that cover a whole Member State shall, "by their very nature", imply "the reinforcement of national thresholds". Usually the members of a national cartel shall try to restrict competition coming from other Member States.[177] A seemingly national cartel shall fall within the scope of application of Article 81 EC Treaty, if it can be demonstrated that there is a market outside this particular Member State for the given products or services and that foreign competitors are interested in importing or exporting. This so called "threshold" criterion is applied in several types of situations by the Commission and by the Courts.[178]

In other words, the extensive interpretation of the condition of interstate trade from the beginning of EC competition law and policy, made it easy for the provisions to be applied in internal situations. This meant not only that the Commission could in such cases enforce the prohibition, but also that Articles 81 and 82 EC Treaty could be invoked easily in a dispute between two national parties before a national judge. The alternative approach of the "effect on the structure of competition" was obviously also a facilitating factor to apply EC prohibitions in internal situations because it makes it even less necessary to prove impact on trade.

3.5 Turning point?

In the Dutch Banks case and in Bagnasco, the Commission, and later on the Court of Justice, seem to be somewhat more reticent and the question arose whether this was to be seen as a change in the interpretation of the interstate trade condition.[179]

Both cases concern the financial sector and in both cases the conclusion was that the particular agreements between the banks did not have, or hardly had, a significant influence on the trade between Member States. In the Dutch case the national system of transfers was at stake: in that system e.g. uniform fees were agreed between banks. In the second case, an Italian judge asked questions about a number of uniform conditions of banks

---

176 Cited by Mulder and Mok (above n 152) [216]

177 ECJ Case 61/80, *Coöperatieve Stremsel en Kleurselfabriek* [1967] ECR 851; ECJ Case 246/86, *Belasco* [1989] ECR I-2117.

178 ECJ, *LTM* (above n 154); see Van Gerven (above n 154).

179 Commission Decision of 19 July 1989 relating to a proceeding under Article 85 of the EEC Treaty [1989] OJ L 253, p. 1; ECJ, *Bagnasco* (above n 166).

regarding the unilateral right of banks to change the interest rates on client accounts.

It is not quite clear why in these two cases the conclusion was finally reached that there was not sufficient effect on interstate trade. This goes particularly for the Dutch case. It would have been very easy to construct another reasoning arriving to the contrary conclusion. In the light of other decisions and case-law in the following years however, it can not be said that there was a persistent change. Rather, the both cases seem to be exceptions: in most cases it is quite easily to assume that there is effect on interstate trade.

However, the seemingly automatic way in which the jurisprudence accepted affectation of interstate trade in internal situations, might be under pressure. There is no longer a *per se* approach in the presence of national cartels. In each case it shall have to be demonstrated that the condition is fulfilled. The extensive definitions remain applicable but there seems to be a cautious trend which is also expressed in the recent guidelines of the Commission discussed hereinafter. The Commission and national judges have to be sure that in national cases there is substantial evidence of interstate effect. This will be discussed below.[180]

4. The meaning of the effect on trade criterion

It is often said in competition law that the effect on trade criterion has a double meaning. It is said to be both a competence clause as well as a substantive condition for the application of Articles 81 and 82 EC Treaty.

First of all, it is an autonomous criterion of competence which determines the application of Community competition law. The Court had already stated this in Consten and Grundig.[181]

It also says so explicitly and clearly in Hugin:

> *"The interpretation and application of the condition relating to effects on trade between Member States contained in articles 85 and 86 of the Treaty must be based on the purpose of that condition which is to define, in the context of the law governing competition, the boundary between the areas respectively covered by Community law and the law of the member states. Thus Community law covers any agreement or any practice which is capable of constituting a threat to freedom of trade between Member States in a manner which might harm the attainment of the objectives of a single market between the member states, in particular by partitioning markets or by affecting the structure of competition within the common market. On the*

180 In that sense: Faull and Nikpay (above n 170).

181 ECJ, *Consten Grundig* (above n 153).

other hand, conduct the effects of which are confined to the territory of a single member state is governed by the national legal order."[182]

Furthermore, the criterion also determines the scope of application of Articles 81 and 82 EC Treaty: only agreements or behaviour having a minimum of cross-border effects shall fall within reach of the provisions. If the conditions of application are not met, enforcement is out of the question at whichever level (national or Community).

The distinction between both dimensions seems somewhat artificial. It has to be said that the meaning of the concept of interstate trade has certainly evolved over the last years, especially as a criterion for competence. Focus is now entirely on the demarcation of Community competition law and national competition law. At the time of the older case-law of the Courts, there were hardly any systems of national competition law in force, except in Germany where the Consten Grundig case occurred. Until the nineties, the absence of interstate effect meant therefore also the absence of national competition law and therefore a lack of sanctions for agreements or behaviour that were restrictive of competition.

A point that should be made in particular in this contribution about interstate trade and competition law is that the term "criterion of competence" is not appropriate. Competence rather refers to whom shall enforce the particular case. However, in the case of Articles 81 and 82 EC Treaty, the question is rather which law shall be implied. The English term "jurisdictional criterion" seems more appropriate.

There is no system of exclusive jurisdiction in competition law. This has to do with the system of parallel competences: an infringement of European competition rules can be sanctioned both at a national level (judge or authority), or at an EC level by the Commission. In the absence of effect on interstate trade, possibly national competition law shall be applied. In the presence of effect on interstate trade, it is not determined who can or should enforce.

5. Regulation 1/2003 and the new system of decentralised application

5.1 Spontaneous harmonisation

It is well known that the introduction of national systems of competition law was accelerated in the nineties. All Member States now have some system of national competition law. In fact, they are all very similar. The Commission has obviously played a role in this development: in the new Member States

---

182 ECJ Case 22/78, *Hugin Kassaregister AB and Hugin Cash Registers Ltd v Commission of the European Communities* [1979] ECR 1869.

that joined the European Union in these last years, the introduction of an adequate system of national competition law was strongly stimulated.

Remarkable in that context is that the broad interpretation of the interstate criterion played a decisive role in these developments. The Netherlands is a good example: the Commission attacked a number of typically national cartels with the European provisions and could do so on the basis of the extensive interpretation in the case-law on interstate trade.[183] This allowed the Commission to act in cases where the territory of one Member State was affected. The decisions of the Commission clearly show that there was a lack of market supervision and perhaps also a lack of political will to sanction cartel behaviour in the particular Member State. The harsh European policy clearly also contributed to the enactment of the Dutch Competition Act which entered into force quite late compared to other Member States.

Apart from stimulating competition legislation in existing Member States, the introduction of such legislation was also part of negotiations with new Member States. EC competition law obviously formed part of the "acquis communautaire". However, in practice, the introduction of a national set of competition rules, as well as the establishment of a national competition authority, were also the result of these negotiations. Therefore, since the date of accession all new Member States had national competition legislation based on the EC model.

The "interference" of Europe here seems different than in other areas of law where the law is harmonised in the classical way, through directives. In principle, it is still the case that a Member State has the obligation to implement directives and achieve a certain result but can choose the way in which that result is achieved. The actual wording of substantive rules, the form of the legislation, as well as the procedures for enforcement, are the area of the autonomy of the Member States.

In competition law it has to be noted that a remarkable spontaneous harmonisation has occurred, especially where substantive rules are concerned. All Member States chose a system with directly applicable prohibitions usually formulated in an identical way as in the EC Treaty.[184] Not only the result but also the instruments were based on the European model in the absence of any formal harmonisation measure. As we will discuss afterwards, Regulation 1/2003 is the provisional highlight of this

---

[183] See before under 3.4. The most famous case is the SPO case, CFI Case T-29/92, *Vereniging van samenwerkende prijsregelende organisaties in de bouwnijverheid* [1995] ECR 289.

[184] About the convergence of national systems: Mortelmans (above n 163). It would lead too far to discuss this in the present article but there is without doubt also a movement of harmonisation taking place in relation to procedural competition law. This is related not only to the modernisation of EC competition law, but also to the growing influence of the ECHR and the protection of fundamental rights more in general.

harmonisation movement. Even though the regulation is not as such to be qualified as harmonisation, it does show important similar features and/or in any case has harmonising effects in practice.[185]

5.2 Regulation 1/2003 and interstate trade

5.2.1 General overview

The introduction of Regulation 1/2003 contains a reference to the contribution that European competition law made to spreading the competition culture in the Community. This reference undoubtedly means the introduction of competition enforcement in all Member States as it was discussed in the preceding paragraph. It is interesting to note also the explicit declaration that the regulation does not go further than necessary to achieve its goal, namely an efficient application of Community competition rules. This statement is accompanied by a reference to the subsidiarity principle as well as the principle of proportionality.[186]

It is commonly known that Regulation 1/2003 has established a new procedural framework within which EC competition rules shall be applied in the following years. Regulation 1/2003 has replaced Regulation 17 of 1962 and it entered into force on 1 May 2004.[187]

For the purpose of this contribution, Article 3 of Regulation 1/2003 is especially important.[188] This article aims to regulate the relationship between national competition legislation and Community rules to *"create a level playing field for agreements, decisions by associations of undertakings and concerted practices within the internal market"*.[189] In a way, this statement acknowledges the objective of harmonisation of Regulation 1/2003. It would lead too far in this contribution to discuss all the provisions that demonstrate this objective but the different components of Article 3 as such are particularly noteworthy in that regard. This article is discussed further below.

---

185 In the case of actual harmonisation, this would obviously have had to have an effect on the legal basis chosen in the Treaty. The term "harmonisation" is not used here in the strict meaning of Articles 94 and 95 EC Treaty; see P. Slot and G. Straetmans, 'Harmonisatie van wetgeving in de EG' (2003) 3 *Tijdschrift voor Privaatrecht* 691.

186 Rec. 34 of the preamble.

187 Council Regulation (EEC) No 17 (First Regulation implementing Articles 85 and 86 of the Treaty) [1959-62] OJ Spec Ed 87.

188 Council Regulation 1/2003 of 16 December 2002 on the implementation of the rules on competition laid down in Articles 81 and 82 of the Treaty [2003] OJ L1/1.

189 Rec. 8 of the preamble of Reg. 1. Article 83 under e) of the EC Treaty provides explicitly for the possibility for the Council to regulate the relationship between national legislation and articles 81 and 82 EC Treaty.

5.2.2 Parallel application

First of all, Article 3 contains an obligation for competition authorities and judges of Member States. In a given case they have the obligation to apply both the European cartel prohibition as well as its national equivalent as soon as trade between Member States is affected. A similar obligation exists for the application of the prohibition on abuse of a dominant position.[190]

This is quite a unique provision: it would have been perfectly possible, and more within the logic of Community law, to determine that in such a case Community competition law has priority (primacy) on national law. As soon as there is interstate effect, national law would then have to make place for Community law.

This is also the way it was originally intended in the Commission proposal for the regulation, but apparently this was not acceptable for a number of Member States having a pre-existing strong competition authority.[191] It is questionable what the value of this parallel application is, especially in the light of further obligations imposed by Article 3 on Member States such as the prohibition of contradictory decisions. The parallel obligation of national and European competition law has as a result that the substantive evaluation of commercial behaviour shall hardly be different according to the rules that are applied. Intrastate is equal to interstate.

5.2.3 No contradictory results

Article 3 § 2 ensures similar application of national and European competition rules, in any case where the cartel prohibition is applicable. The application of the national prohibition cannot result in the prohibition of an agreement if one of the conditions of application of article 81 EC Treaty is not met. In other words: when there is not a restriction on competition (in accordance with the policy of the Commission and the jurisprudence) or because the conditions for a legal exception (Article 81 paragraph 3 EC Treaty) or any of the group exemptions are met. It has to be said that this clause seemingly only applies to cases where there is interstate effect. However, if it is read jointly with other obligations contained in the regulation, it is hard to deny that this is in fact quite a far-reaching factual

---

[190] Article 3 § 1: "*Where the competition authorities of the Member States or national courts apply national competition law to agreements,..., within the meaning of Article 81 of the EC Treaty which may affect trade between Member States within the meaning of that provision, they shall also apply Article 81 EC Treaty to these agreements, ...*" The article then continues with a similar obligation for Article 82 EC.

[191] Commission (EC) 'Proposal for a Council Regulation on the implementation of the rules on competition laid down in Articles 81 and 82 of the Treaty and amending Regulations (EEC) No 1017/68, (EEC) No 2988/74, (EEC) No 4056/86 and (EEC) No 3975/87 ("Regulation implementing Articles 81 and 82 of the Treaty") COM (2000) 0582 final 284.

harmonisation of competition law.[192] The Commission itself interestingly refers to it as being the "rule of convergence".[193]

Also, the explanatory remarks in the introduction of the regulation are far more widely formulated than the provision itself: a reference to interstate trade is not made. On the contrary, the introduction emphasises that the application of national competition law may not lead to another result as the application of the European provisions: the (identically formulated) provisions contain autonomous concepts that are interpreted by the Community judiciary and that therefore have to be applied in an uniform way throughout the Member States.[194]

An interesting question in this regard is whether the duty of loyal co-operation laid down in Article 10 of the EC Treaty obliges Member States to deal with an individual case in a similar way as the Commission would do it, even if there is no effect on interstate trade. Is such an obligation necessary for the sake of coherence of the competition policy?[195]

5.2.4 Exceptions

The situation is slightly different for so-called unilateral behaviour. Member States are not precluded under Regulation 1/2003 from adopting and applying on their territories stricter national laws which prohibit or sanction unilateral conduct engaged in by undertakings. This can be seen as a reference to the concept of abusive economical dependence as it exists in some legal systems. Strictly speaking, the provision also implies that national application of competition law to abusive dominance can deviate

192 Reference can be made to the control the Commission carries out on the beginning of investigations and on the decisions that national authorities prepare to take on the basis of Articles 81 and 82 EC Treaty, also the possibilty to take over a case, Article 11 Reg. 1/2003. Furthermore there is the insistence on the uniform application of Community competition law. In that context the remark is made that the obligation for the national judge to refrain from taking contradictory decisions does not mention the effect on trade between member states. It is probable therefore that a judge interpret this obligation to apply in any case where a prohibition is applied.

193 Commission Notice on the cooperation within the network of competition authorities [2004] OJ C 101/43, 3.

194 Rec. 8 of the preamble. An opening that might still exist could be seen in the lack of reference to the concept of restriction of competition as an autonomous concept: there might still be some room here for individual policy but this seems merely theoretical. This has in turn brought up the question whether national judges and national authorities should have the possibility to put preliminary questions to the ECJ (Article 234 EC) in national cases.

195 The question is left unanswered in this contribution but the argument seems to require a very extensive interpretation of Article 10. In that sense J. Temple Lang 'The duties of cooperation of national authorities and Court under Article 10 EC: two more reflections' (2001) 26 *European Law Review* 84; J. Temple Lang, 'The implications of the Commissions leniency policy for national competition authorities' (2003) 28 *European Law Review* 430.

from the Community policy. However, this might be more of a theoretical possibility given the supervision at the Commission has on the basis of provisions, the obligation of uniform application and also the explicit intention of most national legislators to follow the European model.

Article 3 § 3 of Regulation 1/2003 contains two other exceptions to the rules above that shall not be discussed further here. There is an exception for merger control as well as legislation serving another purpose than the purpose of Articles 81 and 82 EC Treaty. This last provision refers to fair trading practices legislation such as it exists in some of the jurisdictions.[196]

5.3 The Commission guidelines of 2004

5.3.1 Providing guidance

A number of guidelines were published after the entering into force of regulation 1/2003. These accompanying measures partly implement the regulation, partly summarizes the state of the law, but also partly indicate a new direction for EC competition policy. The guidelines on the effect on trade concept in articles 81 and 82 of the Treaty contain all these different components.[197]

There was certainly a need for these guidelines, especially for national judges and authorities. Little guidance could be found in the precedents and older Commission decisions. The effect on trade condition was rarely motivated in a sufficient way. The Community courts have never really criticised the Commission for that.

Both at a national level as well as at a (central) EC level the need is now greater to specify in ever particular case whether there is effect on trade or not. At a national level this mostly has to do with the obligations contained in Article 3 of Regulation 1/2003, as briefly discussed before. The regulation obliges its national authorities and judges to apply Articles 81 and 82 EC Treaty as soon as there is effect on trade. One could say of course that this obligation already existed before on the basis of the direct applicability of both articles. The many other obligations however imposed on the national authorities are new.[198]

At the European level, the Commission shall have to motivate in a more accurate way why it feels an agreement or a behaviour has effect on trade. This is to do with the general tendency in recent case-law which show the Community judges to be stricter with regards to burden of proof and

---

196 Rec. 9 of the preamble.

197 Guidelines of the Commission (above n 157).

198 See note 193 and the critical analysis of the regulation by A. Riley, 'EC Antitrust modernisation: the Commission does very nicely-thank you! Part Two: between the idea and the reality, decentralisation under Reg.1/2003' (2003) 24 *European Competition Law Review* 657.

motivation and reasoning of Commission decisions. The Court of First Instance seems to have initiated this trend but it is confirmed certainly by recent cases at the Court of Justice.[199]

Another reason why careful establishment of effect on trade is necessary, has to do with the principle of the "best placed authority" which is at the basis of the network of competition authorities created by Regulation 1/2003.

The different documents on modernisation (regulation and the guidelines) clearly show the intention of the Commission to limit its efforts and resources to major cases and to let other cases be dealt with largely at a national level. The basic principle for allocation within the network is that the case should be dealt with by the authority which is best placed to do so. This principle is explained in a separate Notice.[200] The Commission shall have to justify therefore why it wishes to deal with certain cases on its own, and part of that motivation shall have to be why the Commission considers there to be effect on trade.

5.3.2 The description of the effect on trade concept

The guidelines of the Commission contain a subtle mix of established case-law and new elements and examples. The discussion of the concept of effect on trade between Member States in Articles 81 and 82 EC Treaty is composed of three elements in the guidelines: the concept of "trade between Member States", definition of "may affect" and the concept of "appreciable effect".

Where the possibility to influence trade is concerned, the guidelines lay down a number of objective elements that, as such, do not have to be decisive but can be so in different combinations: the nature of the agreement or behaviour, the nature of the product and the position and importance of the undertakings concerned.[201]

Also, the importance of the broader legal and factual context of an agreement is mentioned: this has to do especially with the possible obstacles or barriers to entry on national markets.

The Commission gives great attention to the fact that trade may be affected also indirectly or potentially.[202] It follows from the guidelines that the threshold is certainly not higher to possibly exclude national situations.

---

199 ECJ Joined Cases C-12/03 & C-13/03, *Tetra Laval* [2005] ECR 987, 1113; T. Ottervanger and I. Veldhuis, 'Europese Commissie/Tetra Laval' (2005) 04/05 *Markt & Mededinging* 152.

200 Commission Notice (above n 193).

201 Rec. 28 and following of the guidelines on cooperation (above n 193).

202 Rec. 36-43 of the Notice.

The guidelines also determine, in line with Article 2 of Regulation 1/2003, that the burden of proof for the effect on trade lies with the authority (in case of public enforcement) or the claimant (in case of private enforcement).[203]

5.3.3 A more quantitative approach?

The most novel aspect in the guidelines is undoubtedly the discussion of the term "appreciability", especially the quantitative elements in that concept. Agreements and behaviour shall fall outside the scope of application of Articles 81 and 82 EC Treaty when they affect the market only in an insignificant way, having regard to the weak position of the undertakings concerned on the market for the products in question. The appreciability of effect on trade can be appraised in particular by reference to the position and the importance of a relevant undertaking on the market for the products concerned.[204]

- negative presumption

The Commission recognises that it is impossible to lay down quantitative rules for all types of agreements, which would allow determining whether trade between Member States has been affected appreciably. However, according to the Commission, it is possible to explain when trade is normally *not* capable of being appreciably affected.

Reference is first made to the PME policy laid down in the de Minimis Notice.[205] Then the "no appreciable effect on trade " rule (NAAT-rule) is introduced. According to the guidelines this rule shall function as an irrebuttable negative presumption. The consequences of its application for companies are important. The Commission refers to the fact that the negative presumption can have as a result that even hardcore restrictions stay outside the scope of Community law.[206] The Commission shall not open proceedings and companies shall not be sanctioned if they assumed, in good faith, that an agreement was covered by the presumption.

It is always necessary to examine on a case to case basis, but in principle trade shall not be affected appreciably if the joint market share of parties on the relevant market is not more than 5% and, for horizontal agreements, the

---

203 Rec. 43 of the Notice.

204 Rec. 44-45 of the Notice.

205 Rec. 50 of the Notice and also the Notice on de Minimis (above n 159).

206 Correct application would imply that a hard core restriction such as for example a price agreement, would not fall under Article 81 EC Treaty for lack of interstate effect. On the basis of the principles laid down in Reg.1/2003 discussed above, it should then still be possible to apply national competition law. However, this possibility seems to be limited substantially by Article 3 § 2 Reg. 1/2003. The interplay of EC and national law that is construed here by the regulation and the notices is not exactly easy as is illustrated by a judgment of the Court of Appeal of Brussels which clearly did not understand its scope, Brussels Court of Appeal 2004/MR/8, Judgment of 10 November 2005, not reported.

total Community turnover of the undertakings concerned does not exceed 40 million Euro. The same presumption shall apply if this turnover threshold is not exceeded in the two following years by more than 10% or if the market share is not increased by more than 2%.

- positive presumption

There shall be a rebuttable positive presumption where an agreement, by its very nature, is capable of affecting trade between Member States (for example because it concerns import and export or covers several Member States). In such cases where there are already evident indications of interstate effect, an agreement shall be assumed to have an appreciable effect on trade between Member States if parties have a joint turnover of 40 million Euros. In case of these agreements that already by their nature, affect trade between Member States, it can be assumed that they will have appreciable effect if the market share of 5% is exceeded.[207]

In the guidelines the Commission therefore uses the concept of "capable of affecting trade between Member States by its very nature" or "normally having such effect". This resembles a type of *hardcore* or *per se* approach. Horizontal cartels shall normally have interstate effect. Other types of horizontal co-operation and vertical agreements shall require further examination. Where abuses are concerned, a distinction exists between abuse by exclusion and by exploitation. In the first category the Commission shall, according to the guidelines, assume more readily that interstate effect exists.

- internal situation?

The following can be said where internal situations are concerned.

It appears from the above that the competition law equivalent of the "internal situation" (expression used elsewhere in EU law), given the theory of effect, is the case where an agreement or behaviour only has effect on the territory of one particular Member State. On this point, the guidelines of the Commission do not seem to change anything. There are no indications that there will be more reticence to apply the EC provisions in such cases.

Of course this would have been entirely possible: now that all Member States have national prohibitions, a more restrictive interpretation of interstate effect would certainly have been plausible. There do not seem to be any hard elements however in the guidelines that point to such a policy choice.

The guidelines do emphasize the importance of a more detailed examination of a case when agreements or abuse precisely only seem to concern one

207 An exception then again exists when the behaviour only concerns part of the territory of a member state.

Member State or part of it. But this is in line with the case-law (see above 3.5). It also clearly appears from the discussion of the different types of agreements and behaviour in the guidelines.[208]

All in all, many agreements and types of behaviour shall still meet the threshold of interstate effect because the wide definition in the case-law is not called into question by the Commission. This raises the question of the impact of modernisation on the concept of interstate effect.

5.4 The consequences of modernisation for the meaning of interstate effect

It has not become easier to evaluate whether there is an effect on trade between Member States since modernisation. It seems that the burden of proof is heavier for cases which "by their very nature" seem to have such effect.

A rigorous application of the complicated guidelines of the Commission is certainly not a simple task. This is especially true if one wishes to apply in a correct way the quantitative elements which are mentioned to measure the appreciability of the interstate effect.

The question is if this difficult task shall actually be carried out in practice. It would be understandable that the safe route is chosen, and that in many cases the conclusion that interstate effect exists, shall be easily drawn. This allows for less quantitative (economical) motivation of decisions. In that way, authorities and judges will play their roles of loyal entities within the new Community network even in cases where there is in fact merely an internal or national situation.[209]

The choice has certainly not been made to restrict the influence of Articles 81 and 82 EC Treaty when evaluating concrete market behaviour in the Member States. The condition of "effect on interstate trade" is still applied in a broad way. The guidelines of the Commission are formulated in such a way that they are in continuity with the established case-law.

Moreover, the choice was not made to have an "or-or" situation (either national law or Community law) but an "and-and" situation. Regulation 1/2003 has introduced the principle of parallel application of Article 81 EC Treaty and its national equivalents. This means the choice was not in favour of the introduction of a one-stop system such as in the case of merger control. In such a system Community law would only apply if it were

---

[208] Rec. 61 of the Notice.

[209] Recent example of a (too) "loyal" application by the NMa (Dutch competition authority) Decision on opposition (besluit op bezwaar) of 15 March 2005, *OSB* case 2021/397.

necessary from the perspective of the common market.[210] In such a reasoning, the condition of "effect on trade between Member States" has no significance anymore in a unified market and it would only be relevant if there is a restriction of competition which is substantial enough to damage the internal market.[211] However, at the present time, the condition of interstate effect is still very much a condition for the application of Articles 81 and 82 EC Treaty.

5.5 A related concept: "Community interest"?

It seems interesting to briefly introduce another concept in this discussion, namely the "Community interest".

It is established case-law that the Commission can reject complaints on the basis of Articles 81 and 82 EC Treaty for lack of Community interest. In some cases, this is done by an explicit reference to the possibility of the complainant to search legal protection from the national judge. This was the case in the famous Automec jurisprudence.[212] The Community judiciary has accepted that the Commission may set priorities.[213] In evaluating the Community interest, the Commission has to consider the importance of the possible infringement for the common market on the one hand, and the probability of proof and the scope of investigation necessary, on the other hand.

This jurisprudence is certainly one of the elements that led to the decentralisation of Community competition law and has to be seen together with the notices on co-operation between the Commission and national judges.[214] In those notices the Commission strongly promotes enforcement

---

210 Bos (above n 168); also Wesseling (above n 172); as well as Faull (above n 163). In merger control, the relevance is measured by a turnover threshold.

211 See already as early as in the Opinion of Advocate General Trabucchi in 1975, Opinion of Advocate General Trabucchi case 73/74 [1975] ECR 1517 and following.

212 ECJ Case T-24/90, *Automec* [1992] ECR 2223.

213 The same can be said of the NMa (Dutch competition authority), see the judgment of the Court of Rotterdam, Court of Rotterdam Judgment of 3 december 2004 *Role 03/2084* LJN:AS3852. The NMa also justifies rejections of complaints by referring to the existence of judicial protection at the level of the civil judge, for example NMa Judgment of 29 June 2005 *Superunie v Interpay* case 2978/147.

214 Commission Notice on cooperation between national courts and the Commission in applying Articles 85 and 86 of the EEC Treaty of 1993 [1993] OJ C 39, 6, now replaced by the Commission Notice on the cooperation between the Commission and the courts of the EU Member States [2004] OJ (2004) C 101, 54. On the relatively unsuccessful first steps towards decentralisation: R. Wesseling, 'The Commission Notice on decentralisation of EC Antitrust Law: In for a Penny, not for a Pound' (1997) 18 *European Competition Law Review* 94.

through the national judge for companies suffering damages from a possible infringement on competition rules.[215]

The question is whether there is a relationship between the condition of interstate effect on the one hand and Community interest on the other. In the traditional practice and jurisprudence such a relationship does not seem to exist: the fact that the Commission renounced from action at a centralised level was often linked to the possibility to obtain judicial protection elsewhere, not so much the absence of interstate effect.[216]

The position taken here is that the concept of Community interest has (or should have) gained importance in the new modernised system after the entry into force of Regulation 1/2003.

First of all, complainants can now not only go to the national judge but also to national competition authorities (if it was not already the case) who are fully competent to sanction infringements of Articles 81 and 82 EC Treaty. The Automec-case law (cited above) is still justified and there is no longer any doubt that complainants can obtain legal protection at a national level.

Secondly, it was the explicit intention of the Commission to free resources for the big cases, therefore those where the Community interest is at stake.

Finally, it seems obvious that the Community interest should play a role for the allocation of cases within the network, in any case between the Commission on the one hand and national authorities on the other. It has been rightfully pointed out in doctrine that the principle of subsidiarity should play a role in this allocation.[217] As it was said before, Regulation 1/2003 also refers explicitly to subsidiarity.

6. Some conclusive remarks

6.1 Intra state equals inter state: the internal situation

It was discussed above that the condition of "effect on trade between Member States" has, since the beginning, and without too much resistance from courts or Member States, been interpreted in a broad way. More precisely, the interpretation of that condition has without any doubt allowed the prohibitions of Articles 81 and 82 EC Treaty to apply in situations where the

[215] Stimulating private enforcement is (again) a priority of the Commission (EC) 'On public-private partnerships and community law on public contracts and concessions' (Green Paper) COM (2004) 327.

[216] It is difficult to evaluate this because rejections of complaints, just like many informal decisions the Commission took before, are not published.

[217] B. Rodger and S. Wylie, 'Taking the Community interest line: Decentralisation and Subsidiarity in Competition Law Enforcement' (1997) 8 *European Competition Law Review* 485.

effects of the behaviour are clearly only felt in one Member State of part thereof.

For a good understanding: this does not mean that the condition of interstate trade no longer applies, on the contrary. The broad interpretation of the condition makes it easy to apply the prohibitions in a national case with little importance. It is defended in this contribution that this is not fundamentally different since the entry into force of Regulation 1/2003 and the guidelines of the Commission published in 2004.

6.2 Intra state equals inter state: harmonised law and convergence of policies

In the current state of competition law, after the entry into force of Regulation 1/2003, the position is that it is hardly relevant anymore for the legal evaluation of an agreement or behaviour whether there is interstate effect or not. The overall question whether there is a sanctionable restriction of competition or not, shall not be influenced by it.

The somewhat bizar parallel application which is introduced by Article 3 § 1 of Regulation 1/2003, shows how exceptional competition law is on this issue: not so much the opposition between Community law and incompatible national law is at stake. When there is interstate effect, it is as though one legal system reinforces the other.

Even in the cases where it can be successfully argued that there is no interstate effect, the individual solution (is there an infringement or not) shall be the same because of the different mechanisms of convergence that are now part of the system. In this respect the prohibition of contradictory decisions is especially important.

In other words, Community competition law can or should also increasingly be applied to internal situations because national law and Community law are barely distinguishable.

It is difficult to deny that the Member States have lost all, if not much of their autonomy in competition policy, most likely in a more far-reaching way than elsewhere in Community law. However, this has not occurred through the gradual fading of interstate effect (the condition does not apply less) but more by the factual harmonisation of Community law.

There is little room for Member States to develop their own competition policy. The creation of the network of authorities with the entry into force of Regulation 1/2003 does not only have an impact on the enforcement in individual cases, but also on the policy in a more general way.

6.3 A new role for interstate effect?

It was also discussed above that the condition of interstate effect is decisive to determine whether national law and/or Community law is applicable. The boundary between Community and national law is not determined on the basis of the primacy of Community law or a "one stop shop principle" but on the basis of the principle of parallel application laid down in Article 3 of Regulation 1/2003. This is a unique characteristic of the modernised Community competition system.

The position here is that the condition of interstate effect should, in the future, in combination with the principle of Community interest, function much more as a real jurisdictional criterion (in the sense of competence). It could have a more explicit significance when cases are allocated in the context of the network of competition authorities. The more effect on interstate trade, the more justified it is that the Commission itself intervenes in a particular case.

It is useful and necessary to reflect further on the usefulness and interpretation of the condition of interstate effect along these lines. This should also be done from the perspective of the decentralisation of competition law. This might allow to eliminate the impression that not only the substance of competition law but also enforcement is, instead of being decentralised, more centrally managed from the European level than ever before.

Chapter 4

Sense and nonsense of rules on proof in cartel cases*

How to reconcile a more economics-based approach to competition law with more attention for rules on proof?

EC competition law has undergone major changes in the last years. A so-called more economic approach has been introduced: for vertical restrictions safe harbours were created for undertakings with low market shares and only a limited number of hard-core restrictions are still considered detrimental for the economy. For horizontal agreements, the Commission adopted guidelines and new group exemptions allowing for more flexibility for certain types of agreements that can have pro-competitive effects. Where hard-core cartels are concerned, there is no question of introducing more flexibility at a policy level. On the contrary, due to procedural reforms, decentralisation and the successful introduction of leniency programs, the focus of the Commission and most national competition authorities is now on cartels and large fines are imposed.

Even in hard-core cases there is some pressure on the competition authorities to have sufficient consideration for economic reality and impact on the market. This pressure is coming from the insights of economic doctrine, but also from the courts upon review. It is the result of a growing attention for issues of proof and evidence that we can observe in the last years in several areas of competition law. Community courts are requiring the Commission to substantiate adequately its findings of infringement of competition law by demonstrating adverse effect on the market place. Similar requirements are imposed by national courts when it comes to decisions by national competition authorities. This stricter approach towards proof is, at least partly, inspired by the seriousness of the sanctions that are imposed on companies. Increasingly high sanctions bring more attention for rights of defence and rules on proof and evidence.

The impression could exist that there is a contradiction between on the one hand more economics and more flexibility, and on the other hand a more stricter approach when it comes to the procedural framework in which specific competition cases are dealt with. The paper addresses how to reconcile a more economics-based approach to competition law with procedural rules, in particular rules on proof and evidence.

---

* This article is based on a paper presented at the Max Planck Institute in Bonn at a workshop on the Law and Economics of Competition Policy on 5-7 December 2007, published as a TILEC Discussion Paper in January 2008, and published in a revised version in *European Competition Journal*, 2008, 4(1), p. 169-199. It was closed on 15 March 2008.

First, a short description is given of the general characteristics of rules on proof and their role in the legal system with special attention for general principles of law. Then the relevant specific characteristics of EC law and of cartel cases are described, as well as a number of recent developments that have their impact on proof. Thirdly, an attempt is made to define the practical features of workable rules on burden of proof and standard of proof and some proposals are made to develop a pragmatic approach that reconciles the different, seemingly contradictory trends in current competition law. This approach requires both economists and lawyers to deviate somewhat from their dogmas for the sake of efficient enforcement of competition law.

1. Rules on proof: overview and concepts

1.1 Proof

What is meant by *proof*? There are several aspects that are relevant.

First is the subjective and active element, better expressed by "to prove" (in other languages, the words for "prove" and "proof", are the same). A party undertaking an action to prove has as its goal "to convince" (persuasion); proving and convincing being inextricably related. Is there proof enough to convict? Has the infringement been proven?

The second dimension is the objective element, wherein proof refers to the object or support that bears the proof (production). From this perspective, the term "proof" is substitutable with the term "evidence": for example a document of some kind or a witness statement.

It is generally presupposed that all proof or evidence is objective in that it cannot be disputed. However, this is not true in practice: both the truthfulness of evidence (especially but not only with non written evidence) and its value and interpretation are subjects of debate in any given case. In fact, in most legal disputes, this debate is the crucial one.

Another misconception is that "proof" only relates to facts and that once these facts are established without doubt, the law can be applied. This is not the reality of legal disputes: the distinction between facts and law is not so clear cut, and proof, certainly in the active sense of the term, also relates to the law: the legal argument that is made must also convince and be corroborated by proof. A good example from competition law showing how difficult it is to distinguish facts from law is the definition of the relevant market. Determining what the relevant market is that shall be the basis for the competitive analysis in a cartel case, is not (merely) the observation of the facts (the market) but is applying a legal definition of what a relevant market is, selecting certain facts and discarding others in view of applying the legal provisions.[218]

To complete the picture, one might consider that there is a third dimension to proof, namely the result of the two aspects mentioned before: the actions on behalf of a party, that bring together certain elements of fact and law, thereby resulting in convincing the judge or authority.[219] The result is proof that the law has (or has not) been infringed.

1.2 Rules on proof

Generally, rules on proof are considered to be part of procedural law, rather than substantive law. However, competition law illustrates how procedural law and substantive law interact and how blurred the distinction between procedural law and substantive law can be. The rules on proof may be perceived as procedural but no one contests that the existence of sufficient proof or not of a cartel, touches on the merits of the case.

When reference is made to "rules on proof", this covers a wide variety of issues and the different dimensions of the term "proof" mentioned above, are reflected. Only certain aspects are covered in this paper, but these are the most common subjects that are dealt with in rules on proof, or rules of evidence:[220]

- Who has to prove (therefore convince)? When does the burden shift?
- When is an infringement of the law considered proven, in other words, when does the conviction of the authority or court have legal consequences?
- How active or passive can or does the authority or court have to be when dealing with proof?
- If the court or authority is to have an active role, which measures can be taken?
- Which types of proof can be accepted, what is their respective value (hierarchy)?

---

218 In some cases this can lead to results that the companies concerned might find peculiar: they might experience competitive restraints for example for competitors that are legally not considered to be in the same market.

219 N. Verheyden-Jeanmart, *Droit de la preuve* (Bruxelles: Larcier, 1991); P. Wéry, *La preuve, Guide juridique de l'entreprise. Titre préliminaire, Livre 2* (Bruxelles: Kluwer, 2003). For an interesting view on procedural law from a more general theoretical viewpoint of principles of law and the main elements of litigation: M. Bayles, *Principles of law, A normative analysis* (Dordrecht: D. Reidel Publishing company, 1987).

220 In the US legal terminology, the term "rules of evidence" is more common. For discussion of the principles of civil and criminal law that rule evidence as well as the role of the judge in that process, S. Guinchard, *Droit et pratique de la procedure civile* (Paris: Dalloz Action, 2006); G. Stefani and G. Levasseur, *Procédure pénale,* (Paris: Dalloz, 2006); I. Dennis, *The law of evidence* (London: Sweet & Maxwell, 2007); M. Malek (ed), *Phipson on evidence.* 15th edn. (London: Sweet & Maxwell, 2000); F. Kuty and D. Mougenot (eds), *La preuve* (Liège: Anthemis, 2007).

- Can all proof be used in all circumstances? What is the consequence of the use of illegitimately found proof? How is confidential material protected?
- How will a court in appeal deal with proof when reviewing a case?

The first subject is commonly referred to as the burden of proof and the second one the standard of proof. These are the main focuses of this paper. The four other questions mentioned above are typically subjects where the legal tradition of the jurisdiction in question plays an important role and where great differences can occur from one jurisdiction to the other.

For example, the role of the judge is to a large degree determined by the legal tradition and culture of a country. In some countries it is much more acceptable than in others that a judge plays an active role in terms of finding proof, on his own initiative and not bound by what the parties before him. Also, rules on proof often differ considerably depending on the area of law: typically, private and contractual law are governed by rules other than criminal law. Finally, the choice of the institutional "format" has an impact on the rules that govern procedure and also proof issues, including general principles of law. For example: if an authority is an administrative body, administrative law applies and certain guarantees for parties that apply only before courts[221], do not.

In most legal systems a distinction can be made between a system of free proof and a system of regulated proof. The distinction relates mostly to the types of proof that can be used and which probative value is attributed to different forms of proof. In a system of free proof generally, the probative value is not regulated and there are no restrictions on the types of proof or evidence that can be used. The only limits are the following principles which are generally the legal limits for the use of certain proof in all systems of proof:

- rules concerning illegitimately obtained proof
- the protection of privacy and of the person
- protection of the rights of defence.

These limits stem from fundamental general principles of law: the principle of legality, the fundamental human right of the protection of the person, the right to a fair trial and the rights of defence following from that.[222]

---

[221] This argument has lead the Commission for a long time to deny the protection of certain fundamental rights such as the rights protecting immunity of homes but the case-law from the European Court of Human Rights has enlarged the scope of application of these rights primarily on the basis of the quasi-criminal nature of the sanctions that the Commission can inflict upon undertakings.

[222] J. Bourgeois and T. Baumé, *Decentralisation of EC competition law enforcement and general principles of Community law* [2004] Research papers College of Europe 4, available at www.coleurope.be; more general: T. Tridimas, *General principles of EC law* (Oxford: OUP, 1999); K. Lenaerts and P. van Nuffel, *Constitutional law of the EU,* 2nd edn (London: Sweet & Maxwell, 2005) p. 711.

In a system of regulated proof, existing in different degrees, there is typically a formal hierarchy whereby the law recognises the superior value of some forms of proof and does not allow just any proof to be used.[223]

One could qualify competition law, at least at the EC level, as a system of free proof. In principle, the courts have accepted that all imaginable types of evidence can be used by the Commission to prove an infringement of competition law. There is no formal hierarchy and there are no limits to the type of evidence the Commission can use, other than those following from the general principles of law mentioned above. The large degree of discretion that the Commission has in terms of collecting proof is mitigated by the standard of proof, as discussed below.

EC competition law can not only be qualified as a system of free proof in terms of the type of evidence that can be used, but it can also be characterised generally by (an almost total) lack of rules on proof or evidence, as is EC law generally (see below). This means that there are few questions of admissibility of proof other than the three categories of limits mentioned above. In other areas of law, and more so in common law jurisdictions, there are fairly detailed rules, for example on the relevance and reliability of proof and evidence.

Finally, it is clear that rules of proof are often decisive for the outcome of a case. This sometimes makes law enforcement incomprehensible to the general public and lawyers can seem out of touch with reality. The typical example from criminal law is the criminal against whom the evidence is indisputable but who is not punished because irregularities occurred during the investigation. Such cases should definitely be exceptional because they do not stimulate the social acceptance of justice. However, normally, in such cases lawyers feel that the result of the case is regrettable (in the individual case) but justified for the sake of the protection of the general principles that are fundamental to the legal system. There is a particular quote that seems useful here in this respect: "procedural rules prescribe a framework whose justification is not necessarily economic but within that framework economic logic may operate."[224]

---

223 For example, in family law and property law in some jurisdictions ownership can only be proven in a limited number of ways, for example by an act drawn up by a notary.

224 R. Cooter and T. Ulen, *Law & Economics* (Boston: Pearson Education Ltd., 2004) 433. In the same chapter the examples to illustrate how the burden of proof and standard of proof work also offer a interesting perspective. Law & Economics literature seems all in all fairly limited when it comes to evidence. See J. Parker, 'Evidence: general economic analysis', in B. Bouckaert and G. de Geest (eds) *Encyclopedia of Law and Economics* (Cheltenham: Edward Elgar, 2000), also available on SSRN at http://ssrn.com/abstract id=1031736.

1.3 Burden of proof

The burden of proof concerns the question of which party must prove what. At first sight this is a fairly obvious concept: it is either one party or the other. Questions arise mostly when it is appropriate that the burden of proof shifts from one party to the other during the course of proceedings. In this respect, the use of presumptions is important and relevant in the context of competition law. This shall be discussed further below.

In principle, in most jurisdictions the rule "actori incumbit probatio" prevails: the claimant bears the burden of proof. In the context of public enforcement of criminal law but also in competition law this means that the authority bears the burden of proof of the infringement. In cases where an investigation is initiated by a complainant who is a competitor for example, this is not different: the more substantiated the complaint the better it is for the authority, but the authority is solely responsible for proving the infringement, the complainant not being a party to the procedure.

1.4 Standard of proof

The standard of proof can be defined as the level of certainty that proof must achieve and that has to be attained for a jurisdiction to establish whether or not the law has been infringed and/or measures have to be taken.

It is generally assumed that in common law countries there are two standards of proof: "preponderance of evidence" in civil cases and "beyond reasonable doubt" in criminal cases. Another standard that has been often referred to in comments about EC competition law recently is the "balance of probabilities" which is equivalent to the preponderance of evidence.

In most civil law countries the concept of standard of proof as such is not well known and certainly not defined by law. This is important in this context given that the vast majority of the Member States of the European Union can be considered as belonging to the civil law tradition.

There is a strong correlation between the standard of proof and the standard of review. The latter is the scope of review that a court upon appeal exercises when dealing with an appeal against, for example, a decision of a competition authority. The two extreme forms are a full review (the court places itself in the position of the authority and entirely repeats the analysis of facts and law) and a marginal review. The latter is commonly perceived as the form of review in administrative law where the courts, upon appeal, leave a large margin of discretion to the public authorities. Although the focus in this paper is rather on the standard of proof, it is clear that standard of proof and standard of review are two aspects of a single control system.

2. Rules on proof in EC cartel cases

This paper is primarily focused on Article 81 of the EC Treaty, and cartels in particular. For the purpose of this paper the term "cartel" means any infringement of Article 81 of the EC Treaty or its national equivalents in the form of a horizontal agreement having as its object and/or effect the restriction of competition.[225]

The paper also focuses on the application of Article 81 of the EC Treaty at the EC level. It highlights mainly the common features that workable rules on proof, and in particular the burden of proof, and the standard of proof should have in Article 81 EC cases, regardless of where the prohibition is enforced.

Finally, it should be mentioned that the present analysis is limited to the application of the prohibition of Article 81 (1) EC and the exception of Article 81 (3) as such. Proof in the context of the sanctions that can be imposed when an infringement is established is another interesting subject, but is beyond the scope of this paper.

2.1 The specifics of EC law

When discussing proof issues in competition law, the specific context of EC law should not be underestimated. As is well known, competition law as it is applied and enforced now throughout the Member States, is largely based on EC law. For most jurisdictions, competition law was a new area of law, and EC competition law was integrated into the legal system just like other areas of material law such as the free movement of goods, but with less difficulty because there was often less conflict between (the often non-existent) pre-existing national law and EC law.

When EC material law is applied in the Member States, this is done in the context of national procedures on the basis of the principle of procedural autonomy of the Member States. The treaties do not contain a body of procedural rules. EC law does not have rules on proof and evidence. Member States each have their own traditions of procedural law, and certainly rules on proof. As competition law developed and companies were sanctioned in an increasingly severe way, the European courts started to develop jurisprudence on procedure, drawing from different sources of law, each judge with a different background, with the European Convention on Human Rights (ECHR) being an important source of inspiration.

---

[225] It has to be said that most of the article shall also be relevant for vertical agreements that fall within the scope of application of Article 81 EC but these agreements nowadays are rarely, if ever, the subject of decisions of competition authorities and therefore of litigation in review courts. However, vertical agreements are often the subject of private litigation, usually in the context of contractual disputes. The law governing issues of proof shall then be that applicable to such disputes in a particular jurisdiction.

Nevertheless, there has been a great impact on national procedural law in recent years for at least three reasons: spontaneous harmonisation occurred because of the substantial harmonisation of competition law and the decentralisation process instigated by Regulation 1/2003.[226] This harmonisation affects the procedural rules that national authorities and courts apply when they apply EC competition law. However, given the fact that most national competition acts are also based on EC law, harmonisation naturally touches procedural competition law, regardless of whether Article 81 EC is applied alone or the two are applied together.

Also, the EC courts' case-law on equivalence and effectiveness has definitely had a certain unifying effect on procedural law.[227] However, where proof is concerned, this should not be overestimated. Harmonisation of procedural law in competition cases has mainly taken place in the area of the rights of defence in the broad sense of the word, leading for example to the protection against self-incrimination, the right to have access to a file, as well as the protection of legal privilege. It is not surprising that spontaneous harmonisation of these aspects of the procedure could occur because it is based largely on rights that are grounded in general principles of law, laid down also in the ECHR. General principles of law in fact play a key role in the construction of a unified set of procedural rules for competition cases.

Until recently, there was very little case-law on proof or evidence. This is changing now, as will be discussed below. It is important to keep in mind when studying the recent cases in relation to proof, that there is little common ground on which this jurisprudence can be based because legal traditions in the Member States show many differences in the actual rules on proof. One factor is the well-known difference between common law and civil law systems. The EC courts, when dealing with issues of proof, are in fact construing new law, in the absence of EC legislation. They have to attempt to draw common principles from the legal systems of the 27 Member States. In doing so, the Courts base their laws on the general principles of law common to all members states (eg the presumption of innocence). However, where the national laws differ greatly, the courts have to look for a sui generis set of rules, based on the specifics of competition law.

The sui generis character of the jurisprudence and developments concerning proof at the EC level, should perhaps make us wary when trying to apply certain concepts such as "burden of proof" and "standard of proof".[228] We

---

[226] Council Regulation 1/2003 of 16 December 2002 on the implementation of the rules on competition laid down in Articles 81 and 82 [2003] OJ L 1/1.

[227] For an overview: K. Lenaerts, D. Arts and I. Maselis, *Procedural law of the EU* (London: Sweet & Maxwell, 2006), chap. 3.

[228] A. Sibony and E. Barbier de La Serre, 'Charge de la preuve et théorie du contrôle en droit communautaire de la concurrence: pour un changement de perspective (2007) 43 *Revue trimestrielle de droit européen* 205. Also from the French perspective but not opposing the use of these terms: H. Legal, 'Standards of proof and standards of judicial review in EU competition law', in B. Hawk (ed.) *Annual*

should at least realize that these concepts are not clearly defined and that they do not have the same meaning in all Member States, if they exist at all. In fact, the few EC judgments show that the Community courts themselves are clearly reluctant to use a number of the concepts used in doctrine, such as burden of proof and standard of proof.

Keeping this in mind, it seems efficient to use those terms that are also widely known outside the legal community, even though they are certainly common law concepts. The majority of doctrine that has been studying these issues since the emergence of case-law about proof, has also generally used these concepts. Finally, and not unimportantly, the Community legislator and the Commission use both "burden of proof" as well as "standard of proof" in important competition texts such as Regulation 1/2003.

2.2 The specifics of cartel cases

2.2.1 Sources of law for proof in cartel cases

Until fairly recently, not many legal provisions at the EC level dealt with rules on proof in competition matters, and none dealt with the burden of proof or the standard of proof. Regulation 17, which governed Commission investigations for more than 40 years, only contained provisions on the investigatory powers that the Commission could exercise, and regulated to some extent what proof could be used.[229]

Regulation 1/2003 however, which Regulation 17 as of 1 May 2004, contains a clear rule on the burden of proof in Article 2: "In any national or Community proceedings for the application of Articles 81 and 82 of the

Proceedings of the Fordham Corporate law Institute: International Antitrust and Policy (New York: Juris Publishing, 2006), p. 107-116. The answers the ECJ shall give to the questions put before it by the College van Beroep voor het Bedrijfsleven (the highest Dutch court in appeal cases against decisions of the Dutch competition authority) are potentially very important in this respect: Case C-8/08, *T-Mobile Netherlands BV, KPN Mobile NV, Orange Nederland NV and Vodafone Libertel NV v Raad van bestuur van de Nederlandse Mededingingsautoriteit* [2008] OJ C92, 11. The referring court clearly adresses the question of procedural autonomy and whether rules on proof should be similar when national courts and authorities apply EC antitrust rules.

[229] J. Joshua, 'Proof in contested competition cases, a comparison with the rules of evidence in common law' (1987) 12 *European Law Review* 315; A. Walker-Smith, 'Collusion, its detection and investigation' 2 (1991) *European Competion Law Review* 71; M. Guerrin and G. Kyriazis, 'Cartels: proof and procedural issues' in B. Hawk (ed.), *Annual Proceedings of the Fordham Corporate law Institute: International Antitrust and Policy*, (Huntington: Juris Publishing, 1993), p. 773; G. Van der Wal, and L. Parret, 'Bewijs in het Europese mededingingsregime, een overzicht' in S. Prechal and L. Hancher (eds.), *Europees Bewijsrecht: een verkenning*, (Deventer: Kluwer, 2001); more general: C. Kerse and M. Khan, *EC Antitrust Procedure*, (London: Sweet & Maxwell, 2005) and M. Siragusa and C. Rizza (ed.), *EU Competition Law, volume III Cartel law, restrictive agreements and practices between competitors* (Leuven: Claeys & Casteels, 2007).

Treaty, the burden of proving an infringement of Article 81 (1) or of Article 82 of the Treaty shall rest on the party or the authority alleging the infringement. The undertaking or association of undertakings claiming the benefit of Article 81 (3) of the Treaty shall bear the burden of proving that the conditions of that paragraph are fulfilled." In other words, this is the rule "actori incumbit probatio" mentioned above.[230]

It seems clear from the preamble of Regulation 1/2003 that the Community legislator is being careful not to interfere with national law: "*This regulation neither affects national rules on the standard of proof nor obligations of competition authorities and courts of the Member States to ascertain the relevant facts of the case provided that such rules and obligations are compatible with general principles of Community law.*"[231]

Proof and evidence is an area where the case-law, due to the lack of legislative sources, has been the most important source of law. The case-law, even though limited in the number of subjects it has dealt with, has also typically been much inspired by the ECHR, other international treaties and (unwritten) general principles of law, most of them more or less common to the legal traditions of the Member States.

What are these general principles of law that could be relevant when it comes to proof in cartel cases? At least two important principles could have an impact: the first is the protection of the rights of defence and the right to a fair trial; the second, the presumption of innocence and the principle of the benefit of doubt (in dubio pro reo) that follows from it.[232] This last principle is a central element in the constructing of rules of proof in cartel cases and it will be revisited later.[233]

Other principles that may play a role are those of equality and proportionality. Proportionality most frequently plays a role in the context of the determination of the sanctions, but it is entirely possible that proportionality should intervene, for example, in the burden of proof and the shift thereof. There is case-law of the Community courts stating that no greater burden should be imposed on individuals than is reasonably

[230] Furthermore, Regulation 1/2003 describes the investigation procedure of the Commission, including again rules related to the collection of proof during the investigation and inspections. As it was said before, this is not the focus of this article.

[231] Paragraph 5.

[232] The rights of defence shall mostly have an impact on the question what proof can be used. For the purpose of this article which shall focus more on burden of proof and standard of proof, the presumption of innocence shall be more important.

[233] It is less certain that this is also true for merger control. In any case, it would work differently. The benefit of the doubt would not require the authority to refrain from taking an (infringement) decision such as is the case for cartels but it would then arguably oblige the authority to approve the merger.

necessary to attain the policy aim intended.[234] In the context of the investigation by the competition authority, regard should also be had for the right to good administration.[235]

Regardless of the respect of the Community legislator for the procedural autonomy of Member States, it is very important from a legal perspective that the preamble of Regulation 1/2003 also subjects national rules on proof to the general principles of Community law. This means that both the Commission at the EC level and the national authorities and courts are subject to the same general principles of law; if necessary, the national authorities and courts should have to put aside their rules of proof should they feel they are not compatible with these principles. This underlines again the great importance of these general principles in the procedural framework of competition law as it exists today.

2.2.2 Some essential characteristics of cartel cases

There are a number of characteristics that differentiate cartel procedures from other legal procedures and also from other competition procedures (mergers and abuse cases).

The type of legal analysis that needs to be carried out by authorities and judges is fundamentally different from that in abuse or merger cases. First of all, the time dimension of the analysis is very different. The analysis is generally focused on the past: only rarely are alleged cartels still ongoing at the time of the scrutiny. In abuse cases this is often not the case. For example, a refusal to supply leaves the complainant of the abuse without supplies. This situation usually continues until it is remedied by an order by the authority or judge or by the dominant undertaking voluntary complying with a decision that qualifies the certain behaviour as abusive. The situation is obviously even more different in merger cases. In that scenario the competition authority has to take a prospective (ex ante) approach, contrary to the ex post analysis in cartel cases.

Furthermore, there is also a "proof paradox" in cartel cases. The paradox is that, certainly nowadays at the EC level and in jurisdictions with a mature system of enforcement, the most serious cartels that the authorities want to discover and end, are those that are usually the most difficult to find and prove. If the goal is to have effective competition law enforcement, this paradox should lead to a cautious approach towards rules on proof that can

---

[234] For example: ECJ case 9/73, *Carl Schlüter v Hauptzollamt Lörrach* [1973] ECR 1135.

[235] This is not an exhaustive list of all general principles that can be relevant. The purpose in this article is to highlight however that general principles play an important role in the area of competition procedure and that this is increasingly so. Also, that there are interesting "side effects" of this trend such as the harmonising effect it has on the law in the Member States.

make it even more difficult for authorities, but there shall be a clear tension with the protection of the rights of parties which has to be resolved.

The difficulty in discovering the most serious infringements of competition law is also one of the reasons why leniency has become such an essential part of current antitrust practice.

It is a common feature of all leniency programmes that they require applicants to provide the authority with evidence of the cartel they claim to have been part of. In short, the importance of leniency programmes has a great impact on fact finding and evidence for two main reasons. The first is that an applicant for leniency has a great interest in "beefing up" the evidence: the more convincing it seems, the greater the reward will be. It goes without saying that the authority will verify all claims brought forward. Nevertheless, there is a risk that a certain amount of exaggeration takes place, for example when naming all the undertakings implicated in a cartel. Secondly, there might be more reliance on oral statements in leniency cases. This is causing the competition authorities to change the methods they use in dealing with proof.

There are a number of other reasons why cartel cases should be treated uniquely, that are important when it comes to proof.

The legal dispute is usually limited de facto to a number of the conditions of application of the cartel prohibition.[236] In many cases the undertakings concerned recognise, at least in part, the existence of a cartel, certainly in the case of leniency.

There are, then, two types of arguments that are becoming increasingly important in cartel cases: the first are arguments relating to the impact on the market (particularly the appreciability of the restriction and the effects on the market). These arguments are increasingly important because of the more economic approach discussed below. It must also be said that in hardcore cartel cases there is usually not much need for economic analysis because the agreements are considered to have the restriction of competition as their objective and therefore the effects on the market need not be proven. Nevertheless, the impression is that this line of case-law has only a limited shelf life.[237]

The other category of arguments are those that concentrate on procedural aspects and individual accountability for the infringement, or even only on

---

236 For example: in many cases the condition that the parties must be "undertakings" within the meaning of Article 81 EC or the existence of an agreement shall not be in dispute.

237 See below about the increasing pressure on authorities to substantiate their claims and on the other hand the decreasing number of hard core restrictions that remain; CFI case T-168/01, *GlaxoSmithKline Services Unlimited v Commission of the European Communities* [2006] ECR II-02969.

the calculation of the fines and the existence of aggravating and attenuating circumstances.

In other words, the questions of proof shall not always concern all the constituent elements of the cartel prohibition. It can be assumed that when facts or legal points are not in dispute, the Commission is discharged from its burden of proof in that respect.[238]

3. Recent developments having an impact on proof

This article aims to highlight some developments in recent competition practice that bear great relevance for issues of proof.

A so-called more economic approach has been introduced: for vertical restrictions, safe harbours were created for firms with a small market share and only a limited number of hardcore restrictions are still considered detrimental for the economy.[239] The recent well-known judgment of the US Supreme Court in the Leegin case, is quite striking in this respect, and goes substantially further.[240] The Supreme Court decided that it was time to abandon the per se rule for vertical resale price maintenance. This was one of the few remaining hardcore restrictions to which US antitrust law did not apply the rule of reason. Currently, under EC competition law, vertical resale price maintenance is blacklisted.[241] Although it is uncertain at this stage whether this will have an impact on the EC policy towards vertical restraints, at the very least it will be a crucial element in the evaluation of the regulations on vertical agreements that are due to start in the near future. The result might be that the list of hard core restrictions in vertical agreements is limited further.

For horizontal agreements, the Commission adopted guidelines allowing for more flexibility for certain types of agreements that can have pro-competitive effects, such as joint production and research and development agreements.[242] The keyword is now "self-assessment": companies are required to assess themselves on a case-by-case basis as to whether their agreements are compatible with Article 81 of the EC Treaty.

---

238 See Sibony and Barbier de La Serre (above n 228).

239 The reform of the policy towards vertical agreements led to a new group exemption, Commission Regulation (EC) No 2790/1999 of 22 December 1999 on the application of Article 81(3) of the Treaty to categories of vertical agreements and concerted practices [1999] OJ L 336, p. 21. The regulation has to be re-evaluated by 2010. Also: Commission notice on Guidelines on Vertical Restraints [2000] OJ C 291/1.

240 *Leegin Creative Leather Products, Inc. v. PSKS, Inc.* 551 US 877 (2007); see first comments by P. Lugard, 'Annotatie: Leegin Creative Leather Products, Inc./PSKS, Inc' (2007) 5/6 *Markt & Mededinging* 156.

241 Article 4 of Commission Regulation (EC) 2790/1999 (above note 239).

242 Commission Guidelines on the applicability of Article 81 to horizontal co-operation agreements [2001] OJ C 3/2, p. 2.

Even in hardcore cartels[243] there seems to be mounting pressure on the competition authorities to have sufficient consideration for economic reality and the impact on the market. This pressure is coming from the courts upon review: there are some signs of that at the EC level, mainly from the Court of First Instance but also tentatively from some national jurisdictions.[244]

The pressure is the result of the growing attention to issues of proof and evidence that has been apparent over the previous last few years in several areas of competition law. Community courts are requiring the Commission to substantiate adequately its findings of infringement of competition law by demonstrating an adverse effect on the marketplace. Similar requirements are imposed by courts when it comes to justifying the sanctions that are imposed by authorities. This stricter approach towards proof is, at least partly, inspired by the seriousness of the sanctions that are imposed on companies. Sanctions require that rights of defence and rules on proof and evidence be respected.

Specifically, at least two trends have been observed. The first took place mainly in merger cases where the CFI was strict on the Commission in terms of the market analysis that is necessary to evaluate whether or not certain effects on the market might reasonably be foreseen in the future to be the result of a merger. The Court requires accuracy, a convincing file and a well-motivated decision that clarifies the information on which the market analysis is based.[245] It has demonstrated a willingness to perform thorough reviews of Commission cases, causing some surprise. This recent case-law was the start of a discussion in doctrine on the standard of proof, which was until then barely discussed at all. There are clear indications that the Court sees little or no reason to conduct limited reviews in cases under Article 81 or 82 EC, rather the contrary.[246]

The second trend is somewhat similar but involves in Article 81 EC cases and goes a step further. In recent case-law the CFI seems to be challenging the quasi-automatic application of Article 81 EC to certain restrictive

---

243 Generally the following list is mentioned: price fixing, production quota, market sharing and clients sharing; see also the introduction of the new Commission Leniency Notice, Commission Notice on Immunity from fines and reduction of fines in cartel cases [2006] OJ C 298/17.

244 This is clear in the Netherlands: much commented judgment of College van Beroep voor het Bedrijfsleven (highest court in administrative affairs), Judgment of 7 December 2005 *G Star Secon Group*, AWB 04/237 and 04/249.

245 See famous judgments CFI case T-342/99, *Airtours* [2002] ECR II-2585; ECJ case C-13/03, *Commission of the European Communities v Tetra Laval BV* [2005] ECR 987. According to some, the general wordings of the ECJ's judgment in Tetra Laval, makes the considerations on proof in that judgment also applicable in other than merger cases, see H. Legal (above n 228).

246 Interesting comments in CFI case T-170/06, *Alrosa Company Ltd v Commission of the European Communities* [2007] II-02601, para. 108; the CFI's judgment in Microsoft could be considered an example of thorough review, case T-201/04, *Microsoft Corp. v Commission of the European Communities* [2007] II-03601.

practices such as measures against parallel trade.[247] Until recently, such practices received a "per se" treatment by the Commission because they were seen as very detrimental from the viewpoint of the internal market.[248] The Court now seems to be saying that it might be time for a new approach, and now requires the Commission to show, even in such cases, that negative effects on the market can be assumed and that the consumer can be harmed. In other words, again there is an emphasis on the burden of proof of the Commission and on the importance of achieving an adequate standard of proof on a case-to-case basis.[249]

4. Workable rules on proof

As already stated, this paper focuses mainly on the burden of proof and the standard of proof. The purpose is to formulate some considerations and thoughts about proof issues, that should be useful for cases involving Article 81 of the EC Treaty, regardless of where the cases are brought, because they are based on general principles of law that apply both at the Community level and at the level of the individual Member States.

4.1 Burden of proof

As said before, Article 2 Regulation 1/2003 contains the principle that the burden of proof of an infringement of Articles 81 or 82 EC rests upon the Commission or, in court proceedings, on the party alleging the infringement. When a party claims the benefit of the exception of Article 81 (3) it shall bear the burden of proof.

This principle applies to the Commission when it applies Article 81 EC to a cartel and the correct application of the principle is the subject of judicial review by the Court of First Instance and the Court of Justice. As will be discussed further on, the rule is less simple in practice than it might appear.

The rule on burden of proof laid down in Article 2 Regulation 1/2003 also applies to national proceedings in which Article 81 or 82 EC are applied, be it before a competition authority or in a court in civil proceedings. There is clearly no room for a different distribution of the burden of proof in national law. Contrary to the standard of proof, no reference is made to the national procedural autonomy in this respect. More so, one can assume that Article 2 Regulation 1/2003 also regulates the burden of proof in proceedings where

---

247 See GSK (above n 237).

248 Many Art. 81 decisions of the Commission in the last years were still related to issues of parallel trade and restriction of import and export is still listed as one of the most serious infringements by the Commission.

249 There are clear signs in national jurisdictions such as the Netherlands that courts are taking a similar approach, G Star Secon Group (above n 244). However, the author realizes this is still somewhat speculative because there has not been a judgment from the ECJ and the GSK judgment is subject to different interpretations.

only the national cartel prohibition shall be applied. In national cases where Article 81 or 82 EC is applied, the actual distribution of the burden of proof and the shift from one party to another, must respect the principles of equivalence and effectiveness: the procedural framework cannot be such as to make it too difficult to invoke and enforce EC law provisions.[250]

It is appropriate here to recall a specific feature of the burden of proof in cartel cases that was briefly mentioned before. The Commission is discharged from its burden of proof when certain relevant legal or factual elements are recognised by the party in question. This also implies that the same party cannot successfully attack the Commission's infringement decision on inadequate proof for a point where there had previously been recognition on behalf of the concerned undertaking. The growing importance of leniency cases makes it important to bear this in mind.

4.1.1 Legal burden and evidential burden

A distinction is generally made between persuasive or legal burden of proof and the evidential burden of proof. Another term sometimes used is the "tactical" burden of proof.

The party required to prove his case and to persuade the decision-maker, bears the burden of proof. This is the persuasive or legal burden of proof. The burden of persuasion can also be qualified as the risk of non-persuasion. When the Commission is of the opinion that an undertaking has infringed Article 81 of the EC Treaty by entering into a price-fixing cartel, the Commission must prove that infringement. The evidential burden of proof is the need to bring sufficient evidence.[251]

This is more than just a theoretical distinction, it helps to understand and define how the burden of proof works and should work in practice, and, more specifically, how the burden of proof can seemingly shift from one party to the other but actually stay with the same. This is clarified by using the distinction between legal burden of proof and evidential burden of proof. An example might clarify this distinction.

> Example:
> two competitors have made an agreement to work together to develop the technology for a new chip. They are the two major players in the market. The Commission considers that their R&D agreement is problematic and fulfils the conditions of Article 81 EC Treaty. The parties invoke the

---

250 There is quite a lot of case-law on the burden of proof in national cases, outside of competition law: for example ECJ case C-242/95, *GT-Link A/S v De Danske Statsbaner (DSB)* [1997] ECR I-4449; for an overview of the impact of EC law on national procedural law and sanctions, Lenaerts, Arts and Maselis, *Procedural law of the EU* (above note 227).

251 D. Bailey, 'Standard of proof in EC merger proceedings: a common law perspective' (2003) 40 *Common Market Law Review* (2003) 845.

exception of Article 81 (3) of the EC Treaty, stating, amongst other things, that the agreements create major technological progress. They have the burden of proof for the conditions of the exception of Article 81 (3). If plausible scientific evidence is presented about the consequences of their agreement, but the Commission is not convinced, the Commission will have to substantiate its argument. Even though the legal burden of proof is still with the undertakings concerned, the evidential burden of proof will have shifted. If the arguments of the parties are not accepted, they shall be subject of the appeal.

4.1.2. Article 81 (1) EC Treaty

The situation is in fact more complicated than the seemingly simple rule of Article 2 of Regulation 1/2003 would indicate, for another reason. In the current state of competition law, there are many types of cases where a balancing exercise is taking place under Article 81 (1) EC. Although the Community courts have refused to recognise that a rule of reason, similar to that in the US system, exists in EC law, there is a well-developed body of case-law in which, at the very least, a similar exercise occurs.

First, there are cases where pros and cons of agreements are weighed and certain restrictions are left outside the scope of Article 81 (1) EC because non-economic considerations outweigh the restriction of competition. The case-law on sport and on restrictions in the market of professional services are the most well known.[252]

Secondly, the so-called more economic approach has led to a policy where certain agreements are considered to stay outside the scope of application if the parties stay below a certain market share threshold.[253] This also brings the use of presumptions into the picture.

Therefore the rule that the Commission bears the burden of proof for the infringement (or the claimant in civil proceedings) oversimplifies the proof issues at stake.

Example:
Article 81 (1): legal and evidential burden of proof on Commission: (a) undertakings, (b) agreement or concerted practice, (c) appreciable (d) restriction of competition, (e) appreciable (f) effect on trade between Member States.
Undertakings:

252 For example ECJ case C-519/04, *David Meca-Medina and Igor Majcen v Commission of the European Communities* [2006] ECR I-06991 not yet published and ECJ case C-309/99, *J. C. J. Wouters, J. W. Savelbergh and Price Waterhouse Belastingadviseurs BV v Algemene Raad van de Nederlandse Orde van Advocaten, intervener: Raad van de Balies van de Europese Gemeenschap* [2002] ECR I- 1577.

253 The Guidelines in horizontal agreements are a good example; see for example joint distribution agreements and joint production (above n 242).

> Strategy One: contest individual conditions a, b, c, d, e and/or f
> And/or
> Strategy Two: acknowledge the restrictive nature of an agreement but claim the agreements escapes from the scope of application of Article 81 for one of the reasons mentioned above.[254]

The undertakings must substantiate their claims, and have the evidential burden of proof. If they prove in Strategy One that one condition is not met, this is sufficient since the conditions are cumulative. If the arguments are contested, the evidential burden of proof shall shift again. However, at that point there is an important change: the party who has the legal burden of proof has been shown not to have sufficient proof. At such a point, the principle of in dubio pro reo (benefit of the doubt) can come into play, certainly in court proceedings.[255] Doubt has been created: for the evidential burden to shift a second time to the undertakings shall require strong evidence from the Commission.

If the undertaking prove in Strategy Two that, for example, the restrictions of the agreements are inherent to the justified non economic goal they pursue, the agreement shall fall outside the scope of Article 81 (1) and recourse to Article 81 (3) will no longer be necessary. It is understandable that, when the evidential burden of proof is upon the undertakings in this respect, more proof is required, because a restriction of competition is established yet it is not forbidden. This can be based on the general principle that exceptions to general prohibitions are interpreted restrictively.

4.1.3 Article 81 (3) EC Treaty

Where Article 81 (3) of the EC Treaty is concerned, Article 2 Regulation 1/2003 provides that the burden of proof rests upon the party claiming the benefit of the exception. Here the cumulative nature of the four conditions that the provision contains[256], works the other way. The undertaking or association of undertakings brings proof for all four conditions. The

---

[254] It is not always so clear cut: staying below a market share threshold can also be the non fulfillment of the condition of the existence of an appreciable effect on competition.

[255] There is no doubt this principle applies in competition procedures, see ECJ case-199/92 *P, Hüls AG v Commission of the European Communities* [1999] ECR I-4287 as well as in front of national authorities and courts applying the EC provisions, ECJ case 5/88, *Hubert Wachauf v Bundesamt für Ernährung und Forstwirtschaft* [1989] ECR 2609; being general principles of EC law as well as fundamental rights protected by international treaties, there is no question that Member States are bound.

[256] The four conditions are: (1) contribute to improving the production or distribution of goods or to promoting the technical or economical progress, (2) allowing consumers a fair share of the resulting benefit, (3) not imposing restriction which are not indispensable to the attainment of these objectives and (4) not have the possibility to eliminate competition in respect of a substantial part of the products in question.

evidential burden of proof then shifts if the Commission contests this proof. If it can show for only one condition that in fact the necessary proof is not available, this is sufficient. Nevertheless, it is remarkable that the Commission will generally stand on all four conditions in an infringement decision, preferring to explain why the exception does not apply.[257] In most cases the Commission will also argue that more than one condition is not fulfilled. The same tendency exists at the national level: authorities and courts prefer to be cautious and are, in any case, under a duty to adequately justify their decisions. However, strictly speaking, the non-fulfilment of one condition of Article 81 (3) is sufficient and the Commission must not examine in detail further arguments under Article 81 (3) as soon as one condition is not fulfilled.

For Article 81 (3) an interesting question on the shift of the burden of proof is whether in general the attitude towards proof should also be severe because it constitutes an exception to a general rule such as was described above for the case-law under Article 81 (1) EC, which does not include certain agreements in the scope of application of the prohibition (see above). In other words: when the Commission casts doubt on the arguments of a party (for example, concerning the existence of an improvement in production), does this mean that a strict attitude is necessary when the evidential burden of proof is shifted back to the undertaking?

On the basis of EC law and the structure of the EC Treaty, this seems plausible. However, it is submitted that it is doubtful. First, the Treaty itself has provided for the possibility of certain restrictive agreements being exempted because they present advantages, predominantly of an economic nature, that outweigh the restrictions of competition. This is important: the idea is that by nature these agreements have a neutral effect on competition in the market. Secondly, there is no justification for allowing the "benefit of the doubt" rule to apply in favour of the authority that is enforcing the law against the undertaking. In other words, the counter-arguments of the Commission should not make it more difficult for the undertaking to bring forward additional elements to prove why the conditions of Article 81 (3) EC are met. Even though the roles are reversed under Article 81 (3) EC, the undertaking is still in the position of the defendant and should have full respect of the rights or defence.

4.1.4 Shifting the burden: some additional remarks

Flexibility in terms of the shifting burden of proof is a good thing, but the difficulty in some cases is at what point the evidential burden is shifted. When is there enough "likeliness", for the other party to have to show that it is "unlikely"? It helps to always keep in mind who bears the initial legal burden of proof, to determine at which point the evidential burden should

[257] A careful attitude of authorities and courts (in anticipation of review) when examining the conditions of Article 81 (3) EC is justified: the CFI was very critical on this point in GSK (above n 237).

shift. It also helps to keep in mind the structure of Article 81 EC and its logic. Furthermore, the examples above show that an indefinite number of shifts in the evidential burden of proof is unlikely and that after a party has successfully contested the arguments of the Commission bearing the legal burden of proof, the standard should change because doubt is created: reasons for a second change in the burden of proof shall not be assumed so readily.

This shows the extent to which the burden of proof and the standard of proof are linked. It also shows how the authority or judge will inevitably have to make several decisions in terms of the burden of proof throughout the procedure of one single cartel case.

The importance of general principles of law has become clear when discussing how the distribution of the burden of proof should work in practice. The presumption of innocence and the rights of defence protect the defendant undertakings and can sometimes lead to mitigating the burden of proof in their favour.

However, it must be underlined that these principles do not put into question the distribution of the legal burden of proof. Nor does it mean that the burden of proof of undertakings when invoking the exception of Article 81 (3) EC is more easily shifted back to the Commission or the national authority than in cases of an infringement of Article 81 (1) EC: this is a widespread misconception amongst lawyers who still tend to give less importance to proof under Article 81 (3) EC than under Article 81 (1) EC.[258]

4.1.5 Presumptions

In order to have a workable system of proof in competition law and certainly for cartels, it is necessary to work with (rebuttable) presumptions. It is submitted that the more economic approach in competition law has increased the importance of presumptions but has also changed their nature.

---

258 Although it has to be said that this has partly to do with the fact that for many years the Commission hardly motivated its decisions when it came to the fulfilment of the conditions of Article 81 (3). But since the introduction of the legal exception by Regulation 1/2003, this exception shall be dealt with mostly in national proceedings and before national courts who might be more worried both about the burden of proof as well as by adequately motivating why an exception to a fundamental rule of the EC Treaty is accepted. Guidance on the interpretation of the cumulative conditions is given in the Commission Commission Notice laying down guidelines on the effect on trade concept contained in Articles 81 and 82 of the Treaty [2004] OJ C 101/97.

– Thresholds

The first type of presumption usually takes the form of thresholds expressed in the market share of turnover of the parties and works as follows: as long as a particular threshold is not met, it is assumed that there is no appreciable effect on competition in the common market. Such thresholds have existed since the first De Minimis Notice of the Commission in 1970 that introduced the idea that Article 81 EC should not apply to agreements having only a negligible effect on competition.[259] The use of thresholds has increased substantially in all areas of competition law, mainly as a result of the modernisation of competition law. A more economical approach includes creating more and more safe harbours under certain thresholds. It is assumed that under those thresholds of (usually) market share no adverse effect on competition is to be expected.

From the point of view of proof, different types of threshold presumptions can be distinguished, mainly according to their legal basis. Such presumptions can be found mostly in group exemptions, and in Commission notices and guidelines. The degree of legal certainty is not equal in both cases.

The first kind of presumption (mostly group exemptions) gives the highest degree of legal security to undertakings and lays the burden of proof entirely upon the authority because the undertakings no longer have to prove that their agreement fulfils the conditions of Article 81 (3) EC. The example is the safe harbour for vertical agreements that stay below a market share threshold of 30 %. An agreement fulfilling the conditions of Regulation 2790/1999 is exempted from Article 81 (1) EC; in principle neither the Commission nor a court could consider the agreements nevertheless infringes Article 81 (1) EC.[260] The only element of proof that undertakings should have concerns the factual basis for the calculation of their market share; otherwise they can be sure to benefit from the exemption.[261]

For the sake of clarity, it is important to emphasise that these presumptions do not work in two directions: in the case of the threshold for vertical agreements mentioned above, the agreements shall not be assumed to be

---

259 Current de Minimis Notice [2001] OJ C 149/18.

260 The only possibility is the exceptional situation where the benefit of the exemption can be revoked because in a certain territory the cumulative effect of similar agreements leads to an unacceptable restriction of competition. Such an action on behalf of the Commission or a national competition authority shall not have retroactive effect (Articles 6 and 7 Regulation 2790/1999).

261 Some jurisdictions have non rebuttable presumptions for SME undertakings: as long as they stay under a certain market share threshold their agreements can never be considered contrary to the cartel prohibition, even if they contain hard core restrictions, see for example Article 7 of the Dutch Competition Act. This goes further then the safe harbour for vertical agreements which makes the exemption conditional to the absence of hard core restrictions.

illegal once the threshold is exceeded. Another example from the guidelines on horizontal agreements: it is generally assumed that joint purchase agreements will not fall under Article 81 (1) EC if parties stay under the market threshold of 15 % market share. This does not mean, of course, that when this threshold is exceeded an agreement is presumed to be restrictive under Article 81 (1) EC. In one sense, presumptions replace the evidential burden of proof that rests on a party, but as soon as they no longer apply, the normal distribution of the burden of proof is revived. However, the legal burden of proof does not shift.

The use of thresholds is generally seen as a good instrument to allow competition law to take into account the economic reality whilst providing for some legal security for the undertakings. It clearly alleviates the burden of proof for companies: under Article 81 (1) EC many presumptions in group exemptions or guidelines now permit the undertaking to counter any argument of the authority or a claimant to substantiate why their agreements do not fulfil the conditions of application of Article 81 (1) EC, usually because it can be assumed they have no adverse effect on competition in the market. Where Article 81 (3) EC is concerned the use of presumptions with market shares will generally discharge the undertaking entirely of his burden of proof.

Finally, the use of these presumptions based on thresholds has one major advantage where proof is concerned, which is again related to the recent developments in competition law: their use limits the number of cases in which the actual effect on competition in the market has to be measured and proven. This advantage should not be underestimated especially considering the growing pressure to pay sufficient attention to market analysis and to prove concrete effects in the market, as was briefly mentioned above.

– Legal presumptions

A second type of presumption can be found in case-law and concerns more the legal evaluation of the proof or evidence that is put forward. It is beyond the scope of this article to enumerate all the presumptions that seem to be established case-law so far,[262] but some examples are given to illustrate again how important the use of presumptions is. The most important legal presumptions of this kind concern the constituent conditions of Article 81 (1) EC. They allow the authority to qualify factual elements into the concepts laid down in that provision (see the example under 4.1.1 above).

The clearest example is perhaps the condition of the existence of an "agreement or concerted practice".

---

[262] See Siragusa and Rizza (eds), chapter 1 and chapter 5 (above n 229) for some more examples.

Example: Companies A, B and C are suspected to have exchanged information during a meeting in Z at time Y with the purpose of coordinating their market behaviour.

The authority will have to prove that, for example:
- the meeting occurred between these persons at the given time and place; and
- that information was exchanged and that there is some link between this exchange and the market behaviour of the parties.

Where the first element is concerned, the authority will have to adduce positive evidence: one cannot ask the undertakings concerned to prove that they were not present.[263] Where the second element is concerned, presumptions can come into play: it can be assumed that if companies exchange information then they will use this to determine their market behaviour.[264] Therefore parallel behaviour may be assumed to be related to this exchange of information and thus be the result of collusion. The presumption has to be rebuttable: a plausible alternative explanation for the parallel behaviour by the undertakings has to be possible but in that case the burden of proof is shifted to the undertakings. Such an alternative explanation should have to be credible and convincing if the authorities had gathered a substantial amount of circumstantial evidence, but shall be possible by any means the party sees fit to use.

Another important example of the use of presumptions relates to the individual accountability of undertakings to a cartel. In the example above, the authority is allowed to presume that A, B and C participated in the cartel once it is established that they were present at the meeting where information was exchanged. Each one of them could be considered individually responsible for its role in this cartel. If A now claims that even though he was there, he did not participate but, on the contrary, tried to convince the others not to exchange certain information, he will have to prove that this is the case. In other words, the evidential burden of proof shifts again. His burden of proof will require proving for example by whatever way that he explicitly distanced himself from the other participants during the meeting.[265]

---

263 See ECJ case C-49/92 P, *Commission of the European Communities v Anic Partecipazioni SpA* [1999] ECR I-4125. This so called "Anic rule" is the subject of the preliminary questions in case C-8/08, (above n 228).

264 T. Wessely, 'Case note: Case C-49/92P, Commission v ANIC [1999] ECR I-4125; Case C-199/92P, Hüls v. Commission [1999] ECR I-4287; Case C-235/92P, Montecatini v. Commission [1999] ECR I-4539; Judgements of 8 April 1999 (together: Polypropylene appeal cases' (2001) 38 *Common Market Law Review* 739.

265 The ECJ in Hüls (above n 255).

4.2 Standard of proof

4.2.1 Definition: where do we stand?

The standard of proof concerns the level of certainty the proof has to achieve. The standard of proof has to be attained by the party bearing the legal burden of proof.

It appears from the legal framework described above that there are no rules on proof in EC law in general and that legislation in the area of competition law contains only the recently adopted general rule on the burden of proof. Also, it was mentioned that Regulation 1/2003 seems to deliberately leave the definition of the standard of proof at a national level to the law of the Member States. However, in reality, there is some quite useful case-law in which the relevant factors to determine the standard of proof can be found.

As was said above, in the absence of legislation, the courts construe the rules on proof in competition cases on the basis of the inherent characteristics of EC law and the specifics of competition law, and in respect of general principles common to both the Community legal order and the national legal systems of the Member States. The standard of proof is the best example of this development which bears relevance for all cases in which competition law is applied, both at the EC and at the national level.

The Community courts have made reference to what is called the "requisite legal standard".[266] On this basis the courts have been willing to annul important merger decisions by the Commission in recent years, but without quite saying what that standard is.

Frustration has been expressed in legal doctrine after the famous merger cases in which the courts were very strict on the Commission.[267] The criticisms were manifold, but one of the main points was that there was no clear choice for a particular standard of proof.[268] The Courts indeed refused to use the concepts of standard of proof that are known in other legal disciplines, such as "beyond reasonable doubt" and "the balance of probabilities" (see above under section 1.4). It is likely that the lack of a common tradition in the different Member States, also describes above, plays a role in the courts reluctance. However, it seems quite clear that in merger cases, the standard resembles most the balance of probabilities. As

---

266 The preamble of Regulation 1/2003 also mentions this "the requisite legal standard" without defining it. For a general overview: Siragusa and Rizza (ed.) (above n 229), chap 5.

267 ECJ Airtours; ECJ Tetra Laval (above n 245).

268 Y. Botteman, 'Mergers, standard of proof and expert economic evidence' (2006) 2 *Journal of Competition Law and Economics* 71; D. Bailey, 'Standard of proof in EC merger proceedings: a common law perspective' (2003) 40 *Common Market Law Review* (2003) 845; B. Louveaux and P. Gilbert, 'The standard of proof under the Competition Act' (2005) 3 *European Competition Law Review* (2005) 173.

expressed recently by Advocate General Kokott, "it is a prospective analysis which makes it necessary to envisage various chains of cause and effect with a view to ascertaining which of them is *more likely*".[269]However, even in merger control, there is no single standard because in the first phase one might consider the standard of reasonable doubt to apply: only serious doubts about the compatibility with the common market can lead to not clearing the merger within the short time limits of the first phase.

In the ECJ's judgment in Tetra Laval (§39) the Court refers to the requirement that the evidence be "accurate, reliable and consistent" and also that it should contain "all the information which must be taken into account in order to assess a complex situation and whether evidence can substantiate the conclusions drawn from it". According to some authors, this is drafted in such a general way that it can also apply outside of merger cases. Even without opening that debate, it is submitted that this important guideline on proof from the ECJ, is compatible with the standard of proof that is discussed below for cartel cases.

This paper defends that, in any event, in Article 81 EC cases, there are enough guidelines in the case-law to form a basis for a workable standard of proof.

In a particularly illustrative judgment in this matter, *JFE Engineering*, the CFI first reminds us of the key importance of the principle of the presumption of innocence, which means that if there is doubt, the benefit of that doubt should always be given to the undertakings accused. This might lead one to believe that the standard of proof resembles the criminal standard of "reasonable doubt", but in fact the CFI then continues and refers to what has become the more or less standard way of the defining what standard proof should achieve in cartel cases. The Commission must produce: "sufficiently precise and consistent evidence to support the firm conviction that the alleged infringement took place".[270]

We should add: "and that the infringement can be attributed to the undertaking accused" to reflect the individual accountability of undertakings which can then, in turn, lead to sanctions.

It appears that there are two components in this standard, reflecting the two dimensions of proof mentioned at the beginning of this paper (production and persuasion):
- the value of the evidence (sufficiently precise and consistent); and
- the capacity to convince the authority or judge (a firm conviction).

---

[269] Opinion of Advocate General Kokott case C-413/06, *Bertelsmann AG and Sony Corporation of America v Independent Music Publishers and Labels Association (Impala)* [2008] ECR I-4951, para. 208 and following.

[270] CFI cases T-67 and 68/00 and T-71/00 and 78/00, *JFE Engineering and others* [2004] ECR II-2501.

As mentioned before, there are no restrictions on the type of evidence that the Commission can use and there is no hierarchy.[271]

The lack of a set of (technical) rules on proof and the fact that we are in a system of free proof, imply that the relevance and the reliability of proof shall not be issues of admissibility of proof, unlike in other areas of the law. All types of proof can, potentially, be relevant, and the reliability of the proof shall be evaluated in the light of the firm conviction that the authority or judge has to reach. This can be a very difficult task when dealing with expert witnesses or reports, or when having to decide whether a certain type of economic analysis is, for example, generally accepted as state of the art or whether it is questionable. Cases where economists themselves can provide an unequivocal answer to such questions are rare.

It is also established case-law that proof need not meet this standard for every element of the infringement but what counts is the overall assessment of the evidence. According to the CFI: "*In most cases, the existence of an anti-competitive practice or agreement must be inferred from a number of coincidences and indicia which, taken together, may, in the absence of another plausible explanation, constitute evidence of an infringement of the competition rules.*"[272]

In other words, indirect and circumstantial evidence may be used: its actual value shall be the contribution it can or cannot make to the firm conviction mentioned above.

4.2.2 The X Factor

There is a particularity to mention in relation to proof: the human factor, referred to here as the X factor. It is perhaps somewhat audacious to mention this explicitly in times when the impression has been created that competition law is a question of applying a set of pre-established rules to the market situation, with the help of advanced economic analysis. There are two dimensions to this X factor.

The first dimension relates to the traditional abstraction that is made of the person of the decision-maker. The model is that the decision-maker, be it an official of an administrative body or a judge, is presupposed to be a "clean slate" upon which the conviction grows as he acquaints himself with the file

---

271 However, it is clear of course that in practice certain types of evidence shall have more value than others: the "age" of the evidence shall also play a role: the obvious example is evidence dating from before the start of an investigation which shall usually be considered more valuable than evidence of a more recent date. As a general rule written evidence shall be higher regarded than oral evidence but this is a subject of rapid evolution.

272 ECJ case C-105/04P, *Nederlandse Federatieve Vereniging voor de Groothandel op Elektrotechnisch Gebied v Commission of the European Communities* [2006] I-08725.

and the proof that is collected. There is no reason in principle to suspect that any person in a decision-making position would let his personal views prevail, as impartiality is protected by general principle of law.[273]However, in terms of evaluating proof, it is not realistic to deny the personal dimension. This can be illustrated by referring to the famous example in doctrine about the lion in the park. If a party alleges that he has seen a lion in the city park, any person would be sceptical -more sceptical, at least, than if the party were to claim that he had seen a dog. Therefore, even though the standard of proof would obviously have to be the same, one can easily understand that the party in question would have to be more convincing in the case of the lion: the decision-maker would find it hard to believe that there really was a lion in the park.[274] This can be applied to numerous subjects in competition law: for example, the substitution of one product by another for the definition of a relevant market or an alternative explanation for market behaviour. The personal knowledge and experience of the decision-maker and the relation to the particular market or conduct that is at stake can play a role. In the example given, perhaps the decision-maker knew that a lion had escaped from the park a day earlier. Analysing products that all consumers know (such as bread, milk or Microsoft Windows) will also not be as difficult as convincing a decision-maker about complex or intermediate products such as chemical products or microchips, unless, of course, the decision-maker has some particular knowledge in this area.

These remarks about the personal dimension should not be misunderstood: the proposition is not at all that the X factor will make a difference in the end result of the decision, nor in the procedure as it is followed or the guarantees that parties will rightfully claim. Nor would it be justified to modulate the legal burden of proof or the standard of proof. However, the X factor should not be denied and can, in some cases, play a role in the mechanisms of proof (such as shifting the evidential burden), especially in the element of persuasion.

The second dimension of the X factor might be referred to as the quest for justice. In competition law, as in any other area of law, the ultimate goal is or should be to reach fair decisions. It is beyond the scope of this paper to relate this objective to the more economic goals of competition policy and consumer protection. However, most lawyers will have no trouble

---

273 If there is any suspicion of the risk of biased judgment, the legal system has to provide for mechanisms to protect the parties and ensure impartiality. The importance cannot be overestimated. A famous quote from R. Posner is that society has very little interest in the factual outcome of any one trial, as long as the fact-finding process is tolerably accurate and systematically unbiased. See the discussion of these issues by J. Parker, 'Daubert's debut: the Supreme Court, the economics of scientific evidence, and the adversarial system' (1994-95) 4 *Supreme Court Economic Review* 1-56, also available as George Mason University Law and Economics Research Paper, also available on SSRN at http://ssrn.com/abstractid=1069923.

274 Also cited by Sibony and Barbier de La Serre (above n 228).

acknowledging that decisions should be fair and just, whilst at the same time admitting that it is impossible to define precisely what justice or fairness means. A quote from J. Joshua illustrates that this certainly plays a role in assessing proof in competition cases: "*The object of any system of proof in adjucatory proceedings must be to reconcile the limitations inherent in the method devised with the search for the truth and to arrive at a fair decision.*"[275] This quote implicitly recognises that justice considerations might intervene within the normal course of the procedure and might have an impact on the final decision and possible sanction. It is submitted that this often happens in competition law through the application of two general principles of law: the first being the benefit of the doubt as already cited, and the second the principle of proportionality which is increasingly important in competition law.[276] Another remarkable quote in this respect is from Judge H. Legal of the CFI; in commenting a recent CFI judgment (British Airways) and the judicial review exercised in that case, he observes "*The Commission actually retains considerable leeway, as long as it approaches a competition case in a way that is unprejudiced, fair and scrupulous.*"[277]

4.2.3 Flexibility and differentiation

It was argued above that the standard of proof that has now been expressed frequently by the Community courts is a sufficient basis for a workable system in cartel cases. It is recalled here: "*sufficiently precise and consistent evidence to support the firm conviction that the alleged infringement took place*".

This standard allows a number of relevant factors to be taken into account, such as the gravity and nature of the infringement and the type of proof or evidence that is brought forward. If competition law is a system of free proof and all types of proof in principle are accepted, it makes sense to have a standard of proof that is sufficiently flexible to allow a global view of all the proof in the case. The fact that proof is more and more difficult to find should also play a role. These are the specifics of cartel cases mentioned above.

The requirements of "sufficiently precise" and especially "consistent" should ensure that the value of the evidence is adequate. For example: if there are contradictory statements from representatives of the participating undertakings in the file, it is clear that supplementary evidence is necessary to corroborate either one or the other version. If not, it is possible that the

---

[275] Joshua (above n 229) [316].

[276] The principle of proportionality shall often play in the phase of determining the sanction for a cartel: the sanction should be fair (and this proportionate) taking into account the size of the undertaking compared to others, its role etc. In leniency cases this is an issue of attention for the future because there can be some tension between proportionality and the reductions given on the basis of leniency programs.

[277] Legal (above n 228).

statements cannot be used as a proof, given that they are not consistent. "Precise" means that the evidence must concern all the relevant elements of the infringement: for example, the evidence must allow the duration of the infringement to be determined. The Commission cannot consider that once the existence of the agreement is proven, this is sufficient and then require the parties to prove that they have ended their agreement.[278]

The flexibility in terms of the value of proof (production) is counterbalanced by the requirement that proof should lead to a "firm" conviction (persuasion). This should be seen together with the fundamental general principles of law that have been shown to play a key role in proof matters.

The standard has been qualified as somewhere halfway between "reasonable doubt" and "the balance of probabilities", resembling most the standard of "clear and convincing evidence", but this paper contends that it is not useful to devote too much effort to qualifying it in that way because the standard is deliberately flexible to allow for it to work in both ways in practice. It then has the advantage of being applicable in all matters of competition law, whilst still being differentiable in practice on a case-to-case basis according to a number of factors.

One of these factors is the seriousness of the infringement and the sanctions that the applicable law provides. This can be illustrated by a quote from the UK Competition Appeal Tribunal: "*The more serious the allegations, the more cogent should be the evidence.. In particular this applies to cases involving the disqualification of directors which is now one of the possible consequences of a finding of an infringement of the Competition Act.*"[279] This is particularly relevant given the tendency in a growing number of countries to introduce criminal sanctions. There is little doubt that the standard should be differentiated in such cases: in other words, it should be higher. Where sanctions are concerned, it would certainly be preferable that sanctions not differ too much according to the jurisdiction which is applying the law. This would require harmonisation of procedure and sanctions throughout the EU, but discussion of the advantages and disadvantages of such a harmonisation is beyond the scope of this paper.

As was also mentioned above, in the discussion of the specifics of cartel cases, the analysis in such cases is usually different from that in abuse and merger cases. A strict and uniform standard of proof is not possible because of the difference between ex post and ex ante analyses. The standard that is defended here has the advantage of being sufficiently flexible for use in both types of situations but, again, should be differentiated.

It also seems clear that the standard of proof should be differentiated according to whether the proof concerns facts or qualifying the facts to apply

---

[278] CFI "Steamless" tubes cases (above n 270).

[279] JJB Sports Plc v OFT 2004, CAT 17, as cited by Louveaux and Gilbert (above n 268).

the law. Rather, it is the combination of the standard of proof and the standard of review that comes into the picture here. In competition cases, generally a certain discretionary power is left to the Commission when it comes to establishing the (economic) facts or more specifically the economic analysis of those facts. The standard of proof should be the same but the review is more marginal when it comes to the economic analysis of facts than when the court is looking into the legal qualification thereof. This difference is also justified by the respective roles of the administration and of the judiciary.[280]

4.2.4 Duty to state reasons

The duty to state reasons is laid down in Article 253 of the EC Treaty and can also be found in Article 41 of the Charter on Fundamental rights: the obligation for the administration to give reasons for its decisions. Where the courts and tribunals are concerned, there is no explicit legal basis in the treaties for the duty to motivate judgments at the EU level but there is clearly consensus about the fact that adequate reasoning is a fundamental part of the role of the judiciary.

There are some interesting aspects of the duty to state reasons that deserve brief mention here.

First, it seems useful to draw attention to the scope of this duty and its purpose, as defined by the Court of Justice:

"the duty to state reasons does not merely take formal considerations into account but seeks to give an opportunity to the parties defending their rights, to the Court of exercising its supervisory functions and to Member States and to all interested nationals of ascertaining the circumstances in which the institution has applied the Treaty".[281]

This quote summarises well the importance of adequate reasoning in terms of the rights of the parties and judicial and democratic control. In

[280] Interesting on this point very recently the CFI case T-474/04, *Pergan Hilfsstoffe für industrielle Prozesse GmbH v Commission of the European Communities* [2007] ECR 2007 II-04225, paras. 77-78. According to Advocate General Kokott, there seems to be a three step system: the court on review should verify the factual basis of the decision in detail, then give leeway for the economic analysis of those facts but exercise full review afterwards as to the legal consequences of that analysis, Conclusion above note 267. The author entirely agrees. See the interesting article by R. Wilsher, 'Achieving better decision-making in competition enforcement cases: a public law perspective on the role of the executive and the courts' (2007) 30 *World Competition* 263.

[281] ECJ case 24/62, *Germany/Commission* [1963] ECR 137.

competition cases, where sanctions are imposed, this is particularly important.[282]

Secondly, it is argued that the duty to state reasons is particularly relevant in cartel cases given the developments described in this article. According to the case-law adequate reasoning shall be of even more fundamental importance when the Commission has discretion or power of appraisal. This is because the courts on review have to be able to verify whether the factual and legal elements on which such a discretion can be based, are present in the particular case.[283] This line of case-law seems very relevant here: upon analyzing the judgments in the merger cases mentioned above[284] one realizes that the Courts have criticised not so much the choices the Commission made in terms of economic theory or market analysing but rather the lack of sufficient reasoning. In other words, whilst leaving the actual economic appraisal in complex competition cases to the authority, the courts feel that, in such cases, the Commission has a strong duty to construct a well reasoned decision.[285]

In terms of proof in a case involving the application of Article 81 of the EC Treaty, for some factual elements little doubt exists as to their existence, and parties may even be in agreement. When it comes to the more economics based elements (relevant market, effect on the market, effect on interstate trade, impact on the market to taken into account for the fine, benefit obtained by participants etc..), however, the situation is more complex.

Where the production of proof is concerned, there might not be much material available and if it is, often there will be contradictory interpretations, usually placing lawyers in a difficult position of evaluating economic evidence. Where persuasion is concerned, the authority or court that has to reach a "firm conviction" will often have to make choices based on the "likeliness" of certain market effects. This is more so in merger cases, but is also relevant in cartel cases because not only actual effects on the market but also potential effects have to be taken into account.[286] For these reasons, it is argued here that the duty to state reasons is an essential requirement and that it deserves more attention than the focus on the definition of a standard of proof. Justice must be seen to be done: when choices are made, they have to be well motivated and this will increase their acceptability.

---

282 A parallel is made with the case-law of the ECJ in which it was emphasized that the extent of the requirement to state reasons is influenced by the type of instrument which is used, see Lenaerts and van Nuffel (above n 222) [760].

283 ECJ case C-269/90, *Technische Universität München* [1991] ECR I- 5469.

284 *Airtours and ECJ Tetra Laval* (above n 245).

285 On the duty to state reasons, particularly interesting comments in the Conclusion of Advocate General Kokott, (above n 269), paras. 97 and following; also para. 174 on the requirements for a decision in terms of description of the factual basis.

286 This is true both for the appreciable effect on competition as well as for the effect on trade between Member States.

5. So how to reconcile a more economics-based competition law with rules on proof?

This paper attempts to answer this question on the basis of three main ideas, which summarise the above discussion.

First, it is proposed that there is no contradiction between a system of economics-based competition law and a coherent set of rules on proof. In fact, the development towards a more economic approach was one of the factors that triggered the growing attention for rules of proof and modern competition law requires these rules more than ever.

As shown above, as the economics of competition law have become more advanced and increasingly introduced into law enforcement, the evolution has tended towards a more and more case-to-case type of approach in competition law. There are fewer hardcore restrictions, and market analysis plays a more important role. The experience of the last years has shown that economic insights into market behaviour and its desirability, differ greatly according to the theory that is applied or the person who is applying it. Whether or not this is right, it is the perception of many lawyers in the area of competition law. Therefore, rules on proof often have to be decisive in individual cases as a kind of arbitrating factor. Also, as the law becomes more insecure and its application less predictable, legal security becomes a greater concern.

Secondly, flexible and variable rules of proof, more specifically on the burden of proof and the standard of proof, are not a threat to the traditional legal concepts underlying our legal systems and the general principles of law on which they are based, and at the same time should limit the number of cases where the application of the rules achieves a result far from economic reality. Lawyers must acknowledge the specific nature of competition law that requires less rigid rules. It is submitted that the definition of a specific standard of proof is not a priority, nor is a stricter set of technical rules of proof or evidence.

Such flexible and variable rules on proof require confidence in what I have called the X factor. They also require an institutional structure allowing a review court more than only a marginal review. The courts on review should perhaps generally be restrained when it comes to economic appraisal, but should exercise a full review when it comes to legal and procedural points. Whilst exercising that control, it is, of course, necessary that they apply the rules of proof as adapted to the specific competition law context, as discussed above.

Finally, the duty to motivate and provide adequate reasoning are perhaps more relevant than the traditional concepts of burden of proof and standard of proof. This finding is also partly based on the introduction of more economics into competition law. In the current state of competition law, there are difficult choices to be made in every case. Motivation of a decision is the basis for the accountability of an authority to the undertakings concerned, to the policy-makers and to the legislator. It is also essential to permit adequate review on appeal.

A pragmatic approach with workable rules and sufficient attention for adequate reasoning should allow efficient enforcement of competition. This paper proposes that this requires the legal community and the doctrine, to step back from the need for strict definitions and a strict procedural framework in which the decision-maker has little room for taking a global view on the proof and evidence available. It also requires economists to accept that procedural rules are important because they often express general principles of law that are at the basis of our legal system; this is certainly true for rules on proof. Also, the importance of adequate reasoning has to be recognised if competition enforcement is to be credible and socially and politically acceptable, especially in the light of increasingly severe sanctions.

Chapter 5

Shouldn't we know what we are protecting? Yes we should!*

A plea for a solid and comprehensive debate about the objectives of EU competition law and policy

This article emphasizes that, contrary to what the public debate sometimes might lead to believe, EU competition law has always had, and still has, multiple co-existing objectives.

A brief overview of the different objectives is given and it is proposed that the growing emphasis on consumer welfare has increased the lack of clarity in terms of what the system is protecting and also oversimplifies the state of the law.

An attempt is then made to demonstrate that this is not merely a theoretical debate and some examples are given of how the objectives have an impact on legislation, policy and enforcement.

It is argued that a broader perspective should be taken to include some additional factors in the debate on objectives, also from outside the system itself. Some developments regarding the objectives and their interaction are related to more general trends in EU law and policy. Also, decentralisation and the current enforcement system involving member states, are relevant: they have e.g. an impact on the question of where and how the debate about the objectives of EU competition law and policy should take place and what its consequences will be.

1. The evolving objectives of EC competition policy

1.1 Introduction

This article aims to contribute to the debate on the objectives of EC competition law.

---

* This chapter was published in a longer version as a TILEC Discussion Paper in April 2009. This entirely revised version was closed end of January 2010. It was published in *European Competition Journal* (2010, 6 (2), p. 339-376. It was presented as a paper at the 5th ASCOLA conference in Bonn in May 2010.

In the first part, the evolution of the objectives of competition policy is briefly examined. The purpose is not to give an exhaustive historical overview but to show how many different objectives can be identified in relation to the system of EU competition law. Multiple objectives still exist they are not a thing of the past.

In the second part, the impact of the policy objectives on legislation and decision-making is illustrated briefly to show that this is not merely a theoretical debate. Then the discussion on objectives is presented in a broader perspective. Some more general developments in EU law, concerns of governance and the current structure of competition law enforcement are highlighted. Some concluding remarks are finally formulated that hopefully help take this debate a step forward.

1.2 Definitions

At the outset, it is useful to reflect briefly both on the meaning of both "objectives" and "competition policy". An *objective* is a goal pursued. The origin of the expression is an initiatory one: the point against which a strategic or technical operation is directed. It is inherent to the concept of objectives that they are ideals, which are not or seldom achieved. Where "objectives" is concerned, an approach that distinguishes between ultimate and intermediate goals (operational or direct) seems interesting and useful.[287]

The lack of distinction between the ultimate and intermediate goals can be a cause of confusion. To illustrate this point some might define consumer welfare as the objective of competitive law whilst others might identify the achievement of an effective competitive process as objective. Upon a closer look, the protection of an effective competitive process might be the intermediary or instrumental goal, whereas consumer welfare can be the ultimate goal. Contrary to what European scholars seem sometimes to assume, this debate is also ongoing in the U.S.: there is no general consensus on what the overall objective of competition law is.[288] The discussion is related to that on the distinction, on a temporal basis, between short term and long term objectives.

In an OECD report of 2003, the distinction is made between public interest objectives, core competition objectives and a so-called grey zone.[289] The core

---

287 C.D. Ehlermann and L. Laudati, *European Competition Annual 1997: Objectives of competition policy* (Oxford: Hart Publishing, 1998), introduction. This publication demonstrates that the debate on objectives is not a new one. It contains several contributions on the normative foundations of competition law.

288 See J.B. Kirkwood, and R.H. Lande, 'The fundamental Goal of Antitrust: Protecting Consumers, Not Increasing efficiency' (2008) 84 *Notre Dame Law Review* 191.

289 OECD Secretariate, 'The Objectives of Competition Law and Policy and the Optimal Design of a Competition Agency' (2003) 5 *OECD Journal of Competition Law and Policy* 7.

competition objectives are said to be mainly promoting and protecting the competitive process and attaining greater economic efficiency. Public interest objectives seem to refer primarily to interests that are not or not solely economical but aim, for example at social protection or the protection of certain strategic economical sectors. Finally, there are a number of objectives that seem to fall somewhere in the grey zone between public interest objectives and core competition objectives. Ensuring fair competition and the protection of small and medium sized businesses are the most common examples.

Are the objectives of competition law a source of law or can they be considered binding? This is a typically legal question. We would not usually think of the objectives of a legal system to be, as such, a source of law. The main reason is probably that they seem void of binding effect. However, although it is beyond the scope of this contribution to go into this issue, it should be said that some objectives (as discussed below) are not so different from (general) *principles* which clearly can be a source of law in Community law.[290] Authority for the fact that objectives might have some sort of binding effect, can be found in the case-law of the European Court of Justice (ECJ): it appears throughout various areas of EU law that the Court attaches great importance to the objectives expressed in or deferred from the various European Treaties.[291] When the objectives of the Treaties or a particular policy are referred to by the Court and are decisive when a "lower" principle or rule needs to be explained, it is difficult to deny some legal status as a source of law to such objectives.

In fact, objectives could be also considered to have a certain binding effect in another way. This is not so much as in creating rights and duties and allowing courts to evaluate the legality of specific acts in terms of compatibility with these objectives, but more in terms of expectations and accountability: the legislator and the policymaker can be expected to design and apply a system of legal rules in conformity with the objectives they proclaim to strive for and they can themselves be considered bound in that way.

The other term to be briefly looked at in this introduction is "*competition policy*" which Motta defines as "a set of policies and laws which ensure that competition in the market place is not restricted in such a way as to reduce economic welfare".[292] In an interesting study, Dabbah also rightly emphasises the political dimension: "an element of politics which deals with public authorities' intervention beyond certain market imperfections, such

290 An interesting recent analysis of rights and principles in EU law: C. Hilton, 'Rights and Principles in EU law: a Distinction without Foundation' (2008) 15 *Maastricht Journal of European and Comparative Law* 193.

291 An example often cited is environmental law.

292 M. Motta, *Competition policy, Theory and Practice* (Cambridge: Cambridge University Press, 2004) 30.

as in the case of market failure".[293] The political dimension is further illustrated by the following interesting definition of competition policy: "government measures that directly affect the behaviour of enterprises and the structure of industry". Here it comprises two elements: a set of policies that promote competition in local and national markets, such as a relaxed industrial policy, a liberalised trade policy, reduced controls and greater reliance on market forces: and competition law as such: legislation, judicial decisions and regulations aimed at preventing anticompetitive business practices.[294]

Competition law has also been described as "applying a body of legal rules and standards to deal with market imperfections and restore desirable competitive conditions in the market." Still according to Dabbah, a system of competition law is wider than competition law itself and he rightly includes both the law and the policy.

The term *system of competition law* best fits the purpose of this article. It refers to the law and policy relating only to the regulation and enforcement of competition law (cartels, abuse and, to a lesser extent, merger control) and not the wider concept which also includes other areas such as industrial and trade policy but also sector (liberalisation) regulation.

Since the modernisation process in EU competition law, it is fashionable to narrow down competition policy to a purely economic policy[295] or at most an instrument in the broader industrial policy (discussed further below). It is proposed that the system of EU competition law is not only about regulating the economy along the lines of the free market economy principle but that it has always had "political" goals. This is not necessarily a bad thing, as Dabbah demonstrates.[296] A legal system can have political objectives as long as this does not mean that politics play a role in the way the law is applied to individual cases.

---

[293] M. Dabbah, 'Measuring a System of Competition Law: A Preliminary View' (2000) 21 *European Competition Law Review* 369.

[294] P. Mehta, S. Mitra and C. Dube, 'Competition Policy and Consumer Policy: Complementarities and Conflicts in the Promotion of Consumer Welfare', chapter in United Nations Conference on Trade and Development (UNCTAD) *The effects of anti-competitive business practices on developing countries and their development prospects* (New York and Geneva, 2008), available at UNCTAD website: http://www.unctad.org/en/docs/ditcclp20082_en.pdf (accessed December 2008).

[295] See J. Faull and A. Nikpay, *The EC law of Competition* (Oxford: Oxford University Press, 1999) 4.

[296] Dabbah, 'Measuring a system of competition law' (above n 293).

1.3 Competition law in the context of the Treaties: goals and instruments[297]

The ultimate (economic) goal of the European Community was the wholesome and sustainable development of the economy: economic welfare within a single market. For example Article 2 of the EC Treaty added a high level of employment and of social protection, equality between men and women, growth, a high level of competitiveness and a high standard of living. Less obvious from the text until recently but all the more from the general EU policy context, is the importance of other more political goals such as democracy, pluralism, free enterprise and the protection of human rights.

Article 2 EC Treaty was modified in 1992 by the EU Treaty (Maastricht) which introduced and consolidated certain objectives, such as economic and social cohesion and environmental protection, but also e.g. a high employment rate and sustainable development.[298] Article 2 EC Treaty gave the Community three instruments to attain these higher goals: the establishment of the common market, the establishment of an economic and monetary union and flanking common policies and activities.

Article 3 EC Treaty then went on to state that a competition policy as a common Community policy is an *instrument* with which to achieve these ultimate goals laid down in Article 2. According to Article 3 (g) EC Treaty, the activities of the Community shall include... "a system ensuring that competition in the internal market is not distorted". In the logic of the Treaties, competition policy was therefore itself an instrument with which to achieve the intermediary goal of the common market, which in turn should achieve the ultimate goals laid down in Article 2 described above.

Articles 4 of the EC Treaty stated that "the activities of the Member States and the Community shall be based on the internal market, on the common objectives and that they shall act in accordance with the principle of an open market economy with free competition". Article 98 EC Treaty reiterated this principle and added an interesting reference to the efficient allocation of resources.[299] Although this last provision was part of the chapter on economic policy, it was formulated in a general way.

---

[297] The Lisbon Treaty entered into force on 1 December 2009 and will be discussed later on. However, it is still relevant in this particular section to discuss first the situation under the EC Treaty as it was before the recent new treaties. Throughout this article new names and numbering will be followed as much as possible.

[298] See K. Lenaerts, P. van Nuffel, *Constitutional Law of the European Union* 2nd edn (London: Sweet & Maxwell, 2005) 81.

[299] The second sentence of the article read: "the Member States and the Community shall act in accordance with the principle of an open market economy with free competition, favouring an efficient allocation of resources, and in compliance with the principles set out in Article 4. So what is the significance of this reference to free competition? It is not formulated as an intermediate or ultimate goal, nor as a policy serving these goals such as the reference to competition law contained in Article 3 EC". Its function seems to be that of a guidance principle, a source of

The specific chapter of the EC Treaty that dealt with competition does not discuss specific objectives or goals, nor did its predecessors (EEC Treaty, ECSC Treaty), nor does the current TFEU (see further below). Therefore, the treaties, although defining the intermediate and ultimate goals of the Community, now the European Union, as a whole, and the instrumental role of competition policy in general, do not define the operational objectives of competition law further.

Articles 81 and 82 EC Treaty, now Articles 101 and 102 TFEU, are fairly brief and broadly formulated. The drafters were, to some extent, unaware of the implications of the prohibitions and concepts that were used. It is commonly known also that the US antitrust provisions, and particularly the Sherman Act, were an important source of inspiration for the substantive provisions of the ECSC and later on the EEC Treaty provisions.[300]

Following a systematic approach, this would imply that the competition provisions were to be seen entirely in accordance with the ultimate (Article 2) and intermediate goals (Article 3) of the Community in general, as defined in the introduction of the EC Treaty. It is interesting to note that the ECJ in the early days even defined the concept of "competition" by reference to the objectives of the Treaty: "workable competition is the level of competition necessary to attain the objectives of the Treaty".[301] It is also clear that throughout the important body of case-law in this area, the ECJ has attached great importance to Articles 2 and 3 EC (formerly EEC) and the *instrumental* role that competition policy was given.

The basic provisions of European antitrust law were most likely intended to be implemented gradually, allowing them to evolve according to the needs of the interests of the Community but also of the member states: both in terms of the respective powers (rapports de force) of the supranational European level and of the Member States, as well as from the viewpoint of the substantive law. There is also little doubt that the goal of a unified market dominated the process of constructing the European competition law system for a long time.[302]

According to Gerber, the former Articles 85 and 86 of the EEC Treaty (now Articles 101 and 102 TFEU) were meant to be constitutional, they were brief and broadly perceived and they would have to be given content in

---

inspiration, that is to be used and taken into account at all times by Member States as well as by Community institutions when they act.

300 See also C. Jones, 'Foundations of Competition Policy in the EU and USA: Conflict, Convergence, and Beyond' in H. Ullrich (ed), *The Evolution of European Competition Law- Whose regulation, which competition?* (Cheltenham: Edward Elgar Publishing, 2006).

301 Case C-26/76, *Metro* [1977] ECR 1875.

302 For a thorough analysis, D. Gerber, *Law and competition in twentieth century Europe, Protecting Promotheus* (Oxford: Clarendon Press, 1998) 347.

practice.[303] Generally, open norms allow for more flexibility and discretion in the orientation of their application. The competition provisions in the basic treaty, now TFEU, are such norms. In that respect, it is not without importance that the ECJ very rarely refers to these limits as coming from the drafting process of the treaties.[304]

In terms of the way the treaties, as primary source of law, deal with the objectives, the impact of the Lisbon Treaty will probably continue to be a source of worry and/or speculation in the first period after its entry into force.[305]

The core provisions on cartels and abuses, now Articles 101 and 102 TFEU (Treaty on the Functioning of the European Union), remain unchanged.[306] However, it is well known that the Lisbon Treaty has modified the Treaty when it comes to the goals of the European Union as a whole as discussed above.

Undistorted competition is no longer listed as an objective and a way to achieve the higher goals through the establishment of the common market (now called the internal market), as it was in Article 3 under (g) EC Treaty. However, the Protocol on the Internal Market states that undistorted competition is part of the internal market.[307] Therefore, indirectly, through the reference to the internal market in Article 3 of the Treaty on the European Union (hereinafter: TEU), competition policy is still present. In general, the list of goals of the European Union is streamlined and non-economical goals gain importance throughout the new treaties.[308]

The reference to the open market economy based on the principle of free economy in Article 4 EC also discussed above, has disappeared from the beginning of the Treaty. However, the reference is still present in the new Article 119 TFEU at the beginning of the chapter on economic and monetary policy in a similar way. The place in the Treaty has its significance: the

---

303 Gerber, *Law and competition* (above n 302) 345.

304 G. Marenco, 'Le régime de l'exception légale et sa compatibilité avec le traité' (2001) 37 *Cahiers de droit Européen* 135 ; for a visionary analysis long before modernisation: I. Forrester and C. Norall, 'The laicization of Community law : self help and the rule of reason : how competition law is and should be applied' (1984) 4 *Common Market Law Review* 11.

305 The consolidated texts of the Treaty on the European Union and the Treaty on the Functioning of the European Union were published in [2008] OJ C 115.

306 Except for the replacement of "common market" by "internal market" which has been done throughout the treaties.

307 Protocol 27 reads as follows: "*The High Contracting Parties, Considering that the internal market as set out in Article 3 of the Treaty on European Union includes a system ensuring that competition is not distorted, have agreed that, to this end, the Union shall, if necessary, take action under the provisions of the Treaties, including under Article 352 of the Treaty on the functioning of the European Union.*"

308 An example in the provisions on services of general economical interest, see for example Article 14 TFEU and Protocol 26.

common provisions at the beginning express the fundamental principles that are at the basis of the European Union legal system.

Although the Court has said that the objectives cannot create rights for Member States or for individuals and that they constitute general objectives and should be read together with the treaty provisions that further implement them,[309] the objectives and the text of Article 2 and 3 EC Treaty have been an important source for the interpretation of the Treaty provisions on competition.

The possible impact of the changes brought by the Lisbon Treaty is discussed further below under 2.2.1.

1.4 The different objectives of EC competition policy

In the previous section, the treaty provisions and related case-law of the Community courts concerning the objectives of competition law, were briefly examined. In this section an overview is given of the different objectives that can be attributed to the system of EU competition law. The purpose is to present the objectives briefly in such a way to show that they have all played, and mostly still play a role, even though many of these are hardly ever still mentioned. Some sources of potential tension between different objectives are mentioned along the way.

It is difficult to find a common view in literature on what the goals of EU competition policy have been until now, although the same elements often reoccur, albeit in a different order and with a different interpretation. There is a difference depending on whether lawyers or economists discuss the question. Some examples are given below to illustrate this.

Bishop and Walker consider two main goals: the integration goal and the economic goal. In their opinion, these two goals are potentially in conflict with each other.[310] They also draw attention to the fact that the existence of these dual goals is what differentiates the EU system from other jurisdictions, particularly the U.S. The difference with the U.S. system is often cited, and recent diverging views in specific cases are attributed to the different objectives of the European and U.S. legal system: "we protect competition, you protect competitors" is a famous phrase in this respect.[311] Motta assumes that economic efficiency and European market integration

---

[309] ECJ Case C-9/99, *Echirolles Distribution* [2000] ECR I-8207.

[310] S. Bishop and M. Walker, *Economics of EC Competition Law: concepts, application and measurement* (London: Sweet & Maxwell, 1999) 5.

[311] K. Cseres, *Competition law and consumer protection* (The Hague: Kluwer Law International, 2005) 278; R. Whish also mentions redistribution or economic equity as an objective but cites only American sources in that respect: R. Whish, *Competition law*. 5th edn, (London: LexisNexis, 2003) 18.

are probably the main objectives of competition policy but recognizes that social and political reasons have been taken into account.[312]

Monti, on the other hand, distinguishes three core aims of competition law: the protection of economic freedom, market integration and efficiency (in that order). [313] According to him, the first was in fact the primary aim that the drafters of the EEC Treaty had in mind,[314] the idea being that economic efficiency is automatically the result of the freedom which competition law preserves. Monti also indicates the potential conflicts between the three core objectives but claims that EU competition law contains mechanisms for balancing them. Ahlborn and Padilla also identify three groups of objectives along the same lines: fairness goals, welfare and efficiency goals and market integration goals. [315]

1.4.1 Market integration

The promotion of market integration is a key objective of Community law in general and was obviously the focus of competition law from the start. It is what makes the EU competition law system unique.

The rules of competition laid down in Articles 101 and 102 TFEU that are directly addressed at undertakings, are the necessary complement to the Treaty rules on the four freedoms. Agreements or abusive conduct can create obstacles to trade between Member States in a similar way to the obstacles caused by state measures. Competition rules (including also state aid) and free movement provisions form a complete set of tools with which to realize the integration of the markets of the different Member States. The Commission's most important concern was for the integration of markets, and this was reflected in competition law.

It would be wrong to think that other considerations such as consumer benefit were absent "in the old days". The first decisions of the Commission and the ECJ make reference to the generic benefits of competition[316] such as lower prices, technological progress.[317] However, there seemed to have been a strong belief that the market integration ideal could be assumed as being

[312] M. Motta, *Competition policy, theory and practice* (Cambridge: CUP, 2004) 15.

[313] G. Monti, 'Article 81 and public policy' (2002) 39 *Common Market Law Review* 1057.

[314] An ordoliberal (individual freedom as an end in itself) and a neoclassical approach (maximalization of total welfare) are distinguished. The argument is made that the structure of Article 81 EC demonstrates that an ordoliberal philosophy was present in the minds of the drafters of the treaty at the time.

[315] Monti, 'Article 81 and public policy' (above n 27) 1064; C. Ahlborn and A. Padilla, 'From fairness to welfare: implications for the assessment of unilateral conduct under EC competition law', in C. Ehlermann and M. Marquis (eds) *A reformed approach to Article 82 EC. European Competition Law Annual(EUI) 2007* (Oxford: Hart Publishing, 2008) 55.

[316] Gerber, *Law and competition* (above n 302) 248.

[317] ECJ Cases 54/64 & 58/64, *Consten en Grundig* [1966] ECR (1966) 571.

in the interest of consumers, so there was no need to distinguish between different goals.

The goal of market integration is very particular to the European Union. Is it more of a public interest objective or a core competition objective? According to the definitions in the OECD study, the Treaty of Rome market integration objective is a public interest one.[318] It is usually referred to as a political objective. There is certainly a tension between the (political) objective of market integration on the one hand and economic welfare. Motta uses the example of forbidding price discrimination across national borders to illustrate that there is generally no economic rationale to forbid such practices.[319]

The focus on vertical restraints as well as the attitude towards such restraints were very much motivated by market integration. A strict position on vertical restraints, especially those that were considered to be obstacles to parallel (cross border) trade such as territorial protection of distributors, was one of the main characteristics of EU competition law for decades. The subsequent texts on verticals make this clear.[320]

The area of vertical restraints where the Commissions had a fairly strict policy for many years, is also referred to as a typical example of possible tension between market integration and consumer welfare.[321] In that respect, it will be interesting to see how the debate on the revision of the group exemption regulation on vertical restraints evolves.[322]

As will be argued below, the necessity to reconcile this market integration objective with the currently more prominent objective of consumer welfare, is one of the challenges that competition law in Europe now faces. Recent case-law has shown that this debate is very much alive: contrary to what many might have expected, the Court of Justice is not willing to let go of market integration as a key element in determining how competition law should be

318 OECD report 2003 (above n 289).

319 Motta, *Competition Policy* (above n32) 23; this conflict is also cited by Bishop and Walker, *Economics of EC competition law* (above n 292).

320 For example: Commission Regulation (EC) No 1984/83 on Application of Article 85(3) of the Treaty to categories of exclusive purchasing agreements [1983] OJ L 173/5 (one of the predecessors of Reg. 2790/1999 - Commission Regulation (EC) No 2790/1999 of 22 December 1999 on the application of Article 81(3) of the Treaty to categories of vertical agreements and concerted practices [1999] OJ L 336 - and the Commission (EC) 'On vertical restraints in EC competition policy'(Green Paper) COM (96) 721: analysis by Cseres, *Competition law and consumer protection* (above n 311 [271 et seq.].

321 Cseres, *Competition law and consumer protection* (above n 311) 271.

322 The regulation expires on 31 May 2010 and the Commission has launched the process of consultation on possible reform. A particularly interesting analysis of the policy on verticals, including US developments by A. Jones, 'Resale price maintenance: a debate about competition policy in Europe?' (2009) 5 *European Competition Journal* 2009) 479.

applied, as the recent judgments in Sot Lelos kai Sia EE and GSK have shown.[323] This recent case-law is discussed further under 2.2.1 below.

1.4.2 Economic freedom

The protection of economic freedom, which is associated mainly with ordoliberalism, also resurfaced recently, in the discussions about Article 102 TFEU. In a nutshell: competition is necessary for the economic liberty of individuals and the economic order should protect individual economic freedom and control private economic power and political power. In other words, both strong private power as well as strong power at the (public) state level, are mistrusted and should be avoided. The law plays a central role by providing basic principles of economic conduct, based on an economic constitution in which individual economic freedom is the fundamental principle. Government can only intervene with the purpose of enforcing these principles, ruling out discretionary intervention in the marketplace.

It would lead too far to go into the debate about how ordoliberalism shaped Community competition law but it seems clear that its influence is undisputable, even if only indirectly through German competition law.[324] This influence on the way European competition law was created and evolved further, has perhaps been underestimated somewhat in recent years or has been too easily discarded in favour of more fashionable economic concepts.[325]

When debates took place some years ago about the modernisation of cartel law and the way in which Article 101 TFEU should evolve, thought was given

[323] ECJ Case C- 468/06 to C-478/06, *Sot. Lélos kai Sia EE and Others v GlaxoSmithKline AEVE Farmakeftikon Proïonton* [2008] ECR 2008 I-07139 (also called Syfait II case). The case has reactivated the debate about parallel trade in pharmaceutical products and the ECJ aligns itself with older case-law attaching great importance to parallel trade between Member States as a way of creating competition. It is subject of debate whether this judgment is really in favour of parallel trade in practice but in any case, market integration is very much present in the reasoning of the Court. In GSK the Court of Justice overturned the CFI's reasoning, judgment of 6 October 2009, joined cases C-501/06 P, C-513/06 P, C-515 and 516/06 P *GlaxoSmithKline Services Unlimited and others v Commission of the European Communities,* not yet reported.

[324] L. Gormsen, 'The conflict between economic freedom and consumer welfare in the modernisation of Article 82 EC' (2007) 3 *European Competition Journal* 329. She addresses the debate whether the protection of economic freedom on the one hand and the goal of consumer welfare on the other, are in conflict.

[325] See for a complete analysis: Gerber, *Law and competition* (above n 302). He also highlights how ordoliberals had a major influence by occupying important posts at the Commission for many years and shaping competition law at the European level. An interesting summary of the development of EC competition law over the years in A. Weitbrecht, 'From Freiburg to Chicago – the first 50 years of European competition law' (2008) 29 *European Competition Law Review* 8. On the influence of ordoliberalism, see also A. Pera, 'Changing views of competition, economic analysis and EC antitrust law' 2008 4 *European Competition Journal* (2008) 127.

to the origins and objectives of Article 81 EC and in that context, some attributed the wide interpretation of Article 81 (1) applying to almost all restrictions of competition, to the dominating objective of market integration and the influence of the objective of protecting economic freedom. The readiness with which any restriction of competition was seen as a restriction of competition, demonstrates the importance attached to economic freedom.

The European focus on protecting the opportunities of rivals, is one of the factors most often cited as differentiating European and US antitrust regimes.[326] Ordoliberal thoughts or related ideas are still part of modern EU competition law but the influence is wider than only coming from the ordoliberal school: there is a more general belief in freedom that can be found both in U.S. and EU law: the freedom to produce and the freedom of the consumer to choose. By protecting the competitive order, the state protects the freedom of self-responsible individuals to function in the market.[327]

As mentioned before, an example of these ideas can be found in the discussion on Article 102 TFEU policy reforms but also in the Commission Guidelines on Article 81 (3) EC (now Article 101 TFEU) and in recent decisions.[328] Clearly every agreement restricting economic freedom is no longer qualified as a restriction of competition, but in cartel cases, the presumption will exist that there is a restriction of competition that reduces the efficiency. The presumption can then be rebutted, or not, by analysing the effects of the agreement.[329]

The protection of individual economic freedom has perhaps not been given the status of a general principle of law in an explicit way in the jurisprudence, but the Court of Justice has recognized indirectly the importance of safeguarding free enterprise, particularly in the context of Article 102 TFEU and abuse of dominance where it acknowledges that dominant companies may refuse to sell or licence in certain circumstances.

---

326 See D. De Smet, 'The diametrically opposed principles of US and antitrust policy' (2008) 29 *European Competition Law Review* 356.

327 O. Odudu, *The boundaries of EC competition law, the scope of Article 81* (Oxford: Oxford University Press, 2006)14 with e.g. a reference to Fox and Sullivan. The focus of ordoliberalism was very much on preventing and prohibiting monopoly power, see Gerber, *Law and competition* (above n 302) [251]; R. Van den Bergh and P. Camesasca, *European competition Law and Economics: a comparative perspective*, (London: Sweet & Maxwell, 2006).

328 For so-called restrictions "by object", it is assumed that there shall be negative impact on competition, Commission (EC) 'Guidelines on the application of Article 81(3) of the Treaty' (Communication) [2004] OJ C 101/08 [97], for example at 22 and 23; the discussion on efficiency gains takes place under Article 81 (3) EC, now Article 101 (3) TFEU.

329 G. Monti, *EC competition law* (Cambridge, Cambridge University Press, 2007) 52.

In those cases, the principle of economic freedom is balanced with the prohibition on abuse of dominance.[330]

1.4.3 Economic efficiency

Where EU competition law is concerned, consumer welfare and efficiency are often mentioned together. Efficiency is often seen as the overall, general objective of competition policy although it is not cited as often by the Commission as consumer welfare. No attempt will be made here to define these concepts in detail though a brief description is necessary.

The reference to efficiency can mean ensuring efficient allocation of all resources (allocative efficiency) or the efficiency of a particular firm or industry in ensuring that it exploits all economies of scale and technology and cuts unnecessary costs (productive efficiency). Allocative and productive efficiency are mostly static concepts whereas dynamic efficiency also incorporates looking at the potential of the economy as a whole or of a firm or industry.[331]

Allocative efficiency equals total welfare, distinct from consumer welfare. Many economists in the area of competition law, highlight the potential conflict between efficiency and consumer welfare. Just as is the case for consumer welfare described above, the term efficiency as such is, fairly new, and does not appear in older EC case-law. Efficiency is also increasingly present in merger control and in the discussions surrounding the enforcement of Article 82, but meaning a different thing namely arguments that dominant undertakings can present to justify their behaviour.[332]

It is difficult to distinguish at present, what the role of efficiency has been because the Commission seems to always associate both efficiency and consumer welfare: "Our aim is simple: to protect competition in the market as a means of enhancing consumer welfare and ensuring an efficient allocation of resources. An effects-based approach, grounded in solid economics, ensures that citizens enjoy the benefits of a competitive, dynamic market economy" and "competition is not an end in itself but an instrument

---

330 CFI Case T-41/96, *Bayer/Commission* [2000] ECR II-3383 with reference to the Court of Justice in United Brands, ECJ case 27/76, *United Brands Company and United Brands Continentaal BV v Commission of the European Communities* [1978] ECR 207. Again without referring to free enterprise or economic freedom in an explicit way, the ECJ attaches substantial importance to the possibility for a dominant firm to defend its commercial interests in the recent *Sot. Lelos kai Sia* judgment (above n 323).

331 Monti, 'Article 81 and public policy' (above n 313) 45. On the role of efficiency, Odudu, *The boundaries of EC competition law* (above n 327) chapter 2 and an interesting analysis of Article 81 (3) from an efficiency angle, chapter 6.

332 On possible efficiency « defences » for the different abuses that are identified, Guidance published on 3 December 2008 by the Commission on the enforcement of Article 82, http://ec.europa.eu/competition/antitrust/art82/guidance_en.pdf.

for achieving consumer welfare and efficiency" (Commissioner Kroes[333]). Albeit very appealing and convincing, these type of statements, do not shed any real light on the views the Commission has on objectives that are potentially conflicting.

1.4.4 Industrial policy

Less discussed is the industrial policy dimension of competition enforcement but its relevance cannot be denied. On the one hand, it could even be said to have increased in recent years, or at least the relationship between industrial policy and competition policy has received more attention, both at the level of the Commission as the European policymaker, as well as in the literature.

On the other hand, from a legal point of view, it seems difficult to assess to what extent competition law has been used as an instrument of industrial policy: this seems more self-evident in the area of state aid and dumping legislation where measures are at stake to protect particular industries.

A possible definition of industrial policy is "picking the winners": specific sectors are chosen and a strategy is built on behalf of public authorities to develop and support those sectors.[334] This is also called vertical industrial policy. This type of measures, coming from Member States, are problematic at the European level because of the rules on state aid. Vertical action would then have to be devised at the European level, not discriminating between Member States.

Industrial policy, from an economic point of view, can also be defined as a policy aimed at dealing with market failures in a structural way, whereas competition policy is about making competition on the markets work.[335] One of the reasons why it is quite difficult to pinpoint the role of industrial policy objectives in competition law, is because, other than market integration and liberalisation of regulated sectors, it is not obvious what the industrial policy at the Community level actually was. Merger control is perhaps the area in competition law where the link with industrial policy is potentially most obvious.[336]

---

[333] Speech at Competition Day in London, 15 September 2005, http://ec.europa.eu/competition/speeches/index_2005.html.

[334] V. Curzon Price, 'La politique européenne au XXIième siècle: reflet de l'évolution des idées sur le rôle des pouvoirs publics dans l'économie', in J. Defraigne and V. de Moriamé (eds), *Quelles politiques industrielle et sociale pour l'Europe du XXième siècle ?* (Bruxelles : Academia Bruylant, 2008).

[335] E. de Ghellinck, *La politique industrielle européenne: un concept creux* in Defraigne and De Moriamé, *Quelles politiques industrielle et sociale* (above n 334) 96.

[336] By approving or disapproving future transactions, the Commission carries out a hypothetical exercise of imagining what the effects of a particular merger would be. This process involves assessing current market structure but also reflects how markets are considered best to be. Explicit references to industrial policy considerations can be found in the merger regulation, Council Regulation (EC) No

Within the sphere of Article 101 TEU, elements of industrial policy are fairly difficult to identify in specific cases and the case-law of the Community courts does not often refer to industrial policy considerations (other than market integration and also the protection of SME's, discussed elsewhere). One might consider, however, that the priorities that have been determined by the Commission over the years show that particular sectors of the economy are chosen, such as, for example, the automobile industry, in the 1980's and 1990's. Concerted actions in the area of competition through secondary legislation (group exemptions for example) and harsh decisions against producers, simultaneously with initiatives being taken through internal market legislation (e.g. producer responsibility, mutual recognition etc) indicate considerations of industrial policy.

Other than choosing and focusing on specific sectors, the way in which the Commission dealt with crisis cartels or horizontal agreements aimed at combating overcapacity in a particular sector might be mentioned as proof that industrial policy objectives are pursued but there are only a limited number of cases and there was always (and rightly so) reluctance to accept industrial policy issues in individual cases.[337]

Considerations of industrial policy are not a thing of the past.[338] In fact, European industrial policy was driven by the goal of realizing the internal market and eliminating obstacles to trade. In other words, industrial policy was market integration policy.[339]

139/2004 of 20 January 2004 on the control of concentrations between undertakings (the EC Merger Regulation) [2004] OJ L 24/1, rec.4.

337 A somewhat stand alone reference in the 1991 annual report: XXIst report on Competition Policy, at § 201 on the importance of eliminating structural overcapacity to allow industries to recover profitability. The few examples of individual decisions mostly concern cases where the Commission exempted restructuration agreements under Article 81 (3) EC, for example Commission Decision 84/380/EEC of 4 July 1984 relating to a proceeding under Article [81] of the EEC Treaty (IV/30.810 – *Synthetic fibres*) [1984] OJ 207/17, and also Commission Decision 94/296/EC of 29 April 1994 relating to a proceeding under Article [81] of the EC Treaty (IV/34.456 – *Stichting Baksteen*) [1994] L 131/15. For a recent case where a very orthodox line was followed by the ECJ showing no sign whatsoever of taking into account the arguments about overcapacity: ECJ Case C-209/07, *Beef Industry Development Society* [2008] ECR I-08637. Is this one of the areas where the economical crisis and changing political views shall have their impact on the enforcement of Article 81 EC? The mere fact that the question now arises, demonstrates the principle that the interpretation and application of competition law can serve strategic purposes.

338 J. Galloway, 'The pursuit of national champions: the intersection of competition law and industrial policy'(2007) 28 *European Competition Law Review* 172.

339 E. de Ghellinck, *La politique industrielle européenne* (above n 334); C. Huveneers, 'Politique de la concurrence, soutien ou carcan, pour la politique industrielle?'in J Defraigne et V de Moriamé, *Quelles politiques industrielle et sociale* (above n 333) [107].

In recent years, there is clearly a new dynamic to be observed in the context of the so-called Lisbon Strategy. In 2002, the Commission relaunched the debate on the role of industrial policy.[340] The focus is on achieving a competitive industry with priority for innovation and growth. In turn, this emphasis on innovation is something that can be traced since then as a factor that plays a role in general competition policy and individual cases dealt with by the Commission.

The growing integration of competition policy, as a form of industrial policy, into other policy areas of the European Union is often emphasised.[341] The reference to free competition in the treaty article on industrial policy, Article 173 TFEU, is relevant here. Competition policy is now regularly placed at the heart of industrial policy: "Competition policy - which above all else is designed to ensure the maintenance of competitive markets - is therefore central to an industrial policy aimed at enhancing the competitiveness of industry."[342] The keywords are competitiveness of the European economy and the creation of employment and growth.

1.4.5 SME protection

A specific policy objective that is also reflected in EC competition law, is the protection of small and medium sized enterprises. This might perhaps also be seen as an industrial policy objective.[343]

The specific protection of SME could be found in secondary legislation from quite early on. The Commission Notice on de minimis agreements is the most obvious example.[344] This notice was, amongst other things, an assertion of the importance attached to SME protection. There is no "hard" threshold exempting SME from the application of Article 81 EC.[345] The Commission

340 Commission (EC), 'Industrial Policy in an Enlarged Europe'(Communication) COM (2002) 714 final, 11 December 2002; Commission (EC), 'Fostering structural change: an industrial policy for an enlarged Europe' (Communication) COM (2004) 274 final, 20 April 2004; Commission (EC) 'Proactive Competition Policy for a Competitive Europe' (Communication) COM (2004) 293 final, 20 april 2004.

341 See the Communications mentioned in previous note and also Commission (EC), 'Some key issues in Europe's Competitiveness – towards an integrated approach' (Communication) COM (2003) 704 final, 21 November 2003 ; also the introduction of Commissioners Kroes to the 2007 Annual Competition Report, EC Official Publications, 2008, p. 3.

342 Commissioner Kroes, Fordham, 14 September 2006; see also the 2008 edition of the international conference on 25 September 2008, Commissioner Kroes, via site DG Comp, http://ec.europa.eu/competition/speeches/ (accessed 1 March 2009).

343 J. Galloway, 'The pursuit of national champions' (above n 338).

344 The first Notice was drafted in 1970. Current version of the De Minimis Notice: Commission Notice on agreements of minor importance which do not appreciably restrict competition under Article 81 (1) of the Treaty (de minimis) [2001] OJ C 149 [18].

345 In national competition law such exceptions can exist, at least one example is Article (7) of the Dutch Competition Act which exempts agreements between SME's

has always considered that hard-core restrictions had to be sanctionable, regardless of the size or importance of the undertaking in question. Amongst these hard-core restrictions were traditionally vertical restraints that restricted parallel cross border trade, which can be understood in view of the focus on market integration, referred to above.

The current de minimis Notice provides for a framework based on market shares only. In the past, the de minimis regime had a double threshold: turnover and market share. Below certain percentages agreements are considered normally not to restrict competition in an appreciable way. Obviously, depending on the market definition, it is not excluded that SME have a market share exceeding the thresholds. However, agreements between smaller firms will be able to escape the application of Article 81 (or 82) because they are unlikely to affect trade between Member States in an appreciable way.[346] The de minimis Notice has therefore to be read together with the (new) Notice on interstate trade which reiterates the negative presumption for SME's.[347] This presumption is generalised in the new Notice because effect on trade is now quantified for all undertakings by reference to turnover and market share.

From an economic point of view, the objective of protection of smaller undertakings seems to be criticized to the extent that it is potentially, be it not necessarily, in conflict with the objective of economic welfare.[348]

There are not many other specific instances in secondary legislation or individual cases where SME protection is explicitly mentioned. Nevertheless, the policy objective is still present in EC competition law. This is demonstrated not only by the two notices mentioned above but is also reflected in recent policy documents where the Commission appears to expect a lot from SME's in Europe in terms of innovation and employment. In the context of the economic crisis, the protection of SME's is appearing once again in the Commission' s public statements. [349]

---

that stay under a certain turnover threshold, regardless of the type of restriction at stake.

346 § 3 of de minimis Notice (above n 58). The concept of SME is clearly defined in a quantative way by reference to Commission recommendation 96/80/EC, OJ (1996) L 107, p. 4. Small and medium sized undertakings are defined as undertakings which have fewer than 250 employees and have either a turnover not exceeding 40 million EUR or a balance sheet total not exceeding 27 million EUR.

347 In modernised competition law, the distinction is made more clearly between a minor effect on competition on the one hand and a minor effect on trade between Member States on the other hand. Commission Notice laying down guidelines on the effect on trade concept contained in Articles 81 and 82 of the Treaty [2004] OJ C 101 [81, § 50]

348 M. Motta, *Competition policy, theory and practice* (above n 26); Van den Bergh and Camesasca, *European competition Law and Economics* (above n 41).

349 It appears however to be a disputed issue amongst economists whether small firms are more dynamic than larger firms and whether they are more conducive to innovation. The fact that the protection of SME is present in current policymaking

1.4.6 Justice, fairness and non-discrimination

It is relatively self-evident for a lawyer that fairness or justice is a key driver in any set of legal rules and its application. To a great extent, fairness is certainly the fundamental idea that determines the design of procedural competition law. However, it is also an objective reflected in substantive law.

In competition law, this might be described as granting every company the same opportunities on the market place, ensuring that even smaller companies can remain competitive, even though economically speaking they are weaker on the market. Fairness can come in when competition law protects the competitors, the customers or the consumers. Therefore there is, or can be, overlap between the basic ideas of economic freedom (protecting individual companies' rights to competition on the market) and consumer protection or welfare and also with the objective of protecting smaller firms on the market place. The concept of fairness referred to here is also related to the term distributive or social justice, used mostly in economics.

Many authors refer to fairness now as something to move away from and that is or should be replaced by (consumer) welfare. Fairness is sometimes presented as a thing of the past. This is however nor the reality in the current state of the law, nor desirable over the longer term. Fairness has been and still is one of the cornerstones of the European competition regime.[350]

Fairness, from the perspective not only of the consumer but of other players in the market place, has a lot to do with the fundamental principle of non-discrimination which is at the basis of most legal systems. The importance of this principle in law, probably explains why, even though it might not always be justified from a purely economical perspective, the Commission and the Courts remain critical of discriminatory practices, both under Article 101 TFEU as well as under Article 102 TFEU. There is no reason why the fundamental objective of fairness, based to a large extent on the general principle of non-discrimination, should lose its place in modern competition law and yet it is fairly absent in public rhetoric nowadays. There is support in interesting sources however at an international level for the fact that

---

demonstrates that it is still relevant as an objective. In the U.S. protection of smaller companies is also relevant, contrary to what many might assume, but mostly in the protection against abusive exploitation of small companies by companies with market power, see Kirkwood and Lande, 'The fundamental goal of Antitrust' (above n 288).

350 The debate between Ahlborn and Padilla on the one hand and D. Zimmer on the other, is illustrative in this respect: D. Zimmer, *On fairness and welfare: the objectives of competition policy*, a comment on papers of previously cited authors, in the 2007 European Competition Annual (above n 287). Zimmer qualifies fairness in this context as making sure that the legal system provides for a set of rules guaranteeing that the legitimate expectations of market players are realised.

fairness should still be a concern for policymakers.[351] The idea might be considered old-fashioned at times when the focus is on economic analysis or, it may be perceived as difficult to sell to the general public.

1.5 What about consumers?

The objective of protecting consumers is dealt with last because the growing emphasis on consumers is central in this paper and at the origin of many of the questions that are raised.

1.5.1 Consumers in the Treaty and practice: before modernisation

One could argue that the description of the goals at the beginning of the EEC Treaty and especially later in the EC Treaty refer to consumer welfare in an indirect way by referring to the "quality of life" in Article 2. Consumer welfare could be considered to follow from the general economic welfare purpose that was at the basis of Articles 2 and 3 of the EC Treaty and that can now be found in Articles 2 and 3 of TEU.[352]

It is incontestable that, generally speaking, consumers have always been part of the raison d'être of antitrust provisions in some way. In 1966, Bork argued for US antitrust law on the basis of a study of the legislative intent of the Sherman Act, that there can only be one objective and that is consumer welfare.[353] In early yearly European Commission reports on Competition Policy, the interests of the consumer are mentioned.[354]

The wording of Article 101 TFEU contains one explicit reference to consumers. Article 101(3) TEU requires a fair share for the consumer as one of the four cumulative conditions for an exception to the cartel prohibition. However, Vedder convincingly argues that the purpose of that provision, as well as the implicit references in Article 102 TFEU and the merger regulation, are primarily intended to make sure the benefit of a particular operation or agreement is passed on.[355] The term "consumer" in Article 101

[351] As cited at p. 180 and 181 by J. Galloway, 'The pursuit of national champions' (above n 338).

[352] R. Nazzini, 'Article 81 between time present and time past: a normative critique of "restriction of competition" in EU law' (2006) 43 *Common Market Law Review* 497.

[353] R. Bork, 'Legislative intent of the Sherman Act' (2006) 2 *Competition Policy International* (2006) 233, originally published in (1966) 7 *Journal of Law and Economics*.

[354] European Commission, report on Competition Policy, 1971, p. 11; report for 1976, p. 9: ".. aim is to ensure that business operates along competitive lines, while protecting the consumer by making goods and services available on the most favourable terms possible", cited in Cseres, *Competition law and consumer protection* (above n 311) 241.

[355] H. Vedder,'Competition law and consumer protection: how Competition can be used to Protect Consumers Even better – or Not' (2006) 17 *European Business Law Review* 83; this means passing on to others than the undertakings concerned.

(3) does not refer to the end user and is not the "consumer" that is the subject of consumer protection law.

Until recently, the interpretation of Article 101 (3) TFEU was very much underdeveloped: as long as the Commission was exclusively competent for giving exemption under the old notification system, little attention was given to the reasoning and the actual meaning of the different conditions under Article 101 (3) TFEU. This was especially true for the second condition requiring a fair share of the benefit for the consumer.[356]

Although Articles 101 and 102 TFEU have never been modified and no further references to consumer welfare were ever introduced, reference must made to the so-called integration provision of Article 12 TFEU (former article 153 (2) EC) which requires the EU and its institutions to take into account the protection of consumers when developing their policies in all other areas, therefore including competition policy.[357]

Vedder emphasises the difference between competition law and consumer protection law whilst Stuyck argues that competition law is the cornerstone of consumer law: "EC competition law after modernisation: more than ever in the interests of consumers". Stuyck highlights how he see consumer protection at the heart of competition policy. On the basis of a study of economic authors, he describes the objective of EC competition law as being a compromise: "the fruits of producer innovation, efficiency and skill – from otherwise anticompetitive activity – must be shared with the wider community, namely consumers".[358]

The main and fundamental difference between competition law and consumer protection law seems to be that the first protects what is seen as the public interest (preferably resulting in benefits for the consumers in general), whereas the second is destined to protect the subjective rights of consumers. This was very well described in the context of the OECD Roundtable organised in 2008 on the interface between Competition and Consumer policies. Both policies have different perspectives: competition policy approaches the market from the supply side ensuring that consumers have the widest possible range of choice of goods and services at the lowest possible price. Consumer policy approaches markets from the demand side ensuring that consumers are able to exercise intelligently and efficiently the choices that competition provides.[359]

---

[356] For an analysis see Cseres, *Competition law and consumer protection* (above n 311) 252.

[357] Similar integration provisions exist for other policies, see below under 2.2.1. For a critical analysis of EC consumer law: G. Howells and T. Wilhelmsson, 'EC consumer law, has it come of age?' (2003) 28 *European Law Review* 370.

[358] J. Stuyck, 'EC competition policy after modernisation: more than ever in the interest of consumers'(2005) 28 *Journal of Consumer Policy* 1.

[359] Consumer protection is about the right to safe products, right to redress, right to protection of health etc.. On the sources of conflict between the two policies, see

The relevance of consumer interests was already recognised, be it in different wording, from very early on by the Court, for example in the Consten Grundig judgment.[360]As was mentioned above, the idea was very much that unifying the market by eliminating obstacles to interstate trade would automatically benefit consumers by increasing the number of competitors on European markets. The concept of consumer welfare was not identified as a distinct goal of competition law for the larger part of the history of EC competition law, but that does not mean that consumers were not presumed to be at the heart of what competition law was all about.

1.5.2 The consumer emphasis since modernisation

It is common nowadays for competition authorities to emphasise consumer welfare as the main driver for competition policy.[361] The former Commissioners for Competition, Mario Monti and Neelie Kroes put the consumer at the heart of competition policy. Philip Lowe formulated it in this way: "Good consumer and competition policies have one and the same goal – to help markets work well for consumers and for all the fair-dealing enterprises that serve consumers well."[362] Consumer welfare is mentioned as being the "ultimate objective of the Commissions intervention in the area of antitrust".[363]

Timewise, the focus on the consumer coincides with what is often called the move to a more economic approach and was intensified after 2004 when modernisation was completed with the decentralisation leading to the network of competition authorities.[364] Procedural reform has accelerated the move towards a more economics-based approach: letting go of ex ante control by way of exemptions under Article 81 (3) EC (now Article 101 (3) TFEU) implies that agreements shall usually only be prohibited if they have

---

Mehta, Mitra and Dube, 'Competition policy and consumer policy' (above n 294). The documents relating to the Roundtable of the OECD are accessible via www.oecd.org (accessed on 1 March 2009).

360 *Consten en Grundig* (above n 317).

361 The Commissions wishes to "enhance its dialogue with consumers", see 2004 Communication on a proactive competition policy (above n 340). In the XXIInd Report on Competition Policy (2002) the Commission already declares: "One of the main purposes of European competition policy is to promote the interests of consumers, that is, to ensure that consumers benefit from the wealth generated by the European economy", 12.

362 Also: Sir John Vickers, Chairman OFT, opening remarks at the European Competition and Consumer Day Conference, 15 September 2005, cited by H. Jenkins, 'Protecting consumers: does competition help?' (2005) 4 *Competition Law* 283. It is interesting to note in her contribution that the Office of Fair Trading (OFT) is competent for enforcing both policies (competition and consumer protection).

363 P. Lowe, 'The design of competition policy institutions for the 21st century – the experience of the European Commission and DG Comp' (2008) 3 *Competition Policy Newsletter* 1.

364 Council Regulation (EC) No 1/2003/EC on the implementation of the rules on competition laid down in Articles 81 and 82 of the Treaty [2003] OJ L1/1.

actual negative effects or are likely to have them.[365] This has also been characterised as the “Americanisation” of the Commissions policy, the idea being that the Commission adopted a vision based on its own version of the learnings of the famous Chicago School in which consumer welfare was a central concept.[366]

An interesting reference to the objectives of Articles 101 and 102 TFEU can be found in Reg. 1/2003 in § 9 of the introduction and in Article 3 § 3. The provision of Article 3 Reg. 1/2003 aims at making sure national and Community competition law do not lead to contradictory results. Member States are however allowed, to implement national legislation that “protects other legitimate interests” provided that it is compatible with general principles and other provisions of Community law: “Insofar as that legislation pursues predominantly an objective different from that of protecting competition on the market, the competition authorities and courts may apply such legislation”.[367] This provision assumes knowledge of what the objectives (one or more, see “predominantly”) of legislation are, both at the EU level for competition as well as at the national level, for other sources of legislation. It is believed that this reference aims at protecting unfair trading practices legislation and consumer protection laws. Yet, it is not certain that these laws actually have a different objective and if so, to what extent.

It is certainly true that in public statements the Commission and other authorities often use the terms “interests of the consumer” and “consumer welfare” but these concepts seem to be interchangeable. Not only can no straightforward conclusions be drawn from the way the concept of consumer welfare is used by the Commission, but also there are numerous examples of other objectives being mentioned, especially in relation to the Lisbon Strategy and the competitiveness of European industry. In other words, industrial policy motives have not been outdated by more “modern” consumer welfare considerations, on the contrary. In a similar way, references to the other objectives mentioned above can be found at this time. The guidance document on Article 101 (3) TFEU is especially illustrative in this respect.[368]

---

365 Monti, ‘Article 81 and public policy’ (above n 315) 52.

366 A. Weitbrecht, ‘From Freiburg to Chicago’ (above n 325).

367 Par. 9 of the introduction and Article 3 par. 3.

368 The guidelines seem to attempt to mention as many objectives as possible whilst creating the impression they are all integrated and compatible: at 13, 21 and 33; At 13 a catch all formula is given: “*the objective of Article 81 is to protect competition on the market as a means of enhancing consumer welfare and of ensuring an efficient allocation of resources. Competition and market integration serve these ends since the creation and preservation of an open single market promotes an efficient allocation of resources throughout the Community for the benefits of consumers.*”

1.6 Evolving and multiple objectives: intermediate conclusion

It is proposed that the current situation can be summarized as follows. EU competition policy has multiple objectives that can be found, albeit rarely in an explicit way, in different sources of the law: the treaties, secondary legislation, the jurisprudence and policy documents. Van Den Bergh calls this the "multivalued tradition of European competition law".[369]

Although there is no clear basis for this in the establishing treaties, there seems to be general consensus presently that core competition objectives based on consumer welfare are now the main driver. In principle, the system of European competition law allows for the objectives to evolve and so the "reinvention" of the foundations and objectives of competition law and policy is legally not excluded.

However, the other objectives discussed above are still present: market integration, the protection of small and medium-sized companies, aspects of industrial policy, efficiency, and considerations linked to fairness, non-discrimination and integration with other Community policy objectives. Recent examples above have shown that these other objectives are certainly still relevant and some, such as market integration and industrial policy perhaps even more so in recent years (see also below under 2.2.1).

There has not been a radical shift in objectives. If we assume there have always been multiple objectives, the emphasis has changed. The aim of competition law has probably always been to benefit the consumer, albeit in an indirect way. Therefore the current focus on consumers is in continuity with the past.

However, whilst the focus on the consumer has never been greater, there is some doubt about what is actually meant by this. Consumer welfare, consumer detriment and consumer protection are all different concepts that are used at present and that can have a different meaning. The introduction of more economics in competition law has created a certain degree of confusion because it is often taken for granted that the consumer welfare concept that is now part of daily competition rhetoric is in fact the economical concept of consumer welfare. Furthermore, lawyers have perhaps also underestimated the lack of clear definition of the economic consumer welfare concept.

2. Why should we know what we are protecting?

In this second part, the present article proposes some reasons why the discussion on objectives is of great importance at this time and why it is more than a theoretical debate. First, some perhaps less frequently

---

369 R. Van den Bergh and P. Camesasca, *European competition Law and Economics* (above n 327) [39].

mentioned examples of how objectives have an impact on the day-to-day functioning of the system of competition law are given (2.1). Then we step outside of the system of competition law itself and propose some relevant factors to take into account that broaden the discussion and show the links between competition law on the one hand and wider EU law developments on the other (2.2).

2.1 The impact of the objectives in practice

It is quite self-evident that the objectives of a legal system influence the law and the general policy orientations. Several examples have already been given above in the description of the different objectives in section 1.4. What is perhaps less obvious but relevant in the near future is how objectives can have an impact on various other aspects of the system of competition law such as its institutional framework (2.1) and law enforcement in individual cases (2.2).

2.1.1 Institutional framework

Even though it has been said that a shift in objectives generally does not result in institutional changes[370], some interesting interactions between objectives and institutional issues can be observed.

There seems to be a relationship between the objectives of a competition policy and its institutional implementation, which is related to the way in which the objectives are formulated. It has been found that the broader the objectives, the greater the need for a centralised body to pursue them, and when the objectives are defined in a more narrow way, it is easier to transfer responsibilities to independent agencies or courts. Narrower objectives allow for deconcentration and decentralisation.[371]

These are remarkable findings if one considers the major decentralisation process that took place in the EU with the entry into force of Reg. 1/2003. It raises the interesting question whether there is a direct link between the shift in objectives of EC competition law on the one hand, and the decentralisation of the enforcement of competition law on the other hand. The question has not often been put in these terms. Usually the growing attention for the consumer is linked to substantive modernisation of competition law, meaning the increased use of economics. However, there might also be a relationship between the shift in objectives and institutional modernisation and decentralisation.

Given the shift towards more emphasis on consumers, there is also the question whether it is a good idea to integrate the public authorities

370 See Kirkwood and Lande, 'The fundamental goal of Antitrust' (above n 288).

371 This conclusion was drawn from the different panel discussions and reports at the EUI conference in 1997, reflected in Ehlermann and Laudati, *European Competition Annual 1997* (above n 287) general conclusions at p. xi.

responsible for compliance with consumer protection legislation with the competition authorities. At the level of the Commission, one could argue that these policies are all under the same roof, though in different directorates. The question is whether in certain Member States, the growing emphasis on consumers shall or should lead to such integration.[372] There might be a certain tension with the requirements of independence of competition authorities, of course, but in terms of efficiency of the organisation of public authorities, the question is understandable.

The growing emphasis on consumers has indeed led to changes in the internal organisation at the Community level within the Commission. Again, there are no radical changes but signs that show the shift in the objectives. Examples are worth mentioning the creation of the Consumer Liaison Officer within DG Comp and the call for a more integrated approach of Community policies, which implies coordination and consultation between different directorates of the Commission (also discussed below in 2.2.1 and 2.2.2).

Furthermore, the link between the introduction of a more economically based approach and the consumer focus is clearly made by the Commission. The importance attributed to the contribution of economics and economic objectives is integrated in the organisational structures. The appointment of a Chief Economist is the clearest example of this trend.[373] One of the most challenging issues in the near future is whether the institutional framework of competition law systems (including the courts) is adequate to actually allow for economic analysis to be performed and for economics to contribute in a valuable way. It is beyond this article's scope to go into these questions here but the interesting debate about what Gerber calls the institutional embeddedness of economics, is only in a starting phase.[374]Similar questions concerning the impact of the objectives of competition law on the institutional structures, can be raised at the national level, including in

---

[372] Discussed at the OECD roundtable 2008 on the interface between consumer policy and competition, The documents relating to the Roundtable of the OECD are accessible via www.oecd.org (accessed on 1 March 2009).

[373] The Chief Economist now has a team, which is involved both in policy issues as well as in the daily enforcement of the competition rules (including state aid) in specific cases. About recent reforms: Lowe,'The design of competition policy institutions for the 21st century' (above n 363) and also L. Evans, *The role of economics on modern competition policy,* Speech 26 September 2008 in Hamburg, http://ec.europa.eu/competition/speeches/text/sp2008_06_en.pdf.

[374] In a very stimulating chapter entitled *Competition law and the institutional embeddedness of economics*, in: Economic theory and competition law, J. Drexhel, forthcoming, accessible via SSRN: http://papers.ssrn.com/sol3/papers.cfm?abstract_id=1306482 (accessed 1 March 2009). He shows, amongst other things, that the fundamental differences between US and European court systems, make the use and role of economic analysis in competition cases very different and that therefore we should be more careful in comparing the systems and importing US experiences into Europe.

courts of law where the constraints on the use of economics can be considerable.[375]

2.1.2 Priorities and enforcement policy

The Commission is designated to ensure application of the principles laid down in Articles 101 and 102 TFEU and has far-reaching powers in this area, compared to other areas of EU law. It also determines the enforcement priorities of the competition policy. In this way there is a strong link between the policy objectives and the actual day-to-day application of the rules. Both are the responsibility of the same institution. The Commission of course shares the application of Articles 101 and 102 TFEU with national competition authorities and national courts but as will be discussed further below, the policy objectives as defined at a Community level shall be decisive also on a national level.

The debate on Article 102 TFEU in recent years illustrates well how central the concern of attaining the objectives of competition law can be in shaping competition policy. The coexistence and possible tension of the different goals appears as an issue against which the debate took place about which way the enforcement rules on abuse of dominance should go. With regard to exclusionary abuses, for example, the question arises whether to apply Article 102 TFEU to conduct that harms only competitors or whether there should always be (direct) consumer harm as well.[376] Requiring proof of harm in every case, increases the burden of authorities and claimants. Without going further into this subject that has generated huge amounts of literature, it is proposed here that this discussion shows the concrete effect of an objective on the shaping of a policy and, ultimately, the application of the law in specific cases.

It also shows the difficulty of the Commission to push forward reforms when a clear vision on what the objectives of the system of EU competition law are, is lacking. The struggle clearly also has to do with staying in line with the case-law and the ordoliberal heritage (see above on the objective of economic freedom).[377] The recent Guidance on Article 82 (now Article 102 TFEU) as it

---

[375] Even though perhaps oversimplifying the characteristics of continental court systems, Gerber (previous note) develops some interesting thoughts on this. See for an in-depth analysis of the way the legal system can deal with economic analysis, A. Sibony, *Le juge et le raisonnement économique en droit de la concurrence*, L.G.D.J. Lextenso editions, 2008.

[376] P. Marsden and S. Bishop: *Article 82 Review: "What is your theory of harm"*, European Competition Journal (2006) 2, p. 257. Stimulating and critical analysis also by A. Arpon de Mendivil de Aldama, *'Exclusionary conducts and consumer welfare: effects in competition, justifications and efficiencies. What is the right balance?'*, International antitrust law & policy; Fordham Competition Law Institute 2008, p. p. 1-31, and P. Akman, *Consumer welfare and Article 82: practice and rhetoric*, World Competition (2009), vol. 32, no. 1, p. 71.

[377] C. Ahlborn and A.J. Padilla, cited above in note 315. On ordoliberalism, see above in section 1.5.2. There are clear signs of this also in recent case-law, for example

was finally published by the Commission has inevitably been criticized for not making clear choices.[378]

One of the other subjects placed high on the agenda of the Commission recently is private enforcement.[379]The Commission has devoted considerable resources and effort to setting up a policy which might facilitate private enforcement of EC competition law, in other words: private parties, be it citizens or companies, suing companies in front of national courts for harm they have suffered due to anti-competitive behaviour. This policy priority is mentioned here because it inspired by a consumer-focused approach.

It is central to the private enforcement theme that harm is considered to be caused by anticompetitive behaviour, and that such harm should be repaired and the legal system should provide the instruments for such repair.[380] However, this policy priority might also be inspired by another type of consumer-oriented approach. Making class actions for consumers possible seems, at least in the short term, a way to reconcile public opinion as with competition policy and European policy at a whole and it is a way of demonstrating the relevance for society of what the Commission and other competition authorities are doing. In that sense, consumer welfare as the main objective of the system of competition law, also acquires another

---

in *British Airways*, ECJ 15 March 2007, case C-95/04 P, ECR (2007), p. I- 2331 where the Court discusses discriminatory behaviour (already as such debated as as an abuse by economists) and states that "there is nothing to prevent discrimination between business partners who are in a relationship of competition from being regarded as being abusive as soon as the behaviour of the undertaking in a dominant position tends, having regard to all circumstances of the case, to lead to a distorsion of competition between those business partners. In such a situation, it can not be required in addition that proof be adduced of an actual quantifiable deterioration in the competitive position of the business partners individually" (145 of the judgment). One can add in this reasoning: "let alone that it is necessary to prove harm to consumers".

378 For example J. Killick and A. Komninos, *Schizofrenia in the Commission's Article 82 Guidance Paper: formalism alongside increased recourse to economic analysis*, GCP (2009) February release 1 (online magazine for global competition policy); article by Akman cited in note 90 above; also pessimisitc about the contribution of economics to competition policy so far, J. Briones, *A balance of the impact of economic analysis on EU competition policy*, World Competition (2009), vol. 32, no. 1, p. 27.

379 White Paper on Damages Action for Breach of Antitrust Rules, COM (2008) 165; R. van den Bergh, *Schadevorderingen wegens schending van het mededingingsrecht in het spanningsveld tussen compensatie en optimale afschrikking*, M&M (2006), p. 143-151; C. Hodges, *Competition enforcement, regulation and civil justice: what is the case?*, CMLR (2006), p. 1381. Van den Berghe and Hodges clearly demonstrate the questions about the underlying motives for the focus on private enforcement by the Commission.

380 Whether this is only consumer harm in the narrow sense of the word (end users, consumers) or all parties suffering from anticompetitive behaviour, is then a question to be resolved. In any case, in communicating to the general public, the emphasis is put on consumers.

meaning: making it a priority to sell the policy to consumers by showing direct relevance.

It was said that the objectives pursued by the Commission will determine to a great extent the choices of priorities in its enforcement policy. This affects not only general policy directions but priorities can also play a role in the decision making practice of the Commission.

Broadly speaking, setting priorities can trigger particular investigations and can also determine to a large extent whether a complaint is pursued or a case brought to its attention through the leniency programme. Where complaints are concerned, it is established case-law that the Commission is not under an obligation to pursue every case but can have regard to the Community interest. It is hard to dissociate the Community interest from the objectives that are pursued in the context of the Community policy on competition.[381]

2.1.3 Enforcement in individual cases

It might seem difficult to examine how objectives actually have an impact in specific cases. This would require a particular type of research into the way in which officials or judges dealing with individual cases, are influenced by external factors other than the factual and legal elements of a particular case.[382]Account can only be taken of the way in which individual decisions are drafted and refer to general objectives. This is rarely the case.

However, there are some specific aspects of enforcing the law in individual cases which do come to mind and which are all currently very much subject of debate. Without going into any detail, three examples are given of subjects where fundamental choices as to the interpretation of Articles 101 and 102 TFEU have been made in the past and where discussion is ongoing as to whether these choices are still justified. These discussions on how the law should be interpreted are directly linked to the evolving way enforcers and courts are thinking about objectives.

The first is the interpretation of what is a restriction in the meaning of Article 101(1) TFEU. It is well known that a clear choice was made in Europe to take a very wide view on what constitutes a restriction of competition bringing virtually any restriction under the treaty provisions under the influence of, amongst others, ordoliberal thinking, as described briefly above. Secondly, in

---

381 It is consistently accepted by Community courts that complaints can be rejected for lack of Community interest, for example confirmation in CFI 16 January 2008, case T-306/05, *Scippacercola*, ECR (2008), p. II- 00004 (summary publication); also in recital 18 of Reg. 1/2003, cited in note 372; the Courts have accepted that choices have to be made and that this can be justified by limited resources, CFI 18 September 1992, case T- 24/90, *Automec*, ECR (1992) p.II- 2223.

382 See thoughts on this rare subject in A. Sibony, *Le juge et le raisonnement économique en droit de la concurrence*, (Paris : L.G.D.J. Lextenso editions, 2008).

a similar way, the concept of abuse in Article 102 was always a broad one, covering both exploitative and exclusionary abuses, going further than similar concepts in other systems of competition law.[383] Finally, the burden of proof for parties claiming an exception on the basis of Article 81 (3) (now 101 (3) TFEU) has always been high and the use of the mechanism of granting exemptions perhaps somewhat discretionary.[384]
These three ways of interpreting the open norms in Articles 101 and 102 TFEU obviously have a profound impact of how the law is enforced in individual cases and ultimately on the decision to sanction behaviour or not.

Let us turn then finally to a particular aspect of enforcement, namely sanctions. Increasingly high fines at the Commission level have provoked criticism on sanction policy for competition infringements roar up again and the fines are also usually at the heart of the appeals proceedings brought against cartel or abuse decisions.

It seems inevitable that there be a link between the objectives of competition policy and the way in which the policy is enforced and ultimately infringements are sanctioned. It would be interesting to see how the obligation to have more regard for the economical context in cartel cases for example, impacts on the calculation of the fines.[385]

In this respect, reference can be made to an interesting statement by the ECJ in relation to fining policy in the Dansk Rohrindustrie judgment:

> "*the supervisory task conferred on the Commission by Articles 85(1) and 86 of the EC Treaty* (now Article 102 TEU) *not only includes the duty to investigate and punish individual infringements but also encompasses the duty to pursue a general policy designed to apply, in competition matters, the principles laid down by the Treaty and to guide the conduct of undertakings in the light of those principles*" (par. 170).[386]

---

383 The most obvious and most described difference being with US antitrust law.

384 In any case, until the 2004 Notice on Article 81 (3) - Commission Notice on the cooperation between the Commission and the courts of the EU Member States in the application of Articles 81 and 82 EC [2004] OJ (2004) C 101/04 - now Article 101 (3) TFEU, there was very little guidance on how the four conditions of Article 81 (3) were to be interpreted. Such guidance was of course not a priority given the fact that the Commission was the only one granting exemptions.

385 Korsten highlights that Dutch case-law seems to be going that way and emphasising that the authority must also have sufficient regard for economic effects and context when determining the fine, case note, L. Korsten, 'Annotatie: Deelname aan verboden onderling afgestemd feitelijk gedrag? Ernst van de overtreding' (2007) 7 *Markt & Mededinging* 224.

386 ECJ Cases C-189/02P, C-202/02P, C-205/02P to C-208/02P, C-213/02P, Dansk Rørindustri a.o. v Commission of the European Communities [2005] ECR I-5425.

In the new Notice on the method of setting fines, the Commission refers to this statement.[387] It must be seen in relation with the CFI judgment in first instance where it stated that the Commission may adjust at any time the level of fines to *meet the needs of competition policy.*

What is meant by the "needs of competition policy" and the " principle that the Treaty implies" are matters of conjecture. What seems clear in any effect, is that the Commission is allowed to determine fines in individual cases by taking into account general policy aspects such as deterrence effect. This is quite remarkable and it is perhaps a characteristic which distinguishes competition law from (some systems of) criminal law.

Fining policy is also greatly determined by the qualification of what constitutes the most serious infringements of competition law. It must be assumed in a system of competition law that the qualification of "most serious" infringement is measured according to the objectives one wishes to achieve. For this reason, for many years, territorial restrictions in distribution agreements were blacklisted and sanctioned and the same was true for horizontal agreements in which competitors divided (national) markets.

Finally, related to the sanctions is the subject of remedies which are increasingly used to undo the effects of anticompetitive behaviour. Research shows that in recent instances where remedies were imposed, the choice was inspired very much by the interests of consumers. In other words, the shift in objectives might also be demonstrated in the choice of remedies.[388]

2.2 Market integration and consumer welfare: the larger picture

It follows from the first part that the historically most important objective of competition law, namely market integration, seems to have become less prominent, at least in the view of the Commission. This trend coincides, timewise, with the emphasis on the interests of consumers in its various forms. Yet it is proposed here that the importance of market integration might in fact be increasing.

2.2.1 Market integration and the internal market

It is understandable that the focus on market integration seems less prominent: generally speaking major progress has been made to achieve a common market since the Internal Market programmes launched in the early 1990s. Other themes have been the driving forces of policy and lawmaking. The competitiveness of European industry and also consumer

---

[387] Commission Guidelines on the method of setting fines imposed pursuant to Article 23(2)(a) of Regulation (EC) No 1/2003 [2006] OJ C 210/2.

[388] Examples are given by Jenkins, 'Protecting consumers' (above n 362); one might also consider the recent Microsoft case to be an example; see the CFI judgment Case T-201/04, [2007] ECR II-3601.

protection are much more prominent throughout all policy areas at present, not only in competition law.

However, there are signs that market integration is still very much an objective to take into account. Recent case-law of the Court of Justice and the Lisbon Treaty have been mentioned above in this respect and shall be adressed again briefly here. A related point is the increasing pressure to integrate different EU policy areas.

The statement of the Court of Justice in GSK in October 2009 is very illustrative and shall be cited in full because of its key importance, especially compared to what the Court of First Instance (now General Court) had said in the judgment in first instance:

> *"With respect to the Court of First Instance's statement that, while it is accepted that an agreement intended to limit parallel trade must in principle be considered to have as its object the restriction of competition, that applies in so far as it may be presumed to deprive final consumers of the advantages of effective competition in terms of supply or price, the Court notes that neither the wording of Article 81(1) EC nor the case-law lend support to such a position."*

The Court then goes on to say:

> *"First of all, there is nothing in that provision to indicate that only those agreements which deprive consumers of certain advantages may have an anti-competitive object. Secondly, it must be borne in mind that the Court has held that, like other competition rules laid down in the Treaty, Article 81 EC aims to protect not only the interests of competitors or of consumers, but also the structure of the market and, in so doing, competition as such. Consequently, for a finding that an agreement has an anti-competitive object, it is not necessary that final consumers be deprived of the advantages of effective competition in terms of supply or price. It follows that, by requiring proof that the agreement entails disadvantages for final consumers as a prerequisite for a finding of anti-competitive object and by not finding that that agreement had such an object, the Court of First Instance committed an error of law."* [389]

Brevity prevents further analysis of this judgment here, but it is important to note that it is not a stand-alone case: there is a series of recent cases in which the ECJ has clearly implied that the competition regime of the EU pursues multiple goals and where the market integration dimension is clearly present.[390] Whether or not the Court is merely reluctant to change, in any case this development shows a gap between the strong emphasis on

389 ECJ Case *GlaxoSmithKline Services Unlimited and others v Commission of the European Communities* (above n 323) [rec. 62, 63].

390 The same reasoning was behind the ECJ Case C-8/08, *T-mobile*, not yet reported, as well as ECJ *Csdr Syfait II* (above n 323) on abuse.

consumers by the Commission and the position of the Court of Justice. The cases also show again the practical impact of the objectives discussion, namely the way in which it determines the legal reasoning on what is or is not a restriction (object or effect) and how proof should be brought and evaluated (see above under 2.1.2 on enforcement in individual cases).

The second point to be made here has to do with the Lisbon Treaty changes: it is proposed that there are a number of indications that the link between competition and internal market has been reinforced. First, there is the disappearance of the reference to competition in the list of objectives, the only remaining references are to the internal market and the notorious Protocol 27 explicitly subordinates competition policy to the internal market. It remains to be seen whether the Court of Justice will consider this development as legally relevant. In the past, clearly the mention of the competition regime in the former Article 3 (g) EC Treaty played an important role in its case-law. Regardless of the influence this development might have on the case-law of the EU courts, it is in any case relevant as a political and policy development.

There is also the further emphasis on the necessity to integrate policies in different areas of Union law. In that respect, the general obligation of the Union to take into account requirements of high level of employment, social protection, training etc. in the implementation of all its policies is supplemented by specific similar so-called integration provisions, for example in the area of environment or consumer protection.[391] And whereas these integration provisions have moved forward to the beginning of the Treaty now, the reference to the principle of free market economy for other policies, has moved "backwards" to the specific chapter on economic and monetary policy (see above under 1.3).

The result is that the system will have to come to terms with the fact that the link between competition law and the foundations of the EU as well as other policies the Union pursues, is a reality. Competition law might have gotten somewhat isolated from the rest of EU law, notably because of the far-reaching competences of the Commission in determining and pursuing its policy in an independent way. Another reason might be that the shape and form of competition law is now at least partly determined at a national level where a focus on core competition objectives also seems predominant. It seems nevertheless that the ECJ and the Lisbon Treaty have put market integration, the internal market and the integration of different EU policies high up on the agenda.

---

[391] Article 9 (general obligation) and 11 (environment), 12 (consumers) TFEU. These obligations to take an integrated approach have been moved to the beginning of the treaty as compared to the EEC Treaty. They should at least be implemented by a type of impact assessment procedure when the Commission acts in the area of competition.

2.2.2 The consumers

Generally speaking non-economical, non-market related issues are more prominent on the European agenda, even more so after the Lisbon Treaty. Citizenship is more prominent and citizens are consumers.

The search of the EU to bridge the gap with citizens and make the EU project more credible and acceptable, plays a role.[392] Related to this is the overall trend to involve stakeholders is the political and legislative process, which can be observed both at the national as well as at the Community level.[393]

Consumer protection legislation has developed rapidly at the EU level, in areas such as electronic communication, sale at a distance, product safety etc.[394] A high level of consumer protection has been "promoted" as an explicit general Community objective.

It will be important in the near future to make a clear distinction at a policy level between the increasingly important consumer protection policy on the one hand, and competition policy on the other hand, their respective goals, and how the two areas are or should be complementary. The "consumer" who is being protected in both policy areas is not necessarily the same. In this respect, the importance of coherence between the different policy areas of the Community again comes into the picture: integration of the objectives of different policies such as internal market (including consumer protection), industrial policy and competition, is a priority as discussed in the previous section.[395]

Another point that is made here is also that the attention to consumers is not a novelty that economists have brought to competition law, consumers' interests were already present within the system (first part above) and there are many dimensions to the shift towards consumers that are linked to developments at the more general European level.[396] This more general consumer focus also holds a risk: it might push to a more aggressive competition policy that has in mind the protection of weaker consumers or certain groups of consumers. Seen from this perspective, the focus on consumers can in fact conflict with a more economic approach to

---

392 See e.g. Guilford and others, *How political is Europe's competition policy*, European Antitrust Review 2006, p. 8 (published annually by Global Competition review).

393 L. Senden, 'De lidstaten en de kwaliteit van Europese wetgeving: geen consumenten maar co-actoren' (2006) 54 *Sociaal Economische Wetgeving* 46.

394 The former Commissioner Kuneva contributed to making consumer policies one of the key areas of activity of the Commission; a noteworthy recent initiative showing how consumer driven policy can become is the plan concerning a EU wide complaints classifying system to speed up policy response to failing markets, see press release, IP/09/1092 'Consumers: EU-wide complaints-classifying system to speed up policy response to failing markets', 7 July 2009.

395 See above in section 2.2.1.

396 A cautious warning was expressed above concerning the danger of "consumerism" or populist approach in communication about the European political agenda.

competition law to the extent that the latter privileges a total welfare approach.

2.3 Some additional reasons for a debate on objectives

2.3.1 Governance: quality, efficiency, transparency and independence

If we are unsure about which objectives the system of competition law should pursue or at least unsure about what the balance or hierarchy should be between all the possible objectives, this might also raise more governance-inspired questions. In this section some remarks are made in relation to the quality of legislation and policy; in the next section (2.2.2), some issues related to the decentralised enforcement model are highlighted.

Reference is made to the risk of internal contradiction or a lack of coherence that might result from trying to reconcile different objectives, such as protecting efficiency and protecting small firms. Arguably, if there have always been multiple objectives, this risk will have been around since the beginning of EU competition law. Yet, the system seems to have arrived at a stage where the shifts in objectives can hinder the further development of competition law. Evaluating the quality of legislation requires a clear vision on its purpose.[397]

Related to the quality aspect is the need for efficient policymaking and application of the law.[398] For example, it has been said above that the goals or objectives of competition policy determine to a large extent what the priorities for enforcement are. This means that efficient allocation of resources of an authority requires a clear view on the objectives. In a recent publication, Lowe refers to the importance of efficiency at an organisational level and the need to focus limited resources to the most harmful practices.[399]

Efficient policymaking is also about communicating clearly to the stakeholders what the policy and the law are about. The Commission is certainly aware of this and qualifies this as being the need to explain to citizens what the added value of its actions are. As Odudu convincingly argues, a clear focus on the objective that a legal rule pursues enhances the effectiveness of guiding the conduct of undertakings on the market. A

---

397 See the remarkable speech by H. Tjeenk Willink, vice-president of Dutch Raad van State at the European law Conference in Stockholm, 2001, *Clarity and quality in legislation*, access: http://www.raadvanstate.nl/publicaties/toespraken_vice-president/ toespraak/?speech_id=17; Senden, 'De lidstaten en de kwaliteit van Europese wetgeving' (above n.393).

398 Commission (EC) 'European Governance' (White Paper) COM (2001) 428 final, 27 June 2001. And also the Commission (EC) 'A Europe of Results – Applying Community Law' (Communication) COM (2007) 502 final, 5 September 2007.

399 P. Lowe, 'The design of competition policy institutions for the 21st century' (above n 363).

justiciable norm requires, according to him, a unitary goal.[400] A unitary goal is perhaps a bridge to far but clarity on the objectives of a legal system certainly seems essential. The importance of a focused purpose can be qualified as one of the most important lessons to be drawn from the history of competition enforcement on both sides of the Atlantic.[401]

Also, related to quality and efficiency, a lack of a thorough debate and a clear position on the objectives of competition law, can also be perceived as a lack of transparency. The principle of transparency is one of growing importance in Community law. It is evolving into a general principle of Community law.[402]

Finally, reference was made in the introduction above to the political dimension of a system of competition law and it was said that it is undoubtedly the case, and rightly so, that a system of competition law has political objectives. Political influence however *within* the system and with regards to enforcement, must of course be avoided at all cost. A strong stance on the objectives that the system of competition law in Europe aims to achieve, will also help protect competition authorities from political interference and contribute to their independence, and thereby perhaps counter certain current trends where the protection of free competition is called into question by public opinion. It seems worthwhile therefore also in that respect to invest in this debate.

This very brief survey of governance-related issues is meant to substantiate the position that a debate and proper reflection is needed, not only at the academic level, and not only in the lively but small competition community.

2.3.2 Taking governance a step further: the decentralised enforcement system

If a thorough reflection is needed on what the objectives of EU competition policy are, this is especially true since the so-called modernisation which has resulted in a close co-operation between the 27 national competition

400 O. Odudu, *The boundaries of EC competition law* (above n 327) [170]. He makes the argument to defend that therefore Article 101 TFEU should have one unitary goal. In this article it is defended that for the system of competition law as a whole, it is acceptable that different goals exist but there is currently not sufficient though about the reasons and the consequences of the conflicts this can give rise to.

401 A clear call for focus and also a list of improper purposes, in the comprehensive work by K. Ewing, *Competition rules for the 21st century*, (The Hague: Kluwer Law International, 2006) for example at p. 198, p. 201, p. 331.

402 See S. Prechal, 'Transparency: a general principle of EU law?' in U.Bernitz, C. Cardner and J. Nergelius (eds.), *General principles of Community law in the process of development* (The Hague: Kluwer Law International, 2008). The principle of transparency has been recognized at the international level as applying to the procedures applicable for example in merger control, ICN document on guiding principles for merger control, as cited by Galloway, 'The pursuit of national champions' (above n 338).

authorities and the Commission within the network of competition authorities.

The system set up by Reg. 1/2003 devised a number of mechanisms that encourage and ensure convergence, amongst other things, by giving the Commission the task of monitoring and supervising the application of EU competition law by national authorities and courts. The Commission's role is justified in the regulation by the need for coherence and consistency in the application of the law.

Different objectives can mean different implementation of rules, and that would be undesirable in the context of the network at the different levels described above: legislation, policy, enforcement. Without going into the discussion about whether are not there is a legal obligation to converge, it will suffice to observe that, in practice, strong convergence is well underway in terms both of substantive law and procedures.[403] The same is true for policy and setting priorities.

If one assumes here that maximal convergence is the keyword in the decentralised application of Articles 81 and 82 EC, the difficulties for the functioning of the network are twofold.

When it comes to being European enforcers and taking into account the goal of convergence and the legal obligations in that respect, the national authorities are necessarily in a passive role because the Commission is essentially the policymaker at the EU level. The ECJ recognized this role before Reg. 1/2003 by stating that the Commission is responsible for defining and implementing the orientation of Community law.[404] However, in implementing and applying the law, the EU and the Member States are co-actors.[405] It should also be borne in mind that national authorities and judges have the obligation to ensure effective and consistent application of EC law at all times.

The situation is even more difficult if authorities or judges feel that their national law is not in line with EU law in this respect, or if they have to take into account additional (national) objectives pursued.

In the current set-up, national authorities and courts depend largely on the Commission. The system created by Reg. 1/2003 has been qualified by many

---

403 The Commission takes great pride in the remarkable level of convergence that had been reached in the reports published on Reg. 1/2003, Commission (EC) 'Report on the functioning of Regulation 1/2003' (Communication) COM (2009) 206 final, 29 April 2009 and Commission (EC) 'Communication from the Commission to the European Parliament and Council. Report on the functioning of Regulation 1/2003' (Staff Working Paper) SEC (2009) 574.

404 ECJ Case C- 344/98 *Masterfoods* [2000] ECR I-11369.

405 Expression from L. Senden, 'De lidstaten en de kwaliteit van Europese wetgeving' (above n 397).

commentators as essentially, a "top-down" system in which the influence of the Commission is more important than ever. Enforcement is left, to a great extent, to the national authorities, but competition policy is largely, if not entirely, determined by the Commission. The Commission's position has been reinforced by the combination of procedural and substantial reform in these last years. [406]

The second difficulty that this article wants to draw attention to here is that it might be questionable whether some of the objectives pursued at the European level can be transposed so easily to the level of the Member States. To put it in another way: is it so self-evident that the objectives pursued at the European level (should) coincide with the objectives of Member States?

There has not been much resistance on behalf of the Member States to accept the idea that EU objectives in this area are very similar, if not identical, to the objectives that national competition laws pursue. This can be explained most likely by, on the one hand, the focus on making the network work in terms of enforcement, and on the other hand, the fact that it was taken for granted that competition law objectives have some sort of universal value much determined by the fashionable purely economical definition of objectives.

The importance of the market integration objective is of course the clearest example of the questions this raises. The integration of markets is a European political objective. Clearly, history can not be undone and substantial competition law has been shaped by this objective and largely copied in the Member States as it stood. Nevertheless, is it not a valid concern to know whether and how Member States have to follow orientations decided upon at the EU level when they are clearly inspired by market integration? And is there room for industrial policy at a national level; can competition law be used to achieve specific objectives that are closely linked to one member state?

It might seem contrary to the trend towards more convergence to plead for a reflexion on how much room there is for differentiating EU policy objectives and national objectives. However, this point should be well understood. It is a question of drawing the right conclusions from a sufficiently complete overview of the multiple objectives that are pursued and at least questioning whether or not some degree of differentiation is possible and/or desirable between different existing competition regimes or not.[407]

---

406 Monti, *EC competition law* (above n 329), M. De Visser, *Network-based governance in EC law* (Oxford: Hart Publishing, 2009). On the combination of procedural and substantial modernisation, see D. Gerber, 'Two forms of modernisation in European competition law', 31 *Fordham International Law Journal* (2008) 1235.

407 For a recent, very challenging, view on this question: D. Evans, *Why different jurisdictions do not (and should not) adopt the same antitrust rules*, draft consulted at SSRN (accessed 24 March 2009): http://ssrn.com/abstract=1342797.

The European network of competition authorities presents unique practical features to organise a discussion on the objectives and therefore the foundations of competition law, taking into account all the different legal traditions and systems that exist. A debate on objectives should be allowed to take place. Care should be taken, however, to ensure that it is not only the authorities of Member States that are involved but that also their political, economic stakeholders and academics. to allow for a sufficienty broad perspective. This should happen before the system is embarked in new adventures of major policy reforms.

3. Taking the debate forward: concluding remarks

Reflection on what the objectives of the system of EU competition law are, is already a complex debate when it takes place within the system itself. It is about trying to find a proper balance between law and economics, between the traditional objectives that are typical to the EU competition law system such as market integration and the protection of small and medium sized firms and typically legal objectives such as economic freedom and fairness, and the objectives of consumer welfare and economic efficiency.

This article proposes that the debate also involves more issues that merely those, already quite complex issues, that are inherent in the system of competition law as such. There are links between the shift in objectives in the system of competition law and more general developments, and there are a number of governance-related concerns to be adressed. This should be sufficient to justify a solid debate on how to deal with the multiple objectives of EU competition law, especially as the objectives of the system of competition have a profound impact on the law, the policy and the enforcement of the rules on cartels and abuse of dominance.

(1) Multiple objectives are still pursued after modernisation. A new balance has to be found and has to be seen to be found.

The system of European competition law has always had and still has different objectives. A unitary goal is not desirable and not realistic. The issue at stake in the EU is rather the co-existence of different objectives. Van den Bergh and Camesasca, amongst others, expressed dissatisfaction in 2001 because a coherent discussion on the purpose of EC competition law was not really taking place.[408] This discussion is perhaps starting to develop now, but still not in a very prominent way.

The question of how the trade-off is made between different potentially conflicting objectives, is open. It seems acceptable within a legal system that trade-offs are to be made occasionally between different, conflicting,

---

[408] P. Camesasca and R. Van den Berg *European Competition law and economics: comparative perspective* 1st edn (Antwerpen: Intersentia, 2001), later edition (above n 327)

objectives. However, this requires explicit recognition that such conflicts can exist. This is lacking for the moment at the European level. Also, it requires some indication about the factors that will be decisive in arbitrating conflicting goals, both at the policy level as at the enforcement level in individual cases.

At present, the Commission seems to generally consider consumer welfare to be the primary driver of competition policy. However, the current wording of the treaties, the body of case-law and the political dimension of European integration and European policy, do not allow for such a reorientation to be made easily.

(2) The role of market integration is probably the most important issue to be resolved at the European level.

The EU has a major issue to solve: what place is there still for market integration in the further development of competition law?

The effects of the role of the market integration goal, should not be underestimated: it calls into question the very identity of the system of EU competition law as it has always existed. Yet, no major changes were made to the Treaties, the legislation or the Community institutional structure, both the Commission as well as the Community courts. The enforcement of Articles 101 and 102 EC has been partly decentralised, but this has only made the effects of the shift in the objectives more apparent. Perhaps decentralisation has also accelerated the decline of market integration as a goal of competition law.

And now recent months have shown a revival of market integration through case-law and the Lisbon Treaty as it was described above. The question is high on the agenda.

(3) Is the compromise approach a way forward?

It can probably be assumed that the Commission favours a "compromise approach".[409] A compromise approach "harmonises the immediate consumer interests with the overall welfare of society by subordinating the consumer interest to the national interest", but only temporarily. Consumers must *at some stage*, share meaningfully in the wealth that is created: "the fruits of producer innovation, efficiency and skill – from otherwise anticompetitive activity – must be shared with the wider community, namely consumers".[410]

The term "compromise approach" could be extended to mean that all different objectives that the EU system of competition law presently pursues, should be reconciled as much as possible. This should be done at the policy

---

[409] R. Ahdar, 'Consumers, redistribution of income and the purpose of competition law' (2002) 7 *European Competition Law Review* 341.

[410] Quote from Stuyck 'EC competition policy after modernisation' (above n 358).

level, ensuring sufficient transparency and in the proper procedural framework, involving Member States if and when necessary.

Creating a hierarchy between different values or goals, would be preferable from a legal point of view, but shall not be possible without major changes to the legal framework. A clear distinction between ultimate goals and intermediate goals, however, would be beneficial and a first essential step towards creating more clarity.[411] Consumer welfare can be the ultimate goal, but it should be defined in a sui generis way, in relation with the general welfare objectives of the EU. Then the question of how consumer welfare (or perhaps we should find another term?...) also comes into play as an intermediate goal can be examined, and how to reconcile it with other goals as much as possible. And if specific objectives conflict with each other, it should be clearer how the conflict is arbitrated.

One question discussed above is whether we keep a strict attitude to certain vertical restraints because they are detrimental for the internal market even though not necessarily for consumers? There seems to be nothing wrong with that, but it should be acknowledged explicitly. Do we think consumer welfare, after having defined it, is so essential that consumer harm has to be proven in every single abuse case? Or should we rather ascertain why we also wish to protect competitors in some cases, without trying to avoid the subject of conflicting goals and making it appear as if we can do both at the same time. This last option seems preferable.

(4) After concentrating on modernisation and policy reforms, refocusing the debate and going back to basics.

Adopting a more economical approach should not become less credible if multiple values are put into balance. In fact, taking a clear stance on objectives and the relative importance of consumer welfare might simplify the work of a great many lawyers and economists active in the field of competition.

The presence of other than purely economic factors, means that the success of a system of competition law should also be measured by more than just economic parameters. In times when competition authorities are embarking on exercises to measure the results that they achieve in an attempt to justify their existence, this is something to keep in mind. It might be a comforting thought for enforcers and policymakers, provided that they communicate better on the multiple objectives that the system pursues.

Selling competition policy more as a way of protecting consumers than as a way of ensuring free competition and/or protecting competitors, might also have seemed safer in times where the free market principles underlying the

---

[411] According to Neven the policy pursues ultimate goals, but the intermediate goals are assigned to the institutions that are in charge of applying the law, EUI 1997 (above n 287).

Treaty rules are less evident for some. In the longer run, it is not a good idea however to oversimplify the situation by referring to the consumer without giving it more thought what this actually means. EU competition law is in fact a bit like a multiple personality, fascinating but complicated. For the sake of its own credibility, the system should reflect on its foundations and do so, taking into account the new modernised framework of enforcement, involving all stakeholders and without being afraid of showing the multiple aspects of its personality.

Chapter 6

Decentralisation of competition law: sacrificing procedural autonomy?*

Autonomy versus effectiveness: a well known conflict in EU law revisited and its impact on the question of future harmonisation in the area of enforcement of competition law

Five years after its entry into force on 1 May 2004, the Commission carried out a first evaluation of the functioning of Regulation 1/2003 which has brought about significant changes in the area of competition law. One of the questions is whether harmonisation of procedural law in the Member States is necessary and/or desirable. At the same time many observers point to the remarkable level of convergence in the area of competition law, both in substantive law as well as in terms of procedural law. In a discussion about convergence and further harmonisation, both the well known principles of procedural autonomy as well as the principle of effectiveness can make their appearance.

But is procedural autonomy still really a (satisfactory) standard to build a model of enforcement and what does effectiveness really require? The first purpose of this contribution is to analyze what the role, relevance and value of the principles of procedural autonomy and effectiveness could or should (still) be.

The second purpose of this article is to look at some particularities of the enforcement system of competition law in the EU, and in particular at the mechanisms which are at the origin of the great degree of convergence.

By way of conclusion, some issues will be defined which seem key for further harmonisation, building both on the analysis of more general EU developments as well as the specifics of competition law enforcement. The method and format of this contribution aims at combining general EU law developments and competition law, therefore necessarily implying that neither analysis can be very detailed in the context of this article but hopefully creating new perspectives by linking developments, to contribute to an ongoing discussion.

---

* This article was closed end of March 2010. At the close of the manuscript at the end of June 2010, it had not yet been published.

1. Procedural autonomy and effectiveness: cornerstones of Union law enforcement?

1.1 Introduction[412]

In its first part, this article examines the current status of the principles of procedural autonomy and effectiveness in EU law. The purpose is to assess which role these principles can and should play in the debate about convergence and further harmonisation of procedure in the context of competition law, and to gain some insights in the debate on harmonisation by looking at a broader EU context. The method used in this article tries to give sufficient attention to the relationship between competition law and Union law in general and is therefore interactive in two directions: the general debate on procedural autonomy and effectiveness is approached from the perspective of competition law, and the other way around, the general developments regarding procedural autonomy and effectiveness shall feed into the discussion about the enforcement of competition law.

In terms of defining the scope of research, two preliminary remarks are made. First, this article is focused on public enforcement. Obviously, private enforcement is also an important part of the overall enforcement of EU competition rules. The Commission has launched proposals to enhance private enforcement in the Member States.[413] This development of increasing importance of private enforcement in competition law is also in line with a more general tendency, supported by case-law of the Court of Justice.[414] Hereinafter private enforcement shall only be referred to occasionally but it is not the central subject of this article.

Secondly, the procedural autonomy of the Member States which shall be discussed below, is limited by two principles: equivalence and effectiveness. In this contribution, the focus is on effectiveness. This principle is discussed in a wider sense than only in its capacity of a principle limiting procedural

[412] The new numbering since the Lisbon treaty is followed, except in direct citations of case-law or legislation where the old numbering is used.

[413] These initiatives would possibly also involve harmonisation measures of possibly both substantive law (damages, causal link) and procedure (calculation, proof). For the status of these projects: http://ec.europa.eu/competition/antitrust/actionsdamages/documents.html, there appears to be substantial controverse both on the plans as such as well as on the legal basis that would be appropriate. Latest published documents: Commission (EC) 'Damages Actions for breaches of the EC antitrust rules' (White Paper) COM (2008) 165 and Commission (EC) 'Accompanying the White paper on damages actions for breach of the EC antitrust rules' (Staff Working Paper) SEC (2008) 404; see T. Eilmansberger, 'The Green Paper on damage actions for breach of the EC antitrust rules and beyond: reflections on the utility and feasability of stimulating private enforcement through legislative action', (2007) 44 *Common Market Law Review* 431.

[414] See M. Tulibacka, 'Europeanization of civil procedures: in search of a coherent approach' 46 (2009) *Common Market Law Review* 1527.

autonomy. There are two main reasons why the principle of equivalence is largely absent hereinafter. The first is that the question underlying this article is if and how procedural autonomy and effectiveness -as seemingly opposing forces- are relevant in the discussion on further harmonisation in competition enforcement. The starting point is therefore that (the wider concept of) effectiveness is perceived as a principle which has in itself harmonising effects, and might also require further harmonisation. The second reason to be mentioned here is that equivalence seems to play but a limited role in the area of competition law. The enforcement environment of competition law is such as to make equivalence less relevant, at least in the way the European courts have construed it as a limit to procedural autonomy: it seems relatively unlikely that an action concerning EU law would be more difficult before the national authorities or courts than an action on the basis of national law.[415]

1.2 The principle of procedural autonomy

1.2.1 Definition and relevant developments

Member States are free to determine how to design and implement the procedural framework in which Union law is enforced in their national legal system. This is, in a nutshell, the principle of procedural autonomy of the Member States.[416] The case-law of the Court is not easily understood, it has

---

415 Perhaps the contrary would most likely be the case in many Member States. The particular enforcement system in competition law, discussed below in section 2, explains this: national substantive competition law is quasi identical to EU law and there is considerable convergence in terms of procedure. These factors combined with the directly applicable treaty rules and the enforcement practice at the EU level which serves as a model, also account for a legal environment which is familiar with EU law, although this might vary in Member States. Finally, the concept of equivalence in the case-law was developed mostly from the perspective of individuals invoking (substantive) rights against the state; as it shall be discussed in this article, for competition law, this is not the predominant procedural setting.

416 It is a subject studied by many scholars from different perspectives and using different methods in an attempt to qualify the case-law and to apprehend its continuity and its scope. For this article, particular attention was given to T. Tridimas, 'Enforcing Community rights in National Courts: some recent developments', in C. Kilpatrick, T. Novitz and P. Skidmore (eds) *The future of remedies in Europe* (Oxford: Hart Publishing, 2000), pp. 35-49; A. Ward, *Judicial review and the rights of private parties*, 'chapter 4: The rights of private parties and Member State remedies and Procedural rules Part I: The principles of effectiveness and non-discrimination' (Oxford: Oxford Universty Press, 2007); S. Prechal, 'EC requirements for an effective remedy' in J. Lonbay and A. Bondi (eds) *Remedies for breach of EC law* (Oxford: J. Wiley & Sons, 1997); C. Kakouris, 'Do the Member States possess judicial procedural autonomy?' (2007) 34 *Common Market Law Review* 1389; W. van Gerven, 'Bridging the gap between Community and national laws: towards a principle of homogeneity in the field of legal remedies' (1995) 32 *Common Market Law Review* 679; W. van Gerven, 'Of rights, remedies and procedures' 37 *Common Market Law Review* (2000), 501. An inspiring analysis

evolved at an unstable pace and it has left a number of questions open until this day.[417] It is also probably one of the most controversial areas of the Courts jurisprudence because the Courts judgments have, at several occasions, been perceived as intrusions in the national legal systems, leading to heated debates.

Procedure refers to the enforcement framework in which substantive law is invoked and enforced. In Union law, procedural law is usually perceived as having an ancillary role to substantive law and exists to ensure that substantive law can be effectively applied. On the function of procedure, the following description is appealing: procedure should serve as a means to the end of finding facts and enforcing the substantive law accurately.[418] Substantive law and procedural law are in permanent interaction. Procedural law has its own legitimacy or rather contributes to the legitimacy of the legal system in an independent way because it guarantees a number of fundamental principles.[419] Procedural law contains the more technical rules that govern the exercise of rights and remedies, which make them enforceable. A better, broader term to use might be enforcement rules.

The expression "procedural rules" in EU case-law is an autonomous concept. The Courts seem to give a very broad meaning to procedural rules, involving all substantive and organizational rules and principles being applicable to actions brought to obtain judicial protection.[420] This explains why the difference between procedure and substance is not always easy to identify. It

---

from a U.S. perspective on the role of procedure, Bone, R, *Making effective rules: the need for procedure theory* BU Working School of Law working paper (University School of Law, Boston 2008), online via: http://www.bu.edu/law/faculty/scholarship/workingpapers/2008.html (accessed on 1 March 2010).

417 See also Craig, *EU Administrative law* (Oxford: OUP, 2006), chapter 21.

418 Van Gerven, Kakouris, Prechal (above n 416); J. Delicostopoulos, 'Towards European Procedural Primacy in National Legal Systems' (2003) 9 *European Law Journal* 599: he used the expression "a venue for the realisation of rights". Most definitions take the perspective of the individual; quote on the function of procedure taken from Bone, working paper cited in note 416.

419 The existence of an independent judiciary, access to court, due process, equal treatment are values in themselves guaranteed by procedural rules. On the relationship between procedural rules and national legal culture, see A. Gerbrandy, *Convergentie in het mededingingsrecht: de invloed van het EG recht op materiële toepassing, toegang, bewijs en toetsing bij de Nederlandse mededingingsbestuursrechter, bezien in het licht van effectieve rechtsbescherming* (Den Haag: Boom Juridische Uitgevers, 2009), for example at p. 3.

420 See P. Haapaniemi, 'Procedural autonomy: a misnomer?' in L. Ervo, M. Gräns and A. Jokela (eds) *The Europeanization of Procedural Law and the New Challenges to Fair trial,* (Groningen: Europa Law Publishing, 2009), at p. 94. The large scope of application of the Courts scrutiny has made many authors say for some time that procedural autonomy seems a thing of the past; see the strong opinion of judge Kakouris (above n 5). On the lack of precision and distinction in the European Courts case-law between procedural rules and remedial rules, Van Gerven, 'of rights, remedies and procedures'(above n 416).

is not always efficient to distinguish them and the same is true for rights and remedies, because they are so intertwined.[421]

Turning to procedural autonomy, the distinction between direct and indirect conflict of rules is helpful to understand the case-law and to clarify the difference between primacy and the principle of procedural autonomy.[422] Primacy comes into play when a rule of Union law is in direct conflict with a rule of national law. It should be noted that this could be the case both for a rule of substantive law as well as for a rule of procedural law.[423] In such a case, primacy implies that the national rule, which is contrary to the Union rule, shall inevitably have to be set aside (disapplied).[424] This could be a rule of law laid down in legislation, in an administrative practice or in jurisprudence.

In the case of a national (procedural) rule that possibly hinders the effective application or enforcement of Union law, but in the absence of a corresponding rule of Union law that takes primacy over the national rule, the approach is more careful and the result shall be less predictable.[425] In that scenario the principle of procedural autonomy comes into play. This would be the case of an indirect conflict mentioned above. In the notorious Rewe case the Court used the following ever recurring phrase since then:

> "*Applying the principle of cooperation laid down in Article 5 of the Treaty, it is for the national courts which are entrusted with ensuring the legal protection which citizens derive from the direct effect of the provisions of*

421 Eilmansberger used the term "symbiotic", see T. Eilmansberger, 'The relationship between rights and remedies in EC law": in search of the missing link' (2004) 41 *Common Market Law Review* 1199 [1237]. W. van Gerven, 'Bridging the gap', has qualified the attempt to define and distinguish rights, remedies and procedure as almost impossible (above n 5).

422 See R. Ortlep and M. Verhoeven, 'De voorrangsregel versus het beginsel van nationale procesautonomie' (2008) 56 SEW: tijdschrift voor Europees en Economisch Recht 471. Strictly speaking, primacy is not a conflict rule in a sense that a national rule which is not compatible with EU law is invalidated, but the national rule shall have to be set aside, on this distinction: S. Prechal, 'Domestic legal effects on EU criminal law: variations on three themes' in D. Obradovic and N. Lavranos (eds) *Interface between EU law and national law. Proceedings of the annual Colloquium of the G.K. van Hogendorp Centre for European Constitutional Studies* (Groningen: Europe law Publishing, 2007) pp. 335-345.

423 Such a case shall be rarer given that there are less Union "procedural rules" as there are rules of material law, however the distinction is of no relevance where the application of primacy is concerned. Reg. 1/2003 discussed in section 2 below, provides for examples in competition law.

424 On the far-reaching obligation to disapply, even in a horizontal scenario of directive provisions, see ECJ Case C- 555/07, *Kücükdeveci*, not yet reported.

425 The doctrine of conform interpretation also comes into play in this situation: the national judge will always have to try to interpret and apply the national rules in conformity with EU law; this involves looking at the whole context of the rule in question, see ECJ joined cases C-397/01 and C-403/01, *Pfeiffer*, judgment of 5 October 2004, [2004] ECR I-8835.

Community law. Accordingly, in the absence of Community rules on this subject, it is for the domestic legal system of each Member State to designate the courts having jurisdiction and to determine the procedural conditions governing actions at law intended to ensure the protection of the rights which citizens have from the direct effect of Community law, it being understood that such conditions cannot be less favorable that those relating to similar actions of a domestic nature "(rec. 5).[426]

Apart from the caveat of equivalence expressed in the last sentence, the procedural autonomy is limited from the very beginning of the development of the case law, by effectiveness.

In the same judgment the Court states that: "*In the absence of such measures* (read: Union harmonisation measures) *the right conferred by Community law must be exercised before the national courts in accordance with the conditions laid down by national rules. The position would be different only if the conditions and time-limits made it impossible in practice to exercise the rights which the national courts are obliged to protect.*"[427] The Court regularly stated that the Treaty was not intended to create new remedies in the national courts to observe Union law,[428] but nevertheless the creation of a new remedy can become an obligation for the courts, going against most common views of the division of tasks between the different powers in a legal system.[429]

It is mainly through the application of the principle of effectiveness (the second exception to procedural autonomy) that the case-law of the Court of Justice evolved substantially and, in some cases, resembles a full fletched material screening of the national procedural rule (or absence thereof). The Court is willing to scrutinize *any provision of a national legal system which*

---

426 ECJ Case C-33/76, *Rewe-Zentralfinanz eG and Rewe-Zentral AG v. Landwirtschaftskammer für das Saarland* [1976] ECR 1989; ECJ Case C-45/76 *Comet* [1976] ECR 2043.

427 Not making it practically impossible or "rendering it excessively difficult", refers to both access to court and what the Court often calls the "detailed procedural rules", see for example ECJ case C-432/05, *Unibet* [2007] ECR I-2271, at rec. 43. The need to take into account the whole legal context including the general principles underlying the procedure, at rec. 54.

428 In the second Rewe case: ECJ Case C-158/80 *Rewe-Handelsgesellschaft Nord mbH v Hauptzollamt Kiel* [1981] ECR 1805. Recently in *Unibet* (above n 427) [40].

429 ECJ Case C-213/89, *Factortame* [1990] ECR I-2433; see also: P. Craig (above n 6) [792]; similarily the *Zuckerfabrik* case the ECJ obliges the national judge to "create" interim relief: ECJ Joined Cases C-143/88 and C-92/89 *Zuckerfabrik Süderdithmarschen AG v Hauptzollamt Itzehoe and Zuckerfabrik Soest GmbH v Hauptzollamt Paderborn* [1991] ECR I-415. Reluctance however in *Unibet*, cited above in note 427: the existence of an indirect remedy can be sufficient; whereas in the *Impact* judgment (ECJ case C-268/06 *Impact v Minister for Agriculture and Food and Others* [2008] ECR I-2483) the Court goes quite far and considers that the existence of procedural disadvantages for an individual is sufficient to make the exercise of rights excessively difficult and therefore the jurisdiction of a court was to be enlarged. There is some tension between the two judgments.

might prevent Community rules from having full force and effect.[430] Because of the substantial control that the Court is willing to undertake and the effects this can have on procedural law, the term *judicial harmonisation* is appropriate.[431] This term shall be used and illustrated further below. Although there is also a line of case law, where there was clearly more reluctance on behalf of the Court of Justice to interfere with national procedural law[432], it can nevertheless be said that the test applied by the Court of Justice to national rules of procedure has become more of a reasonability test or a proportionality test, or a procedural rule of reason.[433] In view of the foregoing, it is understandable that over time, the impression has grown that procedural autonomy is very much a relative concept.

The focus in the case-law has been on making sure individuals have remedies to enforce their rights derived from Union law. Having a remedy includes having access to court to obtain a remedy. There is a clear link with the right to judicial protection.[434] This explains why the term national

---

430 ECJ Case C-106/77, *Simmenthal* [1978] ECR 629. Effectiveness is qualified as being the very essence of Community law in that judgment. A clear example of the fact that the Court control is substantive can be found in the cases on time-delays and prescription, recently e.g. ECJ Case C-406/08, *Uniplex,* not yet reported, at 39-43. The case-law of the Court contains the principles on which national time-limits should be based and in the preliminary rulings, the Court often evaluates itself whether the time-limit is acceptable or not; see also ECJ Case C-63/08, *Pontin,* not yet reported. Similarly for sanctions, see below in the third part. Every enforcement rule is subject to scrutiny, this can go beyond what are perceived as procedural rules in a national system.

431 The term judicial harmonisation is taken here e.g. from S. Weatherill, *Cases and materials on EU law,* seventh edition (Oxford: Oxford University Press, 2006), p. 168, citing F. Snyder with reference to the judgment in the Comet case where the Court refers to "substance and form".

432 A remarkable analysis is made by P. Girerd, 'Les principes d'équivalence et d'effectivité: encadrement ou désencadrement de l'autonomie procédurale des Etats membres' (2002) 38 *Revue trimestrielle de droit européen* 75, where he argues that the Courts' reluctance can be observed in particular in cases where setting aside a particular national rule or practice would have financial consequences for the member state, at p. 94 and following. The judgment in *Van der Weerd,* is often referred to as being a more careful judgment in terms of interference with national law, ECJ Cases C-222/05 to C-225/05 *Van der Weerd* [2006] ECR I-4233.

433 W. Eijsbouts, J. Jans and F. Vogelaar, *Europees recht; algemeen deel* (Groningen: Europa Law Publishing, 2009), p. 329, S. Prechal, 'Community law in national courts: the lessons from van Schijndel' (1998) 35 *Common Market Law Review* 681; J. Engström, 'National courts obligation to apply Community law ex officio – the Court showing new respect for party autonomy and national procedural autonomy?' (2008) 1 *Review of European and Administrative Law* 67.

434 The same focus on remedies and judicial protection for individuals can be found in the judgment in the area of competition law when it comes to « material » remedies, namely the availability of damages : ECJ Case C-453/99, *Courage* [2001] ECR I-6297; ECJ Joined Cases C-295/04 until C-298/04, *Manfredi* [2006] ECR I-6619; the Commission found support in these judgments for its plans to encourage private enforcement, cited in note 413 above. On the use of the principle of effective judicial protection to justify intrusion in national procedural law, W.

remedial autonomy is also sometimes used.[435] However, this gives too narrow an impression of the full scope of the Courts' case law: procedures provide for a framework for the exercise of actions leading to remedies but also include many more rules not strictly related to the exercise of action for remedies.[436]

After this brief discussion of the concept and its evolution, the question to turn to now is what the status, role and purpose of the principle of procedural autonomy is in the EU legal system so as to determine what relevance it should be given in the particular area of competition law.

1.2.2 Status, role and purpose

Primacy (or supremacy) of Union law is said to be a constitutional principle.[437] But what is the status of procedural autonomy?[438] The principle is not laid down in the treaties as such. It appears in the case-law of the Court of Justice.[439] Is procedural autonomy a basic principle of Union law, a foundational principle or is it more an expression of the doctrine of residual competences? The nature of the principle can evolve due to political and other developments: for example, the rise of the principle of subsidiarity.[440]

Geursen, 'Handhaving van het objectieve gemeenschapsrecht via het effectiviteitsbeginsel vs. subjectieve rechtsbescherming via het nationaalrechtelijk verbod op reformation in peius' (2009) 4 *Nederlands Tijdschrift voor Europees Recht* 131. The focus on the individual judicial protection is apparent in a number of the recent landmark cases cited above: ECJ Case C-432/05, *Unibet* (above n 16) and ECJ Case C-268/06 *Impact* (above n 18). See also: Case C-426/05, *Tele 2 telecommunication gmbh* [2008] ECR I- 685.

435 For example P. Craig, *EU Administrative law*, cited in note 417 for distinction between procedure and remedies; also van Gerven, 'Bridging the gap' (above n 416).

436 Based on the definitions by W. van Gerven, 'Of rights, remedies and procedures' (above n 416) [502].

437 The denomination "constitutional" might now have a slightly different meaning since the Constitutional Treaty and the entry into force of the Treaty of Lisbon which seems to attempt to deconstitutionalize EC law. However, there is no reason to believe that the Court would retreat from such fundamental principles as the primacy of Union law. Above primacy and procedural autonomy were presented as two ways to deal with a conflict between EU law and national law.

438 There seems to be considerably less attention in doctrine for the meaning of the concept of procedural autonomy than for the extent to which the "exceptions" of equivalence and effectiveness have allowed the Court to "interfere" with national procedural law.

439 P. Haapaniemi traces it back to doctrine in the 70's, (above n 420).

440 The 1997 Protocol 30 to the EC Treaty on the application of subsidiarity and proportionality states that "*While respecting Community law, care should be taken to respect well established national arrangements and the organization and working of the Member States' legal systems*". The new protocol 2 to the Treaty of Lisbon on the same subject however, is much shorter and does not contain this statement anymore.

It is argued that procedural autonomy is, first of all, merely the consequence of the decentralized system which characterizes Union law. Procedural autonomy is not a principle of law, nor is it a norm.[441] It does not allow for the compatibility of lower rules to be assessed. It seems more to be a standard which the Court refers to but without situating it as such in the Union legal order.[442] It is a standard or an organizational or institutional principle, without necessarily being a general principle of law. It is therefore part of what the Court has called *"the general principles on which the institutional system of the Community is based and which govern the relations between the Community and the Member States"*.[443] Taking a very pragmatic view: it was necessary to emphasize procedural autonomy because, in general, there was no enforcement structure, nor a set of enforcement rules, at the European level. Emphasizing the importance of national rules and the role of national judges, was a way (the only way) to maximalize the effectiveness of enforcement. [444]

As it appears clearly from the quotes above, reference is almost always made by the Courts to the phrase: "in the absence of Union law, it is up to member states". This resembles the description of a competence of a residual nature: as long as no Union rules exist, the Member States can act. It does seem more appropriate to use the term procedural competence[445]: a national competence that can be exercised dependant on the pre-existence or not of Union rules.

---

441 The idea that is expressed here is mostly based on the idea that procedural autonomy does not appear to be a source of law or a source of legal obligations in itself. The purpose is not to minimalize the political or organizational significance of the principle of procedural autonomy.

442 B. de Witte describes well that the ECJ uses the term principle in different meanings, both for legal rules having a basis in the Treaty, for general principles of law or for more political or organizational principles, see B. de Witte, 'Institutional principles: a special category of general principles of EC law' in U. Bernitz and J. Nergelius (eds.), *General Principles of European Community Law* (The Hague: Kluwer Law International, 2000), p. 143-159. On the meaning of the term "principle", also O. Wiklund and J. Bengoetxea, *General Constitutional Principles of Community Law*, in the same book.

443 The concept of institutional principles is described by B. de Witte, 'Institutional Principles' (above n 412); Delicostopoulos, 'Towards European Procedural Primacy' (above n 418): he considers national procedural competence in the Courts case-law to be a standard.

444 On the intrinsic limits of a system based on decentralised application: E. Dubout, 'Le contentieux de la troisième génération ou l'incomplétude du système jurisdictionnel communautaire', (2007) 43 *Revue trimestrielle de droit européen* 427.

445 Van Gerven, 'Of rights, remedies and procedures' (above n 416) and Delicostopoulos, 'Towards European Procedural Primacy' (above n 418).

The term national procedural competence is also more adequate, in view of primacy or supremacy of European law:[446] there are a number of instances where national rules or acts shall be set aside on the basis of primacy of the law and in which there will be no question of national procedural autonomy.[447]

The recurring phrase "in the absence of Community law/harmonisation measures, it is up to the member states..", seen in the perspective of the current state of EU law, confirms that the perspective to be taken is not so much one of autonomy but of the division of *competences* between the EU and the Member States. Procedural autonomy as an expression of the residual competence of Member States, fits with the new description of competences that the Lisbon Treaty has introduced: the principle of conferral of powers has been reinforced and appears clearly and prominently from the new treaties.[448] As it will appear below in the next section, the particularity of competition law in this respect is that the division of competences (in terms of enforcement) between the EU and the Member States was different from the start and also that, now since the Lisbon Treaty, it is one of the few areas of exclusive competence of the Union.

It is a natural evolution that the more substantial the impact EU law has had throughout the years, the more procedural autonomy is eroded through judicial harmonisation (examples below in section 2) and more and more legislative harmonisation.[449] Where the possibilities of legislative harmonisation of procedure at the EU level is concerned, clearly the recent

---

446 Prechal, 'EC requirements for an effective remedy' (above n 416); Van Gerven, 'of rights, remedies and procedures' (above n 416); Delicostopoulos, 'Towards European Procedural Primacy' (above n 418).

447 This is also due to the broad sense that the ECJ has given to the notion of procedural rules. Example of burden of proof, discussed also below under 2.3.2, the example of damages case law; example given by Delicostopoulos on the articles in Reg. 1/2003 about compliance to decisions by national judges. Many examples of procedural harmonisation in Eilmansberger, 'The Green Paper on damage actions' (above n 413).

448 Article 5 TEU: "*The limits of the Union competences are governed by the principle of conferral. The use of Union competences is governed by the principles of subsidiarity and proportionality.* Also noteworthy in this respect: protocol 2 on subsidiarity and proportionality and protocol 25 on the exercise of shared competence, emphasizing the limits on the EU competences; on the division of competences in this respect, R. van Ooik, 'The European Court of Justice and the division of competence in the EU', in D. Obradovic and N. Lavranos (eds) *Interface between EU law and national law.Proceedings of the annual Colloquium of the G.K. van Hogendorp Centre for European Constitutional Studies* (Groningen: Europe law Publishing, 2007). Any competence not attributed to the Union, remains with the Member States: this can be seen as another way of giving the same message as the one given by the Court in Rewe.

449 See also as discussed by M. Tulibacka, 'Europeanization of civil procedures' (above n 414).

case-law of the EU courts provides opportunities for pushing forward the adoption of enforcement rules at the EU level.[450]

The principle of procedural autonomy is presented here as a necessary organizational standard on the one hand, and as an expression of the Member States residual competence on the other hand. A remaining question is then what (other) purpose it serves. Procedural autonomy is not the one and only standard for the enforcement of EU law anymore. [451] Are there nevertheless compelling reasons to preserve as much national autonomy as possible in any case (*in casu* in the area of the enforcement of competition law), thereby accepting a certain level of divergence amongst the Member States? A very brief answer is given, from a strictly legal perspective.

It would seem that national procedural autonomy in general does not protect an (another) objective Union interest as such. The arguments that are generally made to favor procedural autonomy and therefore oppose the Courts intrusions on it, include the close relationship between procedure and cultural and social roots of a legal system, legal certainty, conferred powers, proportionality and subsidiarity.[452] Many of these are principles enshrined in the Union legal order and therefore their protection would be in the Union interest.[453] Arguments are usually inspired not so much by an

---

[450] ECJ Case C-176/03, *Commission/Council* [2005] ECR I-7879 and ECJ Case C-440/05, *Commission/Council* [2007] ECR I-9097. Simplifying: the Court supports the idea of implied powers: if the adoption of rules on sanctions is a necessary measure for combatting serious environmental offences, then these rules might be adopted on the basis of the legal basis allowing for measures of environmental protection (the basis therefore for substantive harmonisation). These judgments were rendered in the context of a discussion of the right legal basis, discussed briefly below for competition enforcement under 3.3.

[451] This might seem a controversial point of view because the ECJ still performs lip service to the principle of procedural autonomy but even the Lisbon Treaty and its protocols discussed before, which are perceived as containing more emphasis on the Members States' role and a rebalancing of the relationship between EU and Member States, has not consecrated the principle explicitly. It is acknowlegded that this view might be influenced by the perspective of competition law where procedural autonomy seems a thing of the past, see hereinafter. This impression is reinforced by the fact that in recent important cases concerning proof issues in competition law, no mention of procedural autonomy is made by the ECJ, see ECJ Joined Cases C-295/04 until C-298/04 *Manfredi* (above n 23) and case C-8/08, *T-mobile*, not yet reported.

[452] See Delicostopoulos, 'Towards European Procedural Primacy' (above n 418) and C. Kilpatrick, 'The future of remedies in Europe', in C. Kilpatrick and others (above n 416); Placing the erosion of national procedural law in a more global perspective: G. Della Cananea, 'Beyond the State: the Europeanization and Globalization of Procedural Administrative law' (2003) 9 *European Public Law* 563. On link between law and culture, discussion and references in Gerbrandy, *Convergentie in het mededingingsrecht* (above n 419) [79], also in her article 'Procedural convergence in competition law: Towards a spontaneous ius commune'(2009) 2 *Review of European and Administrative Law* 105.

[453] In developing the general principles of Union law as an important source of law, the Court has drawn intensively on the constitutional traditions of the Member

analysis of the raisons d'être of procedural autonomy (and therefore procedural divergence) but often rather constitute criticism on the alleged activism of the Court of Justice in this area. Although many of the (often non-legal) concerns are valid, it is unclear which purpose the principle or procedural autonomy serves as such from a purely legal point of view, or, to put it in another way, why divergence, as a result of autonomy, should be protected.[454]

1.3 Effectiveness

1.3.1 Definition and relevant developments

The principle of effectiveness as a limit to procedural autonomy was already discussed in the previous section. Some more thoughts will be developed about the principle and its scope more in general, again to allow for better assessing what its significance should be when reflecting on the need for further harmonisation in the field of competition law. The starting point is the common (mis)use of effectiveness as an argument to defend more convergence and more harmonisation in procedural competition law. Is this in line with the way the concept has developed generally?

The principle of effectiveness is clearly of essential importance for the functioning of the European legal order and it is generally acknowledged that its importance in the case-law of the Court has increased over the last years.[455] Effectiveness is often considered to be a general principle of Union law; one can wonder however if its scope is sufficiently clear to actually give it that status (see below). It is not, as many other principles given that status by the Court, common to most domestic legal systems of the Member States as such or derived from national systems by the Courts. This has to do with the fact that it is very much linked to the specific characteristics of Union law: enforcement of Union law is dependant on decentralised application through the existing structures in the Member States.

The focus of its application has been on the national level. Effectiveness works in two ways: it is a way of shaping the enforcement of the law but also a way of measuring its enforcement.[456]

States. A good example of how a general principle in procedural law of Member States is given the status of general principle of EU law by the Court (application of more lenient sanction), judment in *Berlusconi* (below n 492).

454 Legal certainty is of course also a general principle of Union law, and obviously it is conceivable to argue that procedural divergence can lead to a decrease in legal certainty. However, if that were the argument, it would plead in favor of harmonisation at the EU level in an appropriate and foreseeable way.

455 The distinction between procedural and substantive effectiveness is discussed by F. Snyder in his authoritative article 'The effectiveness of European Community Law: institutions, processes, tools and techniques' (1993) 56 *Modern Law Review* 19; also M. Accetto and S. Zleptnig, 'The principle of effectiveness: rethinking its role in Community law' (2005) 11 *European Public Law* 375 [377].

456 Accetto and Zleptnig, 'The principle of effectiveness' (above n 455) [379].

The relationship between effectiveness and the principle of effective judicial protection is obvious but not easy to qualify.[457] It appears already from the brief discussion above that the principle of effective judicial protection has enhanced the development and the scope of the Courts case-law in relation to national procedural law. The protection of the individual' access to a court has been a central point of attention. Whereas it is often presented the other way around (effectiveness as simply a specific application of the right to (effective) judicial protection[458]), the approach in this article, from the perspective of procedure, is that effectiveness goes much beyond effective judicial protection. In short: effectiveness is about implementation, enforcement and compliance of Union law.[459] If we add on the broader, non-legal connotations of effectiveness, the formula would be "implementation, enforcement, impact and compliance."[460] Effectiveness as a broader concept, can also mean fulfilling the objectives of the European Union.

1.3.2 Status, role and significance

The principle of effectiveness is easily invoked but difficult to apprehend. Part of the confusion surrounding it is due to the question of the legal basis of the principle. If effectiveness is a general principle of law, this question becomes less important but even that status is unclear. Reference is often made to Article 10 EC Treaty (now Article 4 (3) TEU: the duty of loyalty of Member States). The obligation for Member States to create an efficient system of legal remedies (Article 19 (1) TEU) follows up on the duty to cooperate and from that perspective effectiveness, or more exactly effective judicial protection, is related to the principles laid down in the treaties mentioned before. There is a relationship also with Articles 6 and 13 ECHR and the EU Charter on fundamental rights in that same perspective of protecting rights of individuals.[461]

---

457 See S. Prechal, 'EC requirements for an effective remedy' (above n 416). Part of the confusion comes from the fact that the Court sometimes uses both as interchangeable, for example in *Safalero*, the Court examines a national rule directly on the basis of effective judicial protection without even mentioning effectiveness, Case C-13/01 *Safalero Srl v Prefetto di Genova* [2003] ECR I-08679 [49-50].

458 Perhaps it is a question of perspective: from the perspective of individual judicial protection, that right encompasses more than only effectiveness; but from the perspective of procedure as a whole (more than only access and remedies for individuals), effectiveness is the broader principle.

459 Accetto and Zleptnig, 'The principle of effectiveness' (above n 455).

460 Expression used by Snyder, 'The effectiveness of European Community Law' (above n 455).

461 Article 47 of the Charter on fundamental rights: it describes the right to an effective remedy; see also P. Oliver, 'Le règlement 1/2003 et les principes d'efficacité et d'équivalence' (2007) *41 Cahiers de droit européen* 351 [356]. For a recent mention of the link to Articles 6 and 13 ECHR in an area related to competition, ECJ Cases C-317 to 320/08, *Alassini and others*, not yet reported.

It can be argued that this is only part of the story because the provisions cited above only cover certain aspects of effectiveness, namely the most visible (or most controversial) ones focusing on individual effective judicial protection.[462] Even though the case-law might concern primarily the private enforcement of Union law by individuals[463], the scope is broader: effectiveness is a general principle that goes beyond the obligations laid down in Article 4 (3) TEU and the requirements of individual judicial protection.

Snyder has distinguished at least seven types of effectiveness: the enactment of Union policy through Union legislation, the application of Union rules by Member States, the implementation of directives and other legislation into national law or administrative practices, the use of Union law by individuals that orient their behaviour in relation to Union law, litigation in national course on the basis of Union law, and enforcement of Union law by national courts and authorities.[464] These are all ways of optimalizing the enforcement of the law.

Effectiveness of Union law is realized through a complex interaction of legislation, case-law and policy and both at the Union and at the national level. Effectiveness is about structures, about optimalizing the institutional balance, especially in a federal or supranational system. Decentralisation and centralisation forces are part of every legal systems' search for effectiveness.[465] These forces also explain to a large extent the developments in competition law discussed below: decentralisation of enforcement as a way to make enforcement more effective. Effectiveness is therefore also about efficiency, the efficiency of a legal system, in this case the Union legal order.[466]

Two further specific questions about the role and significance of effectiveness shall be adressed here. They are inspired by the debate on further harmonisation in competition law and the answers should contribute to this debate (third part below). The first is whether effectiveness also comprises effective enforcement of the state against the individual and the second whether effectiveness requires uniformity (the latter is discussed below in 1.3.3).

---

462 The unsatisfactory nature of these legal basis, also argued by Eilmansberger 'The relationship between rights and remedies in EC law' (above n 421).

463 Kilpatrick, 'The future of remedies in Europe' (above n 452).

464 Snyder, 'The effectiveness of European Community Law' (above n 455) [25-26].

465 Snyder, 'The effectiveness of European Community Law' (above n 455) and for an interesting description of this search in another area of law, see B. Keirsblick, 'The limits of consumer law in Europe', in E. Claes, W. Devroe and B. Keirsblick (eds) *Facing the limits of the law* (Berlin: Springer, 2009).

466 The EU is a comprehensive and distinct legal order, ECJ Case C-50/00P *UPA* [2002] ECR I-6677; see K. Lenaerts, 'The rule of law and the coherence of the judicial system of the European Union' (2007) 44 *Common Market Law Review* 1625.

Effective enforcement is not always about enforcing the rights an individual derives from EU law against the state or another individual but enforcement can necessitate actions by the state *against* the individual. If effectiveness is a broad principle as proposed above, it should include this dimension. However, given the focus on effective judicial protection and the doubts about how both concepts relate to each other, it is not clear how and to what extent effectiveness comprises effective enforcement in the above sense. There are very few examples of cases where the Court has dealt with the dimension of effective enforcement against individuals.[467] The question is crucial because in competition law rules are enforced against undertakings and infringements are sanctioned. The enforcement rules that are potentially the subject of harmonisation (see below) also include rules that do not protect rights of individuals or provide remedies. Their application might be to the detriment of individuals or affect them negatively. It is argued here that effectiveness as a broad concept which is meant to contribute to fulfilling the objectives of the European Union, should logically include this specific dimension of effective enforcement. Nevertheless, these aspects are underdeveloped in the current state of the law and there is no clear basis in the ECJ's case-law to defend this.

1.3.3 Does effectiveness require uniformity and/or convergence?

A second question of interest here is if the principle of effectiveness actually requires convergence, or even uniformity of procedural law? As one author has pointed out, competition specialists, many of which support and call for harmonisation of procedural law[468], might overestimate the case-law on effectiveness.[469]

The scope of application of effectiveness is unclear in the area of procedural law and the case-law discussed above is so open-ended that virtually any rule of procedural law seems potentially subject to being an obstacle to the

---

467 There is the area of state aid that could provide some indications: when the Court insists that procedural rules should be interpreted in such a way as to allow maximum chances to oblige undertakings to reimburse illegal state aid, this could be seen as an example of effective enforcement having an impact on procedural law for the sake of efficient enforcement against individuals. However, the setting is specific: because effective judicial protection shall also be the objective of the intervention of the national judge who shall often intervene and have to order reimbursement at the demand of a competitor, for an overview of the far-reaching responsibilities of judges in this respect, Comission Notice on the enforcement of state aid law by national courts [2009] OJ C 85/1. It is only for sanctions that the CJEU seems to have dealt with this dimension (see on this case-law below 2.3.1) to the extent that the basis principles for sanctions have been set out but that does not allow us to answer the question whether the Court would require a procedural rule to be overruled for the sake of effectiveness if the result affects the individual undertaking negatively.

468 See hereinafter about the recent reports on Reg. 1/2003, in section 2.4.

469 P. Oliver, 'Le règlement 1/2003' (above n 461) [353].

effet utile of Union law.[470] The potential scope is therefore enormous. The Courts approach has been labelled as selectively deferent but the criteria for the selectivity are not very clear.[471] What is clear is that the focal point of the case-law on effectiveness has been on creating standing and remedies to make sure individuals can invoke Union law at a national level.

However, there are no convincing arguments to claim that effectiveness goes so far as to require uniformity of national procedural law. Effectiveness was developed as a limit to national procedural autonomy which is the standard by which enforcement of Union law was organised. If effective application were to require uniformity in procedural rules, large parts of Union law would simply be totally inefficient. Even in those areas where the Treaties provide for harmonisation of national measures for the accomplishment of the internal market, the purpose is not unifying the law. Harmonisation is not equal to uniformization. On the contrary, the case-law of the Courts shows that it is sometimes best to accept some divergence for the sake of allowing national rules to be applied if there are general principles such as legal certainty at stake. [472] The principle of effectiveness, even in its broadest meaning, cannot be said to require uniformity.[473]

If effectiveness does not require uniformity of procedural law, can it be said to require convergence? This is an even more difficult question. If the difference between procedural rules causes an individual's legal position to be substantially different from one Member States to another, this seems problematic. When one thinks of a concrete example in the area of competition law, it might appear wrong that in Member State A the prescription period for cartel investigations is five years whereas in Member State B an authority might be able to go back ten years in time. This impression shall exist even more if an example is taken in the area of sanctions: imagine if the same infringement were to be punishable in Member State A with a sanction going up to maximum 5 % of a company turnover, whereas in Member State B, the fine can go to maximum 10 % turnover and the personnel of the company can be imprisoned. This type of divergence is currently a reality.

From the perspective of the individual market player, the absence of a level playing field and equal procedural conditions in the different Member States,

---

470 A. Ward, *Judicial review and the rights of private parties* (above n 416) [193].

471 T. Tridimas, 'Enforcing Community rights in National Courts' (above n 416).

472 M. Tulibacka calls this the "bottom up" approach where the Court does not pose hard rules for national judges but encourages mutual trust and recognition (above n 414). Her analysis concerns private enforcement but it is based on the ECJ's case-law related also to administrative procedures, e.g. ECJ Case C-455/08, *European Commission v Ireland.* not yet reported.

473 Van Gerven, 'Of rights, remedies and procedures' (above n 416) defends that it would be best for rights to be determined equally for all citizens across Europe by the EU legislature; uniformity is required where the constitutive conditions for remedies are concerned; however for the form and extent of the remedy, it is not realistic to abandon national competence.

might be an obstacle to trade and might create barriers to trade. It is fair to say however that this is quite an indirect relationship with the internal market; it is certainly not self-evident in view of the case law.[474] In any case, this perspective is relevant mostly where the individual is on the demanding side (exercising rights), for example when he is a complainant before an authority or when he notifies an agreement or requests leniency. Related to the absence of a level-playing field is an argument based on equal treatment and non-discrimination. It does not seem right that rules would be different and therefore companies in a similar situation might be treated differently without being able to choose themselves in which jurisdiction their case is dealt with. The examples above (prescription and sanctions) appeal to this type of reasoning.

However, strictly speaking, the effectiveness of the enforcement of EU (antitrust) law is not at stake when the procedural law of two Member States is different. This would be the case if in a particular case the enforcement rules were such as to render the application of competition rules very difficult, or if they are not equivalent to the rules applicable to similar national cases. Equivalence between the laws of *different* Member States is not part of the test of effectiveness (effet utile) of Union law, even in its most intrusive form (see above).

The purpose here is not to minimalize the negative effects of divergence between procedural laws in the Member States but merely to show that the principle of effectiveness of Union law cannot serve so easily as an argument to condemn divergence and push for convergence or harmonisation.

The arguments above however do bring the principle of equivalence back into the picture, of which it was said in the introduction that is is not the primary focus of this article. Another type of equivalence appears here: not the equivalence of the case-law of the ECJ which has to do with coherence within the domestic law system (comparing claims based on national law and EU law)[475] but coherence and consistency of the enforcement of EU law throughout the EU, making sure undertakings are treated equally in the Member States. The Court sometimes refers to equivalence in this way in relation to the importance of uniform interpretation.[476] This type of

---

474 We refer here to the judgment in Case C-412/97 *Fenocchio* [1999] ECR I-3845. The Court stated very categorically in relation to an Italian rule (rec. 11): "*It is true that the effect of the national provision is to subject traders to different procedural rules according to whether they supply goods within the Member State concerned or export them to other Member States. However, the possibility that nationals would therefore hesitate to sell goods to purchasers established in other Member States is too uncertain and indirect for that national provision to be regarded as liable to hinder trade between Member States*". And in this case there was a difference within the *same* Member State.

475 The principle is very much (still or again) present in recent cases on procedural autonomy, for example ECJ Case C-445/06, *Danske Slagterier*, not yet reported.

476 See in *Tele2* (above n 434) [26].

equivalence resembles what one would expect in a perfectly integrated market.

1.4 Intermediate conclusion on procedural autonomy and effectiveness

This overview shows that neither the principle of procedural autonomy, nor the principle of effectiveness are clear-cut concepts that can be readily applied. Their scope and definition are subject to discussion and they are evolving concepts. In a discussion on harmonisation there shall not be a simple choice between one or the other, they are not clearly opposite forces either. Procedural autonomy is a standard which is generally under pressure in EU law, especially when it comes to standing and remedies for individuals. Effectiveness potentially has a large scope of application but its boundaries are unclear. It is unlikely that effectiveness can be construed to require uniformity of procedural law and it is too straightforward to claim that procedural divergence is in itself a problem in view of the principle of effectiveness as it stands now.

2. The enforcement model of EU competition law

The discussion above already integrated some developments and examples from the area of competition law. Now, before addressing the question of further harmonisation, the relevant context of the enforcement of competition law shall be discussed. The following features of the relevant legal environment shall be highlighted in that respect: the different layers of enforcement, the existing mechanisms of convergence and harmonisation and the recent evaluation of Reg. 1/2003 which has put the question of further harmonisation on the agenda again.

2.1 Division of tasks, competences and layers of enforcement

Both the prohibition on cartels and restrictive agreements in Article 101 TFEU (former 81 EC) and the prohibition on the abuse of dominant provisions in Article 102 TFEU (former 82 EC) are directly applicable and therefore enforceable in private litigation before the national judge.[477] It is equally well known that Reg. 17 of the Council (1962) enabled the Commission to enforce Articles 81 and 82 EC Treaty (85 and 86 EEC at the time) in individual cases and sanction the undertakings responsible for the infringements.[478] The Council also laid down the framework for the investigative and decision-making procedure that the Commission was to follow. In 2004, Reg. 1/2003 replaced Reg. 17 and consolidated a number of

[477] ECJ Case 13/6, *Bosch* [1962] ECR 93. With the exception of course of the third paragraph of Article 85 (the exception with four conditions) EEC (now 101 TFEU) for which, on the basis of Reg. 17/62 only the Commission was competent.

[478] Council Regulation (EEC) No 17 (First Regulation implementing Articles 85 and 86 of the Treaty) [1959-62] OJ Spec Ed 87.

rules concerning the procedural framework at the level of the Commission whilst also extending its investigative powers.[479]

Reg. 1/2003 is most well known for the decentralisation of enforcement of competition law, bringing in the picture the third player in the field of the enforcement of EU competition law, the national competition authorities.[480] On the basis of Article 35 of the regulation, each Member state designated the institution that is to be considered as "national competition authority" and responsible for the application of Article 81 and 82 EC "in such a way that the provisions of this regulation are *effectively* complied with".

The simultaneous enforcement through private enforcement and public enforcement, and, in particular, the existence of a strong enforcement agency with important powers at the European level, is characteristic for this area of Union law. The decentralisation of this enforcement by using the parallel competences of the Commission on the one hand, and the national competition authorities that now exist in all Member States on the other hand, is also a typical feature in terms of enforcement.

The point to keep in mind here is therefore that we are dealing with enforcement of a set of directly applicable rules in a multi-layer context: the different levels of enforcement complement each other but also reinforce each other: the procedures in front of the Commission, the authorities and the courts each have specific features but they all have the power to establish infringements by individuals to EU competition rules and to sanction such an infringement in some way or another. In other words, enforcement of EU competition rules (Articles 101 and 102 TFEU) is not solely in the hands of the national judge; he or she is much less the *premier juge communautaire* in that sense.[481]

---

479 Council Regulation (EC) No 1/2003/EC on the implementation of the rules on competition laid down in Articles 81 and 82 of the Treaty [2003] OJ L1/1. For an analysis of the network based ECN enforcement model from a governance perspective, see M. de Visser, *Network-based governance in EC law* (Oxford: Hart Publishing, 2009); on the background of the reform and its impact: C. Ehlermann, 'The modernisation of EC antitrust policy: a legal and cultural revolution' (2000) 37 *Common Market Law Review* 537.

480 More and more observers have since then rightly pointed out that the so-called decentralisation also carries in it a number of centralising elements giving the Commission a more prominent role than ever in determining competition policy. This is in fact already clear from the text of the regulation itself; recital 34 is striking in that respect: "*The principles laid down in Articles 81 and 82 of the Treaty, as they have been applied by Reg. 17, have given a central role to the Union bodies. This central role should be retained, whilst associating the Member States more closely with the application of Union competition rules.* "

481 According to recital 7 of Reg. 1/2003 the role of the national courts complements that of the competition authorities of the Member States when deciding disputes between private individuals. The complementary character here refers mostly to the fact that one of the main differences of private and public enforcement is that the judge can *also* protect subjective rights and award damages, something competition authorities, acting in the public interest, can generally not do.

2.2 Convergence mechanisms

The terms convergence and harmonisation can cover a variety of situations. Convergence is used here to qualify a relatively spontaneous process, stimulated by various forms of cooperation between the Member States and with the Union institutions. Convergence can be triggered by direct or indirect pressure but it is not so much a directed process.

In this area specifically, convergence at a procedural level is stimulated by the similarity of the material rules that are being enforced: the prohibition on cartels and abuse of dominant position, the control on concentrations. This similarity enhances spontaneous convergence due to the interaction between substance and procedure.[482]

For the sake of this contribution, harmonisation refers to a process which is more directed and follows an intervention either by the Courts formulating legal principles that are binding on Member States, or an intervention by the legislator. In other words, the term is used in a broader way than the strict legal definition which refers to a particular instrument of legislation designed and used at the level of the European Union, following specific procedures that are laid down in the treaties.

It is clear that defined in this way, the difference between harmonisation and convergence is nuanced. The two terms are used especially to indicate the difference in origin of the process and the degree of spontaneity: convergence is a “bottom up” process, whereas, harmonisation is a “top down” process: the origin might be legislation but also other explicit initiatives taken at the European level, e.g. by the Commission, or by judgment rendered by the Courts. The “bottom up” aspect of convergence is what possibly differentiates this development from convergence in other areas such as for example in civil law where there can be a horizontal movement,[483] bringing the law of Member States closer together but without going towards an existing model (see below, this is different in competition law, 2.2.1).

Two related mechanisms of convergence specific to competition shall be briefly discussed: convergence towards the Commission model of enforcement and convergence due to the existence and the activities of the ECN network. Both are reinforced by the fact that the Member States made a

---

482 Gerbrandy, *Convergentie in het mededingingsrecht* (above n 413), containing a detailed study of convergence in Dutch administrative law in the area of competition law; also in her article cited in note 452 on the way towards a procedural ius commune.

483 On the attempts to develop a ius commune, often based on a comparative approach searching for underlying common or general principles, Gerbrandy, *Convergentie in het mededingingsrecht* (above n 419) and Tulibacka, ‘Europeanization of civil procedures’ (above n 416).

choice to align their national substantive law to EU law, which then often supposes the support for maximal convergence in practice.[484]

2.2.1 Convergence as a result of the specific role of the Commission

As it was said above, the area of competition law is one of the few areas where enforcement is not left entirely to the legal systems of the Member States but where the Commission itself has important operational powers.[485] In fact, the Commission is the most important enforcer of competition rules in the EU, even more so since decentralisation. Enforcement is based on parallel competences of the Commission, the national judges and the national authorities but the features of the system are such that the Commission not only takes the lead in high profile cases but also supervises national enforcement.

From this perspective, competition law enforcement was, from the beginning, an exception to the general enforcement framework in Union law, which was based on decentralized enforcement. Procedural autonomy was not the (only) standard for the organization of enforcement. Apart from the national judge who was under the same obligations to ensure direct effect and effectiveness as in other areas, there was a central enforcement body with its own set of procedural rules.[486] The division of competences in this area of law is different in terms of enforcement and now also clearly specific in terms of competences: reference is made to Article 3 TFEU: competition law has been included in the (short) list of exclusive competences of the Union. This exclusive competence can be seen to reinforce the role of the Commission.

The tendency of national systems to converge towards the enforcement model of the Commission's procedures then seems logical and natural. There is usually an explicit choice on behalf of the national legislator not only to adopt a national competition law similar or identical to the relevant EU provisions, but often also a desire to align the further interpretation and enforcement of the national law to the EU practice. The result is often convergence of national institutional structures and procedural rules going towards the "Commission model". This can be through adoption of national legislation, or by way of case-law of the national courts, who, when in doubt, interpret national rules in line of the EU enforcement system.

---

484 On the explicit choice of the Dutch legislator to align its law, its interpretation and application to the EU model, see Gerbrandy, *Convergentie in het mededingingsrecht* (above n 413); also F. Vogelaar on the margin that remains for national rules or policy, 'Interface: EC and Dutch competition law', in D. Obradovic and N. Lavranos *Interface between EU law and national law* (above n 422) [187-201].

485 The term operational powers is taken from J.A.E. Vervaele, *The Europeanisation of Criminal law and the Criminal law dimension of European integration*, research paper (College of Europe, 2005, Brussels) accessible via http://www.coleurop.be/template.asp?pagename=lawpapers (accessed on 1 March 2010).

486 See M. Tulibacka, 'Europeanization of civil procedures' (above n 414).

2.2.2 Convergence through the network of competition authorities

One of the great novelties of Reg.1/2003 was the creation of the ECN network. It is in itself a very important source of convergence. The mere fact of the existence of the network and the exchanges between authorities it implies, is already a trigger for convergence.[487]

Attention is drawn specifically also to more explicit "quasi legislative" initiatives taken in this respect. The ECN model program for leniency is the best example.[488] The work inside the network creates involvement of the Member States, but of course in a specific way: the Member States are represented by their competition authorities, even though in some cases the government is involved directly or indirectly. The work is carried out without the involvement of the Union legislator, or the national legislators. These last institutions might be involved in a later stage if and when an initiative to change the (formal) national legislation is necessary as a consequence of the work done inside ECN.

2.3 Harmonisation mechanisms

In the enforcement system of competition law as it stands today, there are a number of different mechanisms of harmonisation that can be identified and that should not be underestimated. Judicial harmonisation is briefly situated first and is of course not unique to competition law; secondly some remarks shall be made about the harmonising effects of Regulation 1/2003.

2.3.1 Judicial harmonisation: different forms and different actors

Judicial harmonisation of procedural law takes place by way of case law. A perhaps less controversial term for the same phenomenon would be the regulating effect of the Courts case law.[489] In this particular context, this case-law does not only originate in the ECJ in Luxemburg but there is

---

[487] See M. de Visser, *Network-based governance in EC law* (above n 479), on the network also the thorough study by S. Brammer, *Cooperation between national competition agencies in the enforcement of EC competition law* (Oxford: Hart Publishing, 2009).

[488] The model program was designed within the network, then published, and after a few years an evaluation was recently carried out to measure the degree of convergence, see for status, DG Comp website: http://ec.europa.eu/competition/ecn/documents.html (accessed on 1 March 2010). It was no surprise that many Member States chose not only to adopt a form of leniency containing similar if not identical terms as the model program but that also many chose to use the format also used by the Commission, namely soft law (notice, communications etc.). The model program was drafted in such a way that it could just be copied and translated.

[489] This term is used by J. Vervaele, *The Europeanisation of Criminal law* (above n 485).

definitely also the influence of the ECHR and its judgments in the area of fair trial and due process.[490] Some categories shall be distinguished very briefly.

First of all, there is the case-law of the ECJ based on effectiveness, discussed briefly above (sections 1.2. and 1.3). This case-law has had an effect both on institutional aspects as well as on actual procedural rules, especially regarding access to court and remedies, but also time-delays and jurisdiction, the obligation to raise arguments ex officio etc.[491]

A clear example of the case-law based on effectiveness is related to sanctions. In an area like competition law where fines can be very substantial, this case-law is crucial so it will be discussed a bit further. When it comes to sanctions, the Courts general case-law on effectiveness, provides for broad principles: sanctions for infringement of Union law should be effective, dissuasive and proportionate.[492] In the context of public enforcement, there is no doubt that these general principles have been incorporated into the practice of the Commission and endorsed in the General Court's (formerly the Court of First Instance) and the ECJ's case-law on fines.[493] Moreover, even if certain Member States have not yet adopted specific guidelines for the calculation of fines, the requirements of "effective, dissuasive and proportionate" sanctions will usually be applied by national authorities. If they are not laid down in legislation, guidelines or national soft law equivalents, they simply apply by way of the case-law of the EU Courts. This is one of the clearest examples of the judicial harmonisation.

There is an additional reason why the case-law of the CJEU has considerable impact in the area of sanctions. Whilst sometimes leaving quite some margin to the Commission in terms of its substantive analysis of a restrictive practice, the Courts use their full jurisdiction when it comes to fines (Article 261 TFEU) and there is substantial case-law on fining practices, especially at

[490] Van Gerven distinguishes europeanization and communautarization of procedural law; the first including the influence of the ECHR and the Strasbourg jurisprudence in that respect; Van Gerven, 'Bridging the gap' (above n 416).

[491] In the pending case VEBIC, ECJ case C-439/08, *VEBIC*, a Belgian preliminary reference concerning the role of the NCA in appeal proceedings, OJ 2008, C 313/19, institutional autonomy is at stake: the ECJ shall have to decide how far the application of the principle of effectiveness can lead.

[492] See Prechal, 'EC requirements for an effective remedy' (above n 416); see also ECJ cases C-387/02, C-391/02 and C-403/02, *Berlusconi* [2008] ECR I-3565, where the Court discussed the principle of the retroactive application of the more lenient penalty. The principle having been consecrated as a general principle of EU law, is thus part of the legal rules applying, in a uniform way, to all authorities fining an infringement of Articles 101 and 102 TFEU.

[493] See the most recent guidelines on the calculation of fines: Commission Guidelines on the method of setting fines imposed pursuant to Article 23(2)(a) of Regulation [2006] OJ C 210/2; extensive case-law on fines in the last years at the level of the CFI confirming these principles, some references in section 3.5 of the guidelines.

the level of the General Court.[494] Combined with the voluntary convergence of the Member States to follow the European model discussed above, this case-law can have harmonising effects.

It is self-evident however, that broadly formulated principles set the scene for the calculation of fines and are binding both on national judges and on competition authorities but are not capable by themselves to create sufficient transparency on the method of calculation, all the different factors to take into account and the final result. Therefore these examples show the impact of the Courts case-law but also its limits. In practice, there appear to be substantial differences amongst Member States, both in terms of methods of calculation and procedure, as well as in terms of the actual result, the actual fine.[495]

The case-law of the Courts has also had a substantial impact on national procedural law, on the basis of the right to effective judicial protection. The subjects include the rights of complainants, the right of access to file, the right to a hearing, the duty to motivate etc.[496] The harmonising effect of these principles is inevitable and comes from cumulated sources of law: national law, the ECHR, EU law.[497] This is again a strong example of judicial harmonisation. Large parts of procedural rules have been harmonised without any formal harmonisation taking place.

Last but not least, attention should be drawn to the case-law emphasizing consistency and uniform application of EU law, and more specifically the

---

[494] See for some important recent cases at the level of the General Court: T-174/05, *Elf Aquitane* not yet reported, on the same day: T-175/05, *Akzo Nobel* and *Arkema,* not yet published: in all these cases the role of fundamental rights and principles developed in the case-law is very clear; (more rare) a judgment of the ECJ: ECJ Cases C-322/07 P, C-327/07 P and C-338/07 P, *Bolloré and others* not yet reported.

[495] This point is elaborated because the subject of sanctions is one of the most important subjects of divergence identified in the reports on Reg. 1 for further convergence or harmonisation, see below in section 2.4.

[496] It would lead to far in this article to give an extensive overview of the vast amount of case law, reference is made to overview of antitrust procedure in: L. Ortiz Branco, *EC competition procedure* (Oxford: OUP, 2006), C. Kerse and N. Khan, *EC antitrust procedure* (London: Sweet & Maxwell, 2005).

[497] Access to the investigation file for the plaintiff (subject of the investigation) is an example: derived from Article 6 ECHR, recognized in the case-law of the European Courts, laid down in guidelines of the Commission and now consolidated in Reg. 1/2003 and following regulations (more specifically Commission Regulation (EC) No 773/2004 of 7 April 2004 relating to the conduct of proceedings by the Commission pursuant to Articles 81 and 82 of the EC Treaty [2004] OJ L 123/18). Procedural law in the 27 Member States and at the EU level contain the same rule. Only the technicalities of the access might still be different. This example also shows the links between competition law and other areas of law where the rights of plaintiffs shall be construed on the basis of the same case law, such as for example criminal law. On this point, overview by Kerse and Khan, *EC Antitrust procedure* (above n 496) [214].

obligation for courts and authorities to interpret their procedural law in conformity with EU law as much as they possibly can when they are dealing with the application of EU law: this is a powerful mechanism which can be at the basis of the movement towards convergence described under 2.2.[498]

2.3.2 Harmonisation by legislation: Reg.1

Whether or not the term harmonisation is appropriate when a regulation is used, it is clear that Regulation 1/2003 itself contains a number of provisions that can be considered equivalent to harmonisation measures, in the sense that national laws are approximated, or rather, even uniformized. Disputes about the implementation like in the context of directives are avoided; the harmonising effect is stronger because regulations are binding in their entirety and transposition measures are not required.

If we turn now to the two key concepts analyzed above in part 1, Regulation 1/2003 contains frequent direct or indirect references to effectiveness, but no explicit mention of procedural autonomy. There is however a statement in rec. 34 referring to subsidiarity and proportionality: "... *this regulation does not beyond what is necessary in order to achieve its objective, which to allow the Community competition rules to be applied effectively*".

There are a few examples of references to the Member States competence in the area of procedure but not many. The clearest and most explicit, reference is, interestingly, related to the institutional structure of the national competition authorities.[499] In recital 35 of the regulation:

> "*In order to attain a proper enforcement of Community competition law, Member States should designate and empower authorities to apply Articles 81 and 82 of the Treaty as public enforcers. They should be able to designate administrative as well as judicial authorities to carry out the various functions conferred upon competition authorities in this regulation. This regulation recognises the wide variation which exists in the public enforcement systems of the Member States. ...*"

This phrase acknowledges institutional divergence ("recognizes") but not more than that. It is not a statement recalling procedural autonomy; it expresses more an acknowledgment of a factual situation which can be the subject of further evolution. The underlying assumption at the time of the adoption of the regulation that naturally more convergence would occur in

---

498 The message coming from the EU Court that EU-conform interpretation is a general obligation under EU law, can reinforce legislators, courts and authorities in their 'spontaneous' will to converge, and in the same movement procedure in national cases, can be influenced.

499 The idea was already expressed above that there is more reluctance to interfere with institutional autonomy than with procedural autonomy. On this distinction, Kakouris, note 416 above.

this respect, is now confirmed by the reports of the Commission on the functioning of the regulation (see under the next session).[500]

There are a number of provisions in the regulation that directly or indirectly touch on national procedures. Three different examples shall be given: it is not an exhaustive overview but the examples are chosen because they each illustrate a different type of intervention in national procedural law.

First, Article 2 of Reg. 1/2003 which lays down a rule on the burden of proof. It is clearly formulated as a rule that should apply in any proceedings related to Articles 101 TFEU and 102 TFEU, be it before the courts, before national competition authorities, in a Commission investigation or before the Union courts.[501] Such an explicit rule of procedure formulating a basic principle which impacts the whole course of proceedings, is remarkable.[502]Although it is difficult to reconstruct the discussions about this, it is likely that this article was fairly uncontroversial because the rule it formulates is a long established one in Union law and in the majority, if not all, legal systems of the Member States (actori incumbit probatio). Therefore it merely consolidates a pre-existing rule "common to the traditions of all Member States". Also, because it is a pre-existing rule, most Member States will not have felt it was necessary to take measures for modifying theirs laws to incorporate it. Nevertheless, as a precedent of pure and simple harmonisation of procedural law its importance cannot be underestimated.

---

500 This assumption at the time of the regulation that convergence of procedural laws was to occur, appears clearly from the discussions at the EUI conference of 2002: proceedings published in C. Ehlermann and I. Atanasiu (eds) *European Competition Law Annual 2002: Constructing the EU Network of Competition Authorities* (Oxford: Hart Publishing, 2004); see the contribution of C. Gauer, 'Does effectiveness of the EU network of competition authorities require a certain degree of harmonisation of national procedures and sanctions?', also a noted call for convergence from the Economic and Social Committee in its opinion, Opinion of the Economic and Social Committee on the 'Proposal for a Council Regulation on the implementation of the rules on competition laid down in Articles 81 and 82 of the Treaty and amending Regulations (EEC) No 1017/68, (EEC) No 2988/74, (EEC) No 4056/86 and (EEC) No 3975/87 ("Regulation implementing Articles 81 and 82 of the Treaty") [2001] OJ 155/73; F. Vogelaar observes a conscious choice of the Community institutions to have no top down harmonisation but to wait for a bottom up approximation of the laws (above n 484).

501 Article 2 reads as follows: *In any national or Community proceedings for the application of Articles 81 and 82 of the Treaty, the burden of proving an infringement of Article 81(1) or of Article 82 of the Treaty shall rest on the party or the authority alleging the infringement.* The burden of proof is then reversed for the exception of Article 81(3): *The undertaking or association of undertakings claiming the benefit of Article 81(3) of the Treaty shall bear the burden of proving that the conditions of that paragraph are met.*

502 Reference should be made again here to the relationship between substance and procedure; it is far from clear that the rule on the burden of proof is only a rule of procedure, see also: L. Parret, 'Sense and nonsense of rules on proof in cartel cases' (2008) 4 *European Competition Journal* 169.

Another instance where the regulation intervenes in procedural law in a direct way is by the creation of the amicus curiae system. On the basis of Article 15 of the Regulation, the Commission, and national authorities can intervene in proceedings before national courts.[503] This system again implies both consequences for the procedural rules governing private enforcement (how and when can they intervene) as well as for the rules on public enforcement (how and when does the national authority intervene).[504]

Thirdly, Article 16 of the regulation can be cited: both national judges as well as national competition authorities, are obliged to ensure that do not take decisions that are contrary to a decision taken by the Commission on the same facts. The obligation to avoid conflicting decisions is justified by reference to the principles of legal certainty and uniform application of Union law.[505] This provision can have serious procedural implications. For example, it might require setting aside important rules of procedure (be it for the judge or authority) to avoid giving a decision or to stay proceedings. In most legal systems, it is hardly imaginable that a court would refuse to render a decision on the merits when it has been asked to do so by a claimant. For an authority, it might also sometimes be questionable whether the mere fact that the Commission has taken a decision would be sufficient statement of reasons for its own decision.

These three examples each show, in three different ways, how the regulation has an impact on national procedural law. The first (burden of proof) by regulating directly and imposing a specific rule which does not require further implementation; the second (amicus curiae) by creating a specific procedural modality, new to most legal systems and most probably requiring modifications of national law to make the effective application possible;[506] the third (avoiding conflicting decisions) is the most vague in terms of its procedural implications but has the potential to conflict with existing procedural rules both for courts or for authorities, as the examples above indicate.

We can finally further illustrate this by one more remarkable example in the regulation. Article 3 §2 basically states that the application of national

---

503 The possibility for a national court to ask the Commissions assistance is also confirmed but already existed and was promoted by a Commission Notice on cooperation between national courts and the Commission in applying Articles 85 and 86 of the EEC Treaty of 1993 [1993] OJ C 39/6, now replaced by a new Commission Notice on the cooperation between the Commission and the courts of the EU Member States in the application of Articles 81 and 82 EC [2004] OJ (2004) C 101/04. The possibility to ask for assistance is much less radical in terms of interference with procedural law because it is up to the court to assess the possibility, the necessity and the modalities to do so.

504 The Commission declared from the beginning that it would make scarce use of this possibility, perhaps also because of the controversial nature of it.

505 Recital 22 of the regulation.

506 Or alternatively requiring the judge to set aside any procedural rule hindering an amicus curiae intervention on the basis of effectiveness?

competition law cannot lead to a different result than the application of the corresponding EU provisions. Although strictly speaking this provision only concerns the result/outcome of a case, it seems to be given a much broader meaning. It is significant that the Commission itself calls it the "convergence rule", the idea being that not only the result should be similar but the reasoning leading to the result and the modalities of application should be consistent.[507] According to the Commission in its Communication, this is a question of primacy of European law. If that were the case, it seems that there is hardly any margin left for differences between national and EU law enforcement.

2.4 The current situation and the call for more convergence

The purpose of the previous sections (2.2 and 2.3) was not to give a detailed overview of which provisions are more or less harmonised[508] but to show the variety of mechanisms that have an impact on the enforcement of EU competition rules today. Some of these mechanisms exist in various forms in all areas of EU law (judicial harmonisation by the Courts for example), others are more typical for competition law (the various forms of convergence related to the role of the Commission and the network).

As it was provided for by the regulation itself, the Commission undertook a first evaluation of the application of Reg.1/2003 and prepared reports for the Council and the European Parliament.[509] There is a strong emphasis on institutional and procedural convergence in the reports, even implying that convergence of procedures was the objective of the regulation.

First, when it comes to the institutional framework for the implementation of EU competition rules, the Commission notes that although the regulation does not compel Member States to adopt a specific framework and "accomodates diversity", many Member States have reinforced or reviewed their enforcement structures to "optimise their effectiveness".[510]

---

[507] Report Reg. 1/2003, cited below, par 156 is remarkable and perhaps partly more wishful thinking than entirely in line with the case-law described above. According to the Commission, conduct to which Article 101 TFEU is not applicable, cannot be forbidden by national law; but if EU law is not applicable, how exactly can primacy come into play?...

[508] This type of comparative study would be very comprehensive but immensely useful in view of further harmonisation; some work will be done within ECN and by the Commission, as announced in the reports.

[509] Commission (EC) 'Report on the functioning of Regulation 1/2003' (Communication) COM (2009) 206 final, 29 April 2009 and the Commission (EC) 'Communication from the Commission to the European Parliament and Council. Report on the functioning of Regulation 1/2003' (Staff Working Paper) SEC (2009) 574.

[510] Communication (n 509 above) [33-35]. This is further substantiated in the Staff Working paper, Chapter 5.1.2. entitled Evolving Structure of National Competition Authorities (above n 509) [58].

Again, there is no mention of procedural autonomy as a principle to be protected as such. It is emphasized that in five years there has been a significant degree of evolution in enforcement structures with a movement to a system of one administrative authority investigating and deciding cases, in other words a system that resembles the Commission model.[511] It is interesting to note that, apparently, the differences in institutional structure of the national competition authorities have not raised any particular issues in the application of Articles 101 and 102 TFEU.[512] In other words, the (remaining) institutional divergence is not identified as a major problem.

Secondly, when it comes to procedural rules, the reports start by qualifying the system set up by Reg. 1 as one where (pre-existing) substantive coherence is reconciled with procedural divergence and all in all the system is considered a success.[513] Just as in the case of the institutional framework, the Commission then emphasises the "unprecedented degree of voluntary convergence" that has occurred.[514] The tone is different here when divergence is discussed. A number of subjects of divergence are identified as subjects for further examination and reflection.[515] Subjects mentioned include[516] fines, criminal sanctions, liability of undertakings or associations, succession of undertakings, prescription periods, standard of proof, types of decisions and the possibility to set priorities. According to the Commission stakeholders have placed a "strong call for further harmonisation of procedures in the ECN".[517] In particular, different rules on sanctions seem to be an important source of concern, and in addition to the list mentioned above, other procedural subjects such as deadlines and the admissibility of evidence are mentioned.

It appears from the above that the reports definitely seem to be more careful in their wording when it comes to institutional divergence/convergence than when it comes to procedural rules. Where these last rules are concerned, the Commission clearly announces that work will be undertaken in the ECN to explore how further convergence can be promoted and in which areas.

---

511 Par. 193 for an overview of the Member States and their current systems. In par. 54 the Commission explicitly states that the majority of the Member States have chosen the Commission model.

512 The Commission does refer to the case of VEBIC, case C-439/08 (above n 481).

513 Communication (above n 509) [31], Staff Working Paper (above n 509) [200].

514 Overview in Staff Working Paper (above n 509) [202]. Examples include leniency practice where convergence was stimulated by the ECN Model program, the introduction of inspections in private premises, sector enquiries and commitment decisions.

515 Communication (above n 509) [33], Staff Working Paper (above n 509) [200]. The Staff Working Paper indicates that the still existing divergences should not be underestimated and concern important procedural issues that may influence the outcome of individual cases.

516 Staff Working Paper (above n 509) [203-207].

517 Id. [206].

3. The question of further harmonisation

The analysis of the relevance of the principles of procedural autonomy and effectiveness (section 1) and the description of some of the particularities of the existing system of enforcement of competition law (section 2) are intended as a contribution to the debate on whether or not further harmonisation of procedural competition law should be undertaken and if so, how. Based on these two parts, the question of further harmonisation of procedure (or enforcement rules) shall now be adressed. The following subquestions shall be briefly introduced: is harmonisation is actually required by virtue of the principle of effectiveness (3.1); is such harmonisation desirable (3.2); if so, would there be a legal basis for such harmonisation (3.3) and, finally by way of conclusion, if it is undertaken how should it be done and which are the essential issues that should be addressed (3.4). The current situation is a particular one, simplifying somewhat: substantive EU and national law are identical and national procedural law has undergone considerable influence through various European mechanisms of convergence and harmonisation: these mechanisms are interrelated and they reinforce each other.

3.1 Does effectiveness require harmonisation in a legal sense?

If one presupposes that a solid legal basis could be found for harmonisation by Union legislation (see section 3.3. below), the question is whether effectiveness requires such a harmonisation.

Eilmansberger argues that there are no general principles of law that require the creation of specific legal remedies.[518] Is this reasoning valid in general for procedural rules? It was carefully suggested above that in any case effectiveness does not require uniformity or even convergence as such (above under section 1.3.3); some examples from the area of competition law were given. The answer therefore to the question whether further harmonisation is legally required is that, although the effectiveness of Union law might be endangered in one or the other specific national case by the application of a specific rule, it is far from evident that the principle requires that procedural law in the Member States be (further) harmonized. Arguments based on effectiveness are often made in competition circles but it is submitted that they require careful (re-)consideration. It is not a given fact that the current level of procedural divergence endangers the principle of effectiveness as it has been developed in the case-law so far.

---

518 Eilmansberger, 'The relationship between rights and remedies in EC law' (above n 421): he mentions consistency, uniformity, loyalty, effectiveness.

3.2 Is harmonisation otherwise necessary or desirable?

It follows from the above that the starting point for answering this question is the following. The scope for harmonisation is determined by the different mechanisms of convergence and harmonisation described above in section 2. Otherwise resumed: the primacy of EU law (e.g. for the subjects regulated in Reg. 1/2003, see section 2.3.2), the harmonising effects of the case-law (section 2.3.1) and the more or less spontaneous convergence mechanisms (section 2.2), shall determine how much scope is left for harmonisation by legislation.

The first consideration here is a very pragmatic one: further harmonisation simply seems to be the continuation of a natural process. As it was described above, the adoption and the recent evaluation of Reg. 1/2003 demonstrate this: the remaining subjects of divergence seem now to be the few exceptions to the rule (in terms of quantity) and they might as well be taken away. The tendency towards convergence is so strong that it also seems almost counterintuitive to put a halt to this development.

Harmonisation not only seems natural (in which ever form) but can indeed also be desirable from a viewpoint of equality and equivalence, effective enforcement, and consistency and coherence of EU and national law.

We should be sensitive to the fact that in this area of law, the legal subjects (the undertakings concerned) are subject to sanctions, both at the EU level and at the level of the 27 Member States. In other words, there is enforcement at different levels, possibly simultaneously, also at the level of the courts including possible damage claims. In an environment where undertakings are subject to important sanctions, in some Member States even criminal sanctions, procedural divergence can be more problematic than in other areas of law.

This is reinforced, again, by the fact that the substantive rules that are applied are very similar, if not almost identical when the different levels of enforcement are compared. More so, the difference between cases where Articles 101 and 102 TFEU are applied, and those where only national law shall be applied, is hardly perceivable for the individual undertakings. For the acceptance and the credibility of the system, this can make procedural divergence more problematic from the viewpoint of the individual legal subject.[519] For the sake of equality and equivalence (see above in section 1.3.3), there is a case to be made for further harmonisation aiming specifically at the remaining procedural divergence affecting legal subjects.

519 Reg. 1/2003 (above n 479) recognizes that the difference in the type of sanctions can modulate procedure, see for example in Article 12 §3 where it is said that exchange of information between authorities is only possible if the legal protection of the undertaking is similar in both jurisdictions.

In extension, in terms of consistency and from a viewpoint of efficient enforcement, cooperation within the network and with the Commission can be optimalized if rules are brought even closer together. It makes sense to minimalize the impact of different procedural rules in different jurisdictions and to give all authorities the same tools. A broad concept of effectiveness was proposed in section 1.3 above. Such a concept includes effective enforcement and efficiency. From that perspective, even though effectiveness was said not to strictly require harmonisation, it can be an objective to strive for.

Finally, related to the need for consistency which protects both the individuals legal position and the effectiveness of the enforcement system as such, is the need for coherence. Internal coherence within the system of competition enforcement is the most obvious and most discussed: between the EU and the national systems of competition law and amongst national systems. However, there is also external coherence: even though it has specific features, enforcement of competition law should not be isolated from other areas of EU law. There are already considerable links to other areas of law, for example through the process of judicial harmonisation described above. This need for coherence also becomes apparent in private enforcement: interaction with (general) procedural law and other types of legal rules may be applicable in the same case (contract law, tort law etc). Private enforcement and public enforcement are partly alternative routes to achieve the same result, namely establishing an infringement of competition rules, and in terms of coherence it is not optimal that the procedural context be too different.

3.3 Would there be a legal basis?

The present analysis would not be complete without briefly addressing the question of legal basis. Before doing so, it is recalled (see above under 2.2.1 and on competences under 1.2.2) that since the Lisbon Treaty, the establishment of competition rules is one of the areas of exclusive competence mentioned in Article 3 TFEU. This means, according to Article 5 (3) TEU, that the principle of subsidiarity does not come into play here as long as the EU measures are in line with the description of the exclusive area of competence. This development can also be seen as a reinforcement of the EU level of enforcement, and of the particular situation of competition law. The exclusive nature of the competence might have an impact on any future discussion on the possible legal basis for harmonisation.[520]

[520] Reference is made to the Courts judgment in Commission/Council, cited above in note 39: if the competence is exclusive, does it mean that the competence to harmonise procedure shall be more easily assumed (implied powers)? See also Eilmansberger, 'The Green Paper on damage actions for breach of the EC antitrust rules and beyond' (above n 413) on the legal basis for the Commission plans to take legislative initiatives in the area of private enforcement.

A distinction can be made between a specific legal basis and general legal basis.[521] The most obvious specific legal basis would seem to be Article 103 TFEU (former Article 83 EC). This provision allows for Council regulations or directives to give effect to the principles set out in Articles 101 and 102 (former 81 and 82 EC).

The subjects of the regulations mentioned in Article 103 TFEU however seem to be limited by the Treaty text: reference is made ("in particular") to the enforcement and policy at the European level, in other words at the level where the Commission operates. Article 103 TFEU refers to compliance, detailed rules for the application of 101(3) (former 81 (3)) as well as defining the scope of application of the prohibitions in Articles 101 and 102 as well as the respective functions of the Commission and the European courts. Also, reference is made to the relationship between national laws and the competition provisions of the Treaty.[522] This provision was used as a legal basis for Reg. 1/2003 discussed above.

Harmonising national law, even in cases where there is interstate effect, does not seem to fall within the subjects described in the treaty provision. However, it has been argued that, certainly given the evolution towards shared enforcement with the national competition authorities, that this provision could serve as a basis to lay down a common procedure for the enforcement of Articles 101 and 102 TFEU.[523]

In any case, the use of this provision as a legal basis shall be limited to the application of the EU antitrust provisions and limited to the enforcement by authorities, rather than also covering private enforcement in courts.[524] Such a measure might very well also result in spillover effects in to the law applicable in "national cases", given the convergence mechanisms already in place and described above. In fact, the desired result might be to harmonize national law in a more general way; the likeliness that this shall be the effect is significant given the advantages of consistency between enforcement in purely national cases and cases involving interstate effect dealt with by the same authorities.

---

521 W. van Gerven, 'Over codificatie, convergentie en algemene beginselen in een meergelaagd privaatrecht' (2008) 56 *SEW: Tijdschrift voor Europees en Economisch Recht* 414.

522 A) to E) of Article 103 TEU (unchanged since the first text of the EEC Treaty).

523 See S. Brammer, *Cooperation between national competition agencies* (above n 487). If the form of a directive is chosen, the result of the harmonisation in terms of remaining divergence will depend very much on the type of harmonisation as well as on the way the directive is implemented in the Member States. The use of this legal basis for Reg. 1/2003 without formal opposition from institutions or Member States is a relevant precedent. According to Eilmansberger the list of subjects in Article 103 (former 83) is not exhaustive: Eilmansberger, 'The Green Paper on damage actions for breach of the EC antitrust rules and beyond' (above n 413).

524 For matters concerning private enforcement, Article 81 TFEU (65 EC) dealing with judicial cooperation in civil matters, is an option.

The specific legal basis might be supplemented by the flexibility clause of Article 352 TFEU which allows for measures to be adopted if they are necessary for the attainment of the objectives of the Treaties. A combination of legal basis in this way was used to adopt the merger regulation but the downside is that its use requires unanimity.[525]

A so-called general legal basis could be considered a safer option and one that might allow also to cover a wider scope of rules such as procedure relating to courts. The most obvious provision would then be Article 114 TFEU (former Article 95 EC) which allows for measures for the approximating of national laws which have their object the establishment of the internal market as described in Article 26 TFEU.[526] But here again, the interstate aspect can be an obstacle. The current state of competition law allows for some cases that are seemingly national to be construed as having interstate effect in order to fall within the scope of application of the EU competition rules, but nevertheless there are still real national, regional or local cases of course, to which national competition law is applied. The link with the internal market referred to in Article 114 TFEU will then be difficult to argue.[527] The use of this article would require the willingness of the Member States, supported at the EU level, to go beyond rules applicable to cross-border situations. This route seems less adequate than the use of the competition-specific provisions mentioned above.

The question of legal basis deserves a more thorough examination but is not the purpose of this article. It should not be an obstacle based on the very brief examination above. The difficulty of finding a solid legal basis shall depend very much on the scope of the harmonisation that is undertaken.[528] In a way it might be argued that in competition law, there are so many mechanisms in play that have led to harmonisation and convergence, that it might seem unnecessarily burdensome to embark in formal harmonisation. Using (more) soft law instruments might lead the way to more "spontaneous

---

[525] Council Regulation (EC) No 139/2004 of 20 January 2004 on the control of concentrations between undertakings (the EC Merger Regulation) [2004] OJ L 24/1. There is a little point of doubt: competition is no longer mentioned as an objective of the Union (Article 3 TEU) but only appears in an indirect way through the reference to the internal market and Protocol 27. Apart from that, it seems that the scope of this clause is larger than before (wording of Article 352 TFEU as opposed to 308 EC).

[526] This article was used for the directive on the enforcement of IP rights, which is said to clearly have an impact on cases of a domestic nature, comments in M. Tulibacka, 'Europeanization of civil procedures' (above n 414).

[527] See S. Brammer, *Cooperation between national competition agencies* (above n 487).

[528] There is the aspect of the presence of cross border effects, discussed in this section but also the combination of procedure in public enforcement and in private enforcement: it seems unlikely that both could be covered by the same harmonisation measures in view of this brief overview of legal basis, see note 521 above also. The difficulties that have occurred in materializing the plans on actions for damages at the EU level also illustrated how difficult especially harmonisation of aspects of private enforcement shall be (above n 413).

convergence" and that might simply be sufficient. On the other hand, the counterarguments for such a way forward are democratic legitimacy, the institutional balance, the division of competences between the EU and Member States and e.g. the fact that further harmonisation of procedure would have implications far beyond competition enforcement and should involve more stakeholders than only competition authorities. It is clear from the broader EU perspective[529] that a correct implementation of the division of competences between the EU and its Member States and the involvement of national parliaments are precisely considerations that are of concern in the post Lisbon era.

3.4 By way of conclusion: defining the issues

The following remarks draw on the analysis above, contain some conclusions whilst defining at the same time the issues which could or should be the subject of further research.

(1) Procedural autonomy is not an obstacle to further harmonisation and, in the present state of the law, effectiveness of EU law cannot be said to require it.

Procedural autonomy has but limited value as an argument for those who oppose further harmonisation. The strong convergence and harmonisation trends already present in the public enforcement system of competition law reinforce the pressure that the principle of procedural autonomy already encounters in general. At the same time, effectiveness should not be overrated in the present state of the law.

(2) Further harmonisation would be a natural development and it can have its benefits especially in terms of consistency and coherence of EU law.

There is no urgent need for harmonisation measures, nor is there a stringent legal requirement to undertake them. The question is more whether political, economic and policy considerations require harmonisation of remedies and procedures at this time and if so, in what form.[530] It is argued here that further harmonisation would be a desirable objective to strive for, provided it takes into account a number of important issues both in terms of the object and the method: the five points mentioned here by way of a conclusion attempt to define some of these issues. From a political and policy point of view in the area of competition law, it makes sense that procedure should reflect the unity in substantive law.

Legislative harmonisation would be an interesting experiment in Union law, especially because it would be the end of a process instead of the beginning:

---

529 See above in section 1.2.2 on procedural autonomy and competence; on the role of national parliaments: protocol 1 to the Lisbon treaty.

530 Kilpatrick, 'The future of remedies in Europe' (above n 416).

it would complete a process already well underway through convergence and soft harmonisation and fill in the gaps that remain.

(3) It will only be useful if it addresses the remaining points of divergence which can be perceived as problematic for individuals and/or for the enforcement system.

The objective should be to do away with the remaining sources of divergence between the Member States that are identified as problematic, be it from a legal, a political or economic point of view. The recent reports published by the Commission are a starting point of a stock taking exercise that should allow determining which procedural rules are subject to problematic divergence. A broader EU perspective shows that it cannot be assumed that any divergence is problematic. The preparation of harmonisation will require a clear definition of procedure, in itself already a difficult exercise as was shown above.

(4) It shall have to take various forms to be effective because divergence takes various forms.

Harmonisation of the institutional structures and the procedural rules that authorities apply, will most likely not be able to address the current level of divergence alone. The recent evaluation of Reg. 1 illustrates that the divergence concerns enforcement rules in a broad sense but also exceeds procedure. The area of sanctions (often referred to above and for which the call for harmonisation seems strong) covers procedure, substance and policy, without the boundaries being very clear.

A combination of instruments shall be the right way forward: formal harmonisation with a solid legal basis (for the approximation of actual rules of law) combined with further convergence possibly using soft harmonisation (for policy issues). Judicial harmonisation will continue to develop general principles and from time to time, harmonize a specific aspect of procedure, but it is of course inappropriate to systematically deal with procedural divergence. It is also unpredictable as it evolves mostly at the irregular pace of preliminary ruling cases that are brought by national courts. The particularities of competition enforcement and the high degree of convergence that already exists, most likely also influence the type of legislative harmonisation possible: minimum standards would not make sense for most subjects because they have already been attained.

(5) Spillover effects and external coherence require a comprehensive approach and harmonisation should involve stakeholders.

EU and national competition law and policy are totally intertwined. This does not only complicate the possibilities to use EU instruments of harmonisation in the absence of interstate effect. Also, harmonising procedure in EU competition proceedings at the national level, shall de facto mean harmonising all procedures of public competition enforcement (spillover effects). Competition authorities are well aware of this, but perhaps legislators and policymakers at the national level, do not always realize this particular situation and its consequences for national autonomy.

The network of authorities should not be the only forum where further harmonisation is discussed, especially if it concerns actual procedural rules, that are bound to have either direct or indirect spillover effects into national cases and into private enforcement in the courts. The general strong tendency towards convergence within the network cannot replace the involvement of stakeholders in the Member States and the involvement of the legislator, be it at the EU level (Council, European Parliament) or at the national level (government, parliaments). The need for external coherence argued above, also makes it clear that further harmonisation should be prepared not only in competition circles.

Chapter 7

Side effects of the modernisation of EU competition law

Modernisation as a challenge to the enforcement system of EU competition law and EU law in general

1. Introduction

The different articles brought together in this book all concern the impact of the so-called modernisation on the enforcement system of EU competition law.[531]

Several aspects of the enforcement system are covered. One contribution concerns the impact of modernisation on the legal system as such and focuses on the confusion concerning the objectives that the system aims to achieve.[532] Other articles address issues of competences and applicable law (i.e. the interstate clause[533] and the division of tasks between the national and the EU level[534]) and effective procedures. [535] Finally, this book also deals with issues of proof[536] and adequate judicial protection and access to court.[537]

Recapitulating what has been said on modernisation in most of the preceding chapters, this term covers two aspects: on the one hand, substantive modernisation, meaning (oversimplifying) the introduction of a more economics or an effects-based approach, and, on the other hand, decentralisation based on the structure put into place by Reg. 1/2003, the institutional framework for applying EU competition rules. The bottom line of the decentralisation exercise was to achieve a higher level of involvement of national authorities and national judges in the enforcement of Articles 101 and 102 TFEU. Again oversimplifying, in this final chapter this aspect of

---

531 In all chapters (except perhaps chapter 5 on objectives) the focus is on the cartel prohibition of Article 101 TFEU, but the common thoughts brought together in this chapter take a more general approach and can often apply for both cartels and abuse of dominance cases. The area of merger control is not part of the research covered in this book for two reasons Firstly, because it was not the subject of modernisation as such and secondly because the enforcement of merger control regulations has specific features which distinguish it from the enforcement of Articles 101 and 102 TFEU. Examples are: it is an a priori control system taking a forward-looking approach, whereas competition rules focus on existing behaviour. In addition, the division of competences and the jurisdictional organization are substantively different.

532 Chapter 5.

533 Chapter 3.

534 Chapter 6.

535 Chapter 6.

536 Chapter 5 and 3.

537 Chapter 2.

modernisation will also be referred to as decentralisation. The purpose of this decentralisation was not only to move away from a centralised enforcement system and to allow capacity to be freed at the level of the Commission, but it is assumed also to have been aimed at increasing and enhancing the efficiency and effectiveness of the enforcement system as a whole.[538]

This chapter will set out with a summary of the conclusions drawn in the different articles which are, where appropriate, supplemented with a brief update of relevant developments since the initial publication of the articles/chapters (sub-section 7.2).[539]

Following these summaries and conclusions, the four themes which are present in all or some of the chapters will be highlighted in a horizontal approach in sub-section 7.3. These themes are:

(1) The relationship between competition law and the internal market
(2) Substantive modernisation as a challenge to the enforcement system
(3) Modernisation from an organizational perspective: the complicated relationship between decentralisation, convergence and consistency
(4) Modernisation as a challenge to the system of judicial protection.

The four themes contribute towards an overall coherence between the individual chapters. As it shall appear, these themes overlap to a certain extent, thus reinforcing the interconnection between the different contributions and demonstrating how the themes addressed in the individual chapters build on the same ideas. For every one of these themes, some suggestions and critical remarks for the future shall be formulated.

Finally, in a third, short section of this chapter, a more theoretical issue will be presented as a final roundup (sub-section 7.4). It is present in the background of all of the different articles, but was never (or not yet) the

---

538 The study leading to chapter 6 showed that there is relatively little to be found on the goal of effectiveness that one can presume to be underlying the modernisation process. It was suggested that there is definitely a link between effectiveness and decentralisation, but it is unclear how certain mechanisms in Reg.1/2003 are justified by the goal of effectiveness. It was also suggested that the question of the relationship between effectiveness and effective enforcement is underdeveloped because the focus has been on effective judicial protection. Effectiveness requires both effective enforcement as well as effective judicial protection and yet these can be conflicting values. See chapter 6, e.g. p. 151.

539 As it was indicated in the introduction (chapter 1 above), the different articles are reproduced in the exact form in which they were published. Therefore, they were not updated. The purpose of these conclusions is not to provide for an exhaustive update but some more recent developments can be highlighted, to the extent that it allows to make the common themes more apparent and that it allows to harmonize the different pieces. The updates shall be presented in an as neutral way as possible in the first part, more personal observations will be integrated in the parts that follows (section 3).

actual focus of attention: the relationship and the interaction between substantive law and procedural law. In a way, this issue expresses the overarching single subject of this thesis.

2. Key conclusions of the five chapters and some updates

For every chapter the conclusions shall be recalled below and some more recent relevant developments shall be added, either because they confirm the conclusions drawn in the past or because they shed new light on them.[540]

2.1 Chapter 2: Judicial protection after modernisation

The article in the first chapter addressed modernisation in the sense of decentralisation, from the perspective of judicial protection and access to the court. In European law, the years before the entry into force of Reg. 1/2003 (on 1 May 2004) were characterized by heated debates on a private party's right to access the EU Courts. In particular, there was an upsurge of - mostly - criticism against the restricted access to the courts for individuals in direct appeals, which was at the heart of the Court of First Instance's (now General Court) daring judgment in the famous Jégo Quéré case and the Court of Justice's response in UPA.[541]

The state of the law in relation to an individual's right to have access to the European Courts was considered unsatisfactory by many authors, and rightly so, in view of the development of the principle of judicial protection and the case-law of those Courts which continuously stressed the responsibility of national judges to ensure judicial protection at a national level. The restrictive attitude of the Court of Justice in the area of the admissibility of direct appeals on the one hand, seems in contrast and difficult to reconcile with the pressure on national courts in respect ensuring adequate judicial protection and access to court. Against that background, the novelties brought by Reg. 1/2003 were examined.

The conclusion, in 2005, was that it was exaggerated to state that the new decentralized system of enforcement created by that Regulation, in its own right, caused major issues of judicial protection. However, certain features of the new enforcement system designed by Reg. 1/2003 were considered to add to the pre-existing worries in respect of individual judicial protection. A number of new types of formal and informal Commission decisions were discussed and it was established that it was unclear if these decisions were challengeable in the light of the European Courts' jurisprudence. Amongst others, the increasing use of soft law instruments by the Commission was pinpointed as relevant in that respect. Therefore, some new worries

[540] As Chapters 5 and 6 were written and/or revised more recently, they were not updated.

[541] For a brief overview and references, chapter 2, p. 9 and following.

regarding the level of judicial protection of individuals surfaced as a side effect of modernisation.

Since the publication of this article in 2005, two different developments are worth mentioning briefly. First, the further evolution of the issue of access to courts for individuals in general, both in view of the case-law as well as recent modifications to the EC Treaty (now the Treaty on the Functioning of the EU, hereinafter: TFEU). Secondly, the question should be addressed whether there are any cases that concern those aspects of access to the European court mentioned in the article.

First, in terms of access to the EU Courts, in particular the admissibility requirements for individuals, it is well-known that the Constitutional Treaty which was still cited in the article contained in Chapter 2, never saw the light. However, the Lisbon Treaty has modified the relevant provision on direct appeals for individuals, be it in a different way than was proposed before. The well-known requirement of "direct and individual concern" stays for all acts, but Article 263 (4) TFEU has opened the possibility for private parties to instigate proceedings against "regulatory acts which are of direct concern and do not entail implementing measures".[542] As far as known, this new phrase has not yet lead to particular attempts of private parties in the wider area of competition law, to broaden the scope of admissible cases in areas where their application would not have been admissible under the former treaty text. Another relevant change that came with the Lisbon Treaty, is the fact that the Charter on Human Rights is now binding and that the perspective of the accession of the EU to the ECHR has been created.[543] This reinforces the status of principles such as the right to effective judicial protection, laid down in Article 47 of the Charter, and makes it binding upon the EU institutions.

The overview in chapter 2 identified not only the restrictive case-law on "individual concern" for acts of a general nature as a problem in terms of access to court, but also the combination with the case law that deals with which acts can be subject to appeal proceedings.[544] In particular, doubts were raised with regards the case-law on the question when an act can be considered a definitive position or binding act taken by the Commission.

---

[542] The existing categories remained: acts addressed to the applicant or acts which are of direct and individual concern. The impact for the area of competition shall be discussed under the fourth theme, see sub-section 3.4 below.

[543] Article 6 TEU (Treaty on European Union). The right to effective judicial protection is laid down in the Charter, Article 47. It was referred to by the General Court in Jégo Quéré, see in chapter 2 above, at p. 9.

[544] Where acts of a general nature are concerned, the challengeability of soft law instruments was mentioned in chapter 2 and this might fall within the new category for general acts in Article 263 (4) TFEU. The standard of review was also identified as a potential factor of insufficient judicial protection. See further 3.4 below for the question of how access to the court can be improved and what other factors contribute to the lack of judicial protection.

Even though it appears as though the Courts always take a functional approach, disregarding the form of an act, and only considering whether the legal position of the individual was affected by an act of a general nature just like it would have been if it had been a decision,[545] chapter 2 nevertheless shows that there is reluctance to allow appeal proceedings against actions ("prises de position") of the Commission, that do not constitute final decisions.[546] Recent cases might give rise to some speculation, but there have not been any cases to really test whether, in the modernized enforcement system, the Court would be willing to take on cases where there is perhaps not yet a final decision of the Commission on the merits, but where the rights of parties are affected as if is was a final decision.[547]

The second question that emerges a few years after the entry into force of Reg.1/2003 and the publication of the article in chapter 2 is whether cases have appeared that would actually demonstrate an insufficiency in individual judicial protection along the lines suggested. For the moment it seems as though the worries expressed in chapter 2 with respect to access to court have not materialized into many cases that would confirm that there is a problem from a viewpoint of individual judicial protection. In the comments on the system of Reg. 1/2003 these last years, the focus (of worry) has been on the so-called re-allocation decisions: decisions by which a case within the network goes from one authority to another, either a national competition authority or the Commission.[548]

545 A few interesting precedents are described in chapter 2, at p. 25.

546 This line of case-law has also been considered an obstacle to effective judicial protection by S. Brammer, '*Cooperation between national competition agencies in the enforcement of EC competition law*' (Oxford: Hart Publishing, 2009), see for example at p. 212 and following.

547 An example of the willingness to disregard the form of an action when dealing with admissibilty: a judgment of the General Court of 21 May 2010 about state aid, cases T-425/04, T-450/04 and T-456/04, France, France Télécom and others/Commission, see rec. 126-134 and 212-222. The Court is prepared to subject oral declarations to the direct appeal; there is only mention of the phrase "[acte destiné à produire des effets juridiques"]. There is an interesting case pending concerning a request for information by the Commission addressed to Slovak Telekom (this is not a new instrument of investigation, but interesting because it would not seem to qualify as an act open to appeal under traditional case law) see cases T-458/09 and T-171/10, Slovak Telekom/Commission, [2010] OJ C 11/36; the Court will also have to deal with cases concerning a decision ordering an inspection (not a decision on the merits either), but Article 20 of Reg. 1/2003 provides explicitly for the possibility of review in such a case, an example in cases T-135/09, Nexans/Commission, and T-140/09, [2010] OJ C141/48 and 50. The appeal is based entirely on infringement of fundamental rights.

548 An extensive study of these types of decisions and cooperation between competition authorities in S. Brammer, cited above in n 546, amongst the many articles about this issue, an interesting analysis by M. van der Woude, 'Exchange of information within the ECN: scope and limits', and other contributions in D. Ehlermann and I. Atanasiu, cited above in chapter 6, n 500 also W. Wils, '*Principles of European Antitrust Enforcement*' (Oxford: Hart Publishing, 2005), in particular for example at p. 73 and following. The focus on re-allocation decisions

One particularly relevant aspect following from the evaluation reports on the functioning of Reg.1/2003 is that the number of potentially controversial decisions (in view of what was discussed in chapter 2) and the use of certain new instruments of enforcement have been quite limited in practice.[549] As it has been pointed out by many commentators, the largely informal way in which the network operates in practice, has much to do with this.

2.2 Chapter 3: Intrastate equals interstate; the particularities of the role of the interstate requirement in competition law

The requirement of 'effect on interstate trade' exists for all rules pertaining to the internal market, including free movement rules as well as competition rules. However, it seems that the interstate criterion plays a different role in competition law and has also evolved differently. Has the interstate criterion also become less important over time in competition law?[550] Perhaps, but in a different way than elsewhere in EU law.

An overview first showed that the interstate clause was interpreted in a broad sense by the Commission and that the EU Courts supported this

---

is most probably inspired by the fact that most practitioners feel the lack of transparency most when it comes to cases changing forum. Also, it most probably translates the impression that it really does matter where a case is dealt with in the eyes of the business community even though the same rules are applied. In chapter 2 however, more types of more or less decisions were mentioned as potentially raising questions of judicial protection.

549 The following examples can be mentioned: 13 commitments decisions (Article 9 Reg.1) of which one was challenged at the General Court without issues of admissibility (judgment in appeal of the ECJ very recently, case C-441/07 P, Commission/Alrosa, 30 June 2010, interesting for other points below), p. 33 of the Staff Working paper, no use yet of the new decision of "finding of inapplicability" (Article 10), no actual use of the new notice on giving "guidance", see p. 17 of the Staff Working Paper. The amicus curiae system (Article 15) allowing the Commission to intervene has been scarcely used. When it comes to the sensitive area of information exchange and reallocation of cases, it seems as though cooperation is mostly of an informal nature which makes it difficult to measure frequency, but also for companies to assess when decisions are actually being taken. In terms of who is best placed to take on a case, the only major case so far in which an attempt was made to challenge the fact that Commission took on a case instead of a national authority, was Case T-339/04, France Télécom/ Commission, [2007] ECR II-521. Relevant here was that this point could be raised in the context of an appeal against a decision ordering an inspection, for which admissibility is not an issue. In this way the aspect of allocation was addressed as a kind of "plea of illegality" (Article 277 TFEU) in the context of a dispute concerning another decision (ordering the inspection). The very reduced number of instances of re-allocation also appeared from a number of the national reports presented at the FIDE conference of 2008, see for example the Dutch, French and Italian reports in H.F. Koeck and M.M Karollus (eds) *The modernisation of European Competition law – Initial experiences with Regulation 1/2003*, FIDE XXIII Congress Linz 2008 (Vienna: Nomos, 2008).

550 The general assumption of the book in which the article was published was that the interstate requirement became less central in EU internal market law.

interpretation. As a result, it was relatively easy to qualify a seemingly national case as having interstate effect. In general, not much attention was given by the Commission to the reasoning to substantiate this condition in Article 81 (1) EC (now Article 101 (3) TFEU). From a policy perspective, this allowed the Commission to pursue national cases, to set an example (making the law) from a substantive point of view, and also to fill the enforcement gap in many Member States where competition authorities did not (yet) exist.[551]

The requirement of effect on trade between Member States was often said to be both a substantive and a jurisdictional criterion. Where the last dimension is concerned, the article defends the position that jurisdictional is in fact not an optimal term, because it is not so much about who is competent to apply a rule, but about which law applies. This is clearly the case after the entry into force of Reg.1/2003. The regulation introduces a unique rule in this respect: in the presence of effect on interstate trade, EU law does not precede over national law, but judges and authorities are required to apply them in parallel.[552] The obligation of parallel application is supplemented with a series of provisions destined to ensure convergence of application.[553] In terms of the substantive condition, the article explains how the Commission has set out its views on the requirement of effect on interstate trade in the new guidelines that were published along with Reg. 1/2003. The Commission advocates a more quantitative and economical approach to the interstate clause.

It was argued that the guidelines have certainly not made it easier for national authorities and national courts to establish whether interstate trade is affected. And yet, because of the obligations laid down in Reg. 1/2003, now this exercise has to be undertaken with great care in every national case. One might think that given the fact that national competition laws are mostly identical to EU law, there might be reluctance to assume effect on interstate trade as readily as in the past. However, given the difficulty of the factual and economic assessment required in the Commission's guidelines,[554] the desire to follow the EU and the obligations of Reg. 1/2003,

---

551 The enforcement gap was also due to a very low level of private enforcement, see references in Chapter 6 on reports and plans of the Commission in that respect.

552 The feature which makes this a unique system is that the rules that are to be applied in parallel are mostly very similar, if not identical. On this point also Chapter 6 on harmonisation mechanisms. It would require empirical data that compare cases where only national law is applied on the one hand, and cases where both are applied on the other, but the impression is that in many Member States the authorities determine whether there is effect on interstate trade as if it were a formal requirement to be checked, and then proceed in conducting one single substantive assessment of the behaviour for which it makes no difference whether there is effect on trade.

553 These mechanisms are also the subject of chapter 6.

554 The idea being that in terms of stating reasons, it would be more difficult to "justify" not assuming effect on interstate trade, also vis-à-vis the Commission, than to simply assume (potential) interstate trade).

it was proposed that there is more incentive to simply apply national and EU law in parallel.

The conclusion was drawn that it is hardly relevant anymore for the legal assessment of anticompetitive behaviour whether or not there is effect on interstate trade. The result is the same. Contrary to other areas of EU law, national and EU law have not been brought closer through the "fading away" of the interstate effect clause nor by direct harmonisation, but through the particular kind of harmonisation that characterizes competition law. It is not only top down harmonisation by which EU law (sometimes in the form of case-law) replaces national law, but also a variety of other convergence mechanisms having harmonising effects. Finally, it was argued that the requirement of effect on interstate trade should become much more a jurisdictional criterion with a role to play in the allocation of cases in the new, decentralized enforcement system. It was also proposed that there could be a more important role for the concept of Community (now Union) interest.

Since the publication of this article in 2006, no major developments seem to have taken place in relation to the interstate criterion. Where the jurisprudence of the Courts is concerned, there does not seem to be any real change and there are little or no signs that the Courts require a higher and more economical threshold to determine whether interstate trade is affected. The Courts also still fully support the idea that in a seemingly national cartel it is perfectly possible for interstate trade to be affected.[555]

Turning to the role and function of the requirement of interstate trade effect, the first years of application of Reg. 1/2003 confirm that the requirement constitutes a substantive condition of EU competition law but, foremost, it now functions as a factor of convergence[556] together with the convergence

[555] For an example of the classical case law still being the standard: the Manfredi case, case C-295/04, judgment of 13 July 2006, [2006] ECR I-6619, see at rec. 42-52. There is no mention of the Commission guidelines. More recently also an important judgment in a case concerning a "national" cartel in Austria, ECJ Cases 125/07 P, C-133/07 P, C-135/07 P and C-137/07 P (Lombard club), not yet reported. The Commission reports on Reg. 1/2003 state that the guidelines remain valid, and there has been no significant change in the interpretation of the interstate trade criterion, reports cited above at p. 164, n 509, Staff Working Paper, at par. 145.

[556] This is touched on in chapter 6: the obligation for parallel application in Article 3 has created a single legal standard and this is recognized openly by the Commission in the Communication from the Commission to the EP and the Council, containing a report on the functioning of Reg. 1/2003, also cited at p. 164, see par. 21 and in the Staff Working Paper cited above in the same note, at par. 141. In that way, the obligation to apply in a parallel way is much more efficient in terms of harmonisation than a primacy rule could ever have been: primacy would have set the national rule aside; parallel application de facto obliges the national rule to be the same. The combination of the interstate trade criterion and Article 3 of the regulation are very important factors of convergence.

rule in Article 3 Reg. 1/2003. It also has a key function in terms of enforcement and procedure, namely that it triggers the various mechanisms of cooperation (and supervision by the Commission) laid down in Reg. 1/2003.[557] It is therefore, as proposed in chapter 3, not a jurisdictional criterion in the traditional legal sense of division of competences,[558] nor does it determine which law applies (national – EU) in the sense that the application of one would exclude the other. When there is interstate effect, EU law and national law can both be applied[559] and the national authorities and courts become EU enforcers in the system set up by the regulation.

Finally, the concept of Community interest, for which it was suggested in chapter 3 that it might be developed as a relevant factor for the allocation of cases, seems to have remained relevant mostly in the area of complaints and priority setting by the Commission.[560] There seem to be no signs that it functions as a criterion for case allocation.

2.3 Chapter 4: Sense and nonsense of rules on proof in cartel cases; How to reconcile a more economics-based approach to competition law with more attention for rules on proof?

Modernisation is characterized by more use of economic analysis and more attention for economic reality in the legal assessment of cartel behaviour. At the same time there is growing attention for issues of proof, both before the authorities or judges, as well as in the review courts. The burden of proof, the standard of proof and the standard for judicial review are much discussed subjects in recent case-law and doctrine. There seems to be a contradiction between both tendencies: more economics and yet more pressure for, typically legal, rules on proof. Is there too much focus on proof as a side effect of modernisation?

This article highlighted the relevance of proof issues in cartel cases and discussed the key concepts, such as standard of proof, but also the use of certain legal instruments in proof such as presumptions. Some recent developments impacting on proof are discussed. This is all done from the

557 This is an interesting feature of the interstate trade clause in competition law and one which is believed quite unique when compared to other areas of EU law: instead of differentiating between national law and EU law, it triggers cooperation and mechanisms and obligations for authorities and courts regulated by Reg. 1/2003, see chapter 6. Comparison with the other areas covered in the book in which the article appeared, confirms this.

558 The General Court explicitly endorsed the fact that the Commission always stays competent to deal with a case, even when a national authority is dealing with it; it is said that Regulation 1/2003 has not established a division of competences, judgment in France Télécom/Commission, n 547 above.

559 In theory, the application of national law is optional in case of effect on interstate trade, Member States are said to be free to choose parallel application or only EU law as the legal basis for a decision, Staff Working Paper mentioned above, at par. 152.

560 Staff Working Paper mentioned above in n 509, at par. 119-120.

perspective of having to convince non-lawyers why proof rules are important. For that reason, attention is also drawn to the X factor; to demonstrate that proof is not a mathematical or scientific exercise, but that it is all about conviction and conviction depends, to some extent, on the persons involved.[561]

Finally, based on these considerations, a pragmatic view on proof is proposed allowing for flexibility and differentiation. This requires lawyers to accept a system which is not too rigid and adapted to the specifics of competition law. As a counterpart, it requires economists to realize that most rules on proof reflect fundamental principles underlying the legal system and are much more than merely technical obstacles. There should not necessarily be a contradiction between a more economics-based approach and rules on proof provided the suggestions in the article are followed. It is also argued that there is another very important principle in this respect and that is the duty to state adequate reasoning. At the end of the day, solid reasoning protects the rights of parties, it ensures accountability and it allows for efficient judicial review.

In terms of the issues of proof discussed in this article, attention can be drawn to at least one case in which the Court of Justice has rendered judgment since the publication of the article in chapter 4.[562] In the important judgment T-Mobile, the Court had to address two basic types of issues that are relevant here. First, is it (still) appropriate to consider that in the presence of an anti-competitive object, no proof of anti-competitive effect is necessary?[563] Much perhaps to the regret of the referring court, the Court affirmed its traditional case law on this point, namely that no real proof of effects is needed for certain hard restrictions for which the anti-competitive object has been established.[564]

---

[561] See chapter 4 at p. 86.

[562] The case already mentioned as pending above in chapter 4, ECJ Case C-8/08, T-Mobile and others, [2009] ECR I-04529.

[563] The CBB used this case to launch an invitation to the Court to validate its own case law whereby there is strong pressure on the Dutch competition authority NMa to translate a more economic approach in more solid proof of effects in all cases, even in "object" cases. See in chapter 4 at p. 74 above.

[564] See at rec. 28-29. Along these lines also in an abuse case, Wanadoo: ECJ Case C-202/07 P, judgment of 2 April 2009, [2009] ECR I-2369, and the judgment in GSK discussed also in chapter 5, see at p. 125, where clearly the Court confirms the existence of a category of serious breaches of Article 101 TFEU where no extensive demonstration of effects is required to be able to sanction them. Of course there is some schizophrenia in relation to this case-law: whilst realising that it might not be so "modern" to discard the need to prove effects in the market and to continue the use of presumptions, it should be clear to most lawyers concerned that effective enforcement would become quite difficult, if not impossible, if a total market based and case to case approach were required in cartel and abuse cases. This is related to what was called the "proof paradox" in chapter 4, see at p. 71.

Second, are the presumptions that apply in that context[565] a matter of (substantive) EU law, or rather of (procedural) national law?[566] In this context it is not only relevant that the Court clearly confirmed the use of presumptions as an instrument of proof, as discussed in chapter 4, but also that the Court did not want to allow the risk that proof would depend on differences in national (procedural) law. It, therefore, basically stated that the definition and modalities of the presumptions used to establish concerted practices are a question of EU law because they are part of the application of the prohibition of Article 101 TFEU.[567]

This judgment and an increasing number of recent judgments, especially at the level of the General Court, show that the law of proof in competition law is currently being constructed at the EU level and at quite a rapid pace.[568]

2.4 Chapter 5: Shouldn't we know what we are protecting? Yes, we should! A plea for a solid and comprehensive debate about the objectives of EU competition law and policy

Modernisation has had another side effect, namely a consumer welfare focused public message on behalf of e.g. the Commission, at most evolving towards a mixed "discours" created by the reference to other objectives of the EU competition law system, for example competitiveness or market integration. This article examines the objectives of the EU system, describes the variety of objectives that have always been present and shows that they still are in the system at this time. The overview can (hopes to) surprise in

[565] Notably the presumption of a causal link between meetings that take place, on the one hand, and the behaviour in the market, on the other hand, see also in chapter 4, at p. 80.

[566] This question is an excellent demonstration of the fact that for proof issues the difference between substance and procedure is difficult to make. The question is also quite relevant in view of what was discussed in chapter 6, how much autonomy is left for the Member States?

[567] See at rec. 51-52. The result of this reasoning is that proof is seen as an integral part of substantive law, rather than as being part of procedural law. This is quite a far-reaching statement by the Court.

[568] A whole body of case-law is growing with attention for many details in requirements of proof. It is not always clear where the General Court draws inspiration from when it makes the law. There is a lot of common sense involved and a key role for general principles of law, as was already said in chapter 4 and chapter 6. For an extensive recent overview of some of the main issues, F. Castillo de la Torre, 'Evidence, Proof and Judicial review in cartel cases', *World Competition* (2009) 4 p. 505. For a pragmatic view, along the lines of the article in chapter 4, E. Gippini-Fournier, 'The elusive standard of proof' (2010) 33 *World Competition* 187. It is one of the clearest examples of judicial harmonisation, see chapter 6. It also demonstrates the increasing interest for this legal subject. In the area of merger control there have also been a number of much discussed cases, for some comments see P. Szilagyi, 'The ECJ has spoken: where do we stand on standard on proof in merger control', (2008) *European Competition Law Review* 12, p. 726. The question whether to differentiate between the standard of proof in merger cases and in cartel and abuse cases, is still relevant, see at p. 85 above.

two ways: on the one hand, by showing that in "old times" consumer welfare was already quite present in the case-law of the EU courts and is therefore not so new; and, on the other hand, it is demonstrated that despite general belief, there are clear signs that the legal system is resisting a too strong focus on consumer welfare. Examples are given from the case-law and the new Lisbon Treaty.

The article goes on to show that a discussion on objectives really matters and is relevant in practice. The objectives have their impact on policy and on the interpretation and enforcement of the law. Consequently, other factors from outside the area of competition law, that might have played a role in the emphasis on consumers, are discussed in the article. Finally, some other reasons are presented to argue why a debate on the objectives of competition law and policy is necessary. They include governance related issues, coherence and the decentralized enforcement structure created by Reg. 1/2003. This brings us back to the other aspect of modernisation, the decentralisation of enforcement.

2.5 Chapter 6: Decentralisation of competition law: sacrificing procedural autonomy?; Autonomy versus effectiveness: a well known conflict in EU law revisited and its impact on the question of further harmonisation in the area of enforcement of competition law

The last chapter builds on the decentralized enforcement structure where the previous chapter ended. Whether or not it was intended, somewhere along the way in the modernisation process, Member States have lost most of their autonomy when it comes to competition law and policy. This happened quite some time ago for substantive law and seems well under way for procedural law. Effectiveness is the keyword. This is the premise that was the starting point for the last article in this collection. The purpose of the article is to contribute to the ongoing debate on the need for further harmonisation of procedure in EU competition law.

The different convergence mechanisms which have put pressure on autonomy in competition law are described, but first the principles of procedural autonomy and effectiveness in general EU law are assessed critically. Neither the one nor the other is easily understood, even though easily invoked. The article takes the position that neither provide for a conclusive answer to the question whether further harmonisation of procedural competition law should be undertaken and if so, to what extent.

It was concluded that there is no legal or urgent need to harmonize procedural competition law. However, the article recognizes that there might be reasons, such as consistency, coherence and the principle of non-discrimination, which can argue in favour of harmonisation. If undertaken, it would have to be done, however, on the basis of a comprehensive stock taking of the actual problematic differences that still exist. Given the high degree of convergence, harmonisation would also have to be much more detailed than formulating minimum standards. Moreover many of the subjects for which divergence is claimed to be an issue not only concern procedural law, but also the boundary of procedural and substantive law and/or the boundary between law and policy.[569]

3. Common themes in a future-oriented perspective

There are a number of common themes that can be found throughout the different articles, be it to a larger or a lesser extent. Four themes are identified here as they cross cut the chapters. At the same time, it is proposed that these are important subjects for the further development of competition law, more in particular its enforcement. The different themes overlap to some extent, underlining in fact their interconnectedness. They are presented by way of conclusion including some observations or suggestions from a future-oriented perspective.

3.1 The relationship between competition law and the internal market

In chapter 5, the relationship between competition law and the internal market was studied from the perspective of the objectives. Attention was drawn to the fact that within the basic treaties, the competition rules were always part of the rules on the internal market and instrumental to the achievement of that internal market.[570] A second element, one that clearly demonstrates the relationship between competition law and EU law in a more general sense, is the obligation for the EU to integrate different policies; an obligation that is advocated more strongly than ever since the entry into force of the Lisbon Treaty.[571] In chapter 5 some recent case-law was cited to argue that, regardless of what the policy directions of the Commission might be, the Court of Justice is not letting market integration go as a factor of

---

569 In chapter 4 it appears clearly that proof issues can be on the border of substance and procedure and in chapter 6, the example of fines and fining policy is given as one of the clearest examples where law, law enforcement and policy are combined.

570 Chapter 6. It was somewhat surprising to see how low key, if not practically absent, competition policy is in the Monti report on the internal market recently presented to President Barroso ('A new strategy for the single market – At the service of Europe's economy and society', presented on 9 May 2010, l http://ec.europa.eu/bepa/expertises/visitor-programs/mario_monti/index_en.htm), last accessed on 30 June 2010. The fact that former Competition Commissioner Mario Monti was asked to draw up this report shows in itself how important market integration still is.

571 Chapter 6, e.g. at p. 126. More emphasis on the integration of different policies at the EU level might well be, as such, a strategy to better complete the internal market and increase the efficiency, the quality and the coherence of EU legislation and policy. For an attempt to imagine what the concrete effects of the integration clauses can have for the area of competition, see J. Steenbergen, 'Het mededingingsbeleid en het verdrag van Lissabon', in: *De Europese Unie na het Verdrag van Lissabon* (Deventer: Kluwer, 2009).

importance in the area of competition.[572] When we compare EU competition law to other non-European systems, market integration is also what makes the EU unique. It was argued that in the near future competition law and policy has to come to terms with market integration: its (remaining) role in the shaping of EU competition law has to be redefined. This can allow, at least in part, going beyond the differences between the Commission and the Courts that were referred to in chapter 5.[573]

In chapter 3 the interstate effect clause was examined. The requirement that the trade between Member States is affected in order for EU law to apply, is common to e.g. the provisions on free movement as well as competition. It determines the scope of application of EU law. Public barriers to trade and private barriers to trade can both be a hindrance to the internal market objective.

Another point that competition rules and other rules establishing the internal market have in common, appears from the chapters above. Certain questions raised in chapter 5, such as the stronger emphasis on non-economical values and objectives in the basic treaties, are common to all rules aiming at the establishment and the promotion of the internal market. Balancing non-economic considerations, public policy objectives and more economically inspired considerations is not an exclusive worry for the world of competition law. It is a broad debate that has been relaunched and that shall undoubtedly lead to ongoing debate in literature. The same can be said for the preoccupation with the consumer that was also highlighted in chapter 5: it is a more general feature of the current development of EU law.[574]

---

572 Not only the Court, but see also the Opinion of Advocate general Kokott in the T-Mobile case discussed above, see n 562 above. From a more general point of view it is not a good thing for the legal system that there is a perceived gap between the Commission, the General Court and the Court of Justice that lasts too long, and it is not good for the Court of Justice and some of its Advocate Generals to be perceived as clinging on to the past; which is not necessarily the right way to explain this case law, see below at the end of sub-section 3.2.

573 It has to be observed that regardless the debate on their economic soundness and regardless of developments in the US, a number of vertical restraints have been kept in the list of hardcore restrictions in the new block exemption regulation, Regulation 330/2010, [2010] OJ L 102/1, on this debate see in chapter 4 at p. 73 and in chapter 5 on objectives e.g. at p. 104. Whether this is to be seen as a sign that market integration is still prominent, or rather that the value of having a list of hard core restrictions for the sake of legal certainty prevailed, is an open question. A combination of both is most likely the explanation. The recent judgments in which the Court defended a strict attitude against measures impeding parallel imports for the sake of market integration, must have played a role, see chapter 5, p. 124 and following.

574 See in chapter 5 where it was argued that the consumer-driven policy in competition law can be explained by more than only the introduction of more economics.

Here, in this chapter and building on the previous ones, two further points concerning the relationship between competition law and the internal market are addressed.

The first point that appears from the chapters above concerns an interesting element of divergence between developments in the area of competition and developments elsewhere in EU law. The increased application of EU law to internal situations in other areas is often controversial both from a political as well as from a legal point of view.[575] It is also mostly the result of the case-law of the Court of Justice, which adds, according to some commentators, to its controversial nature.[576] This is quite different in competition law: the "expansion" of EU competition law into the national legal orders is the result of different mechanisms of convergence and harmonisation in which the Commission plays a strong and stimulating role, and for which there is generally large support in the Member States.[577] In other words, the expansion of EU law and the spill over effects in internal situations (meaning cases with no effect on interstate trade), is not a scenario of a confrontation between EU law and national law. The origins, the key actors and the evolution of this process of expansion are of a different nature in the area of competition law as opposed to the broader area of the internal market and the free movement provisions.

A second, more future-oriented point touching on competition law and policy and the internal market concerns the possibility of using EU (formal) harmonisation instruments in the area of competition. Chapter 6 contains a brief discussion of the question whether there would be a legal basis for further harmonisation of enforcement issues at the EU level.[578] There is a clear connection with the subject dealt with in this section, namely the stronger the link between competition law and the internal market, the more acceptable the use of the provisions in the Treaty that allow for harmonisation in the context of the internal market might be.[579]

The combined effect of a number of factors is interesting to explore in this respect: first, the explicit exclusive competence of the Union in the area of

---

[575] This is the subject of the book in which chapter 3 appeared in 2006, see the contribution by B. Drijber, at p. 191, expressing serious doubts about case-law in the areas of free movement and public procurement in which the Court expands principles of the Treaty or laid down in directives, to (purely?) national situations.

[576] See also on judicial harmonisation in chapter 6 at p. 158 and following.

[577] The Court can be considered to support these developments, but is not primarily responsible for it in this area.

[578] Chapter 6 at p. 166 The term enforcement issues is used here because the study in Chapter 6 showed that in fact remaining divergence is said to concern not only subjects that are clearly procedural, but also borderline subjects, such as proof, and subjects that also have an important policy component, such as sanctions.

[579] In particular, the general legal basis in Article 114 TFEU. See in comparison on the possible legal basis for introducing prison sanctions at the EU level, W. Wils, *Efficiency and Justice in European Antitrust enforcement* (Oxford: Hart Publishing, 2008), at p. 197.

competition law and policy, as laid down in Article 3 (1) TFEU, and, second, the strong link that is made between competition law and policy and the internal market in the protocol discussed in chapter 5.[580]

Moreover, one could refer to the case-law of the EU Court to argue that the less relevant the interstate trade clause is for the application of the material rule (in this case, for example Article 101 TFEU), the less relevant it should also be to determine whether the legal basis for harmonisation may be used.[581] Finally, it seems as though the Court attaches considerable importance to the objectives of harmonisation measures when it evaluates if the right choice of legal basis has been made.[582] So, reinstating the objective of market integration, or in any case accepting to a certain extent the instrumental role of competition law with a view of establishing/completing the internal market, seems worthwhile as a strategy to give future harmonisation measures or other initiatives a solid legal foundation. The case law can then provide interesting perspectives. This also holds true if there should be willingness to adopt formal harmonisation in the area of sanctions, which was highlighted in chapter 6 as one of the areas were divergence is perceived as problematic.

Now why does it seem somewhat conservative to highlight the relationship between competition law and policy and the internal market? This impression can indeed exist if one looks at the system of competition law from within. This is most probably because, for a number of reasons, competition law and policy have been alienated from the internal market.[583] One of the reasons is the particular enforcement structure in this area of EU law and the role of the Commission, as opposed to other areas of law. Through the central role given to the Commission from the very start of the EEC, the strong mandate from the Council and substantial powers to sanction, competition law could develop itself autonomously. The

580 At p. 101 above. On the relation with the nature of the competence, the Court has accepted that rules on sanctions were adopted as an implied competence, ancillary to the main competence to take measures of e.g. environmental protection in the famous Commission/Council judgments, Case C-176/03, [2005] ECR I-7879, and Case C-440/05, [2007] ECR I-9097. It follows from Article 4 TFEU that environment is a shared competence. Can it then, a fortiori, be accepted that sanctions are harmonized in relation to competition infringements because Article 3 attributes an exclusive competence to the Union in this area?

581 This links back to the "fading out" of interstate trade effect as a differentiating factor between EU law and national law, as discussed in chapter 3. Reference is made to the 'Tobacco case', ECJ Case C-491/01, [2002] ECR I-11453.

582 Establishing what the main objectives are, is part of the exercise to determine which, one or several, legal basis in the treaty should be used. See also ECJ Case C-338/01, [2004] ECR I-4829.

583 The focus on consumer welfare and the influence of economics is, of course, one of the main reasons why market integration got somewhat pushed into the background. Another reason is probably the general impression that market integration has been achieved to a large extent. Both these factors were discussed in chapter 5.

introduction of national competition laws that are quasi-identical to the corresponding provisions at the EU level and also the setting up of the network of NCA's, certainly contribute to the independent existence of competition law and the fact that the link with the internal market can seem something distant in history.[584] And yet, we tried to show it is nevertheless part of reality.

3.2 Substantive modernisation as a challenge to the enforcement system

Others have commented that there appears to be a general shift in focus from substantive issues to institutional and enforcement issues in the area of EU competition law. This is most probably a natural evolution of a relatively young area of the law moving to a more mature system. Throughout the chapters above, it was argued that the growing attention for more procedural issues is also a result of substantive modernisation and bringing in more economics.[585]

In recent years, the coexistence of law and economics has lead to a vast amount of literature. The relationship between law and economics in the field of competition, is often perceived and presented as a struggle.

> "*Economists and lawyers do not often see eye to eye. They are divided by the boundaries of their respective disciplines. Although most of the time they happily lead separate lives, occasional contacts are not always friction-free. Lawyers, for example, bemoan the 'pollution' of their discipline by economists who favour the introduction of cost-benefit criteria in legal decisions, while economists find incomprehensible court rulings that appear to disregard obvious, in their eyes, economic facts.* "[586]

---

584 On the convergence through the adoption of national laws, see chapter 3 and chapter 6. The purpose is clearly not to defend a return to the past and a denial of the evolution of competition law over the last two decades. It is to draw attention to the importance of the link between competition law and the internal market: redefining this relationship will help progress the system.

585 Examples: in chapter 3 on interstate: the introduction of a more quantitative and economical analysis for measuring effect on interstate trade requires more data and makes application of this condition more difficult; in chapter 4: more economic analysis raises questions of proof and challenges lawyers to accept flexibility; in chapter 5: bringing in the input of economics and the concepts of consumer welfare has troubled our vision on what the system aims to protect and also challenges us to adapt our enforcement system.

586 P. Nicolaides, 'An Essay on Economics and the Competition Law of the European Community', (2000) 27 *Legal Issues of Economic Integration*, 7.

A second quote:

> *"There is no sense in attempting to define the relevant market without first identifying what has been done in contravention of the law.."*[587]

Is there a reason for the court to intervene? Has wrong been done? Is there a problem that should be resolved? The latter quote represents the words of a judge describing in a very simple and honest way how the legal process shall often naturally deal with a competition case, as with any case in any area of the law.[588]

Competition law and policy are (hopefully) now beyond the phase described in the first quote above, which is one of confrontation and tension. However, the intuition at the heart of the second quote, is probably still close to reality in many enforcement cases, especially in the area of cartels and abuse of dominance.[589] Nevertheless, the impression exists that over the last years minds have significantly evolved and the second quote is now probably less shocking for some than it was a few years ago.[590] On the legal side, it is good that there is some more consciousness, albeit slowly, of the fact that the introduction of a more economics based approach also presents other challenges to the legal system than the obvious benefits it offers. And, on the economic side, contrary to what is sometimes believed, there are most certainly signs of a rather realistic attitude to what economics can offer to the practical enforcement of the rules on competition.

---

587 Famous quote paraphrased and often cited from Judge J. Deane at par. 5 of his opinion in case Queensland Wire industries Pty Ltd v Broken Hill Pty Ltd (Star Picket Fence Post case), judgment of 8 February 1989, High Court of Australia, accessible via internet: www.austlii.edu.au/au/cases/cth/HCA/1989/6.html (last accessed 1 September 2010). Another quote from the following paragraph in the judgment expresses well how many lawyers will see the the process of market analysis: "*The identification of relevant markets involves value judgments about which there is some room for legitimate differences of opinion*".

588 Reference is made here to the formula of the "X factor" as well, at p. 86 in chapter 4. This was proposed simply to draw attention to the human factor involved. The idea that every legal decision should achieve justice and fairness was also expressed in chapter 6. To some extent the discussion on the balance between economical and non-economical considerations that was touched upon under 3.1 above and which is present in chapter 5, is related to this as well.

589 Although not based on any empirical evidence, it is believed that this is especially true for courts and less so for specialised agencies, but that would depend very much on the institutional setting.

590 Shocking for many lawyers who embraced with (too) great enthusiasm the more economic approach and shocking for economists who found the legal process too formal, abstract and difficult to understand.

At the risk of making either too simple or too controversial a statement here, it is argued that at the end of the day the legal system is a result of fundamental choices in terms of what it wants to protect and it is based on a series of general principles of law for which there is a broad consensus in society.[591] In that respect, economics can and should be a factor of importance at the different levels of designing the system: the objectives, the policy orientations, the legislative process and the enforcement of the law.[592] More than ever, there is agreement that the rules should be based on sound economic principles. But economics shall mostly be instrumental (for example helping design better rules, a better assessment of the right facts, defining markets, predicting (the probability of) effects[593]) and not decisive in itself.[594]

The previous remarks were of a more general nature and concerned the way the system as a whole is developing towards the optimal coexistence of law and economics. Two more specific, related observations are made in that respect, drawing from the preceding chapters and research and experience over the last years.

At the beginning of this chapter it was observed that substantive modernisation has also brought more attention to typically legal issues. This is also demonstrated in the context of what, upon appearance, seem to be discussions on the substance. Recent discussions on new policy orientations, such as how the enforcement of Article 102 TFEU should evolve, provide good examples. Even if everyone agrees that it would be appropriate to include efficiencies into the legal assessment of the behaviour of a dominant undertaking, there is no clear view on or proposal establishing

591 The importance of general principles of law was emphasized in chapter 4 on proof and also follows from the discussion of judicial harmonisation in chapter 6. General principles of law have a universal character and have been an important factor of convergence of procedural law, because they represent higher values that many jurisdictions share. Based on practical experience it must be noted that these fundamental principles, such as equality, non discrimination and fairness, offer a valuable perspective to explain technical legal issues to economists who are used to a more universal approach.

592 The exercise undertaken in chapter 5 tries to demonstrate the impact of a move towards more economics on the different levels of the legal system, seen from the perspective of the objectives.

593 But even the definition of the relevant market in a cartel or abuse case is to a large extent a legal exercise, although it should be based on solid analysis, if the data are available. It resembles the traditional legal tool of "qualification of facts".

594 "*Competition law is still law and it needs the legal mind and the common sense of a judge to interpret those rules and to apply them to a concrete set of facts* " (quote from S. Norberg, cited by B. Vesterdorf, 'Economics in court: reflections on the role of judges in assessing economic theories and evidence in the modernised competition regime' in *Liber Amicorum in honour of Sven Norberg, A European for all seasons* (Brussels: Bruylant, 2006), at p. 530. I would add: in a given procedural framework. The quote is not taken to mean that lawyers have a monopoly on common sense.

who is responsible and how efficiencies can or should be proven.[595] The same might be said for a concept like consumer harm: we do not really know what it means and what its role is as a requirement in a given case.[596]

And yet without finding a way for the procedural framework to adapt to a (substantive) concept that is to become part of the application of a legal norm (prohibition or exception) in a given case, there will not be any real relevance for efficiencies or for other newly advocated concepts.[597] This can lead to frustration and disappointment and it is an unsatisfactory situation: if there is agreement that substantive assessment should evolve, it makes sense for such a choice to have an impact on enforcement.[598] New substantive concepts, if we think they should be part of the legal assessment of behaviour, should be fitted into the procedural framework. Often, as demonstrated by the examples in the area of Article 102 TFEU, this boils down to issues of proof. Chapter 4 dealt with proof issues in cartel cases and demonstrates how substantive modernisation has an impact on the design and the interpretation of proof concepts such as burden of proof and standard of proof. The focus on proof is also a way for lawyers to translate new (economical) substantive issues into concepts they are more familiar with.

---

595 On the confusion surrounding the concept of consumer welfare and consumer harm, see chapter 5.

596 In chapter 4 the example of vertical agreements was also given: whether or not it still makes sense to maintain a ban on vertical price resale maintenance is really a question whether this is economically justified, but it is also very much linked to the question whether we want to keep a list of hard core restriction to provide legal certainty and to what extent we use presumptions. The fact that a sui generis procedure exists at the Commission level with a bit of influence from different legal traditions makes these subjects difficult. For verticals, in the meantime, the new block exemption was adopted that presents very little change for the former one, see Commission regulation 330/2010 of 20 April 2010 on the application of Article 101(3) of the Treaty on the Functioning of the European Union to categories of vertical agreements and concerted practices, (2010) OJ L 102/1.

597 In this respect the idea that could be the subject of further comparative research (different jurisdictions, but especially different areas of law) is whether a legal system is more resistant to accommodate new or economical concepts in the context of the assessment of facts, when the assessment can lead to substantial sanctions. The feeling exists that this would seem to be the case. This more general question is related to the question of the standard of proof and whether it should be stricter according to the type of sanctions, see in chapter 4, at p. 89.

598 It is believed that a lot of the criticism of the Commission in recent cases and on the guidance paper on abuse are inspired by a disappointment in the fact that the Commission has recently claimed that it now wants to follow a more economical approach, but it is felt by some not do so in practice. This is possibly also related to the fact that not enough thought is given to the procedural and legal implications of introducing economical concepts. It would be understandable that this also leads to frustration of economists that see little effects of their contributions in the daily enforcement practice.

The point about integrating new substantive developments into the legal system and into the procedural framework of cases, can also be illustrated by the discussion of the interstate clause in chapter 3. The new Guidelines on the interpretation of effect on interstate trade promote a more economic approach to this condition in Article 101 (1) TFEU.[599] It is a relatively non-contested reorientation because of its form: an existing and well-known concept in the Treaty is used but reinterpreted, reoriented by the Commission, subject to the approval by the Courts. A general and open norm such as Article 101 (1) allows for dynamic interpretation in this way.[600] The impact on the system is of a different nature when compared to introducing new concepts such as efficiencies or consumer harm as an economic concept.

From an institutional perspective, similar remarks can be made. In order for modernisation to have an impact in a proper way, it has to be studied how not only procedural, but also institutional structures have to be adapted.[601] For the time being, reflection on what has been called the institutional embeddedness of economics,[602] is insufficient and in a relatively preliminary stage. The question in which way the institutional format should best be adapted to the introduction of more economics, is relevant both for the enforcement level, as well as for the level of judicial review (see below in 3.4).

Linking this back to the chapters above, it is proposed that this relation between substantive modernisation and the procedural and institutional framework, can also offer an alternative explanation or another insight in

599 See guidelines cited at p. 41, n 157. Interstate trade is quantified, in a similar way as was also done for the condition "restriction" where the criterium of appreciability was introduced in the form of thresholds and a de minimis regime, see the Commission Notice on agreements of minor importance, cited above in n 159.

600 See in chapter 5, at p. 123 The discussion on the interstate trade clause also illustrates a more general point made at several occasions which is the impact of procedure on substance. In practice, the interstate clause has not really given rise to much interpretation problems and it appears that effect on interstate trade is just as easily assumed as before without too much economic analysis. It is proposed that this is because the effects of Reg. 1/2003 is such that it does not matter much whether or not EU competition law is applied or only national competition law (chapter 3 and summary above under 2.2). If at some point the parallel application or single application should be said to matter, for example in view of which sanctions are possible, then the interpretation and analysis of the effect on interstate trade shall become an issue again, see cases pending on ne bis in idem, below in n 626

601 In chapter 5 examples were given of how the Commission has made some changes that reflect the growing importance attached to economics and also to consumers, see in chapter 5 at p. 119.

602 A term taken from D. Gerber, cited above in chapter 5, published now in *Economic theory and Competition law*, J. Drexl, L. Idot and J. Monéger (eds) (Cheltenham: Edward Elgar, 2009). Merely appointing more economists in the competition authorities is clearly not enough or not adequate. Their role in the decision-making process needs to be defined.

some of the recent judgments of the Court of Justice that were discussed. It might be formulated in this way: recent judgments like GSK[603] and T-Mobile,[604] in which the Court is said to be reluctant to go for a more effects-based approach in cartel cases, might not be so much the Court resisting change and (substantive) modernisation.[605] Rather, it might be the Court sending the message that the procedural framework cannot cope with too much emphasis on effects until it is clearer how this will affect effective enforcement, the burden and standard of proof and the rights and duties of parties.

3.3. Modernisation from an organisational perspective: the complicated relationship between decentralisation, convergence and consistency

The different mechanisms of harmonisation and convergence, both with regards to substantive as well as procedural law, were mentioned or discussed in every one of the previous chapters.[606] This also appears from the conclusions as summarized in section 7.1. above.

One characteristic that is certainly remarkable in EU competition law is the position of the Commission.[607] The policy driving and lawmaking role of the

---

[603] Above in chapter 5 at p. 125, n 323 and 389.

[604] Above, see n 562.

[605] Another recent case referred to in this respect is the Wanadoo case, case C-202/07 P, cited above in n 564, rec. 103-113. Again in that case, the Court does not follow the arguments of the parties asking for a more economic and case-specific approach in an abuse case. It is even common practice to present the Court of Justice as conservative and form based, on the one hand, and the Commission and the General Court to be more susceptible to an effects-based approach, on the other hand. Quote: "So, the introduction of a more economic approach did not trigger a revolution after all", E. Loozen, 'The application of a more economic approach to restrictions by object: no revolution after all, T Mobile Netherlands', (2010) 4 *European Competition Law Review* 146. The suggestion made here can provide a (partial) alternative explanation for the perceived gap between the case law and the enforcement practice. In T-Mobile, the Court (as well as the referring Dutch court) focused on typically legal concepts, such as the use of presumptions and the concept of causality. By doing so, the Court does provide for an answer to the question whether in particular markets collusion can be assumed when certain information is exchanged.

[606] In chapter 2 from the perspective of judicial protection; in chapter 3 in substantive terms to explain why the law applied in national or transborder cases is virtually the same; also in chapter 3 a critical note on centralised "top down" convergence when it comes to policy; in chapter 5 attention was also drawn to the existence of convergence of law and policy as a reason why a debate on objectives is necessary and will also have an important impact at the national level; chapter 6 contains the most elaborate perspective on convergence and harmonisation and the way forward.

[607] See also under 3.1. above on the difference with other areas and the link with the internal market.

Commission in this area[608] is combined with an essential role in the actual enforcement of the law at the EU level and the supervisory role within the network of competition authorities. The actual enforcement of the law in individual cases has an impact on national enforcement in at least two ways: by setting an example and creating a precedent in terms of substance, but also by following a certain procedure in the course of the investigation, when deciding a case and, finally, when imposing a sanction.[609]

It is fair to say that the combination of powers and the exercise thereof, together with the support from the Member States through the network, give the Commission a strong and important position in this area of law. Many authors have also argued that the case-law of the Courts supports the guiding role of the Commission.[610] The central role of an EU institution in shaping the law and its enforcement in this way is one of the key elements that explain the mechanisms of harmonisation and convergence mentioned before. The term decentralisation still feels somewhat misleading; it is more a question of a multitude of enforcers driven by the EU level.

As a matter of realism, the basis of further reflection on how best to improve the enforcement system of EU competition law in the future, should take into account its present features as described in more detail in chapter 6: substantive law that is largely harmonized, the various mechanisms of harmonisation and convergence and a unique enforcement system with strong and visible enforcement at the EU level and simultaneous enforcement of the same rules (and their national equivalents) at the national level by specialized agencies. This all operates alongside the national judge who is, of course, also called, as elsewhere in EU law, to play his role of primary enforcer of EU law in private litigation.[611] To complete this picture: it seems to be a given fact that little controversy exists at the

608 Using classical instruments, such as proposals of legislation like in other areas of law, although always in the form of regulations (block exemption regulations for example) which already makes a difference, but also frequent use of soft law instruments.

609 See chapter 6 for harmonisation and convergence at a procedural level in this respect. The impact of the enforcement practice at the EU level well exceeds cases where EU law is applied due to precisely the convergence that has already taken place in terms of substance.

610 Reference is usually made to the judgment in *Masterfoods*, Case C-344/98, judgment of 14 December 2000, [2005] ECR I-11369. Article 85 EC, now 105 TFEU, is often cited where it says that the Commission shall ensure the application of the "principles laid down in Article 101 and 102". On the role of the Commission in the network, see A. Schaub, 'The Commission's position within the network' in: D. Ehlermann and I. Antanasiu, cited above in n 500 p. 237.

611 As it was briefly mentioned in chapter 6, the Commission would like to see more private enforcement, but the plans to take initiatives have some trouble progressing; the resistance to harmonising rules concerning damage actions is said to be important. This confirms what will be said below about how harmonisation becomes much more delicate as soon as it concerns courts, see in section 3.4.

Member State level about the expansion of EU law into national cases and that there is strong support for convergence.

There is one point, however, where some reluctance should be expressed with regards to the strong and partly "top down" driven convergence. This is precisely the point when it comes to institutional structures and procedural law.

Not so much the will or even the need to either converge, or actually harmonise, is called into question. Rather, serious thought and doubt is justified whether we really want the convergence process to take the Commission (institutional) model as the example.[612] It is defended that it is not a given fact that the Commission procedure and the Commission institutional framework as a competition authority, should be the end objective of further convergence, let alone of formal harmonisation.[613] In fact, it is submitted that the natural or somewhat stimulated movement of convergence towards the Commission model should be halted to privilege first a more fundamental reflection on the institutional framework at the EU level. This includes both the role of the Commission and judicial review of its decisions (this point will also be addressed in the next section).

A second observation, again inspired by the attempt to approach this area of the law from a broader perspective, is that it is difficult to understand why there is such an emphasis on (if not to say obsession with) consistency and uniform application in competition law. With emphasis it is meant also that there is large consensus that the need for consistency is a justification for far-reaching consistency mechanisms of various sorts, as introduced by Reg.

---

[612] An unresolved question which was triggered by research is whether convergence in substance and convergence of procedure are concepts or phenomena with characteristic differences. When it comes to convergence and divergence, there is also a risk that chapters 3 and 6 and these conclusions are interpreted as opposing convergence. This would be a wrong impression. Rather, in different ways the question was explored if divergence is necessarily a bad thing and why the system so strongly wants to do away with it. It is also a call for defining more accurately what problematic divergence is, why (for example because of effectiveness or not, see chapter 6) that is so and which divergence is not problematic. Accepting that not all divergence is bad, see P. Larouche and F. Chirico, 'Divergence, Functionalism, and the Economics of Convergence', in: *The coherence of EU law – The search for unity in divergence concepts*, S. Prechal and B. van Roermond (eds) (Oxford: Oxford University Press, 2008).

[613] This is all the more so because the Staff Working Paper frequently referred to above, explicitly states that institutional divergence has not been mentioned in the public consultation as problematic, contrary to procedural divergence and great differences in terms of resources of competition authorities. Cited above at p. 164, at par. 194. The Commission should therefore not create the impression, directly or indirectly, that institutional divergence is a major issue because given the authority it has in the network, this will stimulate spontaneous or quasi-spontaneous convergence which will naturally take the Commission system as an example. This is especially valid in the light of the important criticism on its own system.

1/2003. This great focus on consistency is wide-spread and not only present at the EU institutional level, but also in doctrine. And yet, decentralized application and enforcement is the very essence of the general enforcement system for EU law as it has always existed.[614] Not to say that it is the best system, but no convincing arguments were found in the preparation of the different articles, why there is either more danger for inconsistent application in competition law than elsewhere in EU law, or, alternatively, why competition law inherently has characteristics that make consistency more important.[615]

This observation is not an expression of criticism of the Commission, nor does it presuppose that there is no problem of inconsistent application in the practice of the 27 Member States. It merely expresses authentic surprise and perhaps frustration at not having established exactly why consistency is felt to be such an issue in the area of competition law, but even more so, how such a high level of consensus was reached as to justify, at the legislative and political level that consistency requires particular mechanisms that put serious pressure on procedural autonomy.[616] It is proposed that, from a purely legal point of view, it is far from sure that the concept of consistency is a valid justification as such for measures aiming at furthering convergence

[614] Is monopoly of enforcement a guarantee for consistency? The principle that consistency is an essential principle in the development of a legal system is of course strongly supported. The question at a theoretical level is from which point on (systemic) consistency is challenged by diverging individual decisions at a certain level. On methods of consistency in the network era, see M. de Visser, cited above, in n 479. In EU law the doctrine of consistent application has mainly been advocated in areas where it can serve to compensate the absence of directly applicable rules, it is also referred to then as indirect effect of EU law, see D. Chalmers, C. Hadjiemmanuil, G. Monti and A. Tomkins, *European Union law* (Cambridge: University Press, 2006), p. 381. In competition law, the key provisions are directly applicable and a centralised enforcement system with specific features highlighted above, was in place since the very beginning.

[615] In chapter 6 the question was asked whether effectiveness requires uniformity. To take an example from one of the mechanisms that Reg. 1/2003 contains to "ensure consistency": would one feel the need to allow the Commission to intervene directly in front of an agency applying directly applicable rules on the safety for workers, or pollution or agricultural quota, so as to tell the agency or even the court (see the mechanism contained in Article 15 Reg. 1/2003 discussed in Chapter 6) what the right way to apply the law is? Is a "false negative" (an agreement wrongfully qualified as non-restrictive) so much worse then leaving environmental pollution unpunished because a judge misinterprets a directive? There are always partial justifications for one or the other specific aspects (fines are high, authorities cannot use the preliminary procedure etc.), but none are satisfactory to explain the important, perhaps disproportionate, concern for consistency when compared to other areas of the law.

[616] An "issue" also mentioned as being perceived as a justification for the creation of a number of specific mechanisms like the one mentioned as an example in the previous note. Also, allowing it to be one of the main arguments mentioned by those who favour of (formal) procedural harmonisation. At par. 261 of the Staff Working Paper cited above (p. 164) it is stated yet again, that the stakeholders themselves ask for stronger mechanisms of consistency.

between national enforcement systems. Clearly, there are underlying worries about inconsistencies that provide a basis for a large consensus in this respect both in the legal community as well as in the political arena. In any case, from a broader EU perspective, it is worthwhile looking at the area of competition law to see whether it can serve as an example to design or reorganise the enforcement of other EU rules.

These last two points taken together[617] can also be seen as an encouragement for the Commission to invest further resources in reflecting on divergence in terms of procedure and institutions as well as the actual inconsistencies and their origins. Work in this area is underway in the network, as announced in the 2009 reports on Reg.1/2003, often cited above. When it comes to what the optimal institutional model is for enforcing the law at the EU level, it is perhaps a delicate exercise for the Commission itself, at least in public, to formulate alternatives. That is why the European Parliament, national stakeholders and academics (and not only in competition circles) should take an interest in these issues.

A final point about consistency, convergence and divergence is the difficult question relating to whether, and if so, how much, divergence is still acceptable or even desirable amongst Member States.[618] More in particular, does it not follow from the reasons behind substantive modernisation that there must still be room for Member States to take into account specific national issues? The question here is limited to substantive law:[619] modern competition law requires taking into account economic reality. It seems self-evident that markets are still very different and economic and other market-oriented national policies in 27 countries are not the same. Is it to be reconciled with a more economic approach that there is no room for diverging results in terms of enforcement or for diverging policies (for example in determining priorities)? If, in principle, the feeling exists that there must be some room for national and market specific considerations to come into play, it is totally unclear in the present system how this should best be organized.[620] It is so contrary to the wide-spread belief in

617 The necessary caution in terms of what the model of enforcement is that we are evolving to, on the one hand, and limits of consistency as a legal basis, on the other hand. Chapter 6 also expresses the need for stocktaking of actual remaining divergence.

618 In all the chapters above the assumption has been that there is no or hardly any divergence in terms of substantive law, more substantial divergence is usually assumed to exist in terms of procedure. It was then questioned in several chapters what this means for policymaking.

619 Whether it is also worth protecting divergence for the sake of the different cultural and historical roots of legal systems, was briefly touched on in chapter 5 and is more a concern for procedural harmonisation.

620 Again, the assumption is that, at least amongst the authorities there is no apparent desire to diverge, which does not mean that for political, legal or economical reasons there should not be some room for national priorities. The question is really whether it is only about applying the law to different facts

convergence that it even seems delicate to draw attention to this point. And yet, the questions do seem logical in view of the very essence of the more economical approach to competition law.[621]

3.4. Modernisation as a challenge to the system of judicial protection

In the article in chapter 2 (written and published in 2005), doubts were expressed regarding the question whether the EU legal system, especially from the perspective of the standing of individuals before the Courts, was well adapted to the developments in competition law. The expectation was that the creation of the decentralized system could give rise to some new problems because a series of new types of decisions, possibly affecting the rights of individuals, would be created. [622] The different articles in this thesis also try to convey the general idea that there is little (judicial) control at all on the coordinating and supervisory role that the Commission has been given within the network. This is all the more so when there is not even a formal or informal decision that could (possibly) be challenged. That is why not only soft law instruments were mentioned, but also Commission interventions e.g. in proceedings in national courts, decisions to undertake sector investigations etc.

Given the extent to which worries were expressed at the time of the entry into force of the regulation, one might have expected that the activities of the new enforcement system would have inevitably lead to litigation before the national courts, attempts of direct appeals in Luxemburg to test the standing conditions, or preliminary questions on judicial protection to the Court of Justice. Nevertheless, as far as known, six years after the entry into force of Regulation 1/2003, there has not been a run to the courts to challenge

---

(different markets with different economical policies) or should this difference in markets also result in divergence in policy or even the law?

621 The great degree of convergence will also make it difficult for stakeholders to accept remaining or new divergence at some point if this is not discussed publicly. This is already the case: it is argued that the call for more convergence can be explained by this: the more convergence there is, the less the remaining divergence seems acceptable for legal subjects.

622 A number of examples are recalled here: decisions to exchange information amongst authorities, the reallocation of a case by the Commission (to a national authority), the lack of decision on a request for guidance, new decisions such as decisions with structural remedies, finding of inapplicability, request in the context of sector inquiries but also interventions before the national judge. See chapter 2 and figures mentioned in n 17 above. Some worries are still repeated even though, in practice, not many problematic cases seem to have occurred, see several papers made by working groups in the context of the public consultation in 2009, presented at a conference organized by the GCLC Center of the College of Bruges, the presentations are accessible at: http://www.coleurope.eu/template.asp?pagename=gclcfifthannual_docs (accessed last on 25 June 2010). The comments of stakeholders in the consultation, at: http://ec.europa.eu/competition/consultations/closed.html (accessed last 25 June 2010); papers forthcoming in D. Waelbroeck and M. Merola (eds), *Towards the optimal enforcement of Competition rules in Europe*, 2010.

decisions taken within the network, at whichever level. However, it is too early to draw conclusions. It takes time for all those concerned to adapt to a new enforcement system and it takes time for the individual companies in the market to evaluate in reality whether there are indeed certain actions within the network, and more in particular by the Commission, that they feel they should be able to challenge because their rights are affected.[623] It is also quite relevant that there have simply been very few "new" types of decisions as qualified in chapter 2.[624]

The Commission has expressed its overall satisfaction with the functioning of the enforcement system that the regulation has set up. The lack of litigation challenging its basic principles can be perceived as a factor contributing to this success.[625] Slowly interesting cases are now appearing in relation to the network, but, as far as known, not in relation to the challengeability of Commission acts which was the subject of chapter 2.[626] These cases are mostly references concerning preliminary questions regarding the functioning of the network and various aspects of Reg.1/2003, showing that national judges are prepared to play their role in addressing difficult questions when confronted with them in specific litigation, either opposing private parties, or in the context of an appeal against a decision of a national authority.

---

623 The absence of cases pending before the Court is of course a dangerous parameter to measure whether there is a real problem in terms of judicial protection; it might very well depend on the cost-benefit analysis of companies to invest in bringing cases "of principle" to the Court whilst they are, for example, themselves still subject of investigations. One opportunity to test the case law on appealable acts might be in a case where an appeal was brought against a request for information by the Commission, see above n 547. The case does not address a new type of decision following modernisation though.

624 An attempt to guess which acts would be open to appeal and which would not, see overview in C.S. Kerse and N. Khan, *EC Antitrust procedure,* (London: Sweet & Maxwell, 2005, fifth edition), at p. 475-476.

625 The low amount of decisions of the Commission within the network (but also generally few re-allocation decisions reported for national authorities) might also be a good illustration of another trend which is a general decrease in formal decisions. First, many commentators indeed refer to the fact that coordination and cooperation within the network involves many informal contacts, and second, in general there might be a certain trend to more informal competition policy involving advocacy and even settlements.

626 Some examples are given of interesting cases that cannot be discussed in detail here concerning a new question raised by Reg.1: the Belgian pending case VEBIC on the question whether authorities should be involved in appeal decisions against their decisions, see above at p. 159, n 491; a Czech case on *ne bis in idem* and parallel application, case C-17/10, [2010] OJ C 100/14; a German reference on access to files and information exchange, Case C-360/09, [2009] OJ C 297/18, and, on the competences of NCA's under the regulation, a Polish reference, Case C-375/09, [2009] OJ C 297/19. The lack of cases confirmed in the reports for the FIDE 2008, n 549.

With the benefit of hindsight, part of the worries expressed by many commentators at the time, were perhaps inspired by the fear of what is new and a sense of mistrust at the idea that e.g. authorities amongst themselves would discuss and allocate cases in a system that is perceived as non-transparent for the outside world.[627]

And yet, the absence of notorious cases challenging the potential shortcomings of the system of judicial protection anno 2010 does not alter the strong belief at all, that any decision which affects the rights of parties in a substantial way should be subject to judicial review at the appropriate level and through an effective process.

Taking the perspective of accountability[628] and taking into account the network of competition authorities, first a remark about the national level.

If there is a decision at stake for which the national authority is accountable, judicial review should be situated at a national level.[629] However, if there is one area where there is little or no spontaneous harmonisation, it is the scope and organisation of judicial review of decisions of competition authorities in the Member States. The different mechanisms of harmonisation discussed in chapter 6 hardly touch on this subject. Modernisation in terms of enforcement has concentrated on the authorities, their cooperation and how they can ensure efficient and consistent application of EU competition rules.[630] However, amongst the parameters that can be used to measure adequate judicial protection and effective enforcement is, of course, also the judicial review of decisions of competition authorities.[631] This important component of the overall enforcement system

627 The Commission also suggests this explanation on the basis of the reactions of stakeholders after the consultation on the functioning of the regulation, see for example in par. 214 of the Staff Working Paper cited above at p. 177 in n 98. It is plausible to the extent that the legal community tends to focus very much on legal certainty and the combination of substantive modernisation, the abolishment of the notification system and the creation of the network were many new factors all introduced at once. I believe that, including myself at the time chapter 2 was written, this is a valid explanation to a certain extent and that now generally there is less fear of the problems that can arise within the network and views are more moderate. Some commentators still pinpoint many deficiencies in the system of the network however, see S. Brammer, cited above in n 546.

628 See chapter 5 on governance inspired reasons to reflect on goals of competition law, where this approach is also used, at p. 128 and following.

629 This does seem obvious, but is not really so: more evolutionary scenarios are possible; it is worth mentioning that even EU institutions have already, somewhat timidly, called for a European appeal level, EcoSoc opinion, see at p. 162, n 500.

630 See chapter 6 on the extent to which Regulation 1 has in fact harmonized enforcement. Also, there is guidance for national judges in the form of a Commission Notice, cited e.g. above on p. 17, n 39 and of the course the Courts' case-law, but this is aimed mostly at national courts in general and usually deals with private litigation.

631 These aspects cannot be elaborated on further in these conclusions but sufficient and reliable empirical data on the functioning of the national judiciary in public

is a source of divergence, a potential obstacle to effective enforcement and a potential issue in terms of equal access to court amongst the Member States. It is really time to address this delicate aspect of enforcement in some way.[632] The contrast between the degree of convergence and consistency at the first level (authorities) on the one hand, and the total diversity of procedures once the stage of appeals is reached on the other hand, is striking.

In turn, if the responsibility for the decision affecting the legal position of the individual can be attributed to the Commission, the EU courts come into play.

Whilst modernising substantive law and decentralizing enforcement, the judicial system has not been subject to much change from the perspective of competition law. Over the last years, on the other hand, the pressure on national judges has continuously increased in terms of judicial protection.[633] As it was mentioned already in Chapter 2, this trend shows a lack of balance between the obligations of national judges to protect the rights of parties, on the one hand, and the level of individual judicial protection that exists at the EU level, on the other hand.

---

enforcement is necessary. It is clear that it is a delicate exercise in view of the independence of the judiciary. However, the courts responsible for appeal procedures carry the responsibilities described by the Court of Justice in terms of uniform application, consistency and judicial protection. They definitely are part of the system of enforcement of competition law and yet are not part of it in many ways. It is also a well-know fact that in many jurisdictions the appeal courts are very critical of the decisions and policy of the authorities. These aspects of enforcement are uncoordinated, not harmonised and relatively difficult to discern, but yet may have implications in practice.

632 The suggestion made above in the previous section, that the Commission should envisage work in mapping out sources of divergence, could lead to a White or Green Paper on the subject, see a cautious remark on courts in the 2009 reports, cited above on p. 164 n 509, at par. 270. Also for example the Italian report at FIDE 2004, see D. Cahill (ed), The modernisation of Eu competition law enforcement in the EU, FIDE 2004 reports (Cambridge: Cambridge University Press, 2004), 305.

633 This has been discussed extensively elsewhere for general EU law, see A. Ward, Judicial review and the rights of private parties in EU law, cited above in n 416 at p. 139, chapter 6 of the book; often reference is made to “double standards”. In the area of competition law just one supplementary reference here to the Opinion of Advocate General Mengozzi in VEBIC who has no hesitation to oblige a national judge to adopt a far-reaching interpretation of procedural law for the sake of effectiveness of EU competition law; he explicitly mentions that at some point the legislation will have to change, but in the meanwhile, the judge should adopt an interpretation *contra legem* (and contrary to the explicit intentions of the Belgian legislator) if necessary. See above in n 491, Opinion of 25 March 2010. Whether or not the Court follows the Opinion is less relevant here, but the Opinion shows very well how minds have evolved in terms of the heavy responsibilities of national judges.

The system of judicial protection at the EU level does not seem optimally adapted to the modernised era: neither from the general perspective of judicial protection, nor from the viewpoint of developments in competition law enforcement. The Lisbon Treaty which has taken the place that was initially allotted to the Constitutional Treaty still referred to in chapter 2, has not fundamentally altered that view. Whether or not the new wording of Article 263 TFEU will widen access to the European Courts is still an open question at this time.[634] But fundamentally, this is not really the main issue in competition law. It is not only about a more liberal interpretation of admissibility requirements in relation to the requirement of 'individual concern', there are other factors that contribute to the insufficiency of the system.

When it comes to admissibility, both the uncertainty about the individual concern of applicants but also the restrictive case-law on preparatory acts was mentioned above.[635] Furthermore, other factors also appeared such as mainly the slow process of judicial review and the relatively passive role of the Courts when it comes to instructing cases.[636] In other words, there is more reason for concern than only the issues raised most often by practioners, namely case allocation decisions within the network and information exchanges between authorities, and the lack of standing to challenge them. The Court system simply has not evolved sufficiently over the years to keep up with developments both in competition law as well as in judicial protection.[637]

When it comes to judicial review at the request of individuals,[638] the purpose should be, on the one hand, optimising the structure in view of the more economic approach,[639] whilst, on the other hand, ensuring adequate judicial

---

634 But chapter 2 and the brief discussion above in section 2.1, already show that the issue in the area of competition law is not always the seemingly regulatory nature of the act. Rather, the challenge still lies in the individual and/or direct effect and in the definitive nature of an act.

635 The case-law on preparatory acts or non definitive acts not open to appeal, can be an obstacle because the general idea seems to be that many acts performed within the network by the Commission would fall within this category, .. As was said above, the focus has been on re-allocation decisions but more decisions were dealt with in chapter 2 and many of the questions raised there are still valid.

636 Chapter 2 and 4. See also provocative and interesting comments by P. Marsden, 'Checks and balances: EU competition law and the rule of law' (2009) *Competition Law International* 24.

637 Clearly the purpose is not to fall into the trap of what Chalmers calls the "lazy assumption" of lawyers that every denial of locus standi to an individual amounts to a lack of judicial protection, cited above in n 614, see at p. 434. The claims here are not new, but there are a number of factors that, taken together should lead to a reform of the system.

638 When it comes to the supervisory role of the Commission in the network, chapters 5 and 6 also suggest more involvement of stakeholders at a national and EU level, to increase accountability.

639 For the phase at the Commission, this aspect was already partly discussed in section 3.2 above and in the chapters mentioned there. In chapters 4 and 5 some

protection.[640] Both require sufficient flexibility of process and full respect of fundamental rights. Reconciling, on the one hand, the efficiency of the process and an outcome which is as sound as possible from an economic perspective, whilst, on the other hand, trying to achieve a sufficient degree of effective judicial protection, is probably just about the biggest challenge for competition law enforcement in the near future and this challenge is also one the Courts should take up.[641]

Possible solutions at the Court level have been discussed elsewhere and can range from relatively minor changes[642] to more revolutionary ones.[643] In terms of access to the court and the need to ensure accountability of the Commission, also in playing its role in the network as discussed above, serious thought might be given to the creation of a specialized EU Competition Tribunal.[644]

This Tribunal should be willing to review, in fast track procedure if necessary, all acts for which the Commission is responsible and that affect the rights of private parties in a substantial way.[645] The (older) case law

---

hints were given about the impact that more economics should have for judges and the difficulties this can imply.

640 This resumes the overall challenge competition law is confronted with since modernisation, see W. Kerber, 'Should competition law promote efficiency? Some reflections of an economist on the normative foundations of competition law', in: *Economic theory and competition law*, cited above in n 605.

641 As competition law continues to develop and enforcement becomes more effective and visible, the procedural questions are more and more at the heart of every case. Both the general pressure on authorities and courts in terms of ensuring adequate judicial protection and ensuring due process, but also substantive developments are responsible for this, as shown throughout this book. For a very interesting analysis in this respect, A. Louvaris, 'A brief overview of some conflicts between economic efficiency and efffectiveness of the administrative or judicial process in competition law' in J. Drexl, L. Idot, J. Monéger (eds), *Economic theory and competition law* (Cheltenham: Edward Elgar, 2009).

642 Integrating economists in the process somehow or merely taking a more active approach to proof and standard of review as suggested is minimalistic in the sense that it does not require structural institutional reforms.

643 Such as forsaking the exclusive competence of the EU courts to examine the legality of the Commission actions, on the one hand, or the creation of decentralised courts or setting up decentralised courts in all Member States, or for certain larger regions, on the other hand. An overview of various ideas on the reform of the judicial architecture, in D. Chalmers and others, cited above in n 614 p. 122 and following and 303 and following. Debates on the judicial architecture of the EU have often focused on the preliminary rulings. Obviously, if structural reforms were to be envisaged for competition cases, they have to be seen in the light of the general structure and workload of the Courts.

644 Former President of the Court of First Instance (General Court) Bo Vesterdorf has pleaded for such a reform as well, see for example in the contribution cited above in n 594, at p. 511.

645 It is clear that the length of procedures and the great reluctance of the Courts in general to award relief in interlocutory proceedings (Article 278, 279 TFEU, these cases are practically non-existent) are two additional elements that contribute to

should be reviewed, a less rigid approach to admissibility should be seriously considered in such a way as to cover the two lines of case law discussed above: the obstacle of 'individual concern' and the obstacle of what constitutes a challengeable binding act.[646] Either this is done by differentiating competition law from other areas of European law[647] or rather by a more general "revirement de jurisprudence" on behalf of the Courts. It should be possible to have sufficient regard to the content and effects of a decision taken by the Commission in the current enforcement framework: in some cases parties will be able to prove that a decision (whether or not it is technically a final decision) has substantial impact on their legal position.[648] In such a case, review must be possible. Such a solution would necessarily involve a case-to-case approach and the outcome of review might not be foreseeable until a body of case-law will have been built. However, the possibility must exist to challenge certain decisions for which, in any case, an action at a national level shall not exist because the responsibilty for the decision lies with the Commission.[649]

At least as important as issues of access to court, it is proposed that the review system should present the necessary procedural flexibility when it comes to dealing with economical assessment.[650] Reviewing judges should be equipped and willing to review factual and economical appraisal if necessary

---

the insufficiency of the system. Would it be accepted in the legal systems of many Member States that urgent measures are de facto never taken by the competent court, for example suspending a cartel decision imposing a fine? Fast track procedures (or expedited procedures) have existed for a number of years, but seem to be scarcely used.

646 The criterion proposed by Advocate General Jacobs was a good basis: any measure that *has, or is liable to have, a substantial adverse effect on the interests of the individual*, Opinion cited above at p. 9, n 16. One might add "*or on his legal position*". Introducing and developing a criterion like that could cover many of the worries in relation to access to court and combine the two lines of case law mentioned here.

647 This can be justified because competition law, state aid and dumping have always been treated somewhat differently by the Court in the past when it came to admissibility, see for a recent overview and comparison with access to court in competition cases in the Netherlands, A. Gerbrandy, cited at p. 140, n 419 e.g. at p. 141 and following.

648 It can not be excluded that a re-allocation decision can have an impact on the position of an undertaking, it will be up to them to demonstrate substantive impact in fact or in law, but not to forget the other types of decisions mentioned in chapter 2.

649 Regardless of whether one agrees with the outcome of the case and whether regulations should be challengable, it is felt that the judgment in UPA (cited above in n 20) was particularly unstaisfactory where the Court referred to indirect possibilities to challenge a Community act at the national level, as if it were an alternative for a direct challenge before the Community (now EU) judges. Every level should take its responsibility in the system.

650 See the interesting ideas of B. Vesterdorf based on his experience at the Court, on how to adapt procedures to competition cases, cited above in n 594 but also in n 25 in chapter 2.

and in an active way.[651] There is also substantial distance and room for manoeuvre between marginal review, on the one hand, and leaving no discretion to the Commission at the risk of taking the place of the enforcer, on the other. The right balance between full review and marginal review is still yet to be found.

The creation of a specialized tribunal does not actually require such major changes in terms of institutional setup: the creation of specialised courts was already possible and has been made easier[652] and the Statute of the Court, which deals with procedure, can also be modified more easily since the Lisbon Treaty.[653] The other suggestions made above are a question of policy reorientation by the Courts.

It is certainly true that these very brief critical remarks in the context of a conclusion do not provide for an easy-to-use blueprint for a future redesigned enforcement system. This was not the subject of a specific article although judicial protection and the EU court system have always been a source of concern. The belief that the EU judicial system needs a change is confirmed by the study underlying the different articles.

It is proposed that the matter needs to be approached in a comprehensive way: from the perspective of individual judicial protection and the procedural framework, both at the level of the Commission and the EU courts, are to be evaluated together.[654] Recently, an upsurge of serious criticism on the

---

[651] See about the passive role of the Courts in that context already in 2001 article with G. van der Wal, in *Europees bewijsrecht: een verkenning*, cited above in chapter 4, above in n 229. Without even considering radical changes of the enforcement system that might be feasible in the longer term, it should be considered how the instruction of cases could be more active in terms of calling witnesses or organizing confrontation on economical data and analysis. Of course, if the Commission itself should consider important changes to its institutional structure towards a more judicial one, the comprehensive approach to enforcement would require it to take that into account when redesigning the judicial review component: maybe in such a case, for example, a more marginal review of facts and data might be accepted, see below on the need for a comprehensive approach.

[652] Article 257 TFEU. It no longer requires unanimity in the Council since the Lisbon Treaty. For a view doubting the usefulness of a new Court, the report of the House of Lords, Select Committee on European Union, Session 2006-2007 accessible via: http://www.publications.parliament.uk/pa/ld200607/ldselect/ldeucom/75/7506.htm.

[653] Article 281 TFEU: the Court can request that modification and unanimity in the Council is no longer required. There is substantial room for further improvement here as well: the Courts should be able now to organize their procedures more autonomously and in a more flexible way. See for some comments on changes since Lisbon, L. Parret, 'En wat met de rechtsbescherming? Het Verdrag van Lissabon en de communautaire rechter' in: *De Europese Unie na het Verdrag van Lissabon* (Deventer: Kluwer, 2009).

[654] In fact this also means including the third level, the appeal on points of law at the Court of Justice after the appeal at the General Court.

Commission system can be heard again.[655] The main focus of attention is the fact that the Commission is simultaneously investigator and decision-maker.[656] This much publicized debate falls well outside the present conclusions. The point to be made here is that the two levels of enforcement are to be evaluated together when the overall level of individual judicial protection is assessed.[657] A proposal by which, for example, some minor changes are made to the institutional format of the Commission might be more acceptable if the system of judicial review is substantially reinforced. Vice versa, if some of the insufficiencies of the Court system remain in place and no changes occur at that level, a more thorough reform of Commission procedures might be called for.[658] It is not a question of simply communicating vessels, but of two levels that are part of one and the same enforcement system.

Recalling the mindset described in the introduction (namely a consistent questioning if and how competition differs from general EU law and how it interacts with the rest of the legal system) the question might be: why should there be a different judicial system or why should the existing judicial

---

655 The public consultation organised after five years of functioning of Reg. 1/2003 was the opportunity for the market to react and the recent substantially high fines are often referred to as the reasons for criticism on the Commission's procedures and institutional structures.

656 Most comments focus on the deficiencies of the Commission's procedures, but the Courts' responsibilities should not be neglected. In the reports on the functioning of Regulation 1/2003 the Commission addresses some sources of criticism on its own system and refutes them, cited above see p. 164, e.g. at par. 51 and 125. Some fierce criticism is found in papers presented at the GCLC conference mentioned above in n 88. For two different perspectives: A. Riley, 'The modernisation of EU anti-cartel enforcement: will the Commission grasp the opportunity' (2010) *European Competition Law Review* 191, and W. Wils, 'The increased level of EC antitrust fines, judicial review and the European Convention of Human Rights', (2010) 33 *World Competition* 5. If ever criminal sanctions would become possible at the EU level, this would again have a profound impact on institutional choices: if the General Court would then always be the one imposing the fine, it could presumably not be the appeal judge at the same time.

657 Whilst clearly differentiating between the national and EU level, the idea expressed here is, however, a very different one than the one expressed by the Court in the UPA judgment, often cited above, see p. 10, n 20 where the Court seemed to have said that the possibilities the individual has at a national level and at the EU level should be taken together. Unless very revolutionary changes would be made, such as making the Commission accountable in front of national judges, quod non, both levels should be differentiated and each should achieve its own acceptable level of judicial protection.

658 A very recent case (Grand Chamber judgment) gives rise to some pessimism at first sight, in the sense that it is so categorical on the limited review that the General Court should carry out when it reviews Commission decisions, pushing the General Court in a very passive role and leaving substantial leeway for the Commission, judgment of 29 June 2010, Case C-441/07 P. Irrespective of whether the General Court did or did not make a wrong assessment in this case, this line of case law would tend to confirm the fact that serious thought is to be given to improving the system.

system be adapted to competition law?[659] At the EU level, the answer lies in the modernisation and the important changes that the law has undergone, the specific roles that the Commission plays in terms of enforcement and in the network, combined with, finally, the evolving requirements of effective judicial protection.

4. Post scriptum: the relationship between substantive and procedural law and the interaction between competition law and EU law in general

From a theoretical perspective, the key issue that appears from this book is the *relationship and the interaction between substantive law and procedural law*. Although it was never as such the focus of attention in a seperate way, it appeared more and more clearly when the project was undertaken to compile a book by bringing together different articles on competition law enforcement. Together, they hopefully demonstrate the clear existence of interaction between substantive law and procedural law and the idea that every substantive development should include an equal amount of thought on procedural implications and vice versa. Procedure might be instrumental to substance, but the two are strongly linked.

How to adapt the institutional structure in an optimal way to ensure the application of new rules and how will new enforcement rules affect the law that is applied? This question could be part of a standard impact assessment test when new legislation or policy initiatives are envisaged. The area of competition law presents an interesting opportunity to take this issue forward at an EU level because of a number of characteristics described above. It also presents many examples illustrating how intertwined procedure and substance are. In fact, modernisation as defined in the introduction of this thesis, comprising both decentralisation and substantive modernisation, is in itself the best example of how procedure and substance are linked. Regulation 1/2003 might have been about decentralising or reforming enforcement but it is also about adapting the system to substantive reform.

At the same time, whilst ascertaining that interaction is a reality, the thesis shows the need for more fundamental research into this issue. This research could contribute towards optimising enforcement structures and, thus, be useful beyond the field of competition law.

Other than the fact that this general proposition on the existence of interaction between substantive and procedural law, goes beyond the area of

[659] The essence of the remarks on the judicial protection system are the objectives that a reform should achieve: a more active and more rapid process, more flexibility and a wider access to court for review of Commission actions. The suggestion of a separate tribunal was made but is not the focus point: these objectives can be achieved by another type of institutional reform within the Courts.

competition law enforcement, the different side effects discussed in the chapters above, are presented together in the title of this compilation as a challenge to the enforcement system of competition law, but also as a challenge to the enforcement of EU law in general.

The first reason for that is the strong belief that EU competition law is very much part of EU law regardless of the fairly autonomous way it seems to have developed recently. Enforcement of competition law has its own characteristics but it is inevitably the enforcement of EU law, with a role for the EU institutions and a role for the national judges, all bound by primary and secondary EU legislation. There is therefore inevitably interaction between EU law and competition law. The first common theme identified above (the relationship between competition law and the internal market, sub-section 3.1) is already in itself sufficient illustration of the interaction between competition law and EU law in general.

The argument was made at several occasions that competition specialists should not underestimate the fact that competition law is part of EU law. Vice versa, by presenting the side effects of modernisation as a challenge to the enforcement of EU law in general, the purpose is to state that it is worthwhile in many respects for non-competition lawyers to take an interest in these side effects because they can shed a light on more general enforcement issues. The title which aims at broadening the scope of the challenge is meant to trigger interest in that respect.

The impact of developments within competition law on EU law in general is more or less important or direct depending on the subject. The points which were raised in relation to the impact of substantive reform on procedure (second common theme above, sub-section 3.2) are of a general nature, for example the difficulty that a legal system has to integrate non-legal concepts. These points show, amongst other things, the importance of a clear definition of concepts and the evaluation of how they fit into the procedural framework within which the law is enforced.

From the perspective of the optimal integration of EU law into national legal orders, the experiences described under the next common theme (relationship between decentralisation, convergence and consistency, sub-section 3.3 but also the networking aspects of the enforcement system) should also provide for an interesting source of inspiration in a more general way. The use of a large variety of convergence mechanisms outside of the traditional harmonisation instruments and the results that this has achieved, are worth examining. Finally, the doubts about the system of judicial protection that were expressed above (the last common theme, sub-section 3.4) are evidently also related to the broader issue of how the system of judicial protection is best organised at the EU level.

Table of Treaty articles

(chapters 2, 3 and 4 still mention former articles in EC Treaty)

Numbering in EC Treaty	**Numbering since Lisbon Treaty**
Article 2 and 3 EC	Article 3 TEU, various articles in TFEU and protocols
Article 10 EC	Article 4, III TEU
Article 81 EC	Article 101 TFEU
Article 82 EC	Article 102 TFEU
Article 83 EC	Article 103 TFEU
Article 230 EC	Article 263 TFEU
Article 234 EC	Article 267 TFEU
Article 249 EC	Article 288 TFEU
Article 308 EC	Article 352 TFEU

NEDERLANDSE SAMENVATTING

Neveneffecten van de modernisering van EU mededingingsrecht
Modernisering als een uitdaging voor het handhavingssysteem van het Europese mededingingsrecht en van het Europees recht in het algemeen

In dit proefschrift worden vijf artikelen bij elkaar gebracht die geschreven werden tussen 2005 en 2010. De titel "Neveneffecten van de modernisering-modernisering als een uitdaging voor het handhavingssysteem van Europees mededingingsrecht en Europees recht in het algemeen" formuleert het onderwerp van alle verschillende artikels.

Voor alle artikelen geldt dat ze opgenomen werden in de vorm waarin ze werden gepubliceerd. Dat heeft voor gevolg dat de hoofdstukken 2, 3 en 4 nog de oude nummering van de verdragen vermelden. Om die reden werd hierna een tabel opgenomen waarin enkele belangrijke corresponderende artikelen worden weergegeven. Hoofdstuk 6 werd nog niet gepubliceerd op het moment van het afronden van het manuscript voor dit proefschrift.

Voor ingewijden in het mededingingsrecht is de term modernisering bekend, althans veelvuldig gebruikt. In dit kader past het eerst om aan te geven wat hiermee word bedoeld. Modernisering dekt een combinatie van verschillende ontwikkelingen die in de afgelopen jaren plaats hebben gevonden in het Europese mededingingsrecht en die zowel een materiële (inhoudelijke) component als ook meer procedurele en institutionele component hebben. Dit proefschrift raakt aan beide componenten, meer bepaald vanuit het perspectief van de handhaving van het recht. Het samenbrengen van de verschillende artikelen vanuit dit perspectief toont aan dat beide aspecten van de modernisering met elkaar verband houden.

Met inhoudelijke modernisering wordt een proces bedoeld dat, kort gezegd, neerkomt op een meer economische benadering van het mededingingsrecht. Meer aandacht voor economische analyse en de marktomstandigheden maar ook meer samenwerking tussen juristen en economen. De andere component van modernisering doelt, kort gezegd, op een proces van decentralisering dat in gang werd gezet door Verordening 1/2003 van 16 december 2002 van de Raad. In het bijzonder ziet deze decentralisering op een grotere betrokkenheid van nationale rechters en ook nationale mededingings-autoriteiten in de handhaving van Europees mededingingsrecht.

De term neveneffecten werd gekozen omdat er in de verschillende stukken onderwerpen aan bod komen die niet als zodanig de inhoud of de doelstelling van de modernisering waren maar die zich gaandeweg voordeden als neveneffecten. Het gaat om de volgende onderwerpen: problemen van individuele rechstbescherming door nieuwsoortige beslissingen die de Commissie kan nemen (hoofdstuk 2), de veranderende rol van de interstatelijkheid als voorwaarde voor de toepassing van de mededingingsregels (hoofdstuk 3), de toegenomen aandacht voor de bewijsproblematiek (hoofdstuk 4), de verwarring rondom de doelstellingen die het mededingingsrecht beoogt na te streven (hoofdstuk 5), en de trend naar verdere harmonisering van het (nationale) procesrecht in mededingingszaken.

De gemeenschappelijke aanpak in al de artikelen is dat wordt gekozen voor voor een bredere perspectief vanuit het Europese recht. De keuze op zich al van de onderwerpen kan door dit bredere perspectief verklaard worden. Daaraan ligt de overtuiging ten grondslag dat het mededingingsrecht, ondanks zijn zelfstandige ontwikkeling in de afgelopen jaren, integraal deel uitmaakt van het bredere Europees recht en daarmee verbonden is. Het kan interessant zijn voor niet–mededingingsjuristen om een aantal van de neveneffecten die hier worden beschreven, te bestuderen met het oog op het verder ontwikkelen van handhavingsmechanismen elders in het Europese recht. Omgekeerd wordt er ook in verschillende onderdelen op gewezen dat mededingingsjuristen er voor moeten waken om niet uit het oog te verliezen dat het mededingingsrecht deel uitmaakt van de bredere Europeesrechtelijke context.

Het eerste artikel dat in de bundel is opgenomen, betreft rechtsbescherming en meer bepaald toegang tot de rechter voor individuele ondernemingen. De vraag die wordt behandeld is of het handhavingssysteem zoals het opgezet is door Verordening 1/2003 bijdraagt tot een gebrek aan rechtsbescherming zoals dat op andere terreinen in het EU recht was gesignaleerd in de jaren voorafgaand aan het artikel (2005). Het artikel concludeert dat het overdreven zou zijn om te stellen dat het nieuwe gedecentraliseerde systeem op poten gezet door de Verordening, op zichzelf belangrijke problemen van rechtsbescherming veroorzaakt. Echter, er zijn bepaalde kenmerken van het nieuwe systeem die wel reeds eerder bestaande zorgen versterken. Het gaat met name om een reeks nieuwe soorten formele en informele Commissie beschikkingen waarvan het onduidelijk is of ze kunnen worden aangevochten voor het Hof in een rechtstreeks beroep (artikel 263 VWEU). In de conclusies in hoofdstuk 7 van dit proefschrift (onderdeel 2.1) wordt gewezen op enkele ontwikkelingen die sinds 2005 hebben plaats gevonden. Eerst met betrekking tot het belang van het beginsel van adequate rechtsbescherming, en verder wordt bezien of zich sinds 2005 al zaken hebben voorgedaan waaruit kan worden afgeleid of het Hof van Justitie bereid zou zijn om haar rechtspraak met betrekking tot rechtstreekse beroepen door individuele ondernemingen, bij te stellen. Die vraag wordt voorlopig negatief beantwoord maar er wordt gesteld dat het te vroeg is om daaruit conclusies te trekken.

In hoofdstuk 3 is een artikel vervat dat gepubliceerd werd in 2006 en dat handelt over het vereiste van de interstatelijkheid. Net zoals de bepalingen inzake vrij verkeer, is het voor de toepassing van zowel artikel 101 VWEU als 102 VWEU vereist dat de handel tussen lidstaten wordt beïnvloed door de gedragingen die aan de orde zijn. Het uitgangspunt in het artikel is de vraag of in het mededingingsrecht het vereiste van interstatelijkheid ook in belang afneemt zoals dat elders in het Europese recht het geval lijkt te zijn. In het artikel wordt een overzicht gegeven van de wijze waarop de interstatelijkheid wordt geïnterpreteerd door de Commissie en in de rechtspraak. In het algemeen moet gezegd dat de drempel voor het aannemen van interstatelijk effect niet hoog ligt. Dit is eigenlijk niet anders sinds de Commissie in nieuwe richtsnoeren in 2004 haar zienswijze publiceerde over hoe met dit vereiste moet worden omgegaan. De conclusie van het onderzoek in hoofdstuk 3 is dat het voor de juridische analyse van concurrentiebeperkend gedrag nauwelijks uitmaakt of er al dan niet invloed is op de interstatelijke handel. Het resultaat is immers hetzelfde omdat de materiële bepalingen van het nationale en het Europese recht doorgaans identiek zijn. In tegenstelling tot andere onderdelen van het Europees recht, zijn nationaal en Europees recht niet dichterbij gebracht doordat de interstatelijkheid aan belang afnam, maar door specifieke harmonisatiemechanismen die typisch zijn voor het mededingingsrecht (ze komen ook meer uitvoerig aan bod in hoofdstuk 6). Derhalve maakt het voor de toepassing van het recht niet uit of er sprake is van beïnvloeding van de handel tussen lidstaten of niet.

Uit de aanvullingen die in hoofdstuk 7 worden gegeven met betrekking tot de ontwikkelingen die zich voordeden sinds 2006 (in onderdeel 2.2), blijkt dat er aan deze situatie niet veel is gewijzigd. Meer dan ooit is de voorwaarde van interstatelijk effect zelf een factor van convergentie geworden en speelt deze voorwaarde een belangrijke rol bij het bepalen van de regels die nationale rechters en autoriteiten moeten toepassen. Immers, door de werking van artikel 3 van Verordening 1/2003 moeten bij interstatelijk effect, zowel de nationale verbodsbepalingen (de nationale tegenhangers van de artikelen 101 en 102 VWEU) als de Europese verbodsbepalingen samen worden toegepast zoals reeds in hoofdstuk 3 werd beschreven. Vanaf dat moment, treden er verder een aantal bepalingen in werking die voor nationale rechters en nationale autoriteiten belangrijke verplichtingen inhouden, zoals bijvoorbeeld het voorleggen door autoriteiten van hun ontwerpbeslissingen aan de Commissie en de algemene verplichting om ten allen tijde tegenstrijdige beslissingen te vermijden. De vereiste van interstatelijkheid heeft dan ook een hele eigen functie binnen het mededingingsrecht.

In hoofdstuk 4 wordt een artikel weergegeven dat handelt over een typisch juridisch onderwerp, namelijk bewijs. De toegenomen aandacht voor bewijsproblemen en vraagstukken wordt ook gezien als een neveneffect van modernisering. Er lijkt op het eerste gezicht een tegenstelling te bestaan tussen een meer economische aanpak enerzijds en meer aandacht voor traditioneel juridische onderwerpen zoals bewijs. In het artikel wordt gepoogd om aan te geven dat er van dergelijke tegenstelling echter geen sprake is.

Vanuit zowel een breder Europees perspectief (bijvoorbeeld algemene rechtsbeginselen) alsook vanuit de context van een toegenomen samenwerking met economen, wordt ingegaan op een aantal bewijsvraagstukken in kartelzaken en worden twee kernbegrippen gesitueerd: de bewijsstandaard en de bewijslast. Een eerder pragmatische kijk op bewijs wordt voorgesteld. Deze aanpak vereist dat juristen aanvaarden om te functioneren in een systeem dat voldoende flexibel en gedifferentieerd kan zijn om zich aan te passen aan de specifieke kenmerken van het mededingingsrecht. Langs de andere kant, vereist de voorgestelde aanpak dat de economen goed begrijpen dat de meeste regels inzake bewijs in feite de uitdrukking zijn van fundamentele rechtsbeginselen die aan de basis liggen van ons rechtssysteem en dus niet alleen moeten worden gezien als technische obstakels in een kartelzaak. In het artikel wordt ook gewezen op het (onderschatte) belang van de motiveringsplicht. Aangezien de meer economische benadering er vaak toe leidt dat bij de toepassing van de mededingingsregels keuzes moeten worden gemaakt, wordt het belang van een goede redenering en motivering alleen maar groter. Een degelijke motivering beschermt immers de rechten van partijen en zorgt voor "accountability". Het laat bovendien ook toe dat beslissingen het onderwerp kunnen zijn van rechtsmiddelen. In de conclusies wordt er nog op één belangrijke zaak die gewezen is sinds het publiceren van het artikel. Het gaat meer bepaald om het arrest T-Mobile van het Hof van Justitie. Verder wordt gesteld dat de grote stroom van zaken die in de afgelopen jaren handelen over de bewijsproblematiek aantonen dat dit inderdaad één van de voornaamste actuele vraagstukken in het mededingingsrecht is.

In hoofdstuk 5 wordt ingegaan op een ander fenomeen dat als een neveneffect van modernisering wordt aangemerkt. Het gaat namelijk om de nadruk die door de Commissie (daarin gevolgd door de meeste concurrentieautoriteiten) wordt gelegd op de consument en het consumentenbelang, en de verwarring die dat veroorzaakt over de doelstellingen van het Europese mededingingsrecht. In dit artikel (gepubliceerd in 2009 als discussiestuk en in herziene versie in 2010 als artikel) worden de doelstellingen van het Europese mededingingsrecht bekeken. De bedoeling is om aan te tonen dat er, ondanks de huidige sterke nadruk op de consument, altijd een reeks van verschillende doelstellingen zijn geweest in het systeem van het Europese mededingingsrecht. Het overzicht wil in twee richtingen inzicht verschaffen: langs de ene kant door aan te tonen dat ook in vroegere tijden de consument al centraal stond met name in de rechtspraak van het Hof van Justitie, en, anderzijds, door aan te tonen dat het systeem van EU mededingingsrecht onterecht gereduceerd wordt door de te sterke nadruk op het consumentenbelang omdat er een reeks andere doelstellingen zijn die eigen zijn aan het Europese mededingingsrecht. Meer nog, recente rechtspraak alsook de nieuwe bepalingen van het Verdrag van Lissabon worden aangehaald om aan te geven dat andere doelstellingen van het mededingingsrecht zoals de marktintegratie, meer dan ooit aanwezig zijn. Vervolgens probeert het artikel aan te tonen dat een discussie over de doelstellingen van het mededingingsrecht meer is dan alleen een theoretische discussie over de normatieve grondslagen van het recht. De doelstellingen hebben wel degelijk hun concrete impact, zowel op beleid als op de uitlegging en de handhaving van het recht. Verder wordt er vanuit een breder perspectief aandacht gevraagd voor factoren buiten het mededingingsrecht die ook mede hebben geleid tot de huidige nadruk op de consument. Met andere woorden, de 'consumer focus' is niet alleen toe te schrijven aan de meer economische aanpak of aan de voornamere rol die economen thans spelen. Tenslotte worden een aantal redenen opgesomd waarom een debat over de doelstellingen belangrijk is. Het gaat ondermeer om zogenaamde 'governance' argumenten alsook om de coherentie en de goede werking van het gedecentraliseerde handhavingssysteem dat werd opgezet door Verordening 1/2003. Er wordt gepleit voor de erkenning van de veelzijdige persoonlijkheid van het mededingingsrecht en gewaarschuwd voor de verenging van de publieke boodschap tot het consumentenbelang, niet in het minst omdat er nog te veel onduidelijkheid bestaat over wat het nastreven van het consumentenbelang inhoudt.

Tenslotte gaat het artikel in hoofdstuk 6 verder op de decentraliseringsaspecten van de modernisering. Het uitgangspunt is de sterke convergentie of harmonisering die plaatsgevonden heeft tussen het nationale en het Europese mededingingsrecht in de afgelopen jaren. Voor wat betreft het materiële recht is dit al veel langer aan de gang (dit werd ook kort beschreven in eerdere hoofdstukken, 2 en 3). Voor wat betreft procedure is er thans een debat ontstaan over de opportuniteit van verdere harmonisering van het nationale procesrecht (met name in de publieke handhaving) en het wegnemen van de laatste verschillen die bestaan tussen de handhavingsprocessen in de verschillende lidstaten. Een debat is wellicht zelfs een verkeerde term, aangezien er een grote consensus lijkt te bestaan dat verdere harmonisering nodig is, zowel in de markt als bij de autoriteiten. Hierbij wordt zeer regelmatig het effectiviteitsbeginsel aangehaald. Daartegenover wordt dan het beginsel van procesautonomie geplaatst. De tegenstelling tussen beiden is in het Europese recht wel bekend.

De bedoeling van het artikel is om na te gaan wat de huidige stand van het recht nu eigenlijk is ten aanzien van deze beide belangrijke beginselen. Vervolgens kan dan worden nagegaan welke hun waarde is als argument voor of tegen verdere harmonisering van het procesrecht in mededingingszaken. Het artikel beoogt tegelijkertijd een actuele kijk op effectiviteit en procesautonomie te bieden door de bril van het mededingingsrecht, als ook tegelijkertijd deze beginselen dan terug te plaatsen in het huidige debat en enkele gedachten te vormen over de noodzaak of opportuniteit van verdere harmonisering. De uitkomst is een genuanceerde beschouwing dat noch effectiviteit noch procesautonomie doorslaggevende waarde hebben als het gaat over harmonisering van nationaal procesrecht. Het mededingingsrecht wordt gekenmerkt door een dermate sterke trend naar convergentie dat het echter natuurlijk lijkt om naar harmonisering te streven. Het is aannemelijk dat ook de coherentie en de consistente toepassing van het recht er wel bij zouden kunnen varen. Er is voldoende aandacht nodig voor de wijze waarop dit gebeurt: na een accurate inventaris van waar nu nog divergentie bestaat die echt problematisch is en die door harmonisering kan worden opgelost, en met voldoende betrokkenheid van stakeholders, niet alleen in de wereld van het mededingingsrecht.

Hoofdstuk 7 valt uiteen in twee delen. Eerst worden de conclusies van de verschillende artikelen samengevat en voor de oudere artikelen worden kort enkele nieuwe meer recente ontwikkelingen aangehaald (die hierboven in de samenvatting reeds zijn geïntegreerd). In het tweede, uitvoerige, onderdeel wordt de samenhang tussen de verschillende stukken aangetoond aan de hand van vier gemeenschappelijke thema's. Deze thema's komen in mindere of meerdere mate voor in al de verschillende artikelen. De bespreking ervan laat ook toe om een aantal opmerkingen en aanbevelingen naar de toekomst toe te formuleren.

Het gaat om de volgende thema's:

(1) de relatie tussen mededingingsrecht en de interne markt
(2) materiële modernisering (meer economische benadering) als een uitdaging voor het handhavingssysteem
(3) modernisering vanuit een organisatorisch perspectief: de ingewikkelde relatie tussen decentralisering, convergentie en consistentie
(4) modernisering als een uitdaging voor het systeem van rechtsbescherming.

De belangrijkste opmerkingen die bij elk van die thema's aanbod komen, kunnen als volgt kort worden samengevat.

(1) De relatie tussen mededingingsrecht en de interne markt

In hoofdstuk 5 werd het verband aangetoond aan de hand van de discussie van de doelstellingen waarbij werd aangegeven dat met name de rol van de marktintegratie (als typische EU doelstelling) moet worden ge(her)definieerd in het mededingingsrecht. Uit het onderwerp van hoofdstuk 3 (interstatelijkheid) blijkt ook duidelijk het verband tussen het mededingingsrecht en de regels inzake de interne markt. Ook het debat over de plaats van niet-economische belangen bij de invulling van de verbodsbepalingen is een gemeenschappelijk kenmerk van de mededingingsvoorschriften en de (andere) regels inzake de interne markt. Het verband tussen beiden kan ook een interessante factor zijn in de discussie rond de mogelijke rechtsbasis voor verdere (formele) harmonisering van procesrecht (hoofdstuk 6). In hoofdstuk 7 wordt onder dit thema ook nog een verschilpunt besproken dat blijkt uit de verschillende artikelen: de relatie tussen nationaal recht en EU recht is anders geëvolueerd in het mededingingsrecht dan elders. De bestudering van dit verschil is de moeite waard vanuit een brede

Europeesrechtelijke context en kan inzichten brengen in de integratie van het Europese recht in de nationale rechtsorde meer in het algemeen.

(2) Materiële modernisering (meer economische benadering) als een uitdaging voor het handhavingssysteem

In hoofdstuk 7 worden enkele algemene beschouwingen ontwikkeld over het samengaan van recht en economie in het mededingingsrecht. Modernisering heeft het zoeken naar een optimale co-existentie noodzakelijk gemaakt. Er wordt aangegeven dat er duidelijk een evolutie is in de zoektocht naar een optimaal samenwerken tussen juristen en economen.

Het belang van de economische inbreng wordt erkend, maar moet steeds worden gezien in de context van een rechtssysteem dat gebaseerd is op rechtsbeginselen en dat het recht toepast en handhaaft in een specifieke procedurele context. Hoofdstuk 5 over de doelstellingen belichtte de verwarring die kan ontstaan zijn door de "consumer focus" die wordt geïdentificeerd met meer economische inbreng. Hoofdstuk 4 probeerde vanuit de context van samenwerking tussen juristen en economen, enkele basisbegrippen uit het bewijsrecht te bespreken.

Een belangrijke vaststelling is dat de inhoudelijke modernisering, doorgaans de meer economische benadering genoemd, vraagstukken op de voorgrond heeft gebracht die raken aan het procedurele kader waarin het mededingingsrecht wordt toegepast. De interactie tussen het introduceren van nieuwe materiële beginselen enerzijds, en het procesrecht anderzijds, mag niet worden onderschat. Inhoud en procedure zijn nauw met elkaar verbonden. Het komt vaak neer op bewijsvragen, zoals de recente discussie rond de heroriëntering van het beleid inzake misbruik van machtspositie aantoont. In hoofdstuk 7 worden nog enkele voorbeelden gegeven. Als we willen dat het mededingingsrecht inhoudelijke evolueert, moeten nieuwe (economische) concepten worden ingebed in het bestaande juridische kader.

(3) Modernisering vanuit een organisatorisch perspectief: de ingewikkelde relatie tussen decentralisering, convergentie en consistentie

Het handhavingssysteem van het Europese mededingingsrecht kent bijzondere kenmerken waarbij een grote mate van convergentie van materieel recht, procesrecht en beleid de kern vormen. Ook de centrale en sterke positie van de Commissie is een uniek gegeven. Deze aspecten komen in elk van de artikelen aan bod, vaak vanuit een andere insteek belicht. Noch de convergentie als zodanig, noch de rol van de Commissie wordt in de verschillende hoofdstukken fundamenteel in vraag gesteld. Wel wordt gewezen op de vragen die ze oproept (bijvoorbeeld rechtsbescherming in hoofdstuk 2, doelstellingen in hoofdstuk 5).

Als het gaat om convergentie worden hier en daar ook wel kritische bedenkingen geplaatst bij de rechtvaardigingen die juridisch worden aangegrepen om verdere convergentie te "stimuleren": het effectiviteitsbeginsel (hoofdstuk 6) bijvoorbeeld. In hoofdstuk 7 wordt daaraan toegevoegd dat ook de voortdurende verwijzing naar consistente toepassing van het mededingingsrecht wellicht niet helemaal op zijn plaats is. Decentrale handhaving is voor alle domeinen van het EU recht in principe het uitgangpunt en de vrees voor inconsistente toepassing van het recht lijkt overdreven. In de praktijk moet echter worden vastgesteld dat er een zeer brede consensus is die aan consistentie dermate belang hecht dat het een draagvlak creeërde voor verregaande convergentiemechanismen, zoals deze neergelegd in Vo. 1/2003 (binnen het netwerk van autoriteiten, nader besproken in hoofdstuk 2 en 6).

Hoofdstuk 7 bevat op dit ook nog een waarschuwing: op institutioneel vlak moet er voldoende besef zijn dat het handhavingsmodel van de Commissie zeker niet noodzakelijk het model is waarnaar de verdere convergentie moet streven. Het verband tussen inhoud van het recht, het procesrecht en het institutioneel model waarbinnen men handhaaft, zorgt ervoor dat nu eerst moet worden gekeken naar de optimale institutionele structuur van een autoriteit in plaats van verder de convergentie van nationale procesregels na te streven. Immers, de natuurlijke neiging van de convergentiebeweging lijkt te zijn om toe te werken naar het Europese model. Gelet op de groeiende vragen over de verenigbaarheid van het Commissiemodel met fundamentele beginselen, is dat echter geen evidente zaak.

Tenslotte wordt nog de vraag gesteld of de convergentie niet zo ver is doorgeschoten dat er een zekere tegenstrijd ontstaat met de modernisering. De meer decentrale toepassing van het mededingingsrecht zou moeten toelaten om makkelijker de meer economische benadering toe te passen, dichter bij de markt en de concrete marktspelers in een lidstaat. Nochtans lijkt er minder ruimte dan ooit tevoren voor eigen beleid. Zoals gezegd lijken de lidstaten daar weinig bezwaren tegen te hebben en is de convergentie gestoeld op grote consensus, maar toch lijkt dit vragen op te roepen want de markten en de economieën van de lidstaten zijn alles behalve even homogeen als de regels die erop worden toegepast. De vraag is of het juridisch kader voldoende ruimte laat voor differentiëring naargelang de economische realiteit. Het stellen van de vraag lijkt al in te gaan tegen de algemene overtuiging dat het nationaal en het Europees niveau in alle opzichten op elkaar moeten worden afgestemd.

(4) Modernisering als een uitdaging voor het systeem van rechtsbescherming.

Het laatste thema dat wordt besproken in hoofdstuk 7 komt terug op het onderwerp van het eerste hoofdstuk. Het bevat een vrij fundamentele kritiek op het systeem van rechtsbescherming. Daarbij wordt vooral ingegaan op de rol van de Europese rechter, het Hof van Justitie en het Gerecht die in het huidige EU systeem als enigen kunnen instaan voor rechterlijke controle op de handelingen van de Commissie als mededingingsautoriteit. In verschillende hoofdstukken kwam nochtans tot uiting hoe centraal de rol van de Commissie is.

Eerst wordt toch een korte maar erg belangrijke opmerking gemaakt over de nationale rechter: wanneer de nationale autoriteiten handelen binnen het netwerk van autoriteiten, moet hij instaan voor rechtsbescherming. Echter, in tegenstelling tot het niveau van de autoriteiten, lijkt van convergentie nauwelijks sprake op het niveau van de rechters die in de publieke handhaving opereren, vooral als beroepsrechters. Noch in Vo. 1/2003, noch in recente initiatieven van de Commissie heeft men het heikele punt van de harmonisering en convergentie in het gerechtelijke apparaat durven aansnijden. Nochtans is het van belang ook hier aandacht aan te besteden.

Het wordt erkend dat er zich klaarblijkelijk nog weinig zaken hebben voorgedaan waarin tot uiting kwam dat het systeem van rechtsbescherming op Europees niveau faalt. Een belangrijke vaststelling is echter dat er zich überhaupt erg weinig (formele) beslissingen hebben voorgedaan van de types die in hoofdstuk 2 werden besproken. Toch zijn er voldoende redenen om te besluiten dat de rol van de Europese rechter als mede-handhaver onvoldoende mee is geëvolueerd met de ontwikkelingen inzake effectieve rechtsbescherming maar ook met de inhoudelijke evoluties in het mededingingsrecht. In hoofdstuk 7 wordt benadrukt dat het niet enkel gaat om problemen die verband houden met de ontvankelijkheid van individuele nietigheidsberoepen tegen beslissingen waarbij zaken worden verdeeld onder de autoriteiten, ook al is dit het onderwerp dat meestal de meeste aandacht krijgt.

Er is ook de gevestigde rechtspraak die alleen beroepen toelaat tegen zogenaamde definitieve beslissingen, de snelheid (het gebrek eraan) van het systeem, het gebrek aan flexibiliteit in de procedures alsmede de relatief passieve opstelling van het Hof en het Gerecht als het om bewijs, feiten en marktanalyse gaat. De roep naar een hervorming van het systeem wordt ondersteund en de oprichting van een Mededingingstribunaal kan een oplossing bieden. De eigen kenmerken van het mededingingrecht vergen een eigen benadering. De doelstellingen van een hervorming moeten precies toelaten om een voldoende rechterlijke controle te hebben op alle handelingen die de belangen van een individuele onderneming op substantiële wijze raken zonder overdreven formele benadering. De handelingen van de Commissie kunnen immers alleen in Luxemburg worden getoetst. Verder moet de rechters actiever kunnen zijn en moet bekeken worden hoe de meer economische benadering moet vertaald worden naar de rechtsgang voor het Hof en het Gerecht. Daarbij is van belang dat er een globale benadering komt: de handhaving door de Commissie en door de (beroeps)rechter vormen een geheel.

Dit proefschrift wordt afgesloten met een post scriptum. Daarin wordt eerst uitgedrukt dat bij het samenstellen van de bundel met artikelen, duidelijk werd dat de interactie tussen materieel recht en procesrecht als een rode draad door het proefschrift heen loopt. De modernisering van het EU mededingingsrecht, met zijn inhoudelijke en zijn procedurele component, die doorgaans afzonderlijk behandeld worden, is daar op zich al een illustratie van. Er zijn veel voorbeelden aan bod gekomen van de wijze waarop procedure en inhoud op elkaar inspelen. Daarmee is ook aangegeven dat dit een onderwerp is dat, op meer theoretisch vlak verder onderzoek verdient. Ten tweede wordt terug aangeknoopt bij de inleiding en de titel van het proefschrift waarin het verband tussen het mededingingsrecht en het bredere EU recht wordt uitgedrukt. Enkele voorbeelden worden opnieuw gegeven waaruit dit verband moet blijken en de hoop wordt uitgedrukt dat daarmee niet alleen mededingingsjuristen aangespoord zijn om de bredere context niet uit het oog te verliezen maar hopelijk ook omgekeerd enige interesse kan gewekt worden voor de beschreven neveneffecten buiten de wereld van het mededingingsrecht.

Bibliography

BOOKS

A

Arnull, A, *The European Union And Its Court Of Justice*, 2nd edn (Oxford: Oxford University Press, 2006)

B

Bayles, M, *Principles of law, A normative analysis* (Dordrecht: D. Reidel Publishing company, 1987)

Bernitz, U, and Nergelius, J (eds.), *General principles of Community law in the process of development* (The Hague: Kluwer Law International, 2008)

Bishop, S, and Walker, M, *Economics of EC Competition Law: concepts, application and measurement* (London: Sweet & Maxwell, 1999)

Brammer, S, *Cooperation between national competition agencies in the enforcement of EC competition law* (Oxford: Hart Publishing, 2009)

Brealy, M and Hoskins M, *Remedies in EC law* (London: Sweet & Maxwell, 1998)

C

Cahill, D and Cooke, J D (eds), *The modernisation of EU Competition law Enforcement in the EU, FIDE 2004 National Reports*, (Cambridge: Cambridge University Press, 2004)

Camesasca, P and Van den Bergh, R, *European Competition law and economics: comparative perspective* 1st edn (Antwerpen: Intersentia, 2001)

Camesasca, P and Van den Bergh, R, *European competition Law and Economics: a comparative perspective*, 2nd edn (London: Sweet & Maxwell, 2006)

Chalmers, D, Hadjiemmanuil, C, Monti, G and Tomkins, A, *European Union law* (Cambridge: University Press, 2006)

Cooter R and Ulen, T, *Law & Economics* (Boston: Pearson Education Ltd., 2004)

Craig, P, *EU Administrative Law* (Oxford: Oxford University Press, 2008)

Craig, P and de Búrca, G, *EU Law: Text, Cases And Materials*, 3th edn (Oxford: Oxford University Press, 2003)

Cseres, K, *Competition law and consumer protection* (The Hague: Kluwer Law International, 2005)

D

Defraigne, J, and de Morianė, V (eds) '*Quelles politiques industrielle et sociale pour l'Europe du XX ième siècle*' (Brussels: Academia Bruylant, 2008)

Dennis, I, *The law of evidence* (London: Sweet & Maxwell, 2007)

De Visser, M, *Network-based governance in EC law* (Oxford: Hart Publishing, 2009)

Drexl, J, *Economic theory and competition law* (Cheltenham: Edward Elgar, 2009)

E

Ehlermann, C and Laudati, L (eds), *European Competition Annual 1997: Objectives of competition policy* (Oxford: Hart Publishing, 1998)

Ehlermann, C and Atanasiu, I (eds), *European Competition Law Annual 2002: Constructing the EU Network of Competition Authorities* (Oxford: Hart Publishing, 2004)

C. Ehlermann and M. Marquis (eds), *A reformed approach to Article 82 EC. European Competition Law Annual (EUI) 2007* (Oxford: Hart Publishing, 2008)

Eijsbouts, W, Jans, J and Vogelaar, F, *Europees recht; algemeen deel* (Groningen: Europa Law Publishing, 2009)

Ewing, K, *Competition rules for the 21st century* (The Hague: Kluwer Law International, 2006)

F

Faull, J and Nikpay, A, *The EC law of Competition* (Oxford: Oxford University Press, 1999)

G

Gerber, D, *Law and competition in twentieth century Europe, Protecting Promotheus* (Oxford: Clarendon Press, 1998)

Gerbrandy, A, *Convergentie in het mededingingsrecht: de invloed van het EG recht op materiële toepassing, toegang, bewijs en toetsing bij de Nederlandse mededingingsbestuursrechter, bezien in het licht van effectieve rechtsbescherming* (Den Haag: Boom Juridische Uitgevers, 2009)

Goyder, D, *EC Competition Law* (Oxford: Oxford University Press, 2003)

Guinchard, S, *Droit et pratique de la procedure civile,* (Paris: Dalloz Action, 2006)

H

Hartley, T, *The foundations of European Community Law* (Oxford: Oxford University Press, 2003)

Howard, M, Auburn, J and Bagshaw, R, e.a., *Phipson on evidence,* 15th edn (London: Sweet & Maxwell, 2000)

J

Jacobs, F, *Court of Justice Review in Competition cases* (New York: Fordham University, 1987)

Jans, J, De Lange, R, Prechal, S, and Widdershoven, R, *Inleiding tot het Europees bestuursrecht* (Nijmegen: Ars Aequi Libri, 2002)

K

Kerse, C and Khan, N, *EC Antitrust Procedure* (London: Sweet & Maxwell, 2005)

Koeck, H.F. and Karollus, M.M (eds), *The modernisation of European Competition law – Initial experiences with Regulation 1/2003*, FIDE XXIII Congress Linz 2008 (Vienna: Nomos, 2008)

Kuty, F, and Mougenot, D, (eds), *La prevue* (Liège: Anthemis, 2007)

L

Lenaerts, K and Van Nuffel, P, *Constitutional Law Of The European Union*, 2nd edn (London: Sweet & Maxwell, 2005)

Lenaerts, K, Arts, D and Maselis, I, *Procedural law of the EU* (London: Sweet & Maxwell, 2006)

Lonbay, J and Biondi A, (ed.), *Remedies for Breach of EC Law* (Chichester: Wiley, 1997)

M

Malek, M, (ed) *Phipson on evidence.* 15th edn (London: Sweet & Maxwell, 2000)

Manunza, E, and Senden, L, '*De interstatelijkheid voorbij?*' (Nijmegen: Wolf Legal Publishers, 2006)

Monti, G, *EC competition law* (Cambridge: Cambridge University Press, 2007)

Motta, M, *Competition Policy: Theory and Practice* (Cambridge: Cambridge University Press, 2004)

Mulder, M and Mok M, *Kartelrecht* (Deventer: Kluwer, 1962)

O

Odudu, O, *The boundaries of EC competition law, the scope of Article 81* (Oxford, Oxford University Press, 2006)

Ortiz Branco, L, *EC competition procedure* (Oxford: Oxford University Press, 2006)

Ovey, C and White, C, *Jacobs & White: European Convention on Human Rights* (Oxford: Oxford University Press, 2002)

P

Prechal, S and Hancher, L (eds), '*Europees bewijsrecht: een verkenning*' (Deventer: Kluwer, 2001)

R

Ritter, L, Braun, W, and Rawlinson, F, *European Competition Law: a practitioners guide*, 2nd edn (The Hague: Kluwer Law International, 2000)

S

Schermers, H and Waelbroeck, D, *Judicial Protection In The European Communities*, 6th edn (The Hague, Kluwer Law International, 2001)

Senden, L, *Soft Law in European Community Law, its relationship to Legislation* (Oxford: Hart Publishing, 2005)

Sibony, A, *Le juge et le raisonnement économique en droit de la concurrence* (Paris : L.G.D.J. Lextenso editions, 2008)

Siragusa, M, and Rizza, C, (ed.), *EU Competition Law, volume III Cartel law, restrictive agreements and practices between competitors* (Leuven: Claeys & Casteels, 2007)

Stefani, G, and Levasseur, G, *Procédure pénale* (Paris: Dalloz, 2006)

T

Tridimas, T, *General principles of EC law*, 1st edn (Oxford: Oxford University Press, 1999)

Tridimas, T, *The General Principles Of EU Law*, 2nd edn (Oxford: Oxford University Press, 2006)

V

Van Gerven, W, *Kartelrecht: Europese Gemeenschap* (Deventer: Tjeenk Willink, 1997)

Van den Bergh, R and Camesasca, P, *European competition Law and Economics: a comparative perspective* (London: Thomson Sweet & Maxwell, 2006)

Verheyden-Jeanmart, N, *Droit de la preuve* (Bruxelles: Larcier, 1991)

W

Ward, A, *Judicial review and the rights of private parties* (Oxford: Oxford University Press, 2007)

Weatherill, S, *Cases and materials on EU law*, 7th edn (Oxford: Oxford University Press, 2006)

Wéry, P, *La preuve, Guide juridique de l'entreprise. Titre préliminaire, Livre 2* (Bruxelles: Kluwer, 2003)

Whish, R, *Competition law.* 5th edn (London: LexisNexis, 2003)

Wils, W, *Principles of European Antitrust Enforcement* (Oxford: Hart Publishing, 2005)

Wils, W, *Efficiency and Justice in European Antitrust enforcement* (Oxford: Hart Publishing, 2008)

ARTICLES & BOOK CHAPTERS

A

Accetto, M and Zleptnig, S, 'The principle of effectiveness: rethinking its role in Community law' (2005) 11 *European Public Law* 375

Ahdar, R, 'Consumers, redistribution of income and the purpose of competition law' (2002) 7 *European Competition Law Review* 341

Ahlborn, C and Padilla, A, 'From fairness to welfare: implications for the assessment of unilateral conduct under EC competition law', in C Ehlermann and M Marquis (eds) *A reformed approach to Article 82 EC. European Competition Law Annual (EUI) 2007* (Oxford: Hart Publishing, 2008)

Akman, P, 'Consumer welfare and Article 82: practice and rhetoric' (2009) 32 *World Competition* 71

Arnull, A, 'Private applicants and the action for annulment since Codorniu' (2001) 38 *Common Market Law Review* 7

Arnull, A, 'April shower for Jégo-Quéré' (2004) 29 *European Law Review* (2004) 287

Arpon de Mendivil de Aldama, A, 'Exclusionary conducts and consumer welfare: effects in competition, justifications and efficiencies, what is the right balance? In B Hawk (ed) *Annual Proceedings of the Fordham Corporate law Institute: International Antitrust and Policy* (New York: Juris Publishing, 2008) Fordham Competition Law Institute Proceedings 31

Atanasiu, I and Ehlermann, C, 'The modernisation of EC antitrust law: consequences for the future role and function of the EC Courts' (2002) 23 *European Competition Law Review* 72

B

Bailey, D, 'Standard of proof in EC merger proceedings : a common law perspective' (2003) 40 *Common Market Law Review* (2003) 845

Bailey, D, 'Scope of Judicial review under Article 81' (2004) 41 *Common Market Law Review* 1327

Bengoetxea, J and Wiklund, O, 'General Constitutional Principles of Community Law' in U Bernitz and J Nergelius (eds.) *General Principles of European Community Law* (The Hague: Kluwer Law International, 2000)

Bone, R, *Making effective rules: the need for procedure theory* BU Working School of Law working paper (University School of Law, Boston 2008)

Bork, R, 'Legislative intent of the Sherman Act' (2006) 2 *Competition Policy International* (2006) 233

Bos, P, 'Towards a Clear Distribution of Competence between EC and National Competition Authorities' (1995) 16 *European Competition Law Review* 410

Botteman, Y, 'Mergers, standard of proof and expert economic evidence' (2006) 2 *Journal of Competition Law and Economics* 71

Bourgeois, J and Baumé, T, *Decentralisation of EC competition law enforcement and general principles of Community law* [2004] Research papers College of Europe 4

Briones, J, 'A balance of the impact of economic analysis on EU competition policy' (2009) 32 World Competition 27

Burnley, R, 'Interstate revisited: the jurisdictional criterion for articles 81 and 82', (2002) 23 *European Competition Law Review* 217

C

Castillo de la Torre F., 'Evidence, Proof and Judicial review in cartel cases', *World Competition* (2009) 4 p. 505

Commentaire Mégret, *Le droit de la CEE, Tome 4 Concurrence.* 2th edn (Bruxelles: Editions de l'Université de Bruxelles, 1997) 448

Cook, C, 'Commitment Decisions: The Law and Practice under Article 9' (2006) 29 *World Competition* 209

Curzon Price, V, 'La politique européenne au XXIième siècle: reflet de l'évolution des idées sur le rôle des pouvoirs publics dans l'économie' in J Defraigne and V de Moriamé (eds), *Quelles politiques industrielle et sociale pour l'Europe du XXième siècle?*, Brussels, Academia Bruylant, 2008)

D

Dabbah, M, 'Measuring a system of competition law: a preliminary view' (2000) 21 *European Competition Law Review* 369

Davies, G, 'Subsidiarity: The Wrong Idea, in the Wrong Place, at the Wrong Time' (2006) 43 *Common Market Law Review* 63

Delicostopoulos, J, 'Towards European Procedural Primacy in National Legal Systems' (2003) 9 *European Law Journal* 599

Della Cananea, G, 'Beyond the State: the Europeanization and Globalization of Procedural Administrative law' (2003) 9 *European Public Law* 563

De Smet, D, 'The diametrically opposed principles of US and antitrust policy' (2008) 29 *European Competition Law Review* 356

De Witte, B, 'Institutional principles: a special category of general principles of EC law' in U Bernitz and J Nergelius (eds.) *General Principles of European Community Law* (The Hague: Kluwer Law International, 2000)

Drijber, B, slotbeschouwingen in: E Manunza and L Senden (eds), *DE EU: interstatelijkheid voorbij?* (Nijmegen: Wolf Publishers, 2006)

Dubout, E, 'Le contentieux de la troisième génération ou l'incomplétude du système jurisdictionnel communautaire', (2007) 43 *Revue trimestrielle de droit européen* 427

E

Ehlermann, C, 'Community Competition Procedures', in Lord Slynn of Hadley and Pappas S (eds), (1995) *Procedural Aspects of EC Competition Law* (Maastricht: EIPA Institute, 1994)

Ehlermann, C, 'The modernisation of EC antitrust policy: a legal and cultural revolution' (2000) 37 *Common Market Law Review* 537
Eilmansberger, T, 'The relationship between rights and remedies in EC law": in search of the missing link' (2004) 41 *Common Market Law Review* 1199
Eilmansberger, T, 'The Green Paper on damage actions for breach of the EC antitrust rules and beyond: reflections on the utility and feasability of stimulating private enforcement through legislative action', (2007) 44 *Common Market Law Review* 431
Engström, J, 'National courts obligation to apply Community law ex officio – the Court showing new respect for party autonomy and national procedural autonomy?' (2008) 1 *Review of European and Administrative Law* 67

F

Faull, J, 'Effect on trade between Member States and Community: Member State jurisdiction' in B Hawk (ed.) *Annual Proceedings of the Fordham Corporate law Institute: International Antitrust and Policy* (New York: Juris Publishing, 1990) 485
Forrester, I and Norall, C, 'The laicization of Community law : self help and the rule of reason : how competition law is and should be applied' (1984) 4 *Common Market Law Review* 11

G

Galloway, J, 'The pursuit of national champions : the intersection of competition law and industrial policy' (2007) 28 *European Competition Law Review* 172
Gauer, C, 'Does effectiveness of the EU network of competition authorities require a certain degree of harmonisation of national procedures and sanctions?' in C Ehlermann and I Atanasiu, *European Competition Law Annual 2002: Constructing the EU Network of Competition Authorities* (Oxford: Hart Publishing, 2004) 187
Gerber, D, 'Two forms of modernisation in European competition law', (2008) 31 *Fordham International Law Journal* 1235
Gerbrandy, A, 'Procedural convergence in competition law: Towards a spontaneous ius commune' (2009) 2 *Review of European and Administrative Law* 105
Geursen, W, 'Handhaving van het objectieve gemeenschapsrecht via het effectiviteitsbeginsel vs. subjectieve rechtsbescherming via het nationaalrechtelijk verbod op reformation in peius' (2009] 4 *Nederlands Tijdschrift voor Europees Recht* 131
Ghellinck de, E, 'La politique industrielle: un cocnept creux' in Defraigne, J and de Moriané, V, *Quelles politiques industrielle et sociale pour l'Europe du XX ième siècle?* (Brussels : Academia Bruylant, 2008) 96
Gippini-Fournier E, 'The elusive standard of proof' (2010) 33 *World Competition* 187

Girerd, P, 'Les principes d'équivalence et d'effectivité: encadrement ou désencadrement de l'autonomie procédurale des Etats membres' (2002) 38 *Revue trimestrielle de droit européen* 75

Gormsen, L, 'The conflict between economic freedom and consumer welfare in the modernization of Article 82 EC' (2007) 3 *European Competition Journal* 329

Groussot, X, 'The EC System of Legal Remedies and Effective Judicial Protection: does the system really need reform?' (2003) 30 *Legal Issues of Economic Integration* 221

Guerrin, M, and Kyriazis, G, 'Cartels: proof and procedural issues' in B Hawk (ed.), *Annual Proceedings of the Fordham Corporate law Institute: International Antitrust and Policy*, (Huntington: Juris Publishing, 1993)

Guilford, P, Tscherny, M, and Brookes, T, 'How political is Europe's competition policy, (2006) European Antitrust Review (published annualy by Global Competition Review) 8

H

Haapaniemi, P, 'Procedural autonomy: a misnomer?' in L. Ervo, M. Gräns and A. Jokela (eds) *The Europeanization of Procedural Law and the New Challenges to Fair trial* (Groningen: Europa Law Publishing, 2009)

Hanf, H, 'Talking with "the pouvoir constituant" in times of constitutional reform: The European Court of Justice on Private Applicants' Access to Justice' (2003) 10 *Maastricht Journal of European & Comparative Law* 265

Hancher, L and Lugard, P, ' Honey, I Shrunk the Article! A critical assessment of the Commission's Notice on Article 81(3) of the EC Treaty' (2004) 25 *European Competition Law Review* 410

Hilton, C, 'Rights and principles in EU law: a distinction without foundation' (2008) 15 *Maastricht Journal of European and Comparative Law* 193

Hodges, C, 'Competition enforcement, regulation and civil justice: what is the case? (2006) *Common Market Law Review* 1381

Howells, G and Wilhelmsson, T, 'EC consumer law, has it come of age?' (2003) 28 *European Law Review* 370

Huveneers, C, 'Politique de la concurrence, soutien du carcan, pour la politique industrielle?' in J Defraigne et V de Moriamé, *Quelles politiques industrielle et sociale pour l'Europe du XXIe siècle?* (Bruxelles, Academia Bruylant, 2008)

J

Jenkins, H, 'Protecting consumers: does competition help?' (2005) 4 *Competition Law* 283

Jones, C, 'Foundations of Competition Policy in the EU and USA: Conflict, Convergence, and Beyond' in H Ullrich (ed) *The Evolution of European Competition Law- Whose regulation, which competition?* (Cheltenham: Edward Elgar Publishing, 2006)

Jones, A, 'Resale price maintenance: a debate about competition policy in Europe?' (2009) 5 *European Competition Journal* 2009) 479

Joshua, J, 'Proof in contested competition cases, a comparison with the rules of evidence in common law' (1987) 12 *European Law Review* 315

K

Kakouris, C, 'Do the Member States possess judicial procedural autonomy?' (2007) 34 *Common Market Law Review* 1389

Kerber, W, 'Should competition law promote efficiency? Some reflections of an economist on the normative foundations of competition law', in J. Drexl, L Idot, J Monéger (eds), *Economic theory and competition law* (Cheltenham: Edward Elgar, 2009)

Keirsblick, B, 'The limits of consumer law in Europe', in E Claes, W Devroe and B Keirsblick (eds) *Facing the limits of the law* (Berlin: Springer, 2009)

Kerse, C, 'The complaint in Competition Cases: a Progress Report' (1997) 34 *Common Market Law Review* 213

Killick, J and Komninos, A, 'Schizofrenia in the Commission's Article 82 Guidance paper: formalism alongside increased recourse to economic analysis' (2009) *Global Competition Policy* February release (online)

Korsten, L. 'Annotatie: Deelname aan verboden onderling afgestemd feitelijk gedrag? Ernst van de overtreding' (2007) 7 *Markt & Mededinging* 224

Kirkwood, J, and Lande, R, 'The fundamental goal of Antitrust: Protecting Consumers, Not Increasing efficiency' (2008) 1 *Notre Dame Law Review* 191

L

Larouche, P, and Chirico, F, 'Divergence, Functionalism, and the Economics of Convergence', in S Prechal and B van Roermond (eds), *The coherence of EU law – The search for unity in divergence concepts* (Oxford: Oxford University Press, 2008)

Legal, H, 'Standards of proof and standards of judicial review in EU competition law', in B Hawk (ed.) *Annual Proceedings of the Fordham Corporate law Institute: International Antitrust and Policy* (New York: Juris Publishing, 2006)

Lenaerts, K and Vanhamme, J, 'Procedural Rights of Private Parties in the Community Administrative Process' (1997) 34 *Common Market Law Review* 531

Lenaerts, K and Gerard, D, 'Decentralisation of EC Competition Law Enforcement: Judges in the Frontline' (2004) 27 *World Competition* 313

Lenaerts, K, 'The rule of law and the coherence of the judicial system of the European Union' (2007) 44 *Common Market Law Review* 1625

E. Loozen, 'The application of a more economic approach to restrictions by object: no revolution after all, T Mobile Netherlands', (2010) 4 *European Competition Law Review* 146

Louvaris, A, 'A brief overview of some conflicts between economic efficiency and efffectiveness of the administrative or judicial process in competition law' in J. Drexl, L Idot, J Monéger (eds), *Economic theory and competition law* (Cheltenham: Edward Elgar, 2009)

Louveaux, B and Gilbert P, 'The standard of proof under the Competition Act' (2005) 3 *European Competition Law Review* 173

Lowe, P, 'The design of competition policy institutions for the 21st century – the experience of the European Commission and DG Comp' (2008) 3 *Competition Policy Newsletter* 1

Lugard, P, 'Annotatie: Leegin Creative Leather Products, Inc./PSKS, Inc' (2007) 5/6 *Markt & Mededinging* 156

M

Marenco, G, 'Le régime de l'exception légale et sa compatibilité avec le traité' (2001) 37 *Cahiers de droit Européen* 135

Marsden, P, 'Checks and balances: EU competition law and the rule of law' (2009) *Competition Law International* 24

Marsden, P and Bishop, S, 'Article 82 review: what is your theory of harm?' (2006) 2 *European Competition Journal* 257

McKendrick, J, 'Modifying Procedural Autonomy : Better Protection for Community Rights' (2000) 8 *European Review of Private Law* 565

Mehta, P, Mitra, S and Dube, C, 'Competition policy and consumer policy : complementarities and conflicts in the promotion of consumer welfare', chapter in United Nations Conference on Trade and Development (UNCTD) *The effects of anti-competitive business practices on developing countries and their development prospects* (New York and Geneva, 2008)

Monti, G, 'Article 81 and public policy' (2002) 39 *Common Market Law Review* 1057

Mortelmans, K, 'Towards convergence in the application of the rules on free movement and on competition' (2001) 38 *Common Market Law Review* 613

N

Nazzini, R, 'Article 81 between time present and time past: a normative critique of "restriction of competition" in EU law' (2006) 43 *Common Market Law Review* 497

Nihoul, P, 'Le recours des particuliers contre les actes communautaires de portée générale' (2002) 96 *J.T. Droit Européen* 38

O

OECD Secretariate, 'The objectives of competition law and policy and the optimal design of a Competition Agency' (2003) 5 *OECD Journal of Competition Law and Policy* 7

Oliver, P, 'Le règlement 1/2003 et les principes d'efficacité et d'équivalence' (2007) 41 *Cahiers de droit européen* 351

Ottervanger, T and Veldhuis, I, 'Europese Commissie/Tetra Laval' (2005) 04/05 *Markt & Mededinging* 152

Ortlep, R and Verhoeven, M, 'De voorrangsregel versus het beginsel van nationale procesautonomie' (2008) 56 *Sociaal Economische Wetgeving* 471

P

Parker, J, 'Daubert's debut: the Supreme Court, the economics of scientific evidence, and the adversarial system' (1994-95) 4 *Supreme Court Economic Review* 1

Parker, J, 'Evidence: general economic analysis' in B Bouckaert and G de Geest (eds), *Encyclopedia of Law and Economics* (Cheltenham: Edward Elgar, 2000)

Parret, L and Prechal, S, 'Zaak C-50/00 P, Unión de Pequeños Agricultores t. Raad van de Europese Unie' (2003) 1 *Sociaal-Economische Wetgeving* 35

Parret, L, 'Sense and nonsense of rules on proof in cartel cases' (2008) 4 *European Competition Journal* 169

Parret, L, 'En wat met de rechtsbescherming? in R van Ooik en R Wessel (eds), *De Europese Unie na het Verdrag van Lissabon* (Deventer: Kluwer, 2009)

Pera, A, 'Changing views of competition, economic analysis and EC antitrust law' (2008) 4 *European Competition Journal* 127

Prechal, S, 'EC requirements for an effective remedy' in J Lonbay and A Bondi (eds), *Remedies for breach of EC law* (Oxford: J. Wiley & Sons, 1997)

Prechal, S, 'Community law in national courts: the lessons from van Schijndel' (1998) 35 *Common Market Law Review* 681

Prechal, S, 'Domestic legal effects on EU criminal law: variations on three themes' in D Obradovic and N Lavranos (eds) *Interface between EU law and national law.Proceedings of the annual Colloquium of the G.K. van Hogendorp Centre for European Constitutional Studies* (Groningen: Europe Law Publishing, 2007) 335

Prechal, S, 'Transparency: a general principle of EU law?' in U Bernitz, C Cardner and J Nergelius (eds), *General principles of Community law in the process of development* (The Hague: Kluwer Law International, 2008)

R

Ragolle, F, 'Access to justice for private applicants in the Community legal order: recent Revolutions' (2003) 28 *European Law Review* 90

Riley, A, 'EC Antitrust modernisation: the Commission does very nicely- thank you! Part Two: between the idea and the reality, decentralisation under Reg.1/2003' (2003) 24 *European Competition Law Review* 657

Riley, A, 'The modernisation of EU anti-cartel enforcement: will the Commission grasp the opportunity', (2010) *European Competition Law Review* 191

Rodger, B and Wylie, S, 'Taking the Community interest line: Decentralisation and Subsidiarity in Competition Law Enforcement' (1997) 8 *European Competition Law Review* 485

Roth, W, 'Strategic competition policy: a comment on EU competition policy', in H Ullrich (ed), *The evolution of European Competition law, whose regulation, which competition?*, (Cheltenham: Edward Elgar Publishing, 2006)

S

A. Schaub, 'The Commission's position within the network' in: Ehlermann, C and Atanasiu, I (eds), *European Competition Law Annual 2002: Constructing the EU Network of Competition Authorities* (Oxford: Hart Publishing, 2004)

Senden, L, 'De lidstaten en de kwaliteit van Europese wetgeving: geen consumenten maar co-actoren' (2006) 54 *Sociaal Economische Wetgeving* 46

Sibony, A and Barbier De La Serre, E, 'Charge de la preuve et théorie du contrôle en droit communautaire de la concurrence: pour un changement de perspective (2007) 43 *Revue trimestrielle de droit européen* 205

Slot, P and Straetmans, G, 'Harmonisatie van wetgeving in de EG' (2003) 3 *Tijdschrift voor Privaatrecht* (2003) 691

Snyder, F, 'The effectiveness of European Community Law: institutions, processes, tools and techniques' (1993) 56 *Modern Law Review* 19

Steenbergen, J, 'Het mededingingsbeleid en het verdrag van Lissabon', in R van Ooik en R Wessel (eds), *De Europese Unie na het Verdrag van Lissabon* (Deventer: Kluwer, 2009)

Stevens, D, 'The "Comfort letter": Old Problems, New Developments' (1994)15 *European Competition Law Review* 81

Stuyck, S, 'EC competition policy after modernisation: more than ever in the interest of consumers' (2005) 28 *Journal of Consumer Policy* 1

Szilagyi, P, 'The ECJ has spoken: where do we stand on standard on proof in merger control', (2008) 12 *European Competition Law Review* 72

T

Temple Lang, J, 'Community Antitrust law – Compliance and enforcement' (1981) *Common Market Law Review* 335

Temple Lang, J, 'The duties of Cooperation of National Authorities and Courts under Article 10 E.C.: Two More Reflections' (2001) 26 *European Law Review* 84

Temple Lang, J, 'The implications of the Commissions leniency policy for national competition authorities' (2003) 28 *European Law Review* 430

Temple Lang, J, 'Actions for Declarations that Community Regulations are invalid: the duties of National Courts under Article 10 EC' (2003) 28 *European Law Review* 102

Tiili, V and Vanhamme, J, 'The power of appraisal of the Commission vis à vis the powers of judicial review of the Communities Court of First Instance and Court of Justice' (1999) *22 Fordham International Law Journal* 885

Tridimas, T, 'Enforcing Community rights in National Courts: some recent developments', in C. Kilpatrick, T. Novitz and P. Skidmore (eds), *The future of remedies in Europe*, (Oxford, Hart Publishing, 2000)

Tulibacka, M, 'Europeanization of civil procedures: in search of a coherent approach' 46 (2009) *Common Market Law Review* 1527

V

Van den Bergh, R, 'Schadevorderingen wegens schending van het mededingingsrecht in het spanningsveld tussen compensatie en optimale afschrikking (2006) *Markt en Mededinging* 143

Van der Wal, G and Parret, L, 'Bewijs in het Europese mededingingsregime, een overzicht' in S. Prechal, L. Hancher (eds.), *Europees Bewijsrecht: een verkenning*, (Deventer: Kluwer, 2001)

Woude van der, M, 'Exchange of information within the ECN: scope and limits', in C Ehlermann and I Atanasiu (eds), European Competition Law Annual 2002: Constructing the EU Network of Competition Authorities (Oxford: Hart Publishing, 2004)

Van Gerven, W, 'Bridging the gap between Community and national laws: towards a principle of homogeneity in the field of legal remedies' (1995) 32 *Common Market Law Review* 679

Van Gerven, W, 'Of rights, remedies and procedures' (2000) 37 *Common Market Law Review* 501

Van Gerven, W, 'Over codificatie, convergentie en algemene beginselen in een meergelaagd privaatrecht' (2008) 56 *Sociaal Economische Wetgeving* 414

Van Ooik, R, 'The European Court of Justice and the division of competence in the EU', in D. Obradovic and N. Lavranos (eds) *Interface between EU law and national law.Proceedings of the annual Colloquium of the G.K. van Hogendorp Centre for European Constitutional Studies* (Groningen: Europe law Publishing, 2007)

Vedder, H, 'Competition law and consumer protection: how Competition can be used to Protect Consumers Even better – or Not' (2006) 17 *European Business Law Review* 83

Vervaele, J, *The Europeanisation of Criminal law and the Criminal law dimension of European integration*, research paper (College of Europe, 2005, Brussels)

Vesterdorf, B, 'The Community Court system ten years from now and beyond: challenges and possibilities' (2003) 28 *European Law Review* 303

Vesterdorf, B, Economics in court: reflections on the role of judges in assessing economic theories and evidence in the modernised competition regime' in *Liber Amicorum in honour of Sven Norberg, A European for all seasons* (Brussels: Bruylant, 2006)

Vogelaar, F, 'Interface: EC and Dutch competition law', in D. Obradovic and N. Lavranos (eds) *Interface between EU law and national law.Proceedings of the annual Colloquium of the G.K. van Hogendorp Centre for European Constitutional Studies* (Groningen: Europe law Publishing, 2007) 187

W

Waelbroeck, D and Fosselard, D, 'Should the Decision-Making Power in EC Antitrust Procedures be left to an Independent Judge? – The impact of the European Convention of Human Rights on EC Antitrust Procedure', (1994) 14 *Yearbook of European Law* 111

Walker-Smith, A, 'Collusion, its detection and investigation' 2 (1991) *European Competion Law Review* 71

Wezenbeek, R, 'Consumer and competition policy: the Commission's perspective and the example of transport' (2006) 17 *European Business Law Review* 73

Ward, A, 'Judicial Architecture at the Cross-Roads: Private Parties and Challenge to EC Measures Post-*Jégo Quéré*' (2001) 4 *Cambridge Yearbook of European Legal Studies* 413

Weatherill, S, 'Beyond Preemption? Shared Competence and Constitutional Change in the European Community' in D O'Keeffe and P Twomey (eds), *Legal Issues of the Maastricht Treaty* (London, Wiley Chancery Law, 1994)

Weitbrecht, A, 'From Freiburg to Chicago – the first 50 years of European competition law' (2008) 29 *European Competition Law Review* 8

Wesseling, R, 'The Commission Notice on decentralisation of EC Antitrust Law: In for a Penny, not for a Pound' (1997) 18 *European Competition Law Review* 94

Wesseling, R, 'Subsidiarity in Community Antitrust law: setting the right agenda' (1997) 22 *European Law Review* 35

Wessely, T, 'Case note: Case C-49/92P, Commission v ANIC [1999] ECR I-4125; Case C-199/92P, Hüls v. Commission [1999] ECR I-4287; Case C-235/92P, Montecatini v. Commission [1999] ECR I-4539; Judgements of 8 april 1999 (together: Polypropylene appeal cases)' (2001) 38 *Common Market Law Review* 739

Wezenbeek, R, 'Consumers and competition policy: the Commission's perspective and the example of transport' (2006) 17 *European Business Law Review* 73

Wils, W, 'The combination of the investigative and prosecutorial function and the adjudicative function in EC Antitrust Enforcement: a legal and economic analysis' (2004) 27 *World Competition* 201

Wils, W, 'The increased level of EC antitrust fines, judicial review and the European Convention of Human Rights', (2010) 33 *World Competition* 5

Wilsher, R, 'Achieving better decision-making in competition enforcement cases: a public law perspective on the role of the executive and the courts' (2007) 30 *World Competition* 263

CASE LAW OF THE EU COURTS

Case-Law of the Court of Justice

Case 13/62 *Bosch* [1962] ECR 93
Case 24/62 *Germany/Commission* [1963] ECR 137
Cases 54/64 & 58/64 *Consten en Grundig* [1966] ECR 571
Case 56/65 *Société Technique Minière (L.T.M.) v Maschinenbau Ulm GmbH (M.B.U.)* [1966] ECR 416
Case 23/67 *SA Brasserie de Haecht v Consorts Wilkin-Janssen* [1976] ECR 512
Case 5/69 *Franz Völk v S.P.R.L. Ets J. Vervaecke* [1969] ECR 295
Case 9/73 *Carl Schlüter v Hauptzollamt Lörrach* [1973] ECR 1135
Case 8/74 *Procureur du Roi v Benoît and Gustave Dassonville* [1974] ECR 837
Case 17/74 *Transmarine Ocean Paint* [1974] ECR 1063
Case 19 and 20/74 *Kali & Salz* [1975] ECR 499
Case 51/75 *EMI Records Limited v CBS United Kingdom Limited* [1976] ECR 811
Case C-33/76 *Rewe-Zentralfinanz eG and Rewe-Zentral AG v. Landwirtschaftskammer für das Saarland* [1976] ECR 1989
Case C-45/76 *Comet* [1976] ECR 2043
Case C-26/76 *Metro* [1977] ECR 1875
Case 27/76 *United Brands Company and United Brands Continentaal BV v Commission of the European Communities* [1978] ECR 207
Case C-106/77 *Simmenthal* [1978] ECR 629
Case 22/78 *Hugin Kassaregister AB and Hugin Cash Registers Ltd v Commission of the European Communities* [1979] ECR 1869
Case 253/78 and I-3/79 *Guerlain* [1980] ECR 2327
Case 61/80 *Coöperatieve Stremsel- en Kleurselfabriek v Commission of the European Communities* [1967] ECR 851
Case C-158/80 *Rewe-Handelsgesellschaft Nord mbH v Hauptzollamt Kiel* [1981] ECR 1805
Case 172/80 *Gerhard Züchner v Bayerische Vereinsbank AG* [1981] ECR 2021
Case 60/81 *IBM* [1981] ECR 2639
Case 42/84 *Remia* [1985] ECR 2545
Case 193/83 *Windsurfing International Inc. v Commission of the European Communities* [1986] ECR 611
Case 222/84 *Johnston* [1986] ECR 1651
Case C-89/85 *Woodpulp* [1993] ECR I-1307
Case 246/86 *SC Belasco and others v Commission of the European Communities* [1989] ECR I-2117
Case 5/88 *Hubert Wachauf v Bundesamt für Ernährung und Forstwirtschaft* [1989] ECR 2609
Joined Cases C-143/88 and C-92/89 *Zuckerfabrik Süderdithmarschen AG v Hauptzollamt Itzehoe and Zuckerfabrik Soest GmbH v Hauptzollamt Paderborn* [1991] ECR I-415

Case C-213/89 *Factortame* [1990] ECR I-2433
Case C-234/89 *Stergios Delimitis v Henninger Bräu AG* [1991] ECR I-935
Case C-269/90 *Technische Universität München* [1991] ECR I- 5469
Case C-49/92 P *Commission of the European Communities v Anic Partecipazioni SpA* [1999] ECR I-4125
Case C-137/92 P *PVC* [1994] ECR I- 2555
Case-199/92 *P Hüls AG v Commission of the European Communities* [1999] ECR I-4287
Case C-250/92 *Gøttrup-Klim e.a. Grovvareforeninger v Dansk Landbrugs Grovvareselskab AmbA* [1994] ECR I-5641
Joined cases C-215/96 & C-216/96 *Carlo Bagnasco and Others v Banca Popolare di Novara soc. coop. arl. (BNP) (C-215/96) and Cassa di Risparmio di Genova e Imperia* SpA (Carige) (C-216/96) [1999] ECR I-135
Case C-242/95 *GT-Link A/S v De Danske Statsbaner (DSB)* [1997] ECR I-4449
Case C-7/97 *Oscar Bronner* [1998] ECR I-7791
Case C-119/97 P *UFEX* [1999] ECR I-1341
Case C-266/97 P *Vereniging van Groothandelaren in Bloemkwekerijen* [2000] ECR I-2135
Case C-412/97 *Fenocchio* [1999] ECR I-3845
Case C-279/98 P *Langnese* [1998] ECR I-5609
Case C-9/99 *Echirolles Distribution* [2000] ECR I-8207
Case C- 344/98 *Masterfoods* [2000] ECR I-11369
Case C-309/99 *J. C. J. Wouters, J. W. Savelbergh and Price Waterhouse Belastingadviseurs BV v Algemene Raad van de Nederlandse Orde van Advocaten* [2002] ECR I- 1577
Case C-453/99 *Courage* [2001] ECR I-6297
Case C-50/00P *Union de Pequenos Agricultores* [2002] ECR I-6677
Case C-94/00 *Roquette Frères* [2002] ECR 9011
Case C-129/00 *Commission/Italy* [2003] ECR I-14637
Case C-453/00 *Kühne & Heinz,* [2004] ECR I-00837
Case C-13/01 *Safalero Srl v Prefetto di Genova* [2003] ECR I-8679
Case C-397/01 and C-403/01 *Pfeiffer* [2004] ECR I-8835
Case C-263/02 P *Jégo-Quéré* [2004] ECR I-03425
Cases C-189/02P, C-202/02P, C-205/02P to C-208/02P, C-213/02P *Dansk Rørindustri a.o. v Commission of the European Communities* [2005] ECR I-5425
Cases C-387/02, C-391/02 and C-403/02, *Berlusconi* [2008] ECR I-3565
Cases C-12/03 & C-13/03 *Commission of the European Communities v Tetra Laval BV* [2005] ECR 987
Case C-53/03 *Syfait e.a* [2005] ECJ I-04609
Case C-176/03 *Commission/Council* [2005] ECR I-7879
Case C-95/04 *British Airways* [2007] ECR I-2331
Case C-105/04P *Nederlandse Federatieve Vereniging voor de Groothandel op Elektrotechnisch Gebied v Commission of the European Communities* [2006] I-08725
Cases C-295/04 until C-298/04 *Manfredi* [2006] ECR I-6619

Case C-519/04 *David Meca-Medina and Igor Majcen v Commission of the European Communities* [2006] ECR I-06991
Cases C-222/05 to C-225/05 *Van der Weerd* [2006] ECR I-4233
Case C-426/05, *Tele 2 telecommunication gmbh* [2008] ECR I- 685
Case C-432/05 *Unibet* [2007] ECR I-2271
Case C-440/05, *Commission/Council* [2007] ECR I-9097
Case C-268/06 *Impact v Minister for Agriculture and Food and Others* [2008] ECR I-2483
Case C-468/06 to C-478/06 *Sot. Lélos kai Sia EE and Others v GlaxoSmithKline AEVE Farmakeftikon Proïonton* [2008] ECR 2008 I-07139
Case C-445/06 *Danske Slagterier,* [2009] ECR I-02119
Cases C-501/06 P, C-513/06 P, C-515 and 516/06 P *GlaxoSmithKline Services Unlimited v Commission of the European Communities,* [2009] ECR I-09291
Case C-209/07 *Beef Industry Development Society* [2008] ECR I-08637
Case C-125/07, C-133/07 P and C-135/07 P *"Lombard club" Austrian banks,* [2009] ECR I-08681
C-322/07 P, C-327/07 P and C-338/07 P *Bolloré and others,* [2009] ECR I-07191
Case C-441/07 P *Commission/Alrosa,* not yet reported
Case C- 555/07 *Kücükdeveci,* not yet reported
Case C-8/08 *T-Mobile,* [2009] ECR I-04529
Case C-63/08 *Pontin,* not yet reported
Cases C-317 to 320/08 *Alassini and others,* not yet reported
Case C-406/08 *Uniplex,* not yet reported
Case C-455/08 *European Commission v* Ireland, not yet reported

Opinions of Advocate Generals

Opinion of Advocate General Trabucchi Case 73/74 [1975] ECR 1517
Opinion of Advocate General Mischo Case 246/86 *SC Belasco* [1989] ECR I-2117
Opinion of Advocate General Darmon Case C-97/91 *Borelli* [1992] ECR I-6313
Opinion of Advocate General Jacobs Case C-50/00P *UPA* [2002] ECR I-6677
Opinion of Advocate General Poiares Maduro, Case 205/03 *Fenin* [2005] ECR I-06295
Opinion of Advocate General Kokott, Case C-413/06 *Bertelsmann AG and Sony Corporation of America v Independent Music Publishers and Labels Association (Impala)* [2008] ECR I-04951

Case-Law of the General Court

Case T- 64/89 *Automec* [1990] ECR II-367
Case T-138/89 *Nederlandse bankiersvereniging and Nederlandse Vereniging van Banken v. Commission of the European Communities* [1992] ECR II-2181

Case T-138/89 *Nederlandse bankiersvereniging and Nederlandse Vereniging van Banken v. Commission of the European Communities (Dutch Banks)* [1992] ECR II-2181
Case T-24/90 *Automec Srl v Commission of the European Communities* [1992] ECR 2223
Case T-28/90 *Asia Motor France* [1992] ECR II-2285
Case T-5/02 *Tetra Laval* [2002] ECR II-4381
Case T-29/92 *Vereniging van samenwerkende prijsregelende organisaties in de bouwnijverheid* [1995] ECR II-289
Case T-37/92 *BEUC/Commission* [1994] ECR II-285
Case T- 70 and 71/92 *Florimex* [1997] ECR II-693
Case T-74/92 *Ladbroke* [1995] ECR II-115
Case T-87/92 *Kruidvat* [1996] ECR II-1931
Cases T-96/92 and T-12/93 *Comité Central d'Entreprise de la Société Générale des Grandes Sources and others v Commission of the European Communities* [1995] ECR II-2479
Case T-114/92 *Bureau Européen des Médias de l'Industrie Musicale (BEMIM) v. Commission of the European Communities* [1995] ECR II-00147
Case T-3/93 *Air France* [1994] ECR II-121
Case T-17/93 *Matra Hachette* [1994] ECR II-595
Case T-575/93 *Koelman* [1996] ECR II-1
Case T-374/94 *European Night Services* [1998] ECR II-3141
Case T-213/95 *Stichting Certificatie Kraanverhuurbedrijf (SCK) and Federatie van Nederlandse Kraanbedrijven (FNK) v Commission of the European Communities* [1997] ECR II-1739
Case T-41/96 *Bayer/Commission* [2000] ECR II-3383
Case T-65/96 *Kisk Glass & Co. Ltd v Commission of the European Communities* [2000] ECR II-1885
Case T-125/97 and 127/97 *Coca Cola* [2000] ECR II-1733
Case T-241/97 *Stork Amsterdam bv/Commission* [2000] ECR II-309
Case T- 197/97 and 198/97 *Weyl Beef Products BV, Exportslachterij Chris Hogeslag BV and Groninger Vleeshandel BV v Commission of the European Communities* [2001] ECR II-303
Case T-23/99 *LRAF* [2002] ECR II-1705
Case T-342/99 *Airtours* [2002] ECR II-2585
Case T-251/00 *Lagardère Canal+* [2002] ECR I-4825
Case T-67 and 68/00 and T-71/00 and 78/00 *JFE Engineering and others* [2004] ECR II-2501

Case T-177/01 *Jégo-Quéré et Cie SA/Commission* [2002] ECR II-2365
Case T-310/01 *Schneider* [2002] ECR II-4071
Case T-168/01 *GlaxoSmithKline Services Unlimited v Commission of the European Communities* [2006] ECR II-02969
Case T-119/02 *Philips* [2003] ECR 1433
Case T-201/04 *Microsoft Corp. v Commission of the European Communities* [2007] ECR II-03601
Case T-339/04 *France Télécom/Commission* [2007] ECR II-521

Cases T- 425/04, T-450/04 and T-456/04 *France, France Télécom and others/Commission*, not yet reported
Case T-474/04 *Pergan Hilffstoffe für industrielle Prozess GmbH v Commission* [2007] ECR II-04225
Case T-174/05 *Elf Aquitane*, not yet reported
Case T-175/05 *Akzo Nobel* and *Arkema*, not yet reported
Case T-306/05 *Scippacercola* [2008] ECR II-00004 (summary publication)
Case T-170/06 *Alrosa Company Ltd v Commission of the European Communities* [2007] II-02601

Pending cases

Case C-439/08, *VEBIC*, OJ C 313/19
Cases T-458/09 and T-171/10, *Slovak Telekom/Commission*, OJ 2010 C 11/36
Cases T-135/09, *Nexans/Commission*, and T-140/09, OJ 2010 C 141/48 and 50
Case C-360/09, *Pfleiderer*, OJ C 297/18
Case C-375/09, Tele2 Polska, OJ C 297/19
Case C-17/10, *Toshiba*, OJ 2010 C 100/14

European Court of Human Rights

Golder v United Kingdom (Appl no 4451/70) (1975) Series A no 18
Posti and Rahko v Finland (Appl no 27824/95) ECHR Reports 2002 VI

NATIONAL CASE LAW OR DECISIONS

Belgium

Brussels Court of Appeal 2004/MR/8 judgement of 10 November 2005

The Netherlands

College van Beroep voor het Bedrijfsleven (CBB) Judgment of 7 December 2005 *G Star Secon Group*, AWB 04/237 and 04/249

Court of Rotterdam Judgment of 3 december 2004 *Role 03/2084* LJN:AS3852

NMa Decision of 15 March 2005 *OSB* case 2021/397

NMa Decision of 29 June 2005 *Superunie v Interpay* case 2978/147

United Kingdom

JJB Sports Plc v OFT 2004, CAT 117

US case law

Leegin *Creative Leather Products, Inc. v. PSKS, Inc.* 551 *US* 877 (2007)

EU LEGISLATIVE INSTRUMENTS

Treaties/charters

Charter of Fundamental rights of the European Union [2000] OJ C 364/1

Treaty establishing a Constitution for Europe (Constitutional Treaty) [2004] OJ C 310

Consolidated versions of the Treaty on European Union and the Treaty on the functioning of the European Union [2008] C 115 (including several cited protocols)

Regulations

Council Regulation (EEC) No 17 (First Regulation implementing Articles 85 and 86 of the Treaty) [1959-62] OJ Spec Ed 87

Commission Regulation (EC) No 1984/83 On Application of Article 85(3) of the Treaty to categories of exclusive purchasing agreements [1983] OJ L 173/5

Commission Regulation (EC) No 2790/1999 of 22 December 1999 on the application of Article 81(3) of the Treaty to categories of vertical agreements and concerted practices [1999] OJ L 336/21

Council Regulation (EC) No 1/2003/EC on the implementation of the rules on competition laid down in Articles 81 and 82 of the Treaty [2003] OJ L1/1

Commission Regulation (EC) No 2790/1999 of 22 December 1999 on the application of Article 81(3) of the Treaty to categories of vertical agreements and concerted practices [1999] OJ L 336/21

Council Regulation (EC) 1206/2001 of 28 May 2001 on cooperation between courts of the Member States in taking evidence in civil and commercial matters [2001] OJ L 174/1

Commission Regulation (EC) No 773/2004 of 7 April 2004 relating to the conduct of proceedings by the Commission pursuant to Articles 81 and 82 of the EC Treaty [2004] OJ L 123/18

Council Regulation (EC) No 139/2004 of 20 January 2004 on the control of concentrations between undertakings (the EC Merger Regulation) [2004] OJ L 24/1

Council Regulation (EU) 330/2010 of 20 April 2010 [2010] OJ L 102/1

Directives

Council Directive 89/665/EEC of 21 December 1989 on the coordination of the laws, regulations and administrative provisions relating to the application of review procedures to the award of public supply and public works contracts [1989] OJ L 395/33

Council Directive 92/44/EEC on the application of open network provision to leased lines [1992] OJ L96/35

Directive 98/27/EC of the European Parliament and of the Council of 19 May 1998 on injunctions for the protection of consumers interests [1998] OJ L 166/ 51

Directive 1999/44/EC of the European Parliament and of the Council of 25 May 1999 on certain aspects of the sale of consumer goods and associated guarantees [1999] OJ L 171/12

Directive 2000/31/EC of the European Parliament and of the Council of 8 June 2000 on certain legal aspects of information society services, in particular electronic commerce, in the Internal Market ('Directive on electronic commerce') [2000] OJ L 178/1

Decisions

Commission Decision 84/380/EEC of 4 July 1984 relating to a proceeding under Article [81] of the EEC Treaty (IV/30.810 – Synthetic fibres) [1984] OJ 207/17

Commission Decision of 19 July 1989 relating to a proceeding under Article 85 of the EEC Treaty [1989] OJ L 253

Commission Decision 91/299/EEC of 19 December 1990 relating to a proceeding under Article 86 of the EEC Treaty [1991] OJ L 152

Commission Decision 94/296/EC of 29 April 1994 relating to a proceeding under Article [81] of the EC Treaty (IV/34.456 – Stichting Baksteen) [1994] OJ L 131/15

EU Legislative proposals

Commission (EC) 'Proposal for a Council Regulation on the implementation of the rules on competition laid down in Articles 81 and 82 of the Treaty and amending Regulations (EEC) No 1017/68, (EEC) No 2988/74, (EEC) No 4056/86 and (EEC) No 3975/87 ("Regulation implementing Articles 81 and 82 ofthe Treaty") COM (2000) 0582 final, p. 284

COMMISSION NOTICES AND GUIDELINES

Commission Notice on cooperation between national courts and the Commission in applying Articles 85 and 86 of the EEC Treaty of 1993 [1993] OJ C 39/6

Commission Notice on co-operation with national competition authorities [1997] OJ C 313/3

Commission notice on Guidelines on Vertical Restraints [2000] OJ C 291/1

Commission Guidelines on the applicability of Article 81 of the EC Treaty to horizontal cooperation agreements [2001] OJ C 3/2

Commission Notice on agreements of minor importance which do not appreciably restrict competition under Article 81 (1) of the Treaty (de minimis) [2001] OJ C 368/13

Commission Notice laying down guidelines on the effect on trade concept contained in Articles 81 and 82 of the Treaty [2004] OJ C 101/81

Commission Notice on the cooperation between the Commission and the courts of the EU Member States in the application of Articles 81 and 82 EC [2004] OJ (2004) C 101/04

Commission Notice on cooperation within the Network of Competition Authorities [2004] OJ C 101/43

Commission Notice on the co-operation between the Commission and the courts of the EU Member States in the application of Articles 81 and 82 EC [2004] OJ C 101/54

Commission Notice on the handling of complaints by the Commission under Articles 81 and 82 of the EC Treaty [2004] OJ C 101/65

Commission Notice on informal guidance relating to novel questions concerning Articles 81 and 82 of the EC Treaty that arise in individual cases (guidance letters) [2004] OJ C 101/78

Commission Notice - Guidelines on the application of Article 81(3) of the Treaty [2004] OJ C 101/97

Commission Guidelines on the method of setting fines imposed pursuant to Article 23(2)(a) of Regulation [2006] OJ C 210/2

Commission Notice on Immunity from fines and reduction of fines in cartel cases [2006] OJ C 298/17

Comission Notice on the enforcement of state aid law by national courts [2009] OJ C 85/1

OTHER COMMISSION COMMUNICATIONS OR PAPERS

Commission (EC) '21st report on competition policy' 1991
Commission (EC) '25th report on competition policy' 1996
Commission recommendation 96/80/EC, [1996] OJ L 107/74
Commission (EC) 'On vertical restraints in EC competition policy'(Green Paper) COM (96) 721
Opinion of the Economic and Social Committee on the 'Proposal for a Council Regulation on the implementation of the rules on competition laid down in Articles 81 and 82 of the Treaty and amending Regulations (EEC) No 1017/68, (EEC) No 2988/74, (EEC) No 4056/86 and (EEC) No 3975/87 ("Regulation implementing Articles 81 and 82 of the Treaty") [2001] OJ C 155/73
Commission (EC) 'European Governance' (White Paper) COM (2001) 428 final, 27 June 2001
Commission (EC) 'Industrial Policy in an Enlarged Europe'(Communication) COM (2002) 714 final, 11 December 2002
Commission (EC) 'Some key issues in Europe's Competitiveness – towards an integrated approach' (Communication) COM (2003) 704 final, 21 November 2003
Commission (EC) 'Fostering structural change: an industrial policy for an enlarged Europe, COM (04) 274 final, 20 april 2004
Commission (EC) 'Proactive Competition Policy for a Competitive Europe' (Communication) COM (2004) 293 final, 20 april 2004
Commission (EC) 'On public-private partnerships and community law on public contracts and concessions' (Green Paper) COM (2004) 327
Commission (EC) 'A Europe of Results – Applying Community Law' (Communication) COM (2007) 502 final, 5 September 2007
Commission (EC) 'Accompanying the White paper on damages actions for breach of the EC antitrust rules' (Staff Working Paper) SEC (2008) 404
Commission (EC) 'Damages Actions for breaches of the EC antitrust rules' (White Paper) COM (2008) 165
Commission (EC) 'Report on the functioning of Regulation 1/2003' (Communication) COM (2009) 206 final, 29 April 2009
Commission (EC) 'Communication from the Commission to the European Parliament and Council. Report on the functioning of Regulation 1/2003' (Staff Working Paper) SEC (2009) 574

WEBSITES/ INTERNET SOURCES

DG Comp website: http://ec.europa.eu/competition/index_en.html

Bundeskartellamt (Federal Cartel Office): www.bundeskartellamt.de/

Bundesministerium fur Wirtschaft und Technologie (Federal Ministry of Economics and Technology): www.bmwi.de/

Bundesnetzagentur für Elektrizität, Gas, Telekommunikation, Post und Eisenbahnen (Federal Network Agency for Electricity, Gas, Telecommunications, Post and Railway) www.bundesnetzagentur.de/enid/2.html

NMa: http://www.nmanet.nl/nederlands/home/index.asp

Conseil de la Concurrence (French Competition Council), now Autorité de Concurrence : : http://www.autoritedelaconcurrence.fr/user/index.php

OECD Competition Committee:
http://www.oecd.org/competition

Commission (EC) 'Codecision: May 1999 to December 2006: Some Statistical Data' available at ec.europa.eu/codecision/institutional/statistics_en.htm

Report of the House of Lords, Select Committee on European Union, Session 2006-2007 accessible via: http://www.publications.parliament.uk/pa/ld200607/ldselect/ldeucom/75/7506.htm

Statement by the President of the French ARCEP, *Les Echos*, on 20 February 2008, available at www.arcep.fr/index.php

Guidance published on 3 December 2008 by the Commission on the enforcement of Article 82, http://ec.europa.eu/competition/antitrust/art82/guidance_en.pdf.

Monti report on the internal market recently presented to President Barroso ('A new strategy for the single market – At the service of Europe's economy and society', presented on 9 May 2010, 1 http://ec.europa.eu/bepa/expertises/visitor-programs/mario_monti/index_en.htm)

Speech of Commissioner Kroes at Competition Day in London, 15 September 2005, http://ec.europa.eu/competition/speeches/index_2005.html.

Commissioner Kroes, Fordham, 14 September 2006; also at the 2008 edition of the international conference on 25 September 2008, Commissioner Kroes, via site DG Comp, http://ec.europa.eu/competition/speeches/ (accessed 1 March 2009).

Report of the House of Lords, Select Committee on European Union, Session 2006-2007, chapter on the creation of a new Court, accessible via: http://www.publications.parliament.uk/pa/ld200607/ldselect/ldeucom/75/7506.htm

Evans, L, *The role of economics on modern competition policy*, Speech 26 September 2008 in Hamburg, http://ec.europa.eu/competition/speeches/text/sp2008_06_en.pdf.

Evans, D, *Why different jurisdictions do not (and should not) adopt the same antitrust rules*, draft, http://ssrn.com/abstract=1342797

Tjeenk Willink, H, vice-president of Dutch Raad van State at the European law Conference in Stockholm, 2001, *Clarity and quality in legislation*, access: http://www.raadvanstate.nl/publicaties/toespraken_vice-president/toespraak/?speech_id=17

Trimidas, T, Memorandum: proposal for improvement of access to courts: www.publications.parliament.uk/pa/ld200304/lolselect/ldeucom/47/47we20.htm

Wils, W, *The EU Network of Competition Authorities, the European Convention on Human Rights and the Charter of Fundamental Rights of the EU*, paper presented at the EUI in 2002: http://www.iue.it/RSCAS/Research/Competition/2002 (later published, see above)

Papers presented at a conference organized by the GCLC center of the College of Bruges, the presentations are accessible at: http://www.coleurope.eu/template.asp?pagename=gclcfifthannual_docs

Comments of stakeholders in the consultation on the functioning of Regulation 1/2003, at: http://ec.europa.eu/competition/consultations/closed.html

PRESS RELEASES

IP/09/1092 'Consumers: EU-wide complaints-classifying system to speed up policy response to failing markets', 7 July 2009

CURRICULUM VITAE

Laura Parret was born in Leuven (Belgium) on 2 April 1969. She obtained a law degree from the Katholieke Universiteit Leuven in 1992 and a degree in European law in 1993 at the Institut d'Etudes Européennes, Université Libre de Bruxelles (grande distinction). From 1993 until 2004 she worked as an attorney (advocaat) at Barents & Krans as a member of the Brussels bar. She became a partner there in November 2003. In 2004 she moved to Simmons & Simmons in their Brussels office, where she worked as Of Counsel. Since March 2007, Laura is a permanent member of the Belgian Competition Council (a judicial body). She has been appointed as a chamber president, presiding both Dutch-speaking and French-speaking chambers. Since February 1997, Laura is also a lecturer at Tilburg University, in the Department of European and International Public Law, and a member of the Tilburg Law and Economics Center (TILEC, since 2002).

Apart from teaching in many different courses at university and the activities as an attorney and now councillor, activities have also included: publication of legal writings but also articles for the general public, teaching post academic courses at university, teaching competition law course for the Dutch speaking bar in Brussels, presidency of the Flemish Brussels Young Bar (2003-2004), presidency of the European law commission of AIJA (Association Internationale de Jeunes Avocats), being correspondent for "Markt & Mededinging" (Dutch legal periodical) and, since 2007, teaching at the College of Europe.

Council Regulation (EC) No 1/2003 of 16 December 2002 on the implementation of the rules on competition laid down in Articles 81 and 82 of the Treaty (Text with EEA relevance)

Official Journal L 001, 04/01/2003 P. 0001 - 0025

THE COUNCIL OF THE EUROPEAN UNION,

Having regard to the Treaty establishing the European Community, and in particular Article 83 thereof,
Having regard to the proposal from the Commission(1),
Having regard to the opinion of the European Parliament(2),
Having regard to the opinion of the European Economic and Social Committee(3),

Whereas:

(1) In order to establish a system which ensures that competition in the common market is not distorted, Articles 81 and 82 of the Treaty must be applied effectively and uniformly in the Community. Council Regulation No 17 of 6 February 1962, First Regulation implementing Articles 81 and 82(4) of the Treaty(5), has allowed a Community competition policy to develop that has helped to disseminate a competition culture within the Community. In the light of experience, however, that Regulation should now be replaced by legislation designed to meet the challenges of an integrated market and a future enlargement of the Community.

(2) In particular, there is a need to rethink the arrangements for applying the exception from the prohibition on agreements, which restrict competition, laid down in Article 81(3) of the Treaty. Under Article 83(2)(b) of the Treaty, account must be taken in this regard of the need to ensure effective supervision, on the one hand, and to simplify administration to the greatest possible extent, on the other.

(3) The centralised scheme set up by Regulation No 17 no longer secures a balance between those two objectives. It hampers application of the Community competition rules by the courts and competition authorities of the Member States, and the system of notification it involves prevents the Commission from concentrating its resources on curbing the most serious infringements. It also imposes considerable costs on undertakings.

(4) The present system should therefore be replaced by a directly applicable exception system in which the competition authorities and courts of the Member States have the power to apply not only Article 81(1) and Article 82 of the Treaty, which have direct applicability by virtue of the case-law of the Court of Justice of the European Communities, but also Article 81(3) of the Treaty.

(5) In order to ensure an effective enforcement of the Community competition rules and at the same time the respect of fundamental rights of defence, this Regulation should regulate the burden of proof under Articles 81 and 82 of the Treaty. It should be for the party or the authority alleging an infringement of Article 81(1) and Article 82 of the Treaty to prove the existence thereof to the required legal standard. It should be for the undertaking or association of undertakings invoking the benefit of a defence against a finding of an infringement to demonstrate to the required legal standard that the conditions for applying such defence are satisfied. This Regulation affects neither national rules on the standard of proof nor obligations of competition authorities and

courts of the Member States to ascertain the relevant facts of a case, provided that such rules and obligations are compatible with general principles of Community law.

(6) In order to ensure that the Community competition rules are applied effectively, the competition authorities of the Member States should be associated more closely with their application. To this end, they should be empowered to apply Community law.

(7) National courts have an essential part to play in applying the Community competition rules. When deciding disputes between private individuals, they protect the subjective rights under Community law, for example by awarding damages to the victims of infringements. The role of the national courts here complements that of the competition authorities of the Member States. They should therefore be allowed to apply Articles 81 and 82 of the Treaty in full.

(8) In order to ensure the effective enforcement of the Community competition rules and the proper functioning of the cooperation mechanisms contained in this Regulation, it is necessary to oblige the competition authorities and courts of the Member States to also apply Articles 81 and 82 of the Treaty where they apply national competition law to agreements and practices which may affect trade between Member States. In order to create a level playing field for agreements, decisions by associations of undertakings and concerted practices within the internal market, it is also necessary to determine pursuant to Article 83(2)(e) of the Treaty the relationship between national laws and Community competition law. To that effect it is necessary to provide that the application of national competition laws to agreements, decisions or concerted practices within the meaning of Article 81(1) of the Treaty may not lead to the prohibition of such agreements, decisions and concerted practices if they are not also prohibited under Community competition law. The notions of agreements, decisions and concerted practices are autonomous concepts of Community competition law covering the coordination of behaviour of undertakings on the market as interpreted by the Community Courts. Member States should not under this Regulation be precluded from adopting and applying on their territory stricter national competition laws which prohibit or impose sanctions on unilateral conduct engaged in by undertakings. These stricter national laws may include provisions which prohibit or impose sanctions on abusive behaviour toward economically dependent undertakings. Furthermore, this Regulation does not apply to national laws which impose criminal sanctions on natural persons except to the extent that such sanctions are the means whereby competition rules applying to undertakings are enforced.

(9) Articles 81 and 82 of the Treaty have as their objective the protection of competition on the market. This Regulation, which is adopted for the implementation of these Treaty provisions, does not preclude Member States from implementing on their territory national legislation, which protects other legitimate interests provided that such legislation is compatible with general principles and other provisions of Community law. In so far as such national legislation pursues predominantly an objective different from that of protecting competition on the market, the competition authorities and courts of the Member States may apply such legislation on their territory. Accordingly, Member States may under this Regulation implement on their territory national legislation that prohibits or imposes sanctions on acts of unfair trading practice, be they unilateral or contractual. Such legislation pursues a specific objective, irrespective of the actual or presumed effects of such acts on competition on the market. This is particularly the case of legislation which prohibits undertakings from imposing on their trading partners, obtaining or attempting to obtain from them terms and conditions that are unjustified, disproportionate or without consideration.

(10) Regulations such as 19/65/EEC(6), (EEC) No 2821/71(7), (EEC) No 3976/87(8), (EEC) No 1534/91(9), or (EEC) No 479/92(10) empower the Commission to apply Article 81(3) of the Treaty by Regulation to certain categories of agreements, decisions by associations of undertakings and concerted practices. In the areas defined by such Regulations, the Commission has adopted and may continue to adopt so called "block" exemption Regulations by which it declares Article 81(1) of the Treaty inapplicable to categories of agreements, decisions and concerted practices. Where agreements, decisions and concerted practices to which such Regulations apply nonetheless have effects that are incompatible with Article 81(3) of the Treaty, the Commission and the competition authorities of the Member States should have the power to withdraw in a particular case the benefit of the block exemption Regulation.

(11) For it to ensure that the provisions of the Treaty are applied, the Commission should be able to address decisions to undertakings or associations of undertakings for the purpose of bringing to an end infringements of Articles 81 and 82 of the Treaty. Provided there is a legitimate interest in doing so, the Commission should also be able to adopt decisions which find that an infringement has been committed in the past even if it does not impose a fine. This Regulation should also make explicit provision for the Commission's power to adopt decisions ordering interim measures, which has been acknowledged by the Court of Justice.

(12) This Regulation should make explicit provision for the Commission's power to impose any remedy, whether behavioural or structural, which is necessary to bring the infringement effectively to an end, having regard to the principle of proportionality. Structural remedies should only be imposed either where there is no equally effective behavioural remedy or where any equally effective behavioural remedy would be more burdensome for the undertaking concerned than the structural remedy. Changes to the structure of an undertaking as it existed before the infringement was committed would only be proportionate where there is a substantial risk of a lasting or repeated infringement that derives from the very structure of the undertaking.

(13) Where, in the course of proceedings which might lead to an agreement or practice being prohibited, undertakings offer the Commission commitments such as to meet its concerns, the Commission should be able to adopt decisions which make those commitments binding on the undertakings concerned. Commitment decisions should find that there are no longer grounds for action by the Commission without concluding whether or not there has been or still is an infringement. Commitment decisions are without prejudice to the powers of competition authorities and courts of the Member States to make such a finding and decide upon the case. Commitment decisions are not appropriate in cases where the Commission intends to impose a fine.

(14) In exceptional cases where the public interest of the Community so requires, it may also be expedient for the Commission to adopt a decision of a declaratory nature finding that the prohibition in Article 81 or Article 82 of the Treaty does not apply, with a view to clarifying the law and ensuring its consistent application throughout the Community, in particular with regard to new types of agreements or practices that have not been settled in the existing case-law and administrative practice.

(15) The Commission and the competition authorities of the Member States should form together a network of public authorities applying the Community competition rules in close cooperation. For that purpose it is necessary to set up arrangements for information and consultation. Further modalities for the cooperation within the network will be laid down and revised by the Commission, in close cooperation with the Member States.

(16) Notwithstanding any national provision to the contrary, the exchange of information and the use of such information in evidence should be allowed between the members of the network even where the information is confidential. This information may be used for the application of Articles 81 and 82 of the Treaty as well as for the parallel application of national competition law, provided that the latter application relates to the same case and does not lead to a different outcome. When the information exchanged is used by the receiving authority to impose sanctions on undertakings, there should be no other limit to the use of the information than the obligation to use it for the purpose for which it was collected given the fact that the sanctions imposed on undertakings are of the same type in all systems. The rights of defence enjoyed by undertakings in the various systems can be considered as sufficiently equivalent. However, as regards natural persons, they may be subject to substantially different types of sanctions across the various systems. Where that is the case, it is necessary to ensure that information can only be used if it has been collected in a way which respects the same level of protection of the rights of defence of natural persons as provided for under the national rules of the receiving authority.

(17) If the competition rules are to be applied consistently and, at the same time, the network is to be managed in the best possible way, it is essential to retain the rule that the competition authorities of the Member States are automatically relieved of their competence if the Commission initiates its own proceedings. Where a competition authority of a Member State is already acting on a case and the Commission intends to initiate proceedings, it should endeavour to do so as soon as possible. Before initiating proceedings, the Commission should consult the national authority concerned.

(18) To ensure that cases are dealt with by the most appropriate authorities within the network, a general provision should be laid down allowing a competition authority to suspend or close a case on the ground that another authority is dealing with it or has already dealt with it, the objective being that each case should be handled by a single authority. This provision should not prevent the Commission from rejecting a complaint for lack of Community interest, as the case-law of the Court of Justice has acknowledged it may do, even if no other competition authority has indicated its intention of dealing with the case.

(19) The Advisory Committee on Restrictive Practices and Dominant Positions set up by Regulation No 17 has functioned in a very satisfactory manner. It will fit well into the new system of decentralised application. It is necessary, therefore, to build upon the rules laid down by Regulation No 17, while improving the effectiveness of the organisational arrangements. To this end, it would be expedient to allow opinions to be delivered by written procedure. The Advisory Committee should also be able to act as a forum for discussing cases that are being handled by the competition authorities of the Member States, so as to help safeguard the consistent application of the Community competition rules.

(20) The Advisory Committee should be composed of representatives of the competition authorities of the Member States. For meetings in which general issues are being discussed, Member States should be able to appoint an additional representative. This is without prejudice to members of the Committee being assisted by other experts from the Member States.

(21) Consistency in the application of the competition rules also requires that arrangements be established for cooperation between the courts of the Member States and the Commission. This is relevant for all courts of the Member States that apply

Articles 81 and 82 of the Treaty, whether applying these rules in lawsuits between private parties, acting as public enforcers or as review courts. In particular, national courts should be able to ask the Commission for information or for its opinion on points concerning the application of Community competition law. The Commission and the competition authorities of the Member States should also be able to submit written or oral observations to courts called upon to apply Article 81 or Article 82 of the Treaty. These observations should be submitted within the framework of national procedural rules and practices including those safeguarding the rights of the parties. Steps should therefore be taken to ensure that the Commission and the competition authorities of the Member States are kept sufficiently well informed of proceedings before national courts.

(22) In order to ensure compliance with the principles of legal certainty and the uniform application of the Community competition rules in a system of parallel powers, conflicting decisions must be avoided. It is therefore necessary to clarify, in accordance with the case-law of the Court of Justice, the effects of Commission decisions and proceedings on courts and competition authorities of the Member States. Commitment decisions adopted by the Commission do not affect the power of the courts and the competition authorities of the Member States to apply Articles 81 and 82 of the Treaty.

(23) The Commission should be empowered throughout the Community to require such information to be supplied as is necessary to detect any agreement, decision or concerted practice prohibited by Article 81 of the Treaty or any abuse of a dominant position prohibited by Article 82 of the Treaty. When complying with a decision of the Commission, undertakings cannot be forced to admit that they have committed an infringement, but they are in any event obliged to answer factual questions and to provide documents, even if this information may be used to establish against them or against another undertaking the existence of an infringement.

(24) The Commission should also be empowered to undertake such inspections as are necessary to detect any agreement, decision or concerted practice prohibited by Article 81 of the Treaty or any abuse of a dominant position prohibited by Article 82 of the Treaty. The competition authorities of the Member States should cooperate actively in the exercise of these powers.

(25) The detection of infringements of the competition rules is growing ever more difficult, and, in order to protect competition effectively, the Commission's powers of investigation need to be supplemented. The Commission should in particular be empowered to interview any persons who may be in possession of useful information and to record the statements made. In the course of an inspection, officials authorised by the Commission should be empowered to affix seals for the period of time necessary for the inspection. Seals should normally not be affixed for more than 72 hours. Officials authorised by the Commission should also be empowered to ask for any information relevant to the subject matter and purpose of the inspection.

(26) Experience has shown that there are cases where business records are kept in the homes of directors or other people working for an undertaking. In order to safeguard the effectiveness of inspections, therefore, officials and other persons authorised by the Commission should be empowered to enter any premises where business records may be kept, including private homes. However, the exercise of this latter power should be subject to the authorisation of the judicial authority.

(27) Without prejudice to the case-law of the Court of Justice, it is useful to set out the scope of the control that the national judicial authority may carry out when it authorises, as foreseen by national law including as a precautionary measure, assistance from law enforcement authorities in order to overcome possible opposition on the part of the undertaking or the execution of the decision to carry out inspections in non-business premises. It results from the case-law that the national judicial authority may in particular ask the Commission for further information which it needs to carry out its control and in the absence of which it could refuse the authorisation. The case-law also confirms the competence of the national courts to control the application of national rules governing the implementation of coercive measures.

(28) In order to help the competition authorities of the Member States to apply Articles 81 and 82 of the Treaty effectively, it is expedient to enable them to assist one another by carrying out inspections and other fact-finding measures.

(29) Compliance with Articles 81 and 82 of the Treaty and the fulfilment of the obligations imposed on undertakings and associations of undertakings under this Regulation should be enforceable by means of fines and periodic penalty payments. To that end, appropriate levels of fine should also be laid down for infringements of the procedural rules.

(30) In order to ensure effective recovery of fines imposed on associations of undertakings for infringements that they have committed, it is necessary to lay down the conditions on which the Commission may require payment of the fine from the members of the association where the association is not solvent. In doing so, the Commission should have regard to the relative size of the undertakings belonging to the association and in particular to the situation of small and medium-sized enterprises. Payment of the fine by one or several members of an association is without prejudice to rules of national law that provide for recovery of the amount paid from other members of the association.

(31) The rules on periods of limitation for the imposition of fines and periodic penalty payments were laid down in Council Regulation (EEC) No 2988/74(11), which also concerns penalties in the field of transport. In a system of parallel powers, the acts, which may interrupt a limitation period, should include procedural steps taken independently by the competition authority of a Member State. To clarify the legal framework, Regulation (EEC) No 2988/74 should therefore be amended to prevent it applying to matters covered by this Regulation, and this Regulation should include provisions on periods of limitation.

(32) The undertakings concerned should be accorded the right to be heard by the Commission, third parties whose interests may be affected by a decision should be given the opportunity of submitting their observations beforehand, and the decisions taken should be widely publicised. While ensuring the rights of defence of the undertakings concerned, in particular, the right of access to the file, it is essential that business secrets be protected. The confidentiality of information exchanged in the network should likewise be safeguarded.

(33) Since all decisions taken by the Commission under this Regulation are subject to review by the Court of Justice in accordance with the Treaty, the Court of Justice should, in accordance with Article 229 thereof be given unlimited jurisdiction in respect of decisions by which the Commission imposes fines or periodic penalty payments.

(34) The principles laid down in Articles 81 and 82 of the Treaty, as they have been applied by Regulation No 17, have given a central role to the Community bodies. This central role should be retained, whilst associating the Member States more closely with the application of the Community competition rules. In accordance with the principles of subsidiarity and proportionality as set out in Article 5 of the Treaty, this Regulation does not go beyond what is necessary in order to achieve its objective, which is to allow the Community competition rules to be applied effectively.

(35) In order to attain a proper enforcement of Community competition law, Member States should designate and empower authorities to apply Articles 81 and 82 of the Treaty as public enforcers. They should be able to designate administrative as well as judicial authorities to carry out the various functions conferred upon competition authorities in this Regulation. This Regulation recognises the wide variation which exists in the public enforcement systems of Member States. The effects of Article 11(6) of this Regulation should apply to all competition authorities. As an exception to this general rule, where a prosecuting authority brings a case before a separate judicial authority, Article 11(6) should apply to the prosecuting authority subject to the conditions in Article 35(4) of this Regulation. Where these conditions are not fulfilled, the general rule should apply. In any case, Article 11(6) should not apply to courts insofar as they are acting as review courts.

(36) As the case-law has made it clear that the competition rules apply to transport, that sector should be made subject to the procedural provisions of this Regulation. Council Regulation No 141 of 26 November 1962 exempting transport from the application of Regulation No 17(12) should therefore be repealed and Regulations (EEC) No 1017/68(13), (EEC) No 4056/86(14) and (EEC) No 3975/87(15) should be amended in order to delete the specific procedural provisions they contain.

(37) This Regulation respects the fundamental rights and observes the principles recognised in particular by the Charter of Fundamental Rights of the European Union. Accordingly, this Regulation should be interpreted and applied with respect to those rights and principles.

(38) Legal certainty for undertakings operating under the Community competition rules contributes to the promotion of innovation and investment. Where cases give rise to genuine uncertainty because they present novel or unresolved questions for the application of these rules, individual undertakings may wish to seek informal guidance from the Commission. This Regulation is without prejudice to the ability of the Commission to issue such informal guidance,

HAS ADOPTED THIS REGULATION:

CHAPTER I
PRINCIPLES

Article 1
Application of Articles 81 and 82 of the Treaty

1. Agreements, decisions and concerted practices caught by Article 81(1) of the Treaty which do not satisfy the conditions of Article 81(3) of the Treaty shall be prohibited, no prior decision to that effect being required.

2. Agreements, decisions and concerted practices caught by Article 81(1) of the Treaty which satisfy the conditions of Article 81(3) of the Treaty shall not be prohibited, no prior decision to that effect being required.
3. The abuse of a dominant position referred to in Article 82 of the Treaty shall be prohibited, no prior decision to that effect being required.

Article 2
Burden of proof

In any national or Community proceedings for the application of Articles 81 and 82 of the Treaty, the burden of proving an infringement of Article 81(1) or of Article 82 of the Treaty shall rest on the party or the authority alleging the infringement. The undertaking or association of undertakings claiming the benefit of Article 81(3) of the Treaty shall bear the burden of proving that the conditions of that paragraph are fulfilled.

Article 3
Relationship between Articles 81 and 82 of the Treaty and national competition laws

1. Where the competition authorities of the Member States or national courts apply national competition law to agreements, decisions by associations of undertakings or concerted practices within the meaning of Article 81(1) of the Treaty which may affect trade between Member States within the meaning of that provision, they shall also apply Article 81 of the Treaty to such agreements, decisions or concerted practices. Where the competition authorities of the Member States or national courts apply national competition law to any abuse prohibited by Article 82 of the Treaty, they shall also apply Article 82 of the Treaty.
2. The application of national competition law may not lead to the prohibition of agreements, decisions by associations of undertakings or concerted practices which may affect trade between Member States but which do not restrict competition within the meaning of Article 81(1) of the Treaty, or which fulfil the conditions of Article 81(3) of the Treaty or which are covered by a Regulation for the application of Article 81(3) of the Treaty. Member States shall not under this Regulation be precluded from adopting and applying on their territory stricter national laws which prohibit or sanction unilateral conduct engaged in by undertakings.
3. Without prejudice to general principles and other provisions of Community law, paragraphs 1 and 2 do not apply when the competition authorities and the courts of the Member States apply national merger control laws nor do they preclude the application of provisions of national law that predominantly pursue an objective different from that pursued by Articles 81 and 82 of the Treaty.

CHAPTER II
POWERS

Article 4
Powers of the Commission

For the purpose of applying Articles 81 and 82 of the Treaty, the Commission shall have the powers provided for by this Regulation.

Article 5
Powers of the competition authorities of the Member States

The competition authorities of the Member States shall have the power to apply Articles 81 and 82 of the Treaty in individual cases. For this purpose, acting on their own initiative or on a complaint, they may take the following decisions:
- requiring that an infringement be brought to an end,
- ordering interim measures,
- accepting commitments,
- imposing fines, periodic penalty payments or any other penalty provided for in their national law.

Where on the basis of the information in their possession the conditions for prohibition are not met they may likewise decide that there are no grounds for action on their part.

Article 6
Powers of the national courts

National courts shall have the power to apply Articles 81 and 82 of the Treaty.

CHAPTER III
COMMISSION DECISIONS

Article 7
Finding and termination of infringement

1. Where the Commission, acting on a complaint or on its own initiative, finds that there is an infringement of Article 81 or of Article 82 of the Treaty, it may by decision require the undertakings and associations of undertakings concerned to bring such infringement to an end. For this purpose, it may impose on them any behavioural or structural remedies which are proportionate to the infringement committed and necessary to bring the infringement effectively to an end. Structural remedies can only be imposed either where there is no equally effective behavioural remedy or where any equally effective behavioural remedy would be more burdensome for the undertaking concerned than the structural remedy. If the Commission has a legitimate interest in doing so, it may also find that an infringement has been committed in the past.
2. Those entitled to lodge a complaint for the purposes of paragraph 1 are natural or legal persons who can show a legitimate interest and Member States.

Article 8
Interim measures

1. In cases of urgency due to the risk of serious and irreparable damage to competition, the Commission, acting on its own initiative may by decision, on the basis of a prima facie finding of infringement, order interim measures.
2. A decision under paragraph 1 shall apply for a specified period of time and may be renewed in so far this is necessary and appropriate.

Article 9
Commitments

1. Where the Commission intends to adopt a decision requiring that an infringement be brought to an end and the undertakings concerned offer commitments to meet the concerns expressed to them by the Commission in its preliminary assessment, the

Commission may by decision make those commitments binding on the undertakings. Such a decision may be adopted for a specified period and shall conclude that there are no longer grounds for action by the Commission.
2. The Commission may, upon request or on its own initiative, reopen the proceedings:
(a) where there has been a material change in any of the facts on which the decision was based;
(b) where the undertakings concerned act contrary to their commitments; or
(c) where the decision was based on incomplete, incorrect or misleading information provided by the parties.

Article 10
Finding of inapplicability

Where the Community public interest relating to the application of Articles 81 and 82 of the Treaty so requires, the Commission, acting on its own initiative, may by decision find that Article 81 of the Treaty is not applicable to an agreement, a decision by an association of undertakings or a concerted practice, either because the conditions of Article 81(1) of the Treaty are not fulfilled, or because the conditions of Article 81(3) of the Treaty are satisfied.
The Commission may likewise make such a finding with reference to Article 82 of the Treaty.

CHAPTER IV
COOPERATION

Article 11
Cooperation between the Commission and the competition authorities of the Member States

1. The Commission and the competition authorities of the Member States shall apply the Community competition rules in close cooperation.
2. The Commission shall transmit to the competition authorities of the Member States copies of the most important documents it has collected with a view to applying Articles 7, 8, 9, 10 and Article 29(1). At the request of the competition authority of a Member State, the Commission shall provide it with a copy of other existing documents necessary for the assessment of the case.
3. The competition authorities of the Member States shall, when acting under Article 81 or Article 82 of the Treaty, inform the Commission in writing before or without delay after commencing the first formal investigative measure. This information may also be made available to the competition authorities of the other Member States.
4. No later than 30 days before the adoption of a decision requiring that an infringement be brought to an end, accepting commitments or withdrawing the benefit of a block exemption Regulation, the competition authorities of the Member States shall inform the Commission. To that effect, they shall provide the Commission with a summary of the case, the envisaged decision or, in the absence thereof, any other document indicating the proposed course of action. This information may also be made available to the competition authorities of the other Member States. At the request of the Commission, the acting competition authority shall make available to the Commission other documents it holds which are necessary for the assessment of the case. The information supplied to the Commission may be made available to the competition authorities of the other Member States. National competition authorities may also exchange between themselves information necessary for the assessment of a case that they are dealing with under Article 81 or Article 82 of the Treaty.

5. The competition authorities of the Member States may consult the Commission on any case involving the application of Community law.
6. The initiation by the Commission of proceedings for the adoption of a decision under Chapter III shall relieve the competition authorities of the Member States of their competence to apply Articles 81 and 82 of the Treaty. If a competition authority of a Member State is already acting on a case, the Commission shall only initiate proceedings after consulting with that national competition authority.

Article 12
Exchange of information

1. For the purpose of applying Articles 81 and 82 of the Treaty the Commission and the competition authorities of the Member States shall have the power to provide one another with and use in evidence any matter of fact or of law, including confidential information.
2. Information exchanged shall only be used in evidence for the purpose of applying Article 81 or Article 82 of the Treaty and in respect of the subject-matter for which it was collected by the transmitting authority. However, where national competition law is applied in the same case and in parallel to Community competition law and does not lead to a different outcome, information exchanged under this Article may also be used for the application of national competition law.
3. Information exchanged pursuant to paragraph 1 can only be used in evidence to impose sanctions on natural persons where:
- the law of the transmitting authority foresees sanctions of a similar kind in relation to an infringement of Article 81 or Article 82 of the Treaty or, in the absence thereof,
- the information has been collected in a way which respects the same level of protection of the rights of defence of natural persons as provided for under the national rules of the receiving authority. However, in this case, the information exchanged cannot be used by the receiving authority to impose custodial sanctions.

Article 13
Suspension or termination of proceedings

1. Where competition authorities of two or more Member States have received a complaint or are acting on their own initiative under Article 81 or Article 82 of the Treaty against the same agreement, decision of an association or practice, the fact that one authority is dealing with the case shall be sufficient grounds for the others to suspend the proceedings before them or to reject the complaint. The Commission may likewise reject a complaint on the ground that a competition authority of a Member State is dealing with the case.
2. Where a competition authority of a Member State or the Commission has received a complaint against an agreement, decision of an association or practice which has already been dealt with by another competition authority, it may reject it.

Article 14
Advisory Committee

1. The Commission shall consult an Advisory Committee on Restrictive Practices and Dominant Positions prior to the taking of any decision under Articles 7, 8, 9, 10, 23, Article 24(2) and Article 29(1).
2. For the discussion of individual cases, the Advisory Committee shall be composed of representatives of the competition authorities of the Member States. For meetings in which issues other than individual cases are being discussed, an additional Member

State representative competent in competition matters may be appointed. Representatives may, if unable to attend, be replaced by other representatives.
3. The consultation may take place at a meeting convened and chaired by the Commission, held not earlier than 14 days after dispatch of the notice convening it, together with a summary of the case, an indication of the most important documents and a preliminary draft decision. In respect of decisions pursuant to Article 8, the meeting may be held seven days after the dispatch of the operative part of a draft decision. Where the Commission dispatches a notice convening the meeting which gives a shorter period of notice than those specified above, the meeting may take place on the proposed date in the absence of an objection by any Member State. The Advisory Committee shall deliver a written opinion on the Commission's preliminary draft decision. It may deliver an opinion even if some members are absent and are not represented. At the request of one or several members, the positions stated in the opinion shall be reasoned.
4. Consultation may also take place by written procedure. However, if any Member State so requests, the Commission shall convene a meeting. In case of written procedure, the Commission shall determine a time-limit of not less than 14 days within which the Member States are to put forward their observations for circulation to all other Member States. In case of decisions to be taken pursuant to Article 8, the time-limit of 14 days is replaced by seven days. Where the Commission determines a time-limit for the written procedure which is shorter than those specified above, the proposed time-limit shall be applicable in the absence of an objection by any Member State.
5. The Commission shall take the utmost account of the opinion delivered by the Advisory Committee. It shall inform the Committee of the manner in which its opinion has been taken into account.
6. Where the Advisory Committee delivers a written opinion, this opinion shall be appended to the draft decision. If the Advisory Committee recommends publication of the opinion, the Commission shall carry out such publication taking into account the legitimate interest of undertakings in the protection of their business secrets.
7. At the request of a competition authority of a Member State, the Commission shall include on the agenda of the Advisory Committee cases that are being dealt with by a competition authority of a Member State under Article 81 or Article 82 of the Treaty. The Commission may also do so on its own initiative. In either case, the Commission shall inform the competition authority concerned.
A request may in particular be made by a competition authority of a Member State in respect of a case where the Commission intends to initiate proceedings with the effect of Article 11(6).
The Advisory Committee shall not issue opinions on cases dealt with by competition authorities of the Member States. The Advisory Committee may also discuss general issues of Community competition law.

Article 15
Cooperation with national courts

1. In proceedings for the application of Article 81 or Article 82 of the Treaty, courts of the Member States may ask the Commission to transmit to them information in its possession or its opinion on questions concerning the application of the Community competition rules.
2. Member States shall forward to the Commission a copy of any written judgment of national courts deciding on the application of Article 81 or Article 82 of the Treaty. Such copy shall be forwarded without delay after the full written judgment is notified to the parties.

3. Competition authorities of the Member States, acting on their own initiative, may submit written observations to the national courts of their Member State on issues relating to the application of Article 81 or Article 82 of the Treaty. With the permission of the court in question, they may also submit oral observations to the national courts of their Member State. Where the coherent application of Article 81 or Article 82 of the Treaty so requires, the Commission, acting on its own initiative, may submit written observations to courts of the Member States. With the permission of the court in question, it may also make oral observations.
For the purpose of the preparation of their observations only, the competition authorities of the Member States and the Commission may request the relevant court of the Member State to transmit or ensure the transmission to them of any documents necessary for the assessment of the case.
4. This Article is without prejudice to wider powers to make observations before courts conferred on competition authorities of the Member States under the law of their Member State.

Article 16
Uniform application of Community competition law

1. When national courts rule on agreements, decisions or practices under Article 81 or Article 82 of the Treaty which are already the subject of a Commission decision, they cannot take decisions running counter to the decision adopted by the Commission. They must also avoid giving decisions which would conflict with a decision contemplated by the Commission in proceedings it has initiated. To that effect, the national court may assess whether it is necessary to stay its proceedings. This obligation is without prejudice to the rights and obligations under Article 234 of the Treaty.
2. When competition authorities of the Member States rule on agreements, decisions or practices under Article 81 or Article 82 of the Treaty which are already the subject of a Commission decision, they cannot take decisions which would run counter to the decision adopted by the Commission.

CHAPTER V
POWERS OF INVESTIGATION

Article 17
Investigations into sectors of the economy and into types of agreements

1. Where the trend of trade between Member States, the rigidity of prices or other circumstances suggest that competition may be restricted or distorted within the common market, the Commission may conduct its inquiry into a particular sector of the economy or into a particular type of agreements across various sectors. In the course of that inquiry, the Commission may request the undertakings or associations of undertakings concerned to supply the information necessary for giving effect to Articles 81 and 82 of the Treaty and may carry out any inspections necessary for that purpose.
The Commission may in particular request the undertakings or associations of undertakings concerned to communicate to it all agreements, decisions and concerted practices.
The Commission may publish a report on the results of its inquiry into particular sectors of the economy or particular types of agreements across various sectors and invite comments from interested parties.
2. Articles 14, 18, 19, 20, 22, 23 and 24 shall apply mutatis mutandis.

Article 18
Requests for information

1. In order to carry out the duties assigned to it by this Regulation, the Commission may, by simple request or by decision, require undertakings and associations of undertakings to provide all necessary information.
2. When sending a simple request for information to an undertaking or association of undertakings, the Commission shall state the legal basis and the purpose of the request, specify what information is required and fix the time-limit within which the information is to be provided, and the penalties provided for in Article 23 for supplying incorrect or misleading information.
3. Where the Commission requires undertakings and associations of undertakings to supply information by decision, it shall state the legal basis and the purpose of the request, specify what information is required and fix the time-limit within which it is to be provided. It shall also indicate the penalties provided for in Article 23 and indicate or impose the penalties provided for in Article 24. It shall further indicate the right to have the decision reviewed by the Court of Justice.
4. The owners of the undertakings or their representatives and, in the case of legal persons, companies or firms, or associations having no legal personality, the persons authorised to represent them by law or by their constitution shall supply the information requested on behalf of the undertaking or the association of undertakings concerned. Lawyers duly authorised to act may supply the information on behalf of their clients. The latter shall remain fully responsible if the information supplied is incomplete, incorrect or misleading.
5. The Commission shall without delay forward a copy of the simple request or of the decision to the competition authority of the Member State in whose territory the seat of the undertaking or association of undertakings is situated and the competition authority of the Member State whose territory is affected.
6. At the request of the Commission the governments and competition authorities of the Member States shall provide the Commission with all necessary information to carry out the duties assigned to it by this Regulation.

Article 19
Power to take statements

1. In order to carry out the duties assigned to it by this Regulation, the Commission may interview any natural or legal person who consents to be interviewed for the purpose of collecting information relating to the subject-matter of an investigation.
2. Where an interview pursuant to paragraph 1 is conducted in the premises of an undertaking, the Commission shall inform the competition authority of the Member State in whose territory the interview takes place. If so requested by the competition authority of that Member State, its officials may assist the officials and other accompanying persons authorised by the Commission to conduct the interview.

Article 20
The Commission's powers of inspection

1. In order to carry out the duties assigned to it by this Regulation, the Commission may conduct all necessary inspections of undertakings and associations of undertakings.
2. The officials and other accompanying persons authorised by the Commission to conduct an inspection are empowered:
(a) to enter any premises, land and means of transport of undertakings and associations of undertakings;

(b) to examine the books and other records related to the business, irrespective of the medium on which they are stored;
(c) to take or obtain in any form copies of or extracts from such books or records;
(d) to seal any business premises and books or records for the period and to the extent necessary for the inspection;
(e) to ask any representative or member of staff of the undertaking or association of undertakings for explanations on facts or documents relating to the subject-matter and purpose of the inspection and to record the answers.
3. The officials and other accompanying persons authorised by the Commission to conduct an inspection shall exercise their powers upon production of a written authorisation specifying the subject matter and purpose of the inspection and the penalties provided for in Article 23 in case the production of the required books or other records related to the business is incomplete or where the answers to questions asked under paragraph 2 of the present Article are incorrect or misleading. In good time before the inspection, the Commission shall give notice of the inspection to the competition authority of the Member State in whose territory it is to be conducted.
4. Undertakings and associations of undertakings are required to submit to inspections ordered by decision of the Commission. The decision shall specify the subject matter and purpose of the inspection, appoint the date on which it is to begin and indicate the penalties provided for in Articles 23 and 24 and the right to have the decision reviewed by the Court of Justice. The Commission shall take such decisions after consulting the competition authority of the Member State in whose territory the inspection is to be conducted.
5. Officials of as well as those authorised or appointed by the competition authority of the Member State in whose territory the inspection is to be conducted shall, at the request of that authority or of the Commission, actively assist the officials and other accompanying persons authorised by the Commission. To this end, they shall enjoy the powers specified in paragraph 2.
6. Where the officials and other accompanying persons authorised by the Commission find that an undertaking opposes an inspection ordered pursuant to this Article, the Member State concerned shall afford them the necessary assistance, requesting where appropriate the assistance of the police or of an equivalent enforcement authority, so as to enable them to conduct their inspection.
7. If the assistance provided for in paragraph 6 requires authorisation from a judicial authority according to national rules, such authorisation shall be applied for. Such authorisation may also be applied for as a precautionary measure.
8. Where authorisation as referred to in paragraph 7 is applied for, the national judicial authority shall control that the Commission decision is authentic and that the coercive measures envisaged are neither arbitrary nor excessive having regard to the subject matter of the inspection. In its control of the proportionality of the coercive measures, the national judicial authority may ask the Commission, directly or through the Member State competition authority, for detailed explanations in particular on the grounds the Commission has for suspecting infringement of Articles 81 and 82 of the Treaty, as well as on the seriousness of the suspected infringement and on the nature of the involvement of the undertaking concerned. However, the national judicial authority may not call into question the necessity for the inspection nor demand that it be provided with the information in the Commission's file. The lawfulness of the Commission decision shall be subject to review only by the Court of Justice.

Article 21
Inspection of other premises

1. If a reasonable suspicion exists that books or other records related to the business and to the subject-matter of the inspection, which may be relevant to prove a serious

violation of Article 81 or Article 82 of the Treaty, are being kept in any other premises, land and means of transport, including the homes of directors, managers and other members of staff of the undertakings and associations of undertakings concerned, the Commission can by decision order an inspection to be conducted in such other premises, land and means of transport.
2. The decision shall specify the subject matter and purpose of the inspection, appoint the date on which it is to begin and indicate the right to have the decision reviewed by the Court of Justice. It shall in particular state the reasons that have led the Commission to conclude that a suspicion in the sense of paragraph 1 exists. The Commission shall take such decisions after consulting the competition authority of the Member State in whose territory the inspection is to be conducted.
3. A decision adopted pursuant to paragraph 1 cannot be executed without prior authorisation from the national judicial authority of the Member State concerned. The national judicial authority shall control that the Commission decision is authentic and that the coercive measures envisaged are neither arbitrary nor excessive having regard in particular to the seriousness of the suspected infringement, to the importance of the evidence sought, to the involvement of the undertaking concerned and to the reasonable likelihood that business books and records relating to the subject matter of the inspection are kept in the premises for which the authorisation is requested. The national judicial authority may ask the Commission, directly or through the Member State competition authority, for detailed explanations on those elements which are necessary to allow its control of the proportionality of the coercive measures envisaged.
However, the national judicial authority may not call into question the necessity for the inspection nor demand that it be provided with information in the Commission's file. The lawfulness of the Commission decision shall be subject to review only by the Court of Justice.
4. The officials and other accompanying persons authorised by the Commission to conduct an inspection ordered in accordance with paragraph 1 of this Article shall have the powers set out in Article 20(2)(a), (b) and (c). Article 20(5) and (6) shall apply mutatis mutandis.

Article 22
Investigations by competition authorities of Member States

1. The competition authority of a Member State may in its own territory carry out any inspection or other fact-finding measure under its national law on behalf and for the account of the competition authority of another Member State in order to establish whether there has been an infringement of Article 81 or Article 82 of the Treaty. Any exchange and use of the information collected shall be carried out in accordance with Article 12.
2. At the request of the Commission, the competition authorities of the Member States shall undertake the inspections which the Commission considers to be necessary under Article 20(1) or which it has ordered by decision pursuant to Article 20(4). The officials of the competition authorities of the Member States who are responsible for conducting these inspections as well as those authorised or appointed by them shall exercise their powers in accordance with their national law.
If so requested by the Commission or by the competition authority of the Member State in whose territory the inspection is to be conducted, officials and other accompanying persons authorised by the Commission may assist the officials of the authority concerned.

CHAPTER VI
PENALTIES

Article 23
Fines

1. The Commission may by decision impose on undertakings and associations of undertakings fines not exceeding 1 % of the total turnover in the preceding business year where, intentionally or negligently:
(a) they supply incorrect or misleading information in response to a request made pursuant to Article 17 or Article 18(2);
(b) in response to a request made by decision adopted pursuant to Article 17 or Article 18(3), they supply incorrect, incomplete or misleading information or do not supply information within the required time-limit;
(c) they produce the required books or other records related to the business in incomplete form during inspections under Article 20 or refuse to submit to inspections ordered by a decision adopted pursuant to Article 20(4);
(d) in response to a question asked in accordance with Article 20(2)(e),
- they give an incorrect or misleading answer,
- they fail to rectify within a time-limit set by the Commission an incorrect, incomplete or misleading answer given by a member of staff, or
- they fail or refuse to provide a complete answer on facts relating to the subject-matter and purpose of an inspection ordered by a decision adopted pursuant to Article 20(4);
(e) seals affixed in accordance with Article 20(2)(d) by officials or other accompanying persons authorised by the Commission have been broken.
2. The Commission may by decision impose fines on undertakings and associations of undertakings where, either intentionally or negligently:
(a) they infringe Article 81 or Article 82 of the Treaty; or
(b) they contravene a decision ordering interim measures under Article 8; or
(c) they fail to comply with a commitment made binding by a decision pursuant to Article 9.
For each undertaking and association of undertakings participating in the infringement, the fine shall not exceed 10 % of its total turnover in the preceding business year.
Where the infringement of an association relates to the activities of its members, the fine shall not exceed 10 % of the sum of the total turnover of each member active on the market affected by the infringement of the association.
3. In fixing the amount of the fine, regard shall be had both to the gravity and to the duration of the infringement.
4. When a fine is imposed on an association of undertakings taking account of the turnover of its members and the association is not solvent, the association is obliged to call for contributions from its members to cover the amount of the fine.
Where such contributions have not been made to the association within a time-limit fixed by the Commission, the Commission may require payment of the fine directly by any of the undertakings whose representatives were members of the decision-making bodies concerned of the association.
After the Commission has required payment under the second subparagraph, where necessary to ensure full payment of the fine, the Commission may require payment of the balance by any of the members of the association which were active on the market on which the infringement occurred.
However, the Commission shall not require payment under the second or the third subparagraph from undertakings which show that they have not implemented the infringing decision of the association and either were not aware of its existence or have

actively distanced themselves from it before the Commission started investigating the case.
The financial liability of each undertaking in respect of the payment of the fine shall not exceed 10 % of its total turnover in the preceding business year.
5. Decisions taken pursuant to paragraphs 1 and 2 shall not be of a criminal law nature.

Article 24
Periodic penalty payments

1. The Commission may, by decision, impose on undertakings or associations of undertakings periodic penalty payments not exceeding 5 % of the average daily turnover in the preceding business year per day and calculated from the date appointed by the decision, in order to compel them:
(a) to put an end to an infringement of Article 81 or Article 82 of the Treaty, in accordance with a decision taken pursuant to Article 7;
(b) to comply with a decision ordering interim measures taken pursuant to Article 8;
(c) to comply with a commitment made binding by a decision pursuant to Article 9;
(d) to supply complete and correct information which it has requested by decision taken pursuant to Article 17 or Article 18(3);
(e) to submit to an inspection which it has ordered by decision taken pursuant to Article 20(4).
2. Where the undertakings or associations of undertakings have satisfied the obligation which the periodic penalty payment was intended to enforce, the Commission may fix the definitive amount of the periodic penalty payment at a figure lower than that which would arise under the original decision. Article 23(4) shall apply correspondingly.

CHAPTER VII
LIMITATION PERIODS

Article 25
Limitation periods for the imposition of penalties

1. The powers conferred on the Commission by Articles 23 and 24 shall be subject to the following limitation periods:
(a) three years in the case of infringements of provisions concerning requests for information or the conduct of inspections;
(b) five years in the case of all other infringements.
2. Time shall begin to run on the day on which the infringement is committed. However, in the case of continuing or repeated infringements, time shall begin to run on the day on which the infringement ceases.
3. Any action taken by the Commission or by the competition authority of a Member State for the purpose of the investigation or proceedings in respect of an infringement shall interrupt the limitation period for the imposition of fines or periodic penalty payments. The limitation period shall be interrupted with effect from the date on which the action is notified to at least one undertaking or association of undertakings which has participated in the infringement. Actions which interrupt the running of the period shall include in particular the following:
(a) written requests for information by the Commission or by the competition authority of a Member State;
(b) written authorisations to conduct inspections issued to its officials by the Commission or by the competition authority of a Member State;

(c) the initiation of proceedings by the Commission or by the competition authority of a Member State;
(d) notification of the statement of objections of the Commission or of the competition authority of a Member State.
4. The interruption of the limitation period shall apply for all the undertakings or associations of undertakings which have participated in the infringement.
5. Each interruption shall start time running afresh. However, the limitation period shall expire at the latest on the day on which a period equal to twice the limitation period has elapsed without the Commission having imposed a fine or a periodic penalty payment. That period shall be extended by the time during which limitation is suspended pursuant to paragraph 6.
6. The limitation period for the imposition of fines or periodic penalty payments shall be suspended for as long as the decision of the Commission is the subject of proceedings pending before the Court of Justice.

Article 26
Limitation period for the enforcement of penalties

1. The power of the Commission to enforce decisions taken pursuant to Articles 23 and 24 shall be subject to a limitation period of five years.
2. Time shall begin to run on the day on which the decision becomes final.
3. The limitation period for the enforcement of penalties shall be interrupted:
(a) by notification of a decision varying the original amount of the fine or periodic penalty payment or refusing an application for variation;
(b) by any action of the Commission or of a Member State, acting at the request of the Commission, designed to enforce payment of the fine or periodic penalty payment.
4. Each interruption shall start time running afresh.
5. The limitation period for the enforcement of penalties shall be suspended for so long as:
(a) time to pay is allowed;
(b) enforcement of payment is suspended pursuant to a decision of the Court of Justice.

CHAPTER VIII
HEARINGS AND PROFESSIONAL SECRECY

Article 27
Hearing of the parties, complainants and others

1. Before taking decisions as provided for in Articles 7, 8, 23 and Article 24(2), the Commission shall give the undertakings or associations of undertakings which are the subject of the proceedings conducted by the Commission the opportunity of being heard on the matters to which the Commission has taken objection. The Commission shall base its decisions only on objections on which the parties concerned have been able to comment. Complainants shall be associated closely with the proceedings.
2. The rights of defence of the parties concerned shall be fully respected in the proceedings. They shall be entitled to have access to the Commission's file, subject to the legitimate interest of undertakings in the protection of their business secrets. The right of access to the file shall not extend to confidential information and internal documents of the Commission or the competition authorities of the Member States. In particular, the right of access shall not extend to correspondence between the Commission and the competition authorities of the Member States, or between the latter, including documents drawn up pursuant to Articles 11 and 14. Nothing in this

paragraph shall prevent the Commission from disclosing and using information necessary to prove an infringement.
3. If the Commission considers it necessary, it may also hear other natural or legal persons. Applications to be heard on the part of such persons shall, where they show a sufficient interest, be granted. The competition authorities of the Member States may also ask the Commission to hear other natural or legal persons.
4. Where the Commission intends to adopt a decision pursuant to Article 9 or Article 10, it shall publish a concise summary of the case and the main content of the commitments or of the proposed course of action. Interested third parties may submit their observations within a time limit which is fixed by the Commission in its publication and which may not be less than one month. Publication shall have regard to the legitimate interest of undertakings in the protection of their business secrets.

Article 28
Professional secrecy

1. Without prejudice to Articles 12 and 15, information collected pursuant to Articles 17 to 22 shall be used only for the purpose for which it was acquired.
2. Without prejudice to the exchange and to the use of information foreseen in Articles 11, 12, 14, 15 and 27, the Commission and the competition authorities of the Member States, their officials, servants and other persons working under the supervision of these authorities as well as officials and civil servants of other authorities of the Member States shall not disclose information acquired or exchanged by them pursuant to this Regulation and of the kind covered by the obligation of professional secrecy. This obligation also applies to all representatives and experts of Member States attending meetings of the Advisory Committee pursuant to Article 14.

CHAPTER IX
EXEMPTION REGULATIONS

Article 29
Withdrawal in individual cases

1. Where the Commission, empowered by a Council Regulation, such as Regulations 19/65/EEC, (EEC) No 2821/71, (EEC) No 3976/87, (EEC) No 1534/91 or (EEC) No 479/92, to apply Article 81(3) of the Treaty by regulation, has declared Article 81(1) of the Treaty inapplicable to certain categories of agreements, decisions by associations of undertakings or concerted practices, it may, acting on its own initiative or on a complaint, withdraw the benefit of such an exemption Regulation when it finds that in any particular case an agreement, decision or concerted practice to which the exemption Regulation applies has certain effects which are incompatible with Article 81(3) of the Treaty.
2. Where, in any particular case, agreements, decisions by associations of undertakings or concerted practices to which a Commission Regulation referred to in paragraph 1 applies have effects which are incompatible with Article 81(3) of the Treaty in the territory of a Member State, or in a part thereof, which has all the characteristics of a distinct geographic market, the competition authority of that Member State may withdraw the benefit of the Regulation in question in respect of that territory.

CHAPTER X
GENERAL PROVISIONS

Article 30
Publication of decisions

1. The Commission shall publish the decisions, which it takes pursuant to Articles 7 to 10, 23 and 24.
2. The publication shall state the names of the parties and the main content of the decision, including any penalties imposed. It shall have regard to the legitimate interest of undertakings in the protection of their business secrets.

Article 31
Review by the Court of Justice

The Court of Justice shall have unlimited jurisdiction to review decisions whereby the Commission has fixed a fine or periodic penalty payment. It may cancel, reduce or increase the fine or periodic penalty payment imposed.

Article 32
Exclusions

This Regulation shall not apply to:
(a) international tramp vessel services as defined in Article 1(3)(a) of Regulation (EEC) No 4056/86;
(b) a maritime transport service that takes place exclusively between ports in one and the same Member State as foreseen in Article 1(2) of Regulation (EEC) No 4056/86;
(c) air transport between Community airports and third countries.

Article 33
Implementing provisions

1. The Commission shall be authorised to take such measures as may be appropriate in order to apply this Regulation. The measures may concern, inter alia:
(a) the form, content and other details of complaints lodged pursuant to Article 7 and the procedure for rejecting complaints;
(b) the practical arrangements for the exchange of information and consultations provided for in Article 11;
(c) the practical arrangements for the hearings provided for in Article 27.
2. Before the adoption of any measures pursuant to paragraph 1, the Commission shall publish a draft thereof and invite all interested parties to submit their comments within the time-limit it lays down, which may not be less than one month. Before publishing a draft measure and before adopting it, the Commission shall consult the Advisory Committee on Restrictive Practices and Dominant Positions.

CHAPTER XI
TRANSITIONAL, AMENDING AND FINAL PROVISIONS

Article 34
Transitional provisions

1. Applications made to the Commission under Article 2 of Regulation No 17, notifications made under Articles 4 and 5 of that Regulation and the corresponding applications and notifications made under Regulations (EEC) No 1017/68, (EEC) No

4056/86 and (EEC) No 3975/87 shall lapse as from the date of application of this Regulation.
2. Procedural steps taken under Regulation No 17 and Regulations (EEC) No 1017/68, (EEC) No 4056/86 and (EEC) No 3975/87 shall continue to have effect for the purposes of applying this Regulation.

Article 35
Designation of competition authorities of Member States

1. The Member States shall designate the competition authority or authorities responsible for the application of Articles 81 and 82 of the Treaty in such a way that the provisions of this regulation are effectively complied with. The measures necessary to empower those authorities to apply those Articles shall be taken before 1 May 2004. The authorities designated may include courts.
2. When enforcement of Community competition law is entrusted to national administrative and judicial authorities, the Member States may allocate different powers and functions to those different national authorities, whether administrative or judicial.
3. The effects of Article 11(6) apply to the authorities designated by the Member States including courts that exercise functions regarding the preparation and the adoption of the types of decisions foreseen in Article 5. The effects of Article 11(6) do not extend to courts insofar as they act as review courts in respect of the types of decisions foreseen in Article 5.
4. Notwithstanding paragraph 3, in the Member States where, for the adoption of certain types of decisions foreseen in Article 5, an authority brings an action before a judicial authority that is separate and different from the prosecuting authority and provided that the terms of this paragraph are complied with, the effects of Article 11(6) shall be limited to the authority prosecuting the case which shall withdraw its claim before the judicial authority when the Commission opens proceedings and this withdrawal shall bring the national proceedings effectively to an end.

Article 36
Amendment of Regulation (EEC) No 1017/68

Regulation (EEC) No 1017/68 is amended as follows:
1. Article 2 is repealed;
2. in Article 3(1), the words "The prohibition laid down in Article 2" are replaced by the words "The prohibition in Article 81(1) of the Treaty";
3. Article 4 is amended as follows:
(a) In paragraph 1, the words "The agreements, decisions and concerted practices referred to in Article 2" are replaced by the words "Agreements, decisions and concerted practices pursuant to Article 81(1) of the Treaty";
(b) Paragraph 2 is replaced by the following:
"2. If the implementation of any agreement, decision or concerted practice covered by paragraph 1 has, in a given case, effects which are incompatible with the requirements of Article 81(3) of the Treaty, undertakings or associations of undertakings may be required to make such effects cease."
4. Articles 5 to 29 are repealed with the exception of Article 13(3) which continues to apply to decisions adopted pursuant to Article 5 of Regulation (EEC) No 1017/68 prior to the date of application of this Regulation until the date of expiration of those decisions;
5. in Article 30, paragraphs 2, 3 and 4 are deleted.

Article 37
Amendment of Regulation (EEC) No 2988/74

In Regulation (EEC) No 2988/74, the following Article is inserted:
"Article 7a
Exclusion
This Regulation shall not apply to measures taken under Council Regulation (EC) No 1/2003 of 16 December 2002 on the implementation of the rules on competition laid down in Articles 81 and 82 of the Treaty(16)."

Article 38
Amendment of Regulation (EEC) No 4056/86

Regulation (EEC) No 4056/86 is amended as follows:
1. Article 7 is amended as follows:
(a) Paragraph 1 is replaced by the following:
"1. Breach of an obligation
Where the persons concerned are in breach of an obligation which, pursuant to Article 5, attaches to the exemption provided for in Article 3, the Commission may, in order to put an end to such breach and under the conditions laid down in Council Regulation (EC) No 1/2003 of 16 December 2002 on the implementation of the rules on competition laid down in Articles 81 and 82 of the Treaty(17) adopt a decision that either prohibits them from carrying out or requires them to perform certain specific acts, or withdraws the benefit of the block exemption which they enjoyed."
(b) Paragraph 2 is amended as follows:
(i) In point (a), the words "under the conditions laid down in Section II" are replaced by the words "under the conditions laid down in Regulation (EC) No 1/2003";
(ii) The second sentence of the second subparagraph of point (c)(i) is replaced by the following:
"At the same time it shall decide, in accordance with Article 9 of Regulation (EC) No 1/2003, whether to accept commitments offered by the undertakings concerned with a view, inter alia, to obtaining access to the market for non-conference lines."
2. Article 8 is amended as follows:
(a) Paragraph 1 is deleted.
(b) In paragraph 2 the words "pursuant to Article 10" are replaced by the words "pursuant to Regulation (EC) No 1/2003".
(c) Paragraph 3 is deleted;
3. Article 9 is amended as follows:
(a) In paragraph 1, the words "Advisory Committee referred to in Article 15" are replaced by the words "Advisory Committee referred to in Article 14 of Regulation (EC) No 1/2003";
(b) In paragraph 2, the words "Advisory Committee as referred to in Article 15" are replaced by the words "Advisory Committee referred to in Article 14 of Regulation (EC) No 1/2003";
4. Articles 10 to 25 are repealed with the exception of Article 13(3) which continues to apply to decisions adopted pursuant to Article 81(3) of the Treaty prior to the date of application of this Regulation until the date of expiration of those decisions;
5. in Article 26, the words "the form, content and other details of complaints pursuant to Article 10, applications pursuant to Article 12 and the hearings provided for in Article 23(1) and (2)" are deleted.

Article 39
Amendment of Regulation (EEC) No 3975/87

Articles 3 to 19 of Regulation (EEC) No 3975/87 are repealed with the exception of Article 6(3) which continues to apply to decisions adopted pursuant to Article 81(3) of the Treaty prior to the date of application of this Regulation until the date of expiration of those decisions.

Article 40
Amendment of Regulations No 19/65/EEC, (EEC) No 2821/71 and (EEC) No 1534/91

Article 7 of Regulation No 19/65/EEC, Article 7 of Regulation (EEC) No 2821/71 and Article 7 of Regulation (EEC) No 1534/91 are repealed.

Article 41
Amendment of Regulation (EEC) No 3976/87

Regulation (EEC) No 3976/87 is amended as follows:
1. Article 6 is replaced by the following:
"Article 6
The Commission shall consult the Advisory Committee referred to in Article 14 of Council Regulation (EC) No 1/2003 of 16 December 2002 on the implementation of the rules on competition laid down in Articles 81 and 82 of the Treaty(18) before publishing a draft Regulation and before adopting a Regulation."
2. Article 7 is repealed.

Article 42
Amendment of Regulation (EEC) No 479/92

Regulation (EEC) No 479/92 is amended as follows:
1. Article 5 is replaced by the following:
"Article 5
Before publishing the draft Regulation and before adopting the Regulation, the Commission shall consult the Advisory Committee referred to in Article 14 of Council Regulation (EC) No 1/2003 of 16 December 2002 on the implementation of the rules on competition laid down in Articles 81 and 82 of the Treaty(19)."
2. Article 6 is repealed.

Article 43
Repeal of Regulations No 17 and No 141

1. Regulation No 17 is repealed with the exception of Article 8(3) which continues to apply to decisions adopted pursuant to Article 81(3) of the Treaty prior to the date of application of this Regulation until the date of expiration of those decisions.
2. Regulation No 141 is repealed.
3. References to the repealed Regulations shall be construed as references to this Regulation.

Article 44
Report on the application of the present Regulation

Five years from the date of application of this Regulation, the Commission shall report to the European Parliament and the Council on the functioning of this Regulation, in particular on the application of Article 11(6) and Article 17.
On the basis of this report, the Commission shall assess whether it is appropriate to propose to the Council a revision of this Regulation.

Article 45
Entry into force

This Regulation shall enter into force on the 20th day following that of its publication in the Official Journal of the European Communities.

It shall apply from 1 May 2004.

This Regulation shall be binding in its entirety and directly applicable in all Member States.

Done at Brussels, 16 December 2002.

For the Council

The President
M. Fischer Boel

Notes:

(1) OJ C 365 E, 19.12.2000, p. 284.
(2) OJ C 72 E, 21.3.2002, p. 305.
(3) OJ C 155, 29.5.2001, p. 73.
(4) The title of Regulation No 17 has been adjusted to take account of the renumbering of the Articles of the EC Treaty, in accordance with Article 12 of the Treaty of Amsterdam; the original reference was to Articles 85 and 86 of the Treaty.
(5) OJ 13, 21.2.1962, p. 204/62. Regulation as last amended by Regulation (EC) No 1216/1999 (OJ L 148, 15.6.1999, p. 5).
(6) Council Regulation No 19/65/EEC of 2 March 1965 on the application of Article 81(3) (The titles of the Regulations have been adjusted to take account of the renumbering of the Articles of the EC Treaty, in accordance with Article 12 of the Treaty of Amsterdam; the original reference was to Article 85(3) of the Treaty) of the Treaty to certain categories of agreements and concerted practices (OJ 36, 6.3.1965, p. 533). Regulation as last amended by Regulation (EC) No 1215/1999 (OJ L 148, 15.6.1999, p. 1).
(7) Council Regulation (EEC) No 2821/71 of 20 December 1971 on the application of Article 81(3) (The titles of the Regulations have been adjusted to take account of the renumbering of the Articles of the EC Treaty, in accordance with Article 12 of the Treaty of Amsterdam; the original reference was to Article 85(3) of the Treaty) of the Treaty to categories of agreements, decisions and concerted practices (OJ L 285, 29.12.1971, p. 46). Regulation as last amended by the Act of Accession of 1994.
(8) Council Regulation (EEC) No 3976/87 of 14 December 1987 on the application of Article 81(3) (The titles of the Regulations have been adjusted to take account of the renumbering of the Articles of the EC Treaty, in accordance with Article 12 of the Treaty of Amsterdam; the original reference was to Article 85(3) of the Treaty) of the Treaty to certain categories of agreements and concerted practices in the air transport sector (OJ L 374, 31.12.1987, p. 9). Regulation as last amended by the Act of Accession of 1994.
(9) Council Regulation (EEC) No 1534/91 of 31 May 1991 on the application of Article 81(3) (The titles of the Regulations have been adjusted to take account of the renumbering of the Articles of the EC Treaty, in accordance with Article 12 of the Treaty of Amsterdam; the original reference was to Article 85(3) of the Treaty) of the Treaty to certain categories of agreements, decisions and concerted practices in the insurance sector (OJ L 143, 7.6.1991, p. 1).
(10) Council Regulation (EEC) No 479/92 of 25 February 1992 on the application of Article 81(3) (The titles of the Regulations have been adjusted to take account of the renumbering of the Articles of the EC Treaty, in accordance with Article 12 of the Treaty of Amsterdam; the original reference was to Article 85(3) of the Treaty) of the Treaty to certain categories of agreements, decisions and concerted practices between liner shipping companies (Consortia) (OJ L 55, 29.2.1992, p. 3). Regulation amended by the Act of Accession of 1994.
(11) Council Regulation (EEC) No 2988/74 of 26 November 1974 concerning limitation periods in proceedings and the enforcement of sanctions under the rules of the European Economic Community relating to transport and competition (OJ L 319, 29.11.1974, p. 1).
(12) OJ 124, 28.11.1962, p. 2751/62; Regulation as last amended by Regulation No 1002/67/EEC (OJ 306, 16.12.1967, p. 1).
(13) Council Regulation (EEC) No 1017/68 of 19 July 1968 applying rules of competition to transport by rail, road and inland waterway (OJ L 175, 23.7.1968, p. 1). Regulation as last amended by the Act of Accession of 1994.
(14) Council Regulation (EEC) No 4056/86 of 22 December 1986 laying down detailed rules for the application of Articles 81 and 82 (The title of the Regulation has been adjusted to take account of the renumbering of the Articles of the EC Treaty, in accordance with Article 12 of the Treaty of Amsterdam; the original reference was to Articles 85 and 86 of the Treaty) of the Treaty to maritime transport (OJ L 378, 31.12.1986, p. 4). Regulation as last amended by the Act of Accession of 1994.
(15) Council Regulation (EEC) No 3975/87 of 14 December 1987 laying down the procedure for the application of the rules on competition to undertakings in the air transport sector (OJ L 374, 31.12.1987, p. 1). Regulation as last amended by Regulation (EEC) No 2410/92 (OJ L 240, 24.8.1992, p. 18).
(16) OJ L 1, 4.1.2003, p. 1.
(17) OJ L 1, 4.1.2003, p. 1.
(18) OJ L 1, 4.1.2003, p. 1.
(19) OJ L 1, 4.1.2003, p. 1.

16W01725/ T4/ 9789058506191